Bringing Culture Back In

Bringing Culture Back In

Human Security and Social Trust

Edited by
Michael Böss

 AARHUS UNIVERSITY PRESS

Bringing Culture Back In
MatchPoints 7
© The authors and Aarhus University Press 2016
Cover design by Jørgen Sparre
Printed by Narayana Press, Denmark
Denmark 2016

ISBN 978 87 7124 791 6
ISSN 1904-3384

Aarhus University Press
Langelandsgade 177
DK – 8200 Aarhus N
www.unipress.dk

Published with the financial support of
The Aarhus University Research Foundation

INTERNATIONAL DISTRIBUTORS
Gazelle Books Services Ltd.
White Cross Mills
Hightown, Lancaster, LA1 4XS
United Kingdom
www.gazellebookservices.co.uk

ISD
70 Enterprise Drive
Bristol, CT 06010
USA
www.isdistribution.com

PEER REVIEWED

/ In accordance with requirements of the Danish Ministry of Higher Education and Science, the certification means that a ph.d.-level peer has made a written assessment which justifies this book's scientific quality.

Contents

Notes on Contributors 7

Introduction: Culture Matters – as Much as Ever
Michael Böss 11

PART 1 · CULTURE AND COMMUNITY

From Mosaic to Multiculturalism: The Canadian Roots and Character of Multiculturalism
Michael Böss 23

Britishness and Canadian Multiculturalism
Donald Ipperciel 54

Misinterpreting Multiculturalism
Will Kymlicka 70

Too Little Culture – Too Much Culture: The Strange Coexistence of Two Opposite Notions of Culture
Frederik Stjernfelt 88

Community Conceptions and Social Cohesion: Theoretical, Empirical, and Normative Issues
Nils Holtug 102

The Normativity of Culture
Antje Gimmler 121

We Are All Authentic: Multicultural Strategies and Religious Constructions
Jørn Borup 135

PART 2 · CULTURE, CONFLICT, AND WORLD ORDER

Cultural Challenges to the Liberal World Order
Georg Sørensen 149

Culture and Conflict in Global Perspective
Uwe Wagschal 163

The Impact of Human Security on Social Trust and Tolerance
Pippa Norris and Ronald Inglehart 183

PART 3 · DIVERSITY AND THE NATION STATE

Globalisation, Civilisations, and Capitalism
Jan-Erik Lane 207

Gemeinschaft and *Gesellschaft*
or the Life and Death of Proselytising Organisations
Margit Warburg 224

Why not Become Multicultural? Second Generation of Intellectual
Sri Lankan Tamil Hindus in Denmark
Marianne Q. Fibiger 237

The Entanglement between Religion and Politics in Denmark
Niels Kærgård 254

Cultural Diversity and the Resilience of Nations
John Hutchinson 272

■ Notes on Contributors

Jørn Borup holds MA and PhD degrees from the Department of the Study of Religion at Aarhus University, Denmark, where he is also an Associate Professor. He has conducted research on Japanese Buddhism and Buddhism in the West (mainly Denmark and Hawaii), and has been engaged in projects of mapping religion at the Centre of Contemporary Religion (Aarhus University). He is furthermore engaged in the research networks *Critical Analysis of Religious Diversity* and *Religious Diversity in Asia*.

Michael Böss is Associate Professor of History and Social Sciences at Aarhus University, Director of Canadian Studies Centre, and Director of the MatchPoints Seminar. He is also a columnist and author of articles and books on current Danish social, cultural, and political issues. His primary research interests are currently Canadian history, theories of nationality, nationhood, and nationalism and studies of democracy. His most recent books are *Developing Democracies* (2013) and *Det Demente Samfund* (The Amnesic Society) (2014).

Marianne Qvortrup Fibiger is associate professor of religious studies at Aarhus University. Her work focuses on Hinduism in general (and in Denmark and in diaspora in particular), Śāktism, religious plurality and diversity, how notions and worldviews travel between East and West, and on religion in cultural encounters. She has conducted extensive field research among Sri Lankan Tamil Hindus in Denmark and Sri Lanka, and Hindus in Mauritius, India (Kerala, Orissa, Punjab, Uttar Pradesh), Kenya, and England and written articles on themes as Hinduism and Wilderness, Śāktism in Denmark, Second generation of Hindus in diaspora and their relation to the Hindu tradition.

Antje Gimmler is Professor of Applied Philosophy at the University of Aalborg, Denmark. Her main research areas are social theory, philosophy of science and science studies as well as philosophy of technology. With a background in philosophical pragmatism and Critical Theory, she focuses on the interplay between norms, politics, technology, and culture. She is Director of CAF, Center of Applied Philosophy at Aalborg University and head of the PhD program Learning and Philosophy. Selected publications: *Institution und Individuum* (1998); "Deliberative Democracy, the Public Sphere, and the Internet", in: *Philosophy & Social Criticism* (2001, 27); and "Hegel as Pragmatist", in Bill Egginton (ed.), *The Pragmatic Turn in Philosophy* (2004).

Nils Holtug is Professor of Political Philosophy and Director of Centre for Advanced Migration Studies, University of Copenhagen. His main research interests are equality, multiculturalism, migration, secularism, social cohesion, population ethics, global justice, normative ethics, and personal identity. His publications include *Persons, Interests, and Justice* (2010), *Nationalism and Multiculturalism in a World of Immigration* (2009, co-edited with Kasper Lippert-Rasmussen and Sune Lægaard) and *Egalitarianism. New Essays on the Nature and Value of Equality* (2006, co-edited with Kasper Lippert-Rasmussen).

John Hutchinson is Associate Professor (Reader) at the London School of Economics. He has authored and edited several books in the field of nationalism, including *The Dynamics of Cultural Nationalism* (1987), *Modern Nationalism* (1994), and *Nations as Zones of Conflict* (2005). He is currently Vice-President and the Association for the Study of Ethnicity and Nationalism and co-editor of *Nations and Nationalism*. He has recently co-edited *Religions in Movement: The Local and Global in Contemporary Faith Traditions* (2013) and has just completed a monograph on nationalism and war.

Ronald Inglehart is the Lowenstein Professor of Political Science and a research professor at the Institute for Social Research at the University of Michigan. He is also co-director of the Laboratory for Comparative Social Research at the Higher School of Economics in St. Petersburg, Russia. Inglehart helped found the Euro-Barometer surveys, and directs the World Values Survey, which has surveyed representative national samples of the publics of 97 countries, containing almost 90 percent of the world's population. His research deals with changing belief systems and their impact on social and political change.

Donald Ipperciel is a Professor of Political Philosophy at Glendon College, York University, in Canada. He obtained his doctorate at Ruprecht-Karls University in Heidelberg in 1996. He held a Canadian Research Chair in Political Philosophy and Canadian Studies between 2002 and 2012. After an 18-year career at the University of Alberta, where he held many administrative positions (including Associate Dean Research, Associate Dean IT and Innovation, Vice-Dean and Director of the Canadian Studies Institute), he moved to Toronto to become the Principal of Glendon College, York University. His research portfolio comprises well over 60 publications and 60 academic conferences, published in either English, French or German. He specializes in contemporary German philosophy, in particular in Hans-Georg Gadamer's philosophical hermeneutics and Jürgen Habermas' Critical Theory, and has for a number of years focused on the theory of nationalism and the nation, as well as on Canadian nationalism and multiculturalism.

Will Kymlicka is the Canada Research Chair in Political Philosophy in the Philosophy Department at Queen's University in Kingston, Canada, where he has taught since 1998. His research interests focus on issues of democracy and diversity, and in particular on models of citizenship and social justice within multicultural societies. He has published eight books and over 200 articles, which have been translated into 32 languages.

Niels Kærgård has since 1993 been Professor of Agricultural Economics at the Royal Danish Veterinary and Agricultural University (since 2007 Faculty of Life Sciences, University of Copenhagen). 1992-2001 he was a member of the presidency of the Danish Board of Economic Advisors, 1995-2001 as chairman. 2002-2012 he was on the board of the Carlsberg Foundation and Carlsberg Brewery. 2007-2013 on the board of University of Copenhagen, and 2008-2013 vice-president of the Royal Danish Academy of Science. He has published in Danish and international journals on econometrics, ethics, economic history, agricultural economics, and economic policy.

Jan-Erik Lane is a social scientist with permanent residence in Geneva. He has taught politics and economics at many universities around the world. He has been full professor at three universities and visiting professor at many more. He is now a fellow at the Public Policy Institute in Belgrade. He has published some 300 books and articles, and has been on the editorial boards of many journals. In 1996 (and 2009) he received the Humboldt Award by the Humboldt Stiftung, receiving also a Lady Davis Fellowship at the Hebrew University in 2006 and also in 2012.

Pippa Norris is Paul F. McGuire Lecturer in Comparative Politics, and she has taught at Harvard for two decades. She is also ARC Laureate Fellow and Professor of Government and International Relations at the University of Sydney. She is a political scientist focusing on democracy and development, public opinion and elections, political communications, and gender politics. She directs The Electoral Integrity Project, a multimillion dollar six year research project with a team based at Sydney and Harvard. A prolific author and international public speaker, she has published more than forty books (many in translation).

Frederik Stjernfelt is a professor at the Humanomics Center, Department for Communication, Aalborg University, Copenhagen. Recent books include *Diagrammatology* (2007), *The Democratic Contradictions of Multiculturalism* (with J.-M. Eriksen, 2012), and *Natural Propositions: The Actuality of Peirce's Doctrine of Dicisigns* (2014).

Georg Sørensen is Professor of International Politics and Economics at the Department of Political Science, Aarhus University. Among his research interests are the contradictions and tensions of the liberal world order, democratization, fragile states, the future of the sovereign states, and theories of international relations and politics. He has been a visiting professor at a number of European and American universities. He has written numerous books and articles on international relations and development issues. Among his books are *Changes in Statehood* (2001), *Democracy and Democratization* (2008), *A Liberal World Order in Crisis* (2011), *Fragile States*, with L. Brock, H.H. Holm, and M. Stohl (2012), and *Introduction to International Relations. Theories and Approaches*, with R. Jackson (2016).

Uwe Wagschal is Professor of Comparative Politics at the University of Freiburg. His research interests include the comparative research of democracies, policy analysis, conflict research, and analysis of public finances. He is co-author of the books *Culture and Conflict in Global Perspective: The Cultural Dimensions of Global Conflicts 1945-2007* (2010), and *Culture and Politics: An Introduction to the Cultural Analysis of Politics* (2011).

Margit Warburg is Professor of Sociology of Religion, University of Copenhagen. Her research interests are the relationship between religion and migration; religion and globalisation; religion and demography; religious minorities; civil religion. Among her publications are *New Religions and New Religiosity* (1998), edited with Eileen Barker; *Religion and Cyberspace* (2005), edited with Morten T. Højsgaard; *Citizens of the World. A History and Sociology of the Baha'is from a Globalisation Perspective* (2006); *Holy Nations and Global Identities. Civil Religion, Nationalism and Globalisation* (2009), edited with Annika Hvithamar and Brian Jacobsen; *Religion in the 21st Century. Challenges and Transformations* (2010), edited with Lisbet Christoffersen, Hans Raun Iversen, and Hanne Petersen. Her latest article is "Counting Niqabs and Burqas in Denmark: Methodological Aspects of Quantifying Rare and Elusive Religious Subcultures" (2013), with Birgitte Schepelern Johansen and Kate Østergaard.

Introduction: Culture Matters – as Much as Ever

Michael Böss

Since the early 1990s, social and political scientists have increasingly re-engaged in discussions of the role of culture in society, politics, and economic development; "re-engaged", because, in classical sociology, culture was seen as a crucial factor, especially in the works of Weber and Durkheim. In Weber's famous study of *The Protestant Ethic and the Spirit of Capitalism*, he claimed that Protestantism promoted the rise of modern capitalism, especially in its Calvinist version, by sanctioning an ethic of everyday behaviour that led to economic success (Weber 1905). Protestantism produced a new kind of man, a "businessman", who aimed to live and work in a certain way. Riches were only a by-product of a way of life inspired by faith.

It was only in a later age that this Protestant ethic was translated into a general work ethic, which was seen as a recipe for material success and was lauded for its contribution to wealth creation. Its virtues – rationality, orderliness, diligence, productivity – were not completely new at the time, although hardly common. What Protestantism did was to generalise them among adherents of the confession and to make them judge each other by their conformity to these standards. In other words, religion encouraged a special type of personality and values that in time became social values in the rising capitalist economy.

Weber's engagement with the relationship between culture and society was not only historical, of course. It was a central element of his life-long concern with the social effects of modernisation. He believed that modernisation in the form of democratisation, commercialisation, industrialization, and urbanisation would erode the collective and traditional, particularly religious values and communities, which had hitherto secured the social order and social cohesion. As a liberal, he preferred to see the social order preserved without too much state interference. Conscious of the declining significance of religion, he hoped that a national sentiment could provide the social glue that was necessary to prevent society from disintegrating. Émile Durkheim expressed a similar concern. But he was confident that a 'collective consciousness' would encourage members of society to bond (Durkheim 1893).

After a lapse of almost half a century, there was a renewed interest in culture among social scientists of the 1940s and 1950s. The inspiration came from seminal studies of national character and so-called cultural patterns by anthropologists Margaret Mead and Ruth Benedict, and by the development of the concept of "political culture" by Seymour Martin Lipset, Gabriel Almond, and Sidney Verba. However, due to the increasing influence of rational choice theory in political science and methodological materialism in the social sciences, culture more or less disappeared again from the social sciences in the 1960s and 1970s. From the mid-1980s, however, the culture concept was again in vogue, so to speak.

With the decline of Marxist theory, books by Samuel Huntington, Lawrence Harrison, Robert Kaplan, Robert Putnam, and Francis Fukuyama spurred a renewed interest in cultural factors as co-determinants of economic development, social formation, democratisation, geo-politics, and interethnic relations. The publication of Harrison's *Underdevelopment Is a State of Mind* (Harrison 1985) marks the outbreak of a virtual "culture war" between culturalists and economists. The position of the economists – who claimed that material self-interest and the rational choice of the individual were universal factors that transcended cultural values and differences – was increasingly challenged by critics who pointed out methodological and philosophical weaknesses of the positivist approach, and disputed the idea that social order can be explained as the product of the choices of individual agents, or that social agents operate independently of their social and cultural habitus (Green and Shapiro 1994; Bourdieu 2005).

Although there might be wide differences between the ways in which the relationship between society and culture was understood, there had, by 1990, developed a general, but relative consensus among a broad field of social scientists that analyses of cultures and their symbols were crucial to understanding society, economics, and politics (Alexander and Seidman 1990). By 2000, Harrison and Huntington confidently asserted that "culture counts" in economic development (Harrison and Huntington 2000). In International Relations theory, culture and national identity were seen as important causal factors in shaping national security and foreign policies (Katzenstein 1996; Wendt 1999). Students of democracy pointed out how culture, values and institutions, historically and at present, have contributed to modernisation, human empowerment and democratisation processes (Inglehart and Welzel 2005; Welzel 2009). Political theorists and philosophers were concerned with issues of identity and the rights of cultural minorities in globalised, multicultural and postmodern western democracies (e.g., Kymlicka 1995). Finally, the return of religion as an important factor in national and international politics contradicted classical modernisation theory – which predicted secularisation as an inevitable process – and contributed to the surprising revival of the concept of civilisation (Heelas et al. 1996; Huntington 1996; Katzenstein).

Culture is a difficult concept to deal with intellectually. This is chiefly due to the problems of definition and measurement and to the cause-and-effect relationship between culture and other variables like policies, institutions, and economic development. Culture, thus, ought not to be seen as an independent variable, but influenced by numerous factors, like for example, climate, geography, social structures, political power, and historical contingencies. In 2000, Huntington defined culture simply as "the values, attitudes, orientations and underlying assumptions prevalent among people in a society" (Huntington and Harrison 2000: xv). But this definition, which was derived from political culture theory (cf. Almond and Verba 1963), is not quite satisfying.

As Lane and Wagschal rightly point out in *Culture and Politics* (2012), definitions of culture may become so broad that they stop making sense or being operational. Defining culture simply as "a way of life", for instance, is problematic since it makes it difficult to determine what in society does not constitute a way of life. What really counts among the variety of cultural phenomena in society, they claim, are ethnicity, religion, secular values and traditions and their significance for individuals, communities, and politics. Cultural values and traditions, furthermore, should not be seen as secondary or derivative, but as real motivations for individual and collective action. They thus define the cultural approach as dealing with "questions concerning the search for the meaning of life as well as for social and personal identity." They hold that a cultural approach to politics complements a rational choice approach "as it goes beyond action as self-centred rational strategy to delve into the way communities shape individuals and how they share meanings, norms and symbols, including altruism" (Lane and Wagschal 2012: 1, 3).

This collection has been edited on the basis of this assumption. It also inspired the conference "The Culture of Politics, Economics, and Society", which was held at Aarhus University in May 2013. Most of the articles have been selected from this conference. The purpose of the book is to examine how elements of culture, politics, and society intertwine normatively as well as empirically and descriptively. Its special emphasis is on how cultural identities may contribute to as well as challenge social cohesion, states, and the liberal world order.

The book is divided into three parts: It begins with a part consisting of papers on multiculturalism as a policy and a philosophy of how to manage cultural diversity in the postmodern, globalised state. The second part looks at the significance of socio-cultural values for international and global conflicts as well for the ability of individuals, communities, and societies to face the challenges of the contemporary world. The final part of the book consists of three papers which examine how culture interacts with society and politics in a particular nation-state, Denmark, and a concluding chapter which argues that nations and nation-states are likely to survive the challenges of diversity and globalization.

For the remaining part of this chapter, the individual papers of the book will be summarised.

The common point of reference in Part 1 is the Canadian political philosopher Will Kymlicka's liberal multiculturalism and his concept of multicultural citizenship. It opens with a long chapter in my hand offering the historical background of the rise of multiculturalism. The rationale of "From Mosaic to Multiculturalism" is that, in order to understand multiculturalism properly, one might benefit from knowing its Canadian roots, because they are important to the definition and the shaping of its character. Apart from being a historical account, its main thesis is that Canadian multiculturalism is a nation-building project that goes back to the interwar years. Hence, I caution against automatically translating support for multiculturalism into support for multiculturalist policy, theory, and philosophy.

The historical perspective is further detailed and elaborated by the Canadian political philosopher Donald Ipperciel. In "Britishness and Canadian Multiculturalism", Ipperciel argues that Canadian multiculturalism draws its ideological source in a normative multiculturalism characteristic of the Third British Empire in the Canadian interwar period. In order to make this point, the multicultural vision peculiar to the Third British Empire is presented through Alfred Zimmern, a political thinker of the British Empire who highlights multiculturalism's normative dimension from an idealist perspective. The link between the abstract thought of a British thinker and Canadian interwar multiculturalism is next established by way of presenting the views of Canada's representative of the Crown and head of state at the time, Governor General John Buchan. And finally, to dispel the possible impression that Britishness-qua-multiculturalism was an essentially Anglo-centric ideal based on an overly-generous self-assessment on the part of the English, the focus in the last section is on Édouard Montpetit, a French Canadian nationalist representing one fringe minority within the British Empire.

In the next chapter, Will Kymlicka takes a long view back over the history and critiques of multiculturalism. In the paper, which he calls "Misinterpreting Multiculturalism", he notes that, like any real-world political phenomenon, the embrace of multiculturalist policies and principles in the West in the past forty years has been driven by multiple, complex, and perhaps even contradictory motivations. In earlier work, he has argued that the primary impulse was a distinctly liberal-democratic conception of inclusive citizenship, inspired and constrained by core liberal principles of individual freedom and democratic participation. In this chapter, Kymlicka considers two alternative genealogies which propose a less benign account of the origins of multiculturalism. One of these alternative genealogies ties multiculturalism to early 20th century anthropological tenets of cultural relativism; the other ties multiculturalism to late 20th century tenets of neoliberalism. Defenders of these alternative genealogies typically assume that multiculturalism, tied at birth to either cultural relativism or neoliberalism, cannot serve emancipatory goals. Kymlicka argues that these "original sin" accounts of multiculturalism are implausible, and that the historical record does not support either account. Liberal multiculturalism should be judged on its merits, not dismissed on the basis of highly selective and misleading genealogies.

Then the word is passed to one of Kymlicka's critics, the Danish semiotician and social critic Frederik Stjernfelt. His chapter investigates two mirroring arguments, which he calls "too much" and "too little" culture, deriving from anthropology and sociology, respectively. The former is the argument that culture determines the values and behaviour of individuals to the degree that cultures form segregated wholes, completely distinct on the outside, completely homogeneous on the inside. Variants of this view of culture – culturalism – are often taken as a basis for hard multiculturalist arguments for the protection or special rights of cultures. The latter is the argument that culture belongs to the social superstructure and that its real "root causes" lie in socio-economic conditions. This argument exists in Marxist and liberalist variants and enjoys prominence in so-called modernisation theories taking it for granted that a general development from traditional to modern societies is at work. The different views of radicalisation stemming from the two positions are compared, and the strange coexistence of both and the contradictory views in certain observers are analysed: If you think that culture is but icing on the surface (modernisation), you may support special rights (culturalism) because the latter is taken to be without real effects anyway. Finally, Stjernfelt opts for a middle, a "soft multiculturalism", way: Cultures will never become extinct, but they should be forced to reshape themselves so as to accept basic democratic principles, human rights, equality before the law, etc.

In "Community Conceptions and Social Cohesion", the Danish philosopher Nils Holtug critically assesses a number of community conceptions, that is, claims about what bonds between community members tend to promote social cohesion. He first provides a more precise definition of the central concept of a community conception. Secondly, he develops a typology of different particular community conceptions, where these conceptions differ with regard to the values they consider conducive to social cohesion. Holtug labels these conceptions "conservative nationalism", "liberal nationalism", "republicanism", "liberalism", "polity patriotism", and "multiculturalism". Thirdly, he presents what he sees as main theoretical arguments for each of these different community conceptions. Since, at the end of the day, community conceptions are empirical claims about the effects of specific values on social cohesion, he ends up briefly considering the (limited) available empirical evidence for thinking that particular community conceptions affect social cohesion in particular ways.

The classical sociological and political question of "what keeps societies together" has gained new gravity in the context of multiculturalism. The German philosopher Antje Gimmler's aim in her chapter "The Normativity of Culture" is to investigate conceptual frameworks that deal with the complexity of cultural values and practices on the one hand, and the theoretical conceptualizations of "what keeps societies together" on the other. It is argued that a differentiated approach to culture is necessary in order to match the complexity of multicultural societies and their constitutional challenges. As examples of two forms of normative social theory that combine cultural practices and norms, Gimmler discusses Axel Honneth's theory of recognition and Laurent Thévenot's neo-pragmatic sociology of engagements in order to explain the inherent normativity of cultural and social relations as well as artefacts. An understanding of cultural diversity that is neither normatively neutral nor overly-determining in relation to the principles of modern Western democracies, she argues, will show to be a necessary prerequisite to address the challenges of multicultural societies.

Jørn Borup, who is a Danish historian of religion, notes that globalisation has called for cultural universalisation, but also re-traditionalisation and quests for particularisation. Never before have so many ethnicities and cultures been so distinct and close to each other as today, and religious diversity has become a topic to be taken seriously by both scholars, politicians, and religious groups. Borup's chapter addresses the question of managing religious diversity and the relations between religion, ethnicity, and cultural identity formation in migration and multicultural settings. He argues that, although these concepts from a constructionist perspective are not *sui generis*, they do in fact have an impact as living constructs and narratives on broader social and political spheres, where representation and authority claims are part of the game.

The second part of the book, *Culture, Conflict, and World Order*, takes a social science approach to the study of the relationship between culture and politics. The first chapter is by Danish political scientist Georg Sørensen. In "Cultural Challenges to the Liberal World Order", Sørensen starts out reminding us that liberals have always been hopeful about the future; their optimism is based on the process of societal modernisation. That process began in the West unleashed by the scientific revolution which led to improved technologies and thus more efficient ways of producing goods and mastering nature. This was reinforced by the liberal intellectual revolution which had great faith in human reason and rationality. The end of the Cold War would appear to confirm this liberal optimism, especially when combined with the mood, spirit, and changes of the 1990s. The number of democracies in the world doubled, from 43 in the early seventies to 88 by the late nineties. Nearly all countries, democratic or not, committed themselves to liberal market economies based on private property. Most countries wanted to participate in international co-operation through international institutions. The

Millennium Declaration, adopted by UN member states, confirmed universal allegiance to liberal principles. In the new century, things went the other way, and we must now contemplate current cultural challenges to liberal world order. The liberal project currently faces a new set of cultural and other challenges. How serious are these challenges, and is the liberal project ready to give convincing answers to them? Sørensen takes the challenges very seriously, and he thinks that the liberal answers so far have been glaringly insufficient. That bodes ill for any quick return to easy liberal progress. In cultural terms, we must prepare for a world where liberal values are increasingly contested and may far from always win the day. All this does not mean that the liberal world order is on the verge of breaking down or that chaos and anarchy are in the cards. It does mean, however, that history never guarantees progress in a liberal direction. Each historical phase of liberal development must be able to confront the important challenges that emerge in a given historical period.

In "Culture and Conflict in a Global Perspective", German political scientist Uwe Wagschal notes that the attempt to explain cultural conflicts has attracted an increasing amount of attention in the social sciences. In his article, he aims to analyse the empirical evidence of cultural conflicts, for example how often they occur, where they occur, and how they are interrelated to other conflict items. First, the article sums up general descriptive data about global and cultural conflicts and their intensity. Second, two different perspectives on the role of culture in conflicts are presented. One views culture as a main conflict issue or dependent variable, and therefore asks for the determinants of cultural conflicts. The other perspectives regard culture as an independent variable in explaining conflicts, and therefore compare the explanatory power of cultural and other demographic factors. The main findings include the following: Cultural conflicts make up a high and increasingly large share of all conflicts. Furthermore, cultural conflicts are mainly domestic (intrastate) conflicts and not interstate conflicts. It can also be seen that demographic factors, like a greater share of young men within the population, influence the risk of conflict more than cultural fragmentation, even though significant effects were found for cultural variables.

American political scientists Ronald Inglehart and Pippa Norris suggest a new approach to understanding the sources of social trust. They begin their chapter "Human Security and Social Trust" by noting that there is a high degree of consensus among cultural theorists that social trust and tolerance are vital qualities that help build social solidarity, reduce conflict, and strengthen democracy. An extensive body of literature has demonstrated the importance of these phenomena for a variety of social goods ranging from economic growth to democracy. Despite widespread recognition of their value, however, there exists no consensus concerning the conditions most conducive to strengthening social trust and tolerance. Debate continues among several schools of thought. Inglehart and Norris build their own study on theories of existential security, focusing on the risks and vulnerabilities facing individuals, communities, and societies. In particular, they demonstrate how feelings of social trust are strengthened by strong feelings of subjective security (as measured by a new battery of items in the World Values Survey). By contrast, insecure environments – where people feel they face life-threatening risks – quite rationally lead to mistrust of others: under extreme conditions, survival may literally be a zero sum game. This theory is contrasted with other accounts, notably theories of social capital that stress the beneficial effects of voluntary participation in community associations and the negative impact of television watching; and social-psychological accounts that focus on the role of education. The authors' core propositions are tested against new data from the 6th wave of the World Values Survey 2011-2013 in three dozen diverse societies worldwide. In their conclusion they summarise the core findings and consider their implications.

In "Civilisations and the Rule of Law", Swedish political scientist Jan-Erik Lane starts out with the claim that the rise of South East and East Asia to near dominance in economic production in the global market economy calls for a re-consideration of the Weber thesis of a close link between Western civilisation and modern capitalism. However, if one employs the value loaded concept of a civilisation in an enquiry into capitalism today, one will find few traces of the Weber link: Protestantism – rationality – modern capitalism. Instead one finds a clear and unmistakable relation between a parsimonious set of civilisations covering the countries of the world on the one hand and the variation in rule of law on the other hand. Rule of law (Rechtsstaat) is, Lane argues, as a matter of fact the core in legal-rational authority, which Weber erroneously placed in his ideal-type of bureaucracy.

The last four papers of the book take their point of departure in a nation state context. The case analysed is Denmark. It begins with a paper by the Danish sociologist of religion Margit Warburg. In *"Gemeinschaft* and *Gesellschaft* or the Life and Death of Proselytising Organisations"*, Warburg takes her point of departure in the two classical terms introduced by Ferdinand Tönnies in 1887, and which he regarded as ideal types of social relations at all levels. They are often superficially equated with soft (cultural) and hard (economical) aspects of society. But when applied as analytical concepts, they can contribute to a better understanding of the internal dynamics of proselytising organisations, Warburg believes. In her paper, she uses religious organisations as the recurrent case for illustrating that the concepts of *Gemeinschaft* and *Gesellschaft* are complementary to each other and not opposing ideal types of social relations. She also shows that both concepts are crucial to consider in the mobilisation of resources for achieving a sustainable organisation with a potential for long-term growth. This approach can be expanded to many other organisations which share a need to mobilise people in order to achieve their goals. In politics, the obvious parallels to proselytising religious organisations are political parties.

In "Why not Become Multicultural? Second Generation of Intellectual Sri Lankan Tamil Hindus in Denmark", Danish scholar in religious studies, Marianne Q. Fibiger presents a case study of second generation Sri Lankan Tamil Hindus in Denmark. She observes a clear tension between being part of a shared culture or tradition, and wishing to adapt this tradition in response to the receiving society's positive and negative understanding of it. This tension is playing an obvious role in their identity formation. In trying to maintain a sense of cultural belonging, the notion of being part of a special group is articulated and specific aspects of the tradition are identified as particularly important. At the same time, this also leads to varying degrees of intentional compartmentalisation strategies, where the differentiation between the in-group and the out-group's relations becomes more apparent, both in relation to behavioural patterns and what is understood as good conduct in different situations. This process results in a form of cultural hybridity or multiculturality, which, as Fibiger claims, is more easily coped with or even understood as a privilege among bearers of cultures that not only have a universal and inclusive meaning system as part of the normative framework, but also appeal to Western societies as a whole, which makes the relation between in- and out-groups differ from other immigration groups.

In "The Entanglement between Religion and Politics in Denmark", the Danish economist Niels Kærgård argues that when politicians make decisions they must base them on investigations of the facts and on attitudes. Attitudes are formed by a mixture of ideology and religion. It is normally assumed that ideology plays a dominant role in relation to politics, while religion is related to the moral of individuals. However, an exact separation of ideology and religion is not simple; many have participated in political debates with a religious starting point. In his paper, he discusses the relation between politics and religion in Denmark over the last two centuries.

Much nationalist scholarship has argued that nationalism is a homogenising force inventing new forms of solidarity with the aim of achieving independent state-hood. In the final chapter of this part of the book, "Cultural Diversity and the Resilience of Nations", British social scientist and historian John Hutchinson addresses the question of whether cultural diversity will make us give up the idea that states need nations. In his earlier work on nationalism, Hutchinson has argued that, in the past there were often competing nationalist projects, focused on the nation as historical community that also recognised and celebrated diversities within nations as the basis of their vitality. Indeed, in many countries we still see the existence of embedded differences that occasionally erupt into cultural wars. In his chapter, Hutchinson first examines the origins and significance of cultural wars in the making and remaking of nation-states. He argues that intense cleavages may arise out of the experiences of wars, civil wars, colonisations, and revolutions that give rise to competing definitions of the nation and that once institutionalised take on a recurring character. In Russia, France and Greece such divisions can assume a religious versus a secular opposition, but there are other bases of division. He then assesses the significance of these divisions suggesting that although they often result in social polarisation, they also articulate alternative options for populations as they experience the contingencies of the modern world.

■ References

Alexander. J.C. and S. Seidman, eds. *Culture and Society: Contemporary Debates*. Cambridge: Cambridge University Press, 1990.
Almond, G.A. and S. Verba. *The Civic Culture*. Princeton, NJ: Princeton University Press, 1963.
Bourdieu, P. *The Social Structures of the Economy*. Cambridge: Polity, 2005.
Durkheim, É. *De la division du travail social*. Paris: Alcan, 1893.
Green, D.P. and I. Shapiro. *Pathologies of Rational Choice Theory: A Critique of Applications in Political Science*. New Haven: Yale University Press, 1994.
Harrison. L.E. *Underdevelopment Is a State of Mind: The Latin American Case*. Cambridge, MA: Harvard University and Madison Books, 1985.
Harrison, L.E. and S.P. Huntington, eds. *Culture Matters: How Values Shape Human Progress*. New York: Basic Books, 2000.
Heelas. P. et al., eds. *Detraditionalization: Critical Reflections on Authority and Identity*. Oxford: Blackwell, 1996.
Huntington. S.P. *The Clash of Civilizations and the Making of the New World Order*. New York: Simon & Schuster, 1996.
Inglehart, R. and C. Welzel. *Modernization, Cultural Change, and Democracy: Their Human Development Sequence*. Cambridge: Cambridge University Press, 2005.
Katzenstein. P. *Cultural Norms and National Security*. Ithaca, NY: Cornell University Press, 1996.
Katzenstein, P. *Civilizations in World Politics: Plural and Pluralist Perspectives*. New York: Routledge, 2010.
Kymlicka, W. *The Rights of Minority Cultures*. Oxford: Oxford University Press, 1995.
Lane, J.-E. and U. Wagschal. *Culture and Politics*. London and New York: Routledge, 2012.
Welzel, C. "Theories of Democratization." In *Democratization*, ed. C. Welzel et al., 94-90. Oxford University Press, 2009.
Weber, M. *Die protestantische Ethik und der Geist des Kapitalismus*. Tübingen: Mohr, 1904/05.
Wendt, A. *Social Theory of International Politics*. Cambridge: Cambridge University Press, 1999.

ND COMMUNITY
PART 1

CULTURE AND COMMUNITY

1 From Mosaic to Multiculturalism: The Canadian Roots and Character of Multiculturalism

Michael Böss

For many Canadians, multiculturalism is a highly cherished aspect of their country and a source of pride and identity. In 2007, polls showed wide and growing support for multiculturalism since its introduction as a state policy in 1971 (Adams 2008). Between 1997 and 2007 there was a rise from 74 to 85 per cent among those who agreed that multiculturalism was important to Canadian identity. In 2002, 83 per cent agreed that people from different racial and cultural groups were enriching the cultural life of Canada (Focus Canada 2002). Contemporary polls show that 58 per cent believe that "the growing variety of ethnic and racial groups in Canada" is either very good or good. 64 per cent believe that "having a multicultural blend of different cultures provides a richer, more tolerant society", and 75 per cent agree that "it is better for Canada to have a variety of people with different religions". Therefore, Canadians are also likely to answer that immigration is beneficial to their country, and they are less likely to believe that immigrants cause more crime. However, one should be cautious not to overstate the case. Firstly, there is a considerable minority who are skeptical of increasing diversity. 31 per cent of Canadians believe that "too much diversity can weaken a society and it would be better if we all subscribed to the same values and culture", and 39 per cent believe that "Canada is changing too quickly because of all the minorities we have here now..." (Government of Canada 2015).

The acceptance of immigration and cultural diversity has never been unconditional: It has been based on the assumption that immigrants would assimilate or – after 1972 when assimilationist policies were abandoned – that they would integrate into Canadian society over time. When the Liberal Prime Minister Pierre Trudeau officially declared Canada a multicultural state in 1971, it was meant as a gesture towards descendants of "white ethnics", whose leaders had recently, as members of the Royal Commission on Bilingualism and Biculturalism, expressed a demand that their "contribution" to Canada be recognised. However, Trudeau also believed that the policy statement might encourage new immigrants to identify with

Canada and adapt to life in their new country. From the outset, then, multiculturalism was part of a nation-building project.

This is how it has worked, or at least *seems* to have worked, ever since: A large proportion of immigrants apply for Canadian citizenship shortly after their arrival, and are thus incorporated not only into the Canadian jobmarket, but also into the political community, a fact which scholars deem important for civic and social cohesion (Bloemraad 2006). This conclusion may also be drawn from polls that show that immigrants overwhelmingly identify with Canada rather than with their country of origin: In 2010, 78 per cent of those born outside of Canada identified with Canada, 13 per cent with their country of birth and 7 per cent with both equally (Focus Canada 2010: 18).

I want to argue in this chapter, however, that one should be cautious not to ascribe the success exclusively to multiculturalist policies, as Bloemraad does (Bloemraad 2006). A great deal of it should be explained with reference to the both popular and public tradition since the mid-1920s of understanding Canada as an ethnic and cultural "mosaic". As Donald Ipperciel explains in the following chapter, a new, normative and culturally inclusive notion of Britishness developed in the British dominions in this period. In Canada, it merged with a "territorial" and "cultural" Canadianness which acquired its first contours from the time of Confederation in 1867, but became a virtual cultural nationalism among British Canadians in the wake of the First World War (Böss forthcoming). What is important to understand is that the symbol of the mosaic did not connote that Canada was fragmented and nationally disunited. In actual fact, it meant the very opposite: unity in diversity. Trudeau's statement on multuticulturalism represented a re-interpretation of this idea, but it was also a statement about the unique character of Canada in relation to its great neighbour, the United States. Whereas the motto of the United States celebrated a plurality which became a unity (*e pluribus unum*), i.e. the ideas of assimilation in the American melting pot, Canadians were "unmeltable ethnics" (cf. Novak 1972) in the federal salad bowl that ony expected immigrants to integrate. Multiculturalism was a symbol of Canadian exceptionalism.

By declaring Canada a multicultural state in 1971, Trudeau broke with the long tradition of dualism - i.e. Canada as a state founded by two peoples, an anglophone and a francophone. Trudeau believed that dualism prevented Canadians from seeing themselves as members of one political community. Although it sounds paradoxical, multiculturalism - or cultural and ethnic pluralism - was thus part of the Liberals' project to create national unity; indeed multiculturalism was part of a nationalist discourse (Kernerman 2005).

This is why one should be cautioned against automatically translating support for multiculturalism into support for multicultural policy, theory, and philosophy.

It also explains why multiculturalism has sometimes been met with criticism from various groups opposed to this vision: conservatives, Quebec nationalists, indigenous groups, socialists, and lower-case liberals. However, multiculturalism has been a moving target and gone through different phases. And one of the great paradoxes is that, in today's Canada, the Conservatives has taken it to heart.

Multiculturalism today is a set of ideas, principles, and policies that have been discussed and implemented around the world, although mostly in western countries, which have become "globalised" by immigration. However, multiculturalism is of Canadian descent, and in order to understand it fully, one needs to know its origins. The purpose of this paper, therefore, is to give a historical account of the roots, developments, and contradictions of Canadian multiculturalism. The chapter is divided into sections that take the reader chronologically through the phases of Canadian multiculturalism, from its roots in the interwar period to its "symbolic", "legal", and "philosophical" phases 1971-1998. It ends with a section on the critiques of multiculturalism and an assessment of its present state and character.

The Canadian mosaic

Ironically, the image of Canada as an ethnic mosaic was first forged by an American, the journalist and writer Victoria Hayward. She based her travel book from 1922, *Romantic Canada*, on a journey she had just taken across Canada. Coming out of the extended woodlands of the Canadian Shield, she describes how she was taken by surprise when she got to the Prairies of Manitoba and Saskatchewan. She was fascinated by her encounter with the "New Canadians", i.e. the newly arrived immigrants from Germany, Ukraine, Iceland, and "widely different parts of the 'Old Europe'" (Hayward 1922: 187). She describes what she observed as a "mosaic", chiefly referring to the patchwork of material culture, for example the church buildings, which the many religious communities had erected, and which she observed from the train window. She believed that this large-scale mosaic of ethnicities and cultures represented unique riches which Canadians ought not only to tolerate, but also to appreciate.

The next writer to use the metaphor was Kate A. Foster. Foster had been commissioned by the Dominion Council of the YWCA to do a survey of immigration that could be used for the social philanthropy of the organisation. Her report was published in 1926 with the title *Our Canadian Mosaic*. Here the term was used as a description of how Canada was made up of disparate regions and localities with each their characteristics (Foster 1926).

That cultural diversity should be seen as a positive and charming feature of Canada was picked up by the tourist industry, which developed after the First World

War, chiefly targeting the British market. In 1907, the journalist John Murray Gibbon was hired by the newly completed transcontinental Canadian Pacific Railway to promote Canada in the United Kingdom. In 1913, he moved from London to Toronto to work as CPR's general publicity agent. He soon was to become an unofficial cultural ambassador for Canada, enthusiastically reporting about the country's many cultural and natural attractions. In 1938 he produced a series of radio talk shows for the Canadian Broadcasting Company (CBC), which he called "The Canadian Mosaic". The talks were afterward published in the book *Canadian Mosaic: The Making of a Northern Nation*. Here Gibbon describes the Canadian people as "a decorated surface, bright with inlays of separate coloured pieces, not painted in colours blended with brush on palette. The original background in which the inlays are set is still visible, but these inlays cover more space than that background, and so the ensemble may truly be called a mosaic" (Gibbon 1938: viii).

Before the Second World War, Canadians had long got used to seeing their country in terms of the metaphor of a mosaic. But a mosaic was not to be seen as a fragmented picture; there was unity to it, each unit in it being part of a larger picture: Canada. However, at the beginning – when Kate A. Foster wrote her report to the YWCA in the mid-1920s – she was evidently worried whether it would be possible for the dominion to assimilate the many new immigrants from Southern Europe, i.e. if they could find a place within the existing Anglo-Saxon culture of Canada, a country still a dominion with a clear British identity, politically as well as culturally. She found the problem most obvious on the Prairies, where the immigrants had settled in "solid blocs". However, she also noticed how, in the crowded inner cities, they tended to settle with people like themselves, i.e. in ethnic enclaves. This prevented them from a necessary process of "canadianization", she thought. But she chose to trust the long term success of the public school system in "melting these foreigners into Canadians" (Foster 1926: 9, 80).

However charming he found cultural diversity, John Murray Gibbon agreed that it would not remain. The diversity of Canadians was only due to the fact that it was such a young people, and sooner or later they would become more alike: "They are made up of European racial groups, the members of which are only beginning to get acquainted with each other, and have not been blended into one type. Possibly in another two hundred years, Canadians may be fused together and standardized so that you can recognize them anywhere in a crowd" (Gibbon 1938: vii). Like many Canadian politicians in that period, Gibbons favoured assimilation, and he believed that Canada was not different from the United States in that respect. However, he was also aware that some politicians thought that Canadians could develop a unique national identity if they tried "to preserve for the future Canadian race the most worthwhile qualities and traditions that each racial group has brought with it" (vii).

As Donald Ipperciel argues convincingly in the following chapter, this prospective Canadianness, which was also adopted by a few francophone intellectuals, marked a break with the earlier myth of Canada as a British nation built by an Anglo-Saxon master race. In "the dominions of the Third British Empire", Britishness instead became a normative idea that could accommodate many ethnicities and nationalities. It was this tradition that Pierre Trudeau drew on in his attempt to appease Quebec nationalists in 1971.

Quebec nationalism and Charles Taylor's philosophy of recognition

Cultural nationalism had been a feature of French Canadian identity as long back as the so-called Conquest of Nouvelle France in 1763. What was new in the 1960s, was the politicisation of cultural difference, based on the the conviction that the cultural survival of French language and culture depended on a high degree of political autonomy for the province of Quebec. A growing section of Quebec nationalists believed that it was necessary for Quebec to separate from Canada and to create an independent nation state.

This process began with the so-called Quiet Revolution. The historian Lucia Ferretti has defined the Quiet Revolution as a brief moment between 1959 and 1968, during which, "on the strength of a broad social consensus [...] the Quebec state pursued the dual objectives of an accellerated modernization on the Welfare State model and, very clearly, of the national promotion of francophone Québecois'" (Ferretti 1999, quoted from Gossage and Little 2012: 232). The term also alludes to the atmosphere of cultural revival and opposition to the province's repressive and authoritarian regime under Maurice Duplessis (Premier 1944-1959) and to the optimism that characterised the public mood of Quebec in the 1960s symbolised by Expo '67 in Montreal.

In traditional neo-nationalist accounts, the changes that took place in the 1960s were results of their own efforts. Over the past 20 years, however, francophone historians have downplayed the heroic theme and pointed out that the modernisation of Quebec was part of a process of industrialisation and urbanisation which also took place in other parts of Canada, indeed all over the western world, in that period (Migué 1999; Paquet 1999). Nevertheless, what should not be questioned is that, for most of the century, there had been economic imbalances between Quebec and the rest of Canada, and also internally between the province's French Canadian majority and its Anglo-Canadian business elite. The voices which called for social change and fairness did so for good reasons (Oullet 1990: 319).

Quebec nationalists did not represent a particular social group – the growing urban middle class – as it has beeen claimed (Guindon 1967; McRoberts and Posgate 1976). They represented a coalition of the francophone middle class, working class, and intelligentsia, who each had their own reasons for being dissatisfied with the status quo. Nor did they make a united front: They became federalists or separatists depending on the degree to which they saw their needs accommodated or frustrated (Coleman 1984). However, it would be a mistake to explain Quebec nationalism solely with social and economic arguments, as has often been the case in liberal and Marxist analysis. Fundamentally, Quebec nationalism represented both something "new" and something "old". The "old" element was a national identity with far deeper roots in North America than that of British – and anglophone – Canadians. Until the Second World War, British Canadian identity had been rather diffuse, fluid, and multifarious. Only in the late 1950s, partly as a result of the end of the British Empire (Buckner 2005), an exclusive identification with Canada had begun to crystallise, a process which has been called "the Second Quiet Revolution" (Igartua 2006).

The "new" element in Quebec nationalism was that, from having formerly been defined by the Catholic Church, the new nationalists emancipated themselves from their religious and cultural tradition. Instead nationalism became an ideology meant to serve the interests of a population which defined itself as a nation in terms of a shared language and history. Nationalists saw it as a common goal to end its social and economic marginalisation, put a brake on a centralising federal government, which was depriving it of its alleged historical right to govern itself, and protect its language against the increasing dominance of American culture. Many members of Quebec's English speaking intelligentsia sympathised with their cause, among whom the young philosopher Charles Taylor. In 1965, he wrote:

> The old nationalism was defensive; it was oriented around the fence of a way of life that was held already to exist but was in danger of being, if not submerged, at least undermined by the more robust North American culture alongside which it lived. [...] The basis of the new nationalism [...] was not the defence of anything existing; it was the creation of something new. Its aim was not to defend the traditional way of life but to build a modern French society on this continent. In its pure form, practically the only value it had in common with the old was the French language itself. The rest of what has been defined as French-Canadian tradition was seen in a very negative light (Taylor 1965 quoted from Taylor 1993: 5).

Taylor acknowledged that there were limits to how far the nationalist coalition was prepared to go in order to modernise their society. They knew that the process of modernisation might lead to the dissolution of French Canadians as a people. Hence there was a logic in the demand for more political autonomy, or alternatively, national independence.

Taylor himself saw nationalism not as an ideology of the past, but as a political phenomenon of the modern world. Over the following decades, he deveoped a generalised philosophy concerning the right of a nation, an ethnic group, and an individual to cultural recognition. This implied recognition of group rights: Since an individual's rights could not be exercised without the public recognition of the rights of the group to which he or she belonged, Taylor drew on a Romantic conception of identity:

> Since the Romantic insight is that we need a language in the broadest sense in order to discover our humanity, and that this language is something we have access to through our community, it is natural that the community defined by natural language should become one of the most important poles of identification for the civilization that is the heir of the Romantics (Taylor 1993: 47).

From Romantic conceptions of identity spring three notions that characterise modern – post-Romantic – thought, Taylor elaborated: expression, realization, and recognition.

"Expression" in so far as the conditions of an individual's identity are "a horizon of meaning, a language in the broad sense in which I can ask and answer questions of ultimate signicance" and which an individual only has access to through the culture of his or her community (48). It is therefore essential that this culture is rich and healthy. But the long-term health of a language and a culture depends on their being continually "re-created through expression", whether in works of art, public institutions or everyday exchange. Hence, any cultural community must have a right to "receive the scope it needs to maintain or increase its expressive power, which in turn is seen as a common condition of the identity of all speakers of the language" (49).

Since a language only gains expressive power in being used, there must therefore also be scope for "realization". This includes the language being used in public life, in business, in technology, in education, etc.

From this follows the third demand of "recognition" secured by law. This could only happen through a degree of self-rule (50). Because the language/culture needed for developing and maintaining identity is one that is always received from others, from one's surroundings, it becomes very important that the individual is recognised for what he or she is. If this recognition is denied by those who surround us, "it is extremely difficult to maintain a horizon of meaning by which to identify ourselves" (52). Furthermore, if a language and a culture which are considered valuable and indispensable to one's identity are not publically recognised, the individual cannot avoid depreciating himself or herself. The language of the national community must therefore be used in the vital areas of public life. Otherwise it will result in an impoverished culture.

As can be gleaned from these quotes, Taylor's "philosophy of recognition" developed within the context of rising claims of national self-determination in Quebec in the 1960s. It was to be integrated into his larger philosophy of modern selfhood in his masterpiece *Sources of the Self: The Making of the Modern Identity* (Taylor 1989).

Taylor's insistence on the vital need to recognise the cultural sources of individual identity was to have a tremendous impact on multiculturalist theories and the politics of identity in Canada and the United States, not least by virtue of the publication of his essay "The Politics of Recognition" in 1994 (Taylor 1994).

Taylor himself did not find the separatist, republican argument for Quebec independence convincing, however. He believed that, in a federation such as Canada, it was possible to practice a kind of self-rule which was necessary for the health and welfare of the francophone nation. He also emphasised that the principle of recognition must apply reciprocally, i.e. between language communities. The French speaking majority of Quebec would have to recognise the rights of the anglophone community of the province. He trusted they would be convinced of the liberal character of Quebec nationalism. This optimism, however, was not shared by one of the leading political figures of the day, the Liberal politician Pierre Elliott Trudeau. But before depicting his vision of Canada, we need to understand the context in which he acted.

Dualism confirmed: Canada becomes officially bilingual

Until 1969, Canada had been an English speaking country in practical terms. Even though both English and French were used in the Federal Parliament in Ottawa, the two languages did not have real equal status at the level of government. Francophone politicians did get appointed to ministerial positions in proportion to the size of the French Canadian population in Canada as a whole, but they were rarely given heavy, economic offices such as minister of finance, trade, and commerce (Gibson 1970: 165). Cabinet meetings were almost exclusively conducted in English, which was also the working language of public administration, whose upper echelons were dominated by anglophones and where francophones were also numerically underrepresented.

As a response to growing pressure from Quebec, the federal government introduced a bilingual policy in the federal civil service in 1966 (McRoberts 1997: 79-80). The reform was instigated as part of a cross-party strategy to contain the New Nationalism in Quebec. The Liberal Prime Minister Lester Pearson, who had formed his government in 1963, was seriously concerned with the unity of Canada, and therefore acted on the suggestion of the president of the Privy Council to introduce "perfect equality for the two official languages". The government set up a Royal Commission on Bilingualism and Biculturalism already from Pearson's first year in office to support the ambitious effort with a brief to

> inquire into and report upon the existing state of bilingualism and biculturalism in Canada and to recommend what steps should be taken to develop the Canadian Confederation on the basis of an equal partnership between the two founding races, taking into account the contribution made by the other ethnic groups to the cultural enrichment of Canada and the measures that should be taken to safeguard that contribution (Royal Commission 1965: 150).

The B&B Commission, as it would be called, treated "bilingualism" and "biculturalism" within a specific Canadian historical context, not as abstract principles. In accordance with the "dualist" tradition, it emphasised that the two languages of Canada were English and French, not any other language such as the languages of immigrants or indigenous groups (Royal Commission 1965: xxxi).

The commission ended up making recommendations that went beyond Pearson's original plan of "individual bilingualism". Instead it recommended "institutional bilingualism" arguing that "[a] bilingual country is not one, where all the inhabitants necessarily have to speak two languages; rather it is a country, where the principal public and private institutions must provide services in two languages to citizens, the vast majority of whom may very well be unilingual" (Royal Commission 1967 vol. 1: xxviii). In practical terms, this meant that English and French were to be declared "the official languages of the Parliament of Canada, of the federal courts, of the federal government, and of the federal administration" (91).

But there was more to this than an official recognition of French; it was also a recognition of French *culture*. Pearson was aware that language could not be abstracted from culture, and francophone civil servants would therefore be permitted to apply the values of their culture (McRoberts 1997: 80). Already in its preliminary report from 1965, the B&B Commission had defined culture as "a driving force animating a significant group of individuals united by a common tongue, and sharing the same customs, habits and experiences" (Royal Commission 1965: xxxi). Hence "equal partnership" meant equality between cultures. Therefore, a truly "bicultural" public service could only be created if there was "coexistence and collaboration of the two cultures so that both can flourish and contribute to the overall objectives of government" (Royal Commission 1967: 263).

The commission's recommendations led to the Official Languages Act of 1969. In the meantime, however, Lester Pearson had stepped down and passed his office to Pierre Elliott Trudeau. Trudeau was a bilingual Quebecker who had been a leading leftwing intellectual, anti-nationalist and social critic since the early 1950s. Trudeau was a strong supporter of a bilingual Canada as a means to enhance the role of francophones in Canadian society and government, but also as a means to making them less attached to Quebec and identify more with Canada.

Trudeau only supported "individual bilingualism", not special language rights for Quebec. He also disagreed with some of the assumptions behind the commission's arguments. As a liberal universalist and a believer in Canada's need for unity secured by a strong, modernising central government, he was against the notion of collective rights and the associated idea of a French speaking nation in Quebec. His government, therefore, did not take steps towards balancing federal departments on a linguistic basis and segregating workers according to the language of their first choice (McRoberts 1997: 82). Nor did it implement the commission's recommendation to strengthen the position of French in Quebec's private sector. To the degree that the government intervened at all, it was only to protect the English speaking minority. In other respects, however, the government conscientiously saw to it that all regulatives, directives, protections, laws, and public documents were published in both languages, and that all federal institutions were able to serve Canadian citizens in both languages. A new office of Commissioner for Official Languages was created to receive complaints, undertake inquiries, and make recommendations regarding the status of the two official languages.

As for biculturalism, however, the Trudeau government did nothing. He regarded the idea as divisive and preferred instead to define Canada as a culturally plural – or "multicultural" – society. The formal origins of multiculturalism are to be found in the final volume of the B&B Commission, which was published in 1970 as *The Cultural Contribution of the Other Ethnic Groups*. Among its authors were two Canadians of Ukrainian and Polish origin. They had consented to the bilingual policy of the commission's majority, but were opposed to its view of Canada as a bicultural country. They were of the opinion that, in its effort to accommodate French Canadians' demand to have their cultural rights recognised, the majority had neglected other groups who had also "contributed" to Canada. They found their own groups reduced to second-rate citizens by the government's continuation of the dualist tradition. Against that background, the last volume recommended that the government recognise and take appropriate measures to "safeguard" the contribution of "other ethnic groups".

In view of the fact the Canadian population was at that time made up of 26.7 per cent who was neither of British or French ancestry, but originated in other parts of Europe, the "white ethnics" did have a point, and it was taken by Pierre Trudeau.

Canada as a state without cultural identity: Trudeau's Canada

Trudeau liked the report. Not because he entertained a wish to give Canada a new cultural identity, however, but for the very opposite reason: Because he saw that the key to Canada's national unity was to define it as a state without a dominant culture and an official nationality. Culture was a private matter for individuals and groups, he thought. He had expressed this conviction several times in his past life as an intellectual, most cogently in his essay "The New Treason of the Intellectuals", which was published in April 1962 in *Cité Libre*, a major intellectual and political journal, which he had co-founded and edited since 1950.

The intellectuals, whom the title of the essay referred to, were French Canadian separatists, who, he claimed, had failed to make a proper distinction between nation, state, people, and sovereign people believing that states were dependent on the existence of nations. But the very idea of a nation-state was absurd, especially in a federation like Canada, and to insist that a particular nationality must have sovereign power would ultimately lead to its destruction, for there would always be ethnic and national minorities who would want to have their own state. Trudeau was strongly critical of nationalism built on notions of a national culture. Indeed the very idea of nationality had led to two centuries of war. The solution was, therefore, to abandon the concept of nation-state as an outdated idea. Acccording to the same line of thinking, Trudeau rejected Canadian dualism, which was the principle on which Canada had confederated in 1867. Dualism assumed that Canada was a binational federation and had nourished two nationalisms – an Anglo Canadian and a French Canadian nationalism – which were incongruous and had therefore been a block to Canadian unity. He concluded his essay by envisioning a "polyethnic pluralism" and a "regionalism" based on a degree of regional and local autonomy (Trudeau 1968: 165, 178). In 1962, Trudeau still used words and expressions like "nation" and "national characterstics", but he wanted the ties between state and nation to be severed, and he was adamant that there could not be a pan-Canadian nation in other than civic terms (178). As a "truly pluralistic state", Canada would, in the longer term, become "an envied seat of a form of federalism that belongs to tomorrow's world", Trudeau argued: a model superior to the American melting-pot and an example to the new post-colonial states in Asia and Africa. Finally, he offered a good argument for "cold-shouldering the lure of annexation to the United States". Indeed, the Canadian "experiment" could "become a brilliant prototype of the moulding of tomorrow's civilization" (179).

After 1962, however, Trudeau's enthusiasm for increased provincial "autonomy" waned in light of rising Quebec separatism. It convinced him that not even provinces should have the right to protect their "national characteristics". His vision of Canada as an ethnically plural state became one of the factors which motivated him

33

to announce his government's implementation of "a multicultural policy within a bilingual framework" in the House of Commons on October 8, 1971. But, obviously, there were also political concerns behind it. The Liberals were being challenged in Quebec, their traditional base of support, by the rise of separatism, and the party was trying to broaden its appeal. Its leaders hoped that multiculturalism might help them win votes from the ethnic communities in Ontario and to appease opposition to official bilingualism in Western Canada (Wayland 1997).

Trudeau's statement on multiculturalism did not refer to these political considerations, of course. Instead the policy was to serve two purposes. One was to secure the "cultural freedom" of Canadians by breaking down "discriminatory attitudes and cultural jealousies". The other was to restore national unity. He described the importance of individual culture to national identity as follows:

> National unity, if it is to mean anything in the deeply personal sense, must be founded on confidence in one's own individual identity; out of this can grow respect for that of others and a willingness to share ideas, attitudes and assumptions. A vigorous policy of multiculturalism will help create this initial confidence. It can form the base of a society which is based on fair play for all (Trudeau 1971: 134).

In other words, if individuals did not have the freedom to express and live according to their own culture, they would not be able to respect and share with others and participate on equal terms in society. This would erode national unity "from below" so to speak.

In his statement, Trudeau then listed the four main pillars of his government's policy:

- State support of "all Canadian cultural groups that have demonstrated a desire and an effort to continue to develop a capacity to grow and contribute to Canada, and a clear need for assistance," be they small and weak or strong and highly organised.
- Removal of "cultural barriers to full participation in Canadian society".
- Promotion of "creative encounters and interchange among all Canadian cultural groups in the interest of national unity".
- Assistance to immigrants "to acquire at least one of Canada's official language in order to become full participants in Canadian society" (Trudeau 1971: 134).

Trudeau's statement was received with almost unanimous support in Parliament. The members were used to such broad statements since the days of the Conservative Prime Minister John Diefenbaker (PM 1957-1963). Besides, it confirmed he bilingual character of Canada. However, there were dissenting voices outside

Parliament, especially in Quebec and in the media, where Trudeau's replacement of biculturalism with multiculturalism was met with the claim that it represented a betrayal and outdated views (Nemni 2011: 429). French Canadian nationalists winced at the statement's re-definition of what it meant to be a Canadian. Also English Canadian media, which had traditionally supported the Liberals, expressed some concern. The Canadian nationalist *Toronto Star* thus claimed that "no immigrant should be encouraged to think that Canada is essentially a chain of ethnic enclaves like the New Iceland Republic that once flourished on the shore of Lake Winnipeg" (quoted from English 2009: 146).

In spite of the fact that Trudeau never defined what it meant to recognise ethnic cultures – or the very concept of culture – the implications had the potential to go far beyond Trudeau's original intentions. Trudeau was convinced that the recognition of ethnic minorities would encourage them to identify with Canada and thus integrate the better into Canadian society. With the mass influx of non-western immigrants from Asia and the Carribean in the following decades, however, state multiculturalism was to become more than the nation-building project, as he had conceived it.

From lore to law: state multiculturalism phases one and two

State multiculturalism has been a dynamic project developing instutionally and theoretically from 1971 to the present. It has gone through a "symbolic", "legal", and "philosophical" phase and is now in a "conservative" phase. This section will focus on the first two.

To implement his vision of Canada, Trudeau established a special branch within the office of the Secretary of State and appointed a minister of multiculturalism. However, in the 1970s, multiculturalism remained rather marginal as a policy and mostly had a symbolic and "folkloristic" character. Public authorities and institutions would regularly state their recognition and "celebration" of Canada's cultural diversity. Funds would be channelled into a programme which supported language training and cultural festivals – as, for example, the annual Cabana festival in Toronto.

In 1982, the re-elected Trudeau, again motivated by the twin political goals of attracting minority voters and defeating Quebec nationalism (Gwyn 1980; Plamondon 2013: 171), decided to add more substance to the policy, not only by increasing the public funding of ethnic associations, but also by inserting a passage in the Charter of Rights and Freedoms in connection with the patriation of the Constitution in 1982. Section 27 thus read: "This Charter shall be interpreted in a manner consistent with the preservation and enhancement of the multicultural heritage of Canadians." What exactly was intended with the section was never officially stated by Trudeau. But from then on, multiculturalism was no longer just an official policy, but a part of the Canadian Constitution: a national value meant to direct policy making and prevent laws from infringing on the the individual's cultural rights. It was not, however, a collective right (Hogg 1982). All his life, Trudeau had been a firm believer in liberal individualism. He also acknowledged that discrimination of minorities could become a barrier to the individual's ability to choose and express his or her own identity. Trudeau's vision of Canada was never a community of (cultural) communities, but a political community of self-determining citizens.

After the passing of the Constitution Act of 1982, The Canadian Ethnic-Cultural Council (established 1973) criticised what it still regarded as a rather empty gesture. Claiming that the Charter continued the tradition of favouring francophone and anglophone cultures, it began to lobby for a more substantial multiculturalism based on law. In 1987, the Standing Committee on Multiculturalism, created in 1985, concluded in its annual report that multiculturalism as a policy had lost direction. The original idea, that the federal state had committed itself to protecting minority cultures, had been receding and was being replaced by a policy aiming at getting rid of racism and discrimination of so-called visible minorities from Asia and the Carribean, who made up 70 percent of immigrants in the mid-80s. This critique was not misplaced. In fact it was the direction in which state multiculturalism was going from the mid-1980s, when the large majority of immigrants to Canada now came from Asia, Africa, and Latin America (Naidoo and Edwards 1991).

The Conservative Prime Minister, Brian Mulroney (PM 1984-1993) responded to this critique by passing the Multiculturalism Act in 1988 and creating a Department of Multiculturalism and Citizenship. The act charged all federal institutions

- to ensure that Canadians of all origins have an equal opportunity to obtain employment and advancement in those institutions;
- promote policies, programs and practices that enhance the ability of individuals and communities of all origins to contribute to the continuing evolution of Canada;
- promote policies, programs and practices that enhance the understanding of and respect for the diversity of the members of Canadian society;
- collect statistical data in order to enable the development of policies, programs and practices that are sensitive and responsive to the multicultural reality of Canada;
- make use, as appropriate, of the language skills and cultural understanding of individuals of all origins; and
- generally, carry on their activities in a manner that is sensitive and responsive to the multicultural reality of Canada (Government of Canada 1988).

The act thus stated that multiculturalism was a fundamental feature of Canadian society and that it was the state's obligation to increase minority participation in Canada's major institutions. From now on, all government agencies, departments, and Crown corporations had an obligation to provide leadership in designing and implementing plans, programmes, procedures and decision-making strategies that enhanced the inclusion and participation of minorities in institutional structures. In practice, this meant the establishment of quotas and preferences in hiring and recruitment schemes and accommodating minorities in public workspaces.

In the 1990s, the "legal" phase of state multiculturalism was succeeded by a "philosophical phase" in which academics undergirded state multiculturalism with philosophical and theoretical arguments. The most prominent were James Tully and Will Kymlicka.

Tully contrasted "culture" and "nation" arguing that, since cultures are diverse, flexible and overlapping, a cultural politics of recognition will lead to harmonious coexistence among cultural groups, whereas the idea of the nation is exclusive and will therefore lead to social and political division. The implication was that democratic institutions, laws and constitutions should not be treated as if they were set in stone, i.e. as a fixed set of rules, but should be seen as an imperfect form of accommodation of the diverse members of a political association. Tully argued for further democratisation based on negotiations among the members of society's many cultures (Tully 1995: 29). His philosophy was "grounded" in a Canadian context, and his particular interest in how to accommodate Canada's indigenous population gave him a role as special advisor to the Royal Commission on Aboriginal Peoples 1991-1995. Although his "public philosophy" also has a global dimension, he has never had the same impact internationally as Will Kymlicka.

Will Kymlicka's Canada

It was *Multicultural Citizenship* (1995) which made Kymlicka an international household name among political theorists and philosophers in the 1990s. In 2004, he was recognised by the United Nations as an international authority on how to protect cultural freedom in the contemporary world (United Nations 2004). In response to critiques of multiculturalism, both in Canada and Europe, his writings have taken an increasingly defensive character, which is also reflected in his contribution to the present volume. He believes that the critiques are unfair, because they build on misunderstandings and misinterpretations of liberal multiculturalism.

The task that Kymlicka has always been engaged in is to reflect on how it may be possible to create an inclusive society, which is able to accommodate cultural difference without violating liberal principles and jeopardizing social cohesion and democracy. Key to this is defining a differentiated – or as he calls it – a "multicultural" citizenship. He believes that this idea is part of a Canadian tradition. Since Confederation in 1867, he claims, Canada has constantly been engaged in an attempt to find new and creative mechanisms of balancing groups and achieving equality among them. He thinks that this ideal of equality was finally legally recognised in 1989, when the Canadian Supreme Court stated that the "accommodation of difference is the essence of true equality" (quoted in Kymlicka 1996: 153).

Kymlicka does not think that Canada has developed a perfect model, however. He concedes that Canada's international reputation as a tolerant and culturally inclusive state builds on a process, which has only taken place since the 1960s, and he often contrasts the present with a past marked by assimilation policies towards indigenous groups, racist immigration laws, and discrimination of visible minorities (e.g., Kymlicka 2004b). And he grants that Canada has not yet succeeded in eradicating racism against visible minorities (cf. Kymlicka 2001: ch. 9).

What does Kymlicka's vision of Canada look like, then? He describes Canada as a multinational and multiethnic state. Canada's *multinationality* is a result of its history. Before Canada was created as a British dominion in 1867, Canada had had the status of a British colony since 1763. But Canada's history goes even further back: to the building of the British and French empires in North America in the 17th century, which involved the confiscation of the lands of the original inhabitants. In this way, Canada could be said to be made up of three nations: English Canadians, French Canadians, and indigenous peoples (Indians, Inuit, and Metís). These nations have each their own language, but nations are not only based on a common language, Kymlicka holds. He defines a nation as a society which, apart from a language, has its own institutions, homeland, and history. A nation does not need to have its own state, however. But in order to exist and survive, it must possess some political institutions, a particular cultural tradition, and a territory which it regards as its homeland.

To avoid confusing "nation" and "nation-state", Kymlicka initially used the expression "societal culture". He defined it as "a territorially-concentrated culture, centred on a shared language which is used in a wide range of social institutions in both public and private life (schools, media, law, economy, government, etc.)" (Kymlicka 2001: 25). The reason he called it a *societal* culture was to emphasise that it is based on language and social institutions, rather than on common religious beliefs, customs, myths, and lifestyles. Modern nations are pluralistic and culturally diverse, and seldom based on race and ethnicity. They are almost invariably products of nation-building on the part of governments and states. However, after being criticised for its imprecise meaning and its assumption of homogeneity (Benhabib 2002: 60), Kymlicka stopped using it.

Canada's *multiethnic* character is also due to its history; not the history of settlement, but of immigration. Kymlicka prefers "multiethnic" to "multicultural", partly because he finds the latter concept ambiguous, partly because he wants to distance himself from radical multiculturalist thinkers, as for example Bhiku Parekh. But also because the word used in a Canadian context would imply that French Canadians or First Nations (Canadian Indians) would have the same status and rights as ethnic immigrant groups. But ethnic minorities cannot demand the same rights as nations, such as a territory, political institutions, and self-determination. For immigrants are individuals, who voluntarily choose to leave their original homelands, or are descended from those who did. Hence, they must be expected to integrate into their host country. In return, however, the state must offer them fair conditions for their integration. Since it may be a long and difficult process, the majority population has a moral obligation to show patience and goodwill towards them. Furthermore, the state must be prepared to accommodate them by offering them language training, so that they may learn to master the language of the nation, English or French, that they will ultimately become part of. Equally important is it that the state ensures that the national institutions are organised in such a way that they are shown the same degree of respect and recognition as the settled majority population. This requires

> A systematic exploration of our social institutions to see whether their rules and symbols disadvantage immigrants. For example, we need to examine dress-codes, public holidays, even height and weight restrictions, to see whether they are biased against central immigrant groups. We also need to examine the portrayal of minorities in school curricula or the media to see if they are stereotypical, or fail to recognize the contributions of immigrants to national history or world culture. These measures are needed to ensure that liberal states are offering immigrants fair terms of integration (Kymlicka 2001: 30).

Kymlicka thus abandons the traditional liberal idea of universal citizenship that applies equally to all citizens. But this does not abandon liberal values and principles. It is a matter of adapting the liberal values of freedom and equalty to the conditions of diversity, which apply not only in Canada, but all over the world, and which often lead to civil conflicts.

Multicultural citizenship does not tolerate all cultural deviation. Cultural rules and norms must be compatible with basic liberal values, first of all individual freedom and self-determination. But it builds on the assumption that individuals do not only have political and social rights, but also cultural rights. Multicultural citizenship is meant to protect that right, i.e. the individual's right to his or her cultural identity. This involves protecting collective rights. Kymlicka believes that multicultural citizenship should (1) protect members of Canada's three nations; (2)

secure polyethnic rights for members of religious and cultural minorities; and (3) distribute rights of special representation to ensure marginalised regions and groups (women, ethnic groups, and linguistic minorities, e.g.) against being overlooked or discriminated by the federal government or provincial assemblies.

Kymlicka sanctions group rights but sets limits on how far a group can go in order to assert its cultural rights and preserve itself as a group. He distinguishes between two types of collective rights: rights that are meant to protect the group from *internal deviation* and rights that meant to protect the group from *external pressure*. The first type of rights are those that a group may claim in order to limit the freedom of its individual members under the pretext of protecting its culture and securing "cultural purity" and social survival. This claim could involve a limitation of women's or children's right of self-determination. Kymlicka rejects these rights as illiberal. Laws and customs that violate the democratic and constitutional rights of individuals to dissent and exit from the group must be regarded as illicit. The Canadian Charter of Rights and Freedoms must thus be regarded as superior to cultural custom and tradition.

The second type of collective rights – rights against *external pressure* – also serve to enhance the group's ability to survive. But Kymlicka deems them acceptable from a liberal point of view. Such rights may apply, for example, when an indigenous group demands the right to protect its power over its territory and society by regulating the sale and use of land and property, or by regulating the use of the national language. Although such regulations do limit the right of private property or may require settlers to learn the local language, they are legitimate and fully compatible with liberal principles. Indeed, they are even quintessentially liberal, Kymlicka argues, in so far as they contribute to creating a level playing field for indigenous groups and national minorities. He thus gives sanction to the right of Quebec to enforce laws that protect the French language.

Kymlicka thinks that granting ethnic or religious immigrant minorities special rights may be justified by the same argument. An example often referred to in Canada is the right of Sikh members of the Royal Mounted Police to wear turbans. Kymlicka is aware that there are many problems involved in assigning cultural groups special sets of rights, especially rights of self-government and religious rights that exempt members of the group from full participation in society. His argument, also in such situations, is that differentiated citizenship must be organised, so as not to conflict with the individual's right and the integrative goal of citizenship.

Kymlicka remains fairly optimistic about Canada's future as a united polity, and does not believe that multiculturalism leads to its fragmentation, as many of his critics claim. He argues that, since its founding, Canada has experienced a high degree of peace and toleration among its national and ethnic groups. He explains it as a result of a political system which has been sufficiently flexible to accommodate the various groups' demands for self-determination and recognition without risking the collapse of the federation. He also notes that the various demands for cultural protection and recognition have never been meant as a first step towards separating the group from the state. On the contrary, they seem to have been motivated by the group's wish to be included in the larger society and the political community. The demand to be accommodated, in other words, has always been a demand for inclusion, not self-exclusion. The demands for special rights from various cultural groups have gone in different directions, and the groups behind them have been so small that they have, more or less, balanced each other off, creating a kind of ordered chaos.

In recent years, however, Kymlicka has become less optimistic about the future of multiculturalism. He is particularly concerned about its "backlash" in Europe as it is reflected in public statements from Nicolas Sarkozy, Angela Merkel, and David Cameron about the "failure of multiculturalism" (see, e.g., Kymlicka 2007). Canada became a model for Australia, which in the mid-1970s adopted a multiculturalist integration policy under Whitlam and Fraser (Mann 2012; Theophanous 1995). However, Kymlicka is reluctant to use Canadian multiculturalism as a universal model of how to manage national, ethnic, and cultural minorities since, as he argues, the "Canadian model" was a result of special historical circumstances. It is indeed "misleading to talk of 'the Canadian model of diversity', as if there were one overarching policy on diversity from which policies regarding Aboriginal peoples, francophones, and immigrant/ethnic groups could be derived or deduced" (Kymlicka 2007: 3). Canada was founded on the basis of a unique colonial experience, but has also, since the 1960s, had an immigration history which differs from that of Europe (Kymlicka 2004a). Hence, Kymlicka believes, each European state must find its own way of doing it, based on a combination of "best practices" and their own histories.

This does not mean, however, that Kymlicka is complacent about Canada. He is painfully aware that many Canadians are badly informed about the nature and implications of multiculturalism, and that they have taken to it partly because it is a marker of Canadian difference and a source of national pride, which is partly due to the way the Canadian government has used it to "market" Canada internationally (Kymlicka 2007). And in spite of the fact that Canadians support the multicultural character of Canada, multiculturalism as an idea and a policy has never been uncontested in Canada. These critiques will be described in the following section.

The critiques of state multiculturalism

Ever since 1971, there have been both supporters and critics of multiculturalism both as a philosophy and a policy. Supporters have argued that multiculturalism assists in the integration of immigrants and minorities because it removes barriers to participation in Canadian society. It makes them feel more welcome, and therefore they develop a sense of belonging. Critics of multiculturalism argue that it promotes national fragmentation, enourages ethnic enclaves, and makes members of ethnic and religious groups look inward. It makes them emphasise differences between themselves and other groups, rather than develop a sense of shared identity as Canadian citizens.

In the early 1970s, many English Canadians were ready to accept Trudeau's vision of a multicultural Canada, because it expressed a view of "Canadianness" which was recognizable: It was rooted in the tradition of the ethnic mosaic and confirmed them in their belief that Canada was indeed a unique place with its own cultural identity.

As already indicated above, however, Quebec nationalists were strongly critical of multiculturalism; first of all because they rightfully saw it as representing a rejection of Quebec's and the French Canadians' special position in Canada since Confederation. This caused them sincere worries about their future, not only in Canada, but in English speaking North America as a whole. The most cogent critique was articulated by the highly respected sociologist Guy Rocher, who analysed the sociological and philosophical assumptions of the notion of a multicultural society (Rocher 1972).

Rocher castigated multiculturalism because it built on an untenable distinction between language and culture. Since only a minority of Canadians were bilingual – unlike Trudeau, who was the son of a mother of Scottish descent and a French speaking father – official bilingualism in a multicultural context would mean that the French language would gradually lose its social and cultural basis. It would be reduced to an abstract symbol of culture that belonged to the past. Ultimately, such an "artificial" bilingualism would lead to the death of the French language in Canada (Rocher 1972: 137). If Trudeau really meant what he said – that speaking one's vernacular was crucial for an individual's identity – then the logical consequence would be that all languages in Canadian society would have to be put on equal terms. Then one might as well abandon the whole idea of official languages.

Rocher's second argument pertained to the question of preserving national unity in a multicultural society. In Trudeau's definition of the Canadian nation, it had "no central cultural core" which was "clearly definable". This meant, Rocher argued, that Canada was made into "a sort of microcosm or meeting-place for all the nations of the world, represented here by groups of greater or lesser numerical size, all having equal right to recognition and financial support by the Canadian government". In

Rocher's opinion, these ethno-national groups would benefit better if the two major linguistic and cultural communities were maintained as poles around which they might group. Instead they were offered "a nebulous sort of image constituted by an undefined number of different cultures" with "no common denominator" (Rocher 1972: 137). Rocher wondered what kind of nation could exist on a basis so fluid and noncommittal.

Finally, he outlined the consequences for the francophone community. Multiculturalism, he argued, would be a large step backwards in regard to the recognition of French language and culture, which had recently been achieved after a century long struggle for survival and equality on a continent overwhelmingly dominated by an anglophone population and culture. And since also economic forces acted to the advantage of speakers of English, the French community would become "more and more secondary in the midst of all the other culture which will compose the new Canadian mosaic" (Rocher 1972: 138). Rocher predicted that multiculturalism would stoke the fire of Quebec separatism and make the option of an independent state even more attractive to an increasing number of French Canadians. It would thus lead to the destruction of the Canadian Confederation.

Canadian Indians – or First Nations – rejected Canadian state multiculturalism for other reasons. As a young political science student claimed, multiculturalism treated them as immigrants in their own land (Sebastian n.d.). Since the mid-1990s, academics of indigenous background drawing on postcolonial theory have depicted multiculturalism as part of a "politics of settlement", i.e. as colonization of space and meaning and "securing the material and symbolic contours of the state" by other means (Chaza et al. 2011: 1).

Among English Canadians, intellectuals and academics have voiced critiques ranging over the full political scale from conservative-assimilationists over liberal democrats – critical of group rights – to neo-marxists seeing multiculturalism as a veil drawn over socio-economic divisions. These critiques began in the late 1970s and early 1980s (Peter 1978, 1979; Kallen 1982), i.e. before the full unfolding of multicultural policy. In her thorough analysis of multiculturalism as a set of social values (ideology), a federal programme (policy), and an ethnopolitical movement (social reality), the sociologist Evelyn Kallen concluded in 1982 that, on all three counts, evidence indicated that "the concept of multiculturalism is inherently problematic" (Kallen 1982, quoted from Cameron 2004: 89).

The 1990s a period in which Canadians began to worry about immigration from non-western countries – many books and articles questioned the basic assumptions of multiculturalism. Most influential was the book of a recent immigrant, the Carribean Canadian novelist Neil Bissoondath. In his bestselling *Selling Illusions: The Cult of Multiculturalism in Canada* (1994), Bissoondath castigated multicultural ideology as being based on "illusions", first of all the idea that multicultural integration is better than the old assimilationist model of turning immigrants into Canadians. In his opinion the problem with multiculturalism was that it did not expect immigrants to change and adapt to life in their new country, but assumed that the host society was to change in accommodating them. Bissoondath regarded Canadian multiculturalism as a "cult" and a kind of cultural apartheid, which prevented immigrants from realising their dream of becoming Canadians and part of the larger Canadian community. He even went as far as describing it as a covert strategy to keep them on the lower social rungs of the social ladder – an idea that obviously built on leftwing sociologist John Porter's description of Canada as a "vertical mosaic" (Porter 1965). However, to Bissoondath, the most serious problem was the long-term effect of multiculturalism. For, as he asked, is there a point when difference begins to threaten the cohesion of society (Bissoondath 1993: 373)?

On a similar note, the prominent liberal civil servant, journalist, and author Richard Gwyn discussed how multiculturalism limited an individual's identity, trapping him or her within a stereotype of the identity of his alleged group. Multiculturalism had invented a duty not to merge with the Canadian mainstream. But what was particularly problematic was Canadians' loss of control over their "collective citizenship" at a time when society was getting increasingly exposed to globalisation:

> Like all nation-states, the authority and effectiveness of ours has been eroded by the global economy. Our state's down-going matters more to us than to any other people, though, because, lacking a distinctive ethnic identity, we've used the state to give us collective shape. As the state weakens, the 'caring and sharing' concept of Canadianism [...] becomes less and less able to resist the polarizing effect of globalism and technology upon incomes and jobs; the impact of both of these is being magnified further by the contemporary dominance of neo-conservative, free-market ideology. As Canadians become more and more different from each other – not as a function of demography but as a function of their rising demands to be treated as 'differentiated citizens' on the basis of their cultures and values – the less Canadians will be interested in, let alone care about, each other (Gwyn 1992: 8).

Gwyn thus saw multiculturalism and its idea of culturally differentiated citizenship as leading to the erosion of solidarity among citizens and ultimately to a loss of social cohesion and national unity.

The sociologist Reginald Bibby, who monitored Canada's landscape of social values over three decades, described multiculturalism as pluralism gone mad: "Faced with the problem of creating a society in which people of varied linguistic and cultural backgrounds can live together, Canadians have decided to convert a demographic reality into a national virtue" (Bibby 1990: 7). This had led to an excessive combination of individualism and value relativism that, paradoxically, combined with a moral absolutism of a purely formal character: the right to express one's cultural identity. Gone was the idea of shared values and goals, also of the value of traditional national values of coexistence:

> If there is no subsequent vision, no national goals, no explicit sense of coexisting for some purpose, pluralism becomes an uninspiring end itself. Rather than coexistence being the foundation that enables a diverse nation to collectively pursue the best kind of existence possible, coexistence degenerates into a national preoccupation. Pluralism ceases to have a cause. The result: mosaic madness (Bibby 1990: 104; cf. Padolsky 2000).

The Conservative historian Jack Granatstein saw multiculturalism as the root cause of Canadians' loss of their past. Governments at all levels had been

> throwing money for years into multicultural education and, in the process, the history of Canada, where it is even taught, has been distorted out of all recognitioin. Guilt, victimhood, redress, and the avoidance of offence – those are the watchwords that rule today (Granatstein 1998: 83).

The purpose appears to be to destroy the past, Granatstein argued, "so that we can build anew the perfect multicultural society with the new 'core Canadian values' predominant" (93). But this will in reality mean overlooking the state's original cultural traditions and their roots in European civilisation on which it was founded (xiv). Granatstein later observed how, paradoxically, multiculturalism had led to a strange conformity when it came to Canadians expressing themselves on public and social issues: "People are increasingly afraid to speak out lest they be labelled racist. Many Canadians seem to have forgotten that diversity of opinion is at least as important, indeed more important, to democracy as diversity of race, gender, and religion" (Granatstein 2011: 284).

But not only intellectuals criticised multiculturalism. In the 1990s, there was also, on a popular level, growing concerns about the effect of multiculturalist policy on Canadian society (Dasko 2002). And, on the political level, multiculturalist policy developed in a new direction, especially after 2001.

Multiculturalist policy re-oriented

In a report from Citizens' Forum on Canada's Future, the writers noted that, while Canada as a nation of immigrants is recognised and celebrated, there were considerable concerns among the citizens as to multiculturalist programmes. Especially, there was opposition to the continued use of public funds to support heritage language and culture programs. Achieving balance between an evolving multicultural Canada and a secure sense of Canadian identity provoked much discussion among contributors and resulted in comments such as that from the Ontario participant who said: "Ethnic and cultural diversity is an attractive embroidery on our national fabric, but [...] if we really want a country, we must be Canadians first" (Citizens Forum 41-42).

This critique was picked up by the Reform Party, a new conservative party, which had been founded in 1987 in opposition to Brian Mulroney's Progressive Conservatives. The party, which was based in Alberta, was a populist and socially conservative party which fought for constitutional reforms that would create a fairer balance between the West and central provinces of Ontario and Quebec. It was strongly opposed to government-funded and sponsored bilingualism and multiculturalism, which were regarded as Liberal policies. The party's founder, Preston Manning, claimed that efforts to create a bilingual country had not been successful, and that language issues should be dealt with on a provincial level. Multiculturalism was criticised for creating a "hyphenated Canadian" identity, rather than a single Canadian identity (Manning 1992).

Shortly before Mulroney's government left office in 1993, it closed the Department of Multiculturalism that had been established only five years earlier, and in 1996, the Progressive Conservatives officially repudiated multiculturalism as a policy. When it was succeeded by a Liberal Government, the new Prime Minister, Jean Chretien, decided not to revive the department. Instead, the Multiculturalism Act was to be administered by a new Department of Canadian Heritage, which had responsibility for a host of other policies and programmes: the arts, culture, media, communications networks, the official languages, the status of women, and sports.

The transfer signified a downgrading of multiculturalism as a major policy area in its own right, and also reflected how the public support for multiculturalism had decreased throughout the decade (Dasko 2002). In response to growing concerns about the "balkanization", the department began to focus more on the integration of newly arriving immigrants than on promoting a pluralist society. The term "multiculturalism" was removed from prominence, and the goals of multiculturalism were now identified as "build[ing] a more inclusive and cohesive society by addressing three objectives: social justice, identity, and civic participation" (Canada 1997 quoted from Winther 2007). The new emphasis on citizenship signalled a commitment to civil society and an inclusive expression for membership in the Canadian "nation".

After 9/11, the critique of multiculturalism as a policy took another turn upwards as difference in terms of religion rather than ethncity and race challenged the basically liberal assumptions of multiculturalism. A number of cases created strong popular reactions, most prominently the campaign of an Iranian immigrant, Homa Arjoman, against the plans of the Ontario Supreme Court to allow sharia principles to be applied in family conflicts. Arjoman received strong support from feminists, who had long argued that multiculturalism was "bad for women" (Okin 1999).

The mainstream critique focused not only on matters of how to deal with illiberal minority cultures and issues of national security, but also with the policy's inefficiency as a framework for promoting social harmony. In the 2007 hearings in Quebec, conducted by a commission headed by the sociologist Gérard Bouchard and the philosopher Charles Taylor, it appeared as if the whole idea and purpose of multiculturalism was ripe for re-examination and renegotiation as the cornerstone of Canadian identity. The report, which was published the following year, did acknowledge that religious and cultural differences could only be expected to be "reasonably accommodated". The general message of the report thus confirmed the official "intercultural" policy of the province, i.e. a compromise between the polar opposites of multiculturalism and assimilation. Interculturalism emphasises the need for intercultural understanding. It demands respect towards ethno-cultural-religious minorities, and it is in favour of selected measures targeted at disadvantaged situations such as recent immigration. Yet it also aims at securing commitment to the values, history, and traditions of the host country, and is prepared to use integration policies and efforts that water down excessive distinctiveness and self-segregation (Emerson 2011).

When Stephen Harper took office in 2006 as head of the Progressive Conservatives, most political observers expected him to put a final lid on multiculturalism. He had begun his political career in the Reform Party, which, as we saw, had denounced multiculturalism as part of the Liberals' vision for Canada. To the observers' great surprise – but also the continued puzzlement of traditional multiculturalists (Ryan 2010, e.g.) – the Conservative government ended up embracing it, although the embrace was regarded as rather ambiguous and rhetorical by critics (Ryan 2010: ch. 6). Harper saw the grat potential in attracting votes of groups that shared his party's socially conservative values, and created a Secretary of State for Multiculturalism and Canadian Identity and gave it to his loyal aide, Jason Kenney.

As Minister for the new Department of Citizenship, Immigration and Multiculturalism 2008-2013, Kenney had considerable success in unsettling liberal multiculturalism and re-setting it on Conservative terms, while at the same time, changing citizenship and immigration rules and laws (Griffith 2013). Kenney was concerned with what he and his party regarded as an increasing diversity in Canada. "This makes our jobs challenging and complex, so we must work hard to ensure continued social cohesion and focus on what unites us as a country," Kenney said in 2010 (Griffith 2013: n.p). Multiculturalism was now part of the Conservatives' ambitious project of a renewed patriotism. It was about Canadian identity, being proud of Canada and bringing Canadians together and less about minority-majority issues. The government continued to emphasise the need to fight racial discrimination and to "always be vigilant against hatred inspired by race, religion, and ethnicity" (Griffith 2013: note 76). It also stressed the importance of preventing religious – Islamic – extremism and anti-semitism.

The key objective of his department's Multiculturalism Program was to build "an integrated, socially cohesive society, while promoting intercultural and interfaith understanding and fostering citizenship, civic memory, civic pride, and respect for core democratic values" (Government of Canada 2010-11). On the department's website, it said that "through multiculturalism, Canada recognizes the cultural heritage and the potential of all Canadians, encouraging them to integrate into Canadian society and take an active part in its social, cultural, economic and political affairs" (Government of Canada, Citizenship and Immigration). It was still the governement's commitment to reach out to Canadians and newcomers and develop "lasting relationships with ethnic and religious communities in Canada." However, it was up to these communities "to participate fully in society by enhancing their level of economic, social, and cultural integration. Accordingly, immigrants were expected to "adapt to a reasonable degree" to life in Canadian society. Active citizenship and participation in civic life in Canada should enhance the mutual connections of Canadians."

Intellectually, the critiques of multiculturalism continued in the first decade of this century with both liberal and conservative academics denouncing multiculturalism as a "delectable lie" (Mansur 2011), a hindrance to full participation in the Labour Market Council (Garcea 2008), and a threat to democracy in the light of militant islamism (Steyn 2009). The sharpest critique of the ethics of multiculturalism was formulated by the political scientist Janice Gross Stein (Stein 2007). Stein notes that multiculturalism, which began as recognition of ethnic difference, is now being tested by a global resurge of religious orthodoxy, and this does not leave Canada untouched:

> The most obvious fault line is the tension between the treatment of women and homosexuals in different religions and cultures, and their rights to equality that are given voice through the Charter. Multiculturalism is being tested in part because Canadians are uncertain about what limits, if any, there are to embedding diverse religious and cultural traditions within the Canadian context. We know pretty well what the 'multi' in multicultural means, but are much less confident about the 'culture'. [...] There is more than a sniff of smugness in our celebration of our success as multicultural society. Is respect for difference being polluted by a reluctance to set limits, to give positive content to what and who we are as well as to what we recognize and respect? (Stein 2007: 4, 6).

Will Kymlicka's response to this critique was that Stein did not correctly represent either the "ethos" of multiculturalism properly, namely as one of inclusion, or the "policy" of multiculturalism, which, as in The Multiculturalism Act of 1988, was "located squarely within the larger framework of liberal constitutionalism" (Kymlicka 2007d: 139, 145). Kymlicka was definitely not a supporter of the Conservative government. Still, he was occasionally used by it, for example to report on the state of multiculturalism in Canada (Kymlicka 2010). But it is equally true that official multiculturalism today appears in a renegotiated and re-articulated form, and is now implemented as a policy within a new institutional structure which puts emphasis on helping immigrants to integrate into Canadian society.

Conclusion

As officially stated, multiculturalism is today understood as fundamental to the belief that "all citizens are equal". It ensures "that all citizens can keep their identities, can take pride in their ancestry and have a sense of belonging". The official acceptance of diversity is said to give "Canadians a feeling of security and self-confidence, making them more open to, and accepting of, diverse cultures". Finally, it says, "Canadian experience has shown that multiculturalism encourages racial and ethnic harmony and cross-cultural understanding, and discourages ghettoization, hatred, discrimination and violence" (Government of Canada, Multiculturalism). These phrases might have been articulated by Trudeau in the 1970s.

However, as reflected in the citizenship test introduced by the Harper government in 2009, multiculturalism has become part of a national and patriotic discourse. In practical terms, multiculturalist policy must not encourage immigrants and their descendants to self-segregate on the basis of ethnic or religious identity. Whereas for Trudeau, multiculturalism was an instrument of nation-building in a strictly civic sense, it gradually turned part of a project to unite Canadians with reference to a shared history that made them distinct from Americans.

There is no doubt that, today, multiculturalism as a policy is less favourably viewed by Canadians than multiculturalism as a fact of life and a national symbol. There are probably two explanations. As I have argued here, Canada's long tradition of seeing ethnic diversity as a national characteristic makes Canadians support multiculturalism both as a sociological fact and as a symbol of national uniqueness and identity. The other reason is probably: The kind of individuals that Canada attracts and admits are "cherry-picked" voluntary immigrants who have decided to pull up their roots to become Canadians. Seen in this light, however, the success of Canada in creating social harmony among culturally diverse groups might have much less to do with state multiculturalism than often claimed.

References

Adams. M. *Unlikely Utopia*. Toronto: Penguin Canada, 2008.

Banting, K. and W. Kymlicka. *Multiculturalism and the Welfare State: Recognition and Redistribution in Contemporary Democracies*. Oxford: Oxford University Press, 2006.

Benhabib, S. *The Claims of Culture: Equality and Diversity in the Global Era*. Princeton, NJ: Princeton University Press, 2002.

Bibby, R. *Mosaic Madness: The Poverty and Potential Life in Canada*. Toronto: Stoddart, 1990.

Bissoondath, N. *Selling Illusions: The Cult of Multiculturalism in Canada*. Toronto: Penguin Books, 1994.

Bloemraad, I. *Becoming a Citizen: Incorporating Immigrants and Refugees in the United States and Canada*. Berkeley: University of California Press, 2006

Buckner, P. *Canada and the End of Empire*. Vancouver: UBC Press, 2005.

Böss, N. *Canada: State without Nation?: A History of Canadian Identities*. Aarhus: Aarhus University Press, forthcoming.

Cameron, E., ed. *Multiculturalism and Immigration in Canada: An Introductory Reader*. Toronto: Canadian Scholars' Press, 2004.

Canada. *Multiculturalism Program: The Context for Renewal*. Ottawa: Government of Canada, 1997.

Canada. "A Literature Review of Public Opinion Research on Canadian Attitudes Towards Multiculturalism and Immigration, 2006-2009." Ottawa: Government of Canada, http://www.cic.gc.ca/english/resources/research/por-multi-imm/sec02-1.asp.

Chazan, M. et al. "Introduction: Labours, Lands and Bodies." In *Home and Native Land: Unseettling Multiculturalism in Canada*, ed. May Chazan et al., 1-11. Toronto: Between the Lines, 2011.

Citizens' Forum on Canada's Future: A Report to the People and Government of Canada. Ottawa: Government of Canada, 1991.

Coleman, W.D. *The Independence Movement in Quebec 1945-1980*. Toronto: University of Toronto Press, 1984.

Dasko, D. "Public Attitudes towards Multiculturalism and Bilingualism in Canada." Paper Presented at the Canadian and French Perspectives on Diversity, Ottawa, 16 October, 2003, http://www.queensu.ca/cora/_files/diversity_dasko.pdf.

Emerson, M., ed. *Interculturalism*. Brussels: Centre for European Policy Studies, 2011.

English, J. *Just Watch Me: The Life of Pierre Elliott Trudeau 1968-2000*. Toronto: Vintage Canada, 2009.

Ferretti, L. "La Révolution tranquille." *L'Action nationale*, December, 1999.

Focus Canada 2002. Toronto: Environics, 2002.

Foster, K.A. *Our Canadian Mosaic*. Toronto: The Commission Council of the YWCA, 1926.

Garcea. J. "Postulations on the Fragmentary Effects of Multiculturalism in Canada." *Canadian Ethnic Studies* 40, 1 (2008): 141-60.

Gibbon, J.M. *Canadian Mosaic: The Making of a Northern Nation*.Toronto: McClelland and Stewart, 1938.

Gibson, F.W., ed. *Cabinet Formation and Bicultural Relations*, Studies of the Royal Commission on Bilingualism and Biculturalism, no. 6. Ottawa: Queen's Printer, 1970.

Gossage, P. and J.I. Little. *An Illustrated History of Quebec: Tradition and Modernity*. Don Mills, ON: Oxford University Press, 2012.

Government of Canada. "Canadian Multiculturalism Act," 1988, http://laws-lois.justice.gc.ca/eng/acts/C-18.7/page-1.html.

Government of Canada. 2011, Citizenship and Immigration. Annual Report on the Operation of the Canadian Multiculturalism Act 2010-2011, http://www.cic.gc.ca/english/resources/publications/multi-report2011/part1.asp.

Government of Canada. 2015, Citizenship and Immigration, http://www.cic.gc.ca/english/department/.

Government of Canada. Citizens and Immigration. "A Literature Review of Public Opinion Research on Canadian Attitudes towards multiculturalism and immigration, 2006-2009", http://www.cic.gc.ca/english/resources/research/por-multi-imm/sec01-1.asp, Accessed Dec. 15. 2015.

Government of Canada. Citizens and Immigration, "Canadian Multiculturalism: An Inclusive Citizenship", http://www.cic.ca/english/multiculturalism/citizenship.asp, Accessed Dec. 15. 2015.

Granatstein, J. *Who Killed Canadian History?* Toronto: Harper Collins, 1998.

Granatstein, J. "Who Are We Now? A Multicultural Canada in the Twenty-First Century." In *Narrating Peoplehood amidst Diversity*, ed. Michael Böss, 273-88. Aarhus: Aarhus University Press, 2011.

Griffith, A. *Policy Arrogance or Innocent Bias: Resetting Citizenship and Multiculturalism*. Ottawa: Anar Press, Kindle digital, 2013.

Guindon, H. "The Social Evolution of Quebec Reconsidered." *Canadian Journal of Economics and Political Science* xxvi (November 1960): 553-61.

Guindon, H. "Two Cultures: An Essay on Nationalism, Class and Ethnic Tensions." In *Contemporary Canada*, ed. R. Leach. Durham, NC: Duke University Press, 1967.

Gwyn, R. *Northern Magus: Pierre Trudeau and Canadians*. Toronto: McClelland and Stewart, 1980.

Gwyn, R. *Nationalism without Walls: The Unbearable Lightness of Being Canadian*. Toronto: McClelland and Stewart, 1996.

Hayward, V. *Romantic Canada*. Toronto: Macmillan, 1922.

Helmes-Hayes, R. and J. Curtis. *The Vertical Mosaic Revisited*. Toronto: University of Toronto Press, 1998.

Hogg, P.W. *Canada Act 1982 Annotated*. Toronto, Canada: The Carswell Company Limited, 1982.

Igartua, J.E. *The Other Quiet Revolution: National Identities in English Canada, 1945-71*. Vancouver: UBC Press, 2006.

Kallen, K. "Multiculturalism: Ideology, Policy and Reality." *Journal of Canadian Studies* 17, 1 (Spring 1982): 51-63.

Kernerman, G. *Multicultural Nationalism: Civilising Difference, Constituting Community*. Vancouver: UBC Press, 2005.

Kymlicka. W. *Liberalism, Community and Culture*. Oxford: Oxford University Press, 1989.

Kymlicka, W. *Multicultural Citizenship*. Oxford: Clarendon, 1995a.

Kymlicka, W., ed. *The Rights of Minority Cultures*. Oxford: Oxford University Press, 1995b.

Kymlicka, W. "Three Forms of Group-Differentiated Citizenship in Canada." In *Democracy and Difference: Contesting the Boundaries of the Political*, ed. S. Benhabib, 153-70. Princeton, NJ: Princeton University Press, 1996.

Kymlicka, W. *Finding Our Way: Rethinking Ethnic Relations in Canada*. Toronto: Oxford University Press, 1998.

Kymlicka, W. *Politics in the Vernacular: Nationalism, Multiculturalism, and Citizenship*. Oxford: Oxford University Press, 2001.

Kymlicka, W. and W. Norman, eds. *Citizenship in Diverse Societies*. Oxford: Oxford University Press, 2003.

Kymlicka, W. "Citizens, Communities, and Identities in Canada." In *Canadian Politics*, ed. J. Bickerton and A.-G. Gagnon, 35-54. Peterborough, ON: Broadview Press, 2004a.

Kymlicka. W. "Marketing Canadian Pluralism in the International Arena." *International Journal* 59, 4, (2004b): 829-52.

Kymlicka, W. *Multicultural Odysseys: Navigating the New International Politics of Diversity*. Oxford: Oxford University Press, 2007a.

Kymlicka, W. "The New Debate on Minority Rights (and Postscript)." In *Multiculturalism and Political Theory*, ed. A.S. Laden and D. Owen, 25-59. Cambridge: Cambridge University Press, 2007b.

Kymlicka, W. "Marketing Canadian Pluralism in the International Arena." *International Journal* 59, 4 (2007c): 829-52.

Kymlicka, W. "Disentangling the Debate." In *Uneasy Partners*, J.G. Stein et al., 137-56. Waterloo, ON: Wilfrid Laurier Press, 2007d.

Kymlicka, W. *The Current State of Multiculturalism in Canada and Research Themes on Canadian Multiculturalism 2008-2010*. Ottawa: Government of Canada, 2010.

Mann, J. "The Introduction of Multiculturalism in Canada and Australia." *Nations and Nationalism* 18, 3 (2012): 1-21.

Manning, P. *A New Canada*. Toronto: Macmillan Canada, 1992.

Mansur, S. *Delectable Lie: A Liberal Repudiation of Multiculturalism*. Brantford, ON: Mantua Books, 2011.

McRoberts. K. and D. Posgate. *Quebec: Social Change and Political Crisis*. Toronto: Toronto University Press, 1976.

McRoberts, K. *Misconceiving Canada: The Struggle for National Unity*. Toronto: Oxford University Press, 1997.

Migué, J.-L. *Étatisme et decline du Québec: Bilan de a revolution tranquille*. Montreal: Edition Varia, 1999.

Naidoo, J.C. and R.G. Edwards. "Combatting Racism Involving Visible Minorities: A Review of Relevant Research and Policy Development." *Canadian Social Work Review* 8, 2 (Summer 1991): 211-36.

Nemni, M. and M. *Trudeau Transformed: The Shaping of a Statesman, 1944-1965*. Toronto: McClelland and Stewart, 2011.

Novak, M. *Unmeltable Ethnics: Politics and Culture in American Life*. New Brunswick: Transaction Publishers, 1972.

Okin, S.M. et al. *Is Multiculturalism Bad for Women?* Princeton, NJ: Princeton University Press, 1999.

Oullet, F. *Economy, Class, and Nation in Quebec*. Toronto: Copp Clark Pitman, 1991.

Padolsky, E. "Multiculturalism at the Millenium." *Journal of Canadians Studies*, 35, 1 (2000): 138-60.

Paquet, G. *Oublier la Revolution tranquille. Pour une nouvelle socialite*. Montreal: Liber, 1999.

Peter, K. "Multicultural Politics, Money and the Conduct of Canadian Ethnic Studies." *Canadian Ethnic Studies Association Bulletin* 5, 2-3 (1978).

Peter, K. "The Myth of Multiculturalism and Other Political Fables." Paper presented at the Canadian Ethnic Studies Conference, Vancouver, B.C., October 1979.

Plamondon, B. *The Truth about Trudeau*. Ottawa: Great River Media, 2013.

Porter, P. *The Vertical Mosaic: An Analysis of Social Class and Power in Canada*. Toronto: University of Toronto Press, 1965

Rocher, G. "Les ambiguïtés d'un Canada bilingue et multicultural." In *Essential Readings in Canadian Government and Politics*, ed. P. H. Russell et al., 135-38. Toronto: Edmond Montgomery Publications, 2010.

Royal Commission on Bilingualism and Biculturalism, *Preliminary Report*. Ottawa, 1965.

Royal Commission on Bilingualism and Biculturalism. Ottawa, 1967

Royal Commission on Bilingualism and Biculturalism. Ottawa, 1970.

Ryan, P. *Multicultiphobia*. Toronto: Toronto University Press, 2010.

Sebastian, T. "Immigrants in Our Own Land," *Voices*, no date, http://www.darrenduncan.net/archived_web_work/voices/voices_v1_n1/immigrants.html.

Stein. J.G. et al. *Uneasy Partners: Multiculturalism and Rights in Canada*. Waterloo, ON: Wilfrid Laurier Press, 2007.

Steyn, M. *Lights Out: Islam, Free Speech and The Twilight Of The West*. Toronto: Stockade Books, 2009.

Taylor, C. "Nationalism and the Political Intelligentsia: A Case Study." *Queen's Quarterly* 72 (Spring 1965): 150-68.

Taylor, C. *Sources of the Self: The Making of the Modern Identity*. Cambrige MA: Harvard University Press, 1989.

Taylor, C. *Reconciling the Solitudes: Essays on Canadian Federalism and Nationalism*. Montreal and Kingston: McGill-Queen's University Press, 1993.

Theophanous, A.C. *Understanding Multiculticultralism and Australian Identity*. Melbourne: Elikia Books, 1995.

Trudeau, P.E. "Statement on Multiculturalism." In *Essential Readings in Canadian Government and Politics*, ed. P. H. Russell et al., 133-36. Toronto: Edmond Montgomery Publications, 2010.

Tully, J. *Strange Multiplicity: Constitutionalism in an Age of Diversity*. Cambridge: Cambridge University Press, 1995.

United Nations. *Human Development Report: Cultural Liberty in Today's Diverse World*. New York: UNDP, 2004.

Wayland, S.V. "Immigration, Multiculturalism and National Identity in Canada." *International Journal of Group Rights* 5, 1 (1997): 46-47.

Winther, E. "Bridging Unequal Relations, Ethnic Diversity, and the Dream of Unified Nationhood: Multiculturalism in Canada." *Zeitschrift für Kanada-Studien* 1 (2007): 38-57.

2 Britishness and Canadian Multiculturalism

Donald Ipperciel

This chapter seeks to contribute to the debate on the ideological origins of Canadian multiculturalism, which is a different matter, one should note, from analysing its strictly historical origins,[1] the emphasis here being on ideas rather than events. In general, commentators have above all been interested in the proximal causes of Canadian multiculturalism, and in this context, they are right in finding its origins in the aftermath of the Laurendeau-Dunton Commission, in Trudeau's ideas or, indirectly, in the civil rights movement in the United States. Even those who wish to attribute its paternity to Yuzyk[2] are only pushing back its origins by a few years. For my own part, I would like to consider a more distal cause, one that is more conducive to exposing the underlying forces at play. Mindful of the principle that history does not move in leaps and bounds, we have reason to posit prior circumstances having contributed to the emergence of Canadian legislation and public policy on multiculturalism in the 1970s. I will defend the thesis that Canadian multiculturalism finds its ideological source in a normative multiculturalism characteristic of the third British Empire, also known as the British Commonwealth, a political organization that existed between the First and the Second World Wars. In so doing, I do not mean to suggest that Canada was actually, at that time, a multicultural haven. Indeed, much has been written with regard to the prevalence of Anglo-conformity in public as well as private doings in Canada (cf. Kymlicka 1995: 14-15; 1998: 44, 74; Palmer 1990). It will be enough in this context to ascertain the known and established presence of the idea of multiculturalism in the normative landscape of that period. Multiculturalism, here, should not be understood in a descriptive sense as tied to a demographic reality, nor as governmental policy, as they were implemented since the 1970s. Evidently, multiculturalism is meant

---

1. For such a historical analysis of the origin of Canadian multiculturalism, cf. e.g. Wayland 1997.
2. This is the case of the Conservative Party of Canada, perhaps eager to claim, among ethnic communities, some of the credit for multiculturalism normally accorded to the Liberal Party of Canada. Cf. Jason Kenney's speech (2009) as Minister for Citizens, Immigration and Multiculturalism.

here as the ideal of coexistence of cultures within a single state and the resulting identity dimension with regard to nation building.

After the First World War, a new wind was sweeping the world: the principle of self-determination for small nations, as popularised by President Wilson, had come to the fore; the League of Nations, founded on the equality of small and large nations, had been created; the Statute of Westminster, instituting a community of free and equal nations, a Commonwealth of "sister nations", had been promulgated. These are all signs of the emergence of the principle of the equal dignity of peoples and cultures. As Michael Böss describes in the preceding chapter, it was also during this period that the metaphor of the "mosaic" was first introduced to describe Canadian society (cf. Gibbon 1938: viii-ix; Day 2000: 149-153).

I believe that Britishness can be understood as a precursor to Canadian multiculturalism as in that period, the very idea of the former contained a normative notion of the latter. The origin of the term "British" as a political concept dates back to the formal union of Scotland and England in 1707, with the Acts of Union, and encompassed the "English" and the "Scottish". The concept gradually expanded with the Empire, to the point where, formally from 1914, Britishness became the privilege of all the King's subjects, and all individuals born in the colonies were considered British, irrespective of their race or ethnic group. After the Second World War, the notion of Britishness contracted, applying only to the territory of the United Kingdom. It is in its broad sense, however, as it was used during the Third Empire, that Britishness will be understood in this paper.

The multicultural vision peculiar to the Third British Empire will be brought to the fore. To this end, reference will be made especially to Alfred Zimmern who, as an idealist thinker of the British Empire, highlights its normative dimension in a quite distinctive manner. The link between the abstract thought of a British thinker and Canadian interwar multiculturalism will next be established by way of presenting the views of Canada's representative of the Crown and head of state at the time, Governor General John Buchan. And finally, to dispel the possible impression that Britishness-qua-multiculturalism was an essentially Anglo-centric ideal based on an overly-generous self-assessment on the part of the English, the focus in the last section will be on Édouard Montpetit, a French Canadian nationalist representing one fringe minority within the British Empire.

Britishness and the multiculturalism of the third British Empire: Alfred Zimmern

In this section, I would like to focus on one of the first great studies dedicated to the Third Empire,[3] written during the turbulent years of its formation, that is, *The Third British Empire* (1934) by Alfred Zimmern, first written in 1926. At the time, the author was an eminent specialist in international relations. He was the first to hold the Woodrow Wilson chair of International Relations at the University College of Wales, Aberystwyth, the first Montague Burton Professor of International Relations at Oxford and one of the fathers of International Relations as an academic discipline (Rich 2003: 79). A renowned idealist, pacifist, and internationalist, he was an influential architect of the League of Nations and director of its Institute of Intellectual Cooperation, the precursor to UNESCO.[4] In 1946, he was nominated for the Nobel Peace Prize. Zimmern viewed the Third Empire as a model for internationalism.

In his most abstract conception, Zimmern situates the British Empire in a dialectic of unity and diversity. On the one hand, unity is assured by a *political* community symbolized by the Crown, its ideals and its institutions. The guiding ideal is liberty, both individual – as secured by the rule of law protecting individuals against the arbitrary use of powers[5] – and national – as represented by a people's right to self-determination. Even though the principle of liberty has often been flouted in the past, it remains nonetheless in his view a norm to which the Third Empire aspired, and which, in his mind, was gradually being achieved, as evidenced by, among other things, the granting of dominionhood to former colonies of the Empire. Zimmern compares the Empire to a "procession" of communities en route towards complete self-determination (Zimmern 1934: 8). Certainly, the principle of trusteeship favoured by Zimmern and the Empire still constitutes a form of paternalism towards the directly administered territories, but subsequent history will confirm that the Empire's goal of granting formal liberty to peoples under its jurisdiction was indeed genuine. This movement towards ever-expanding liberty originated, according to Zimmern, with the beginning of the Second Empire, as indicated by the Quebec Act of 1774 (cf. ibid.: 180) and the Royal Proclamation of 1794. The latter in particular established that British constitutional rights "were not the exclusive patrimony and privilege of the inhabitants of Great Britain and their

---

3. H. Duncan Hall's work, *The British Commonwealth of Nations*, 1920, was the first to be published on this subject.
4. Cf. Markwell 2004; McIntyre 2009: 31-37 for a short biography; Rich 2003: 80-82 for biographical information. According to Rich 2003, Einstein, Bartok and Bergson were members of the committee chaired by Zimmern (p. 81).
5. In this context, Zimmern takes pleasure in saying that the British Empire "has brought one quarter of humanity under a single law" (p. 104).

descendants at home and overseas, but that they rightfully belonged to all those under the British flag" (Zimmern 1934: 25). Such an understanding of the British Empire will impact the very idea of Britishness. According to Zimmern,

> the content of that adjective "British" [...] defies exact interpretation. It is not an adjective of race. It is not an adjective of nationality. It is not an adjective of territory. [... Rather,] it denotes a political and social tradition and a mode of life in which that tradition is revealed – a mode of life characterized by common habits, common institutions, and a certain unexpressed philosophy of public affairs (ibid.: 96).[6]

Thus, from the outset, Britishness appears in Zimmern as a political concept, as well as a social one.

In contrast to this unity, one also finds a multi-levelled diversity: *geographical*, since the Empire had spread to all continents; *racial*, with members of all races; *religious*, including all the great religions; *cultural*, embracing Germanic (Afrikaners), Latin (French Canadians) and Slavic (especially in Western Canada) cultures; and *governmental*, there being fundamental differences between the governments of the United Kingdom, the dominions and the communities dependent upon the Imperial Government (with this latter group being itself heterogeneous) (cf. ibid.: 6-11).

In this dialectic of unity and diversity, what is at stake is the way in which unity can actually be reconciled with diversity. In other words, how can diversity remain without exerting purely centrifugal and self-destructive forces? Zimmern's response to this question rests on his criticism of political nationalism (or "mazzinism"; cf. Rich 2003: 82). One must keep in mind that Zimmern regards nationalism as one of the major sources of war in the world, along with interracial relations between whites and non-whites and economic relations between the rich and the poor (Zimmern 1934: 108). In his mind, political nationalism is a mistaken ideology originating in the French Revolution of 1789, which conflated political liberty, i.e. free institutions of state, with national consciousness, a process of social psychology (cf. Zimmern 1929: 88). It is this identification of unrelated concepts that has led many to infer the coextension of state and nation. The substance of this argument is well known, since it more or less recasts Lord Acton's criticism of J.S. Mill. Not only do the concepts of liberty and nationality not coincide, argues Acton, but their aims often collide.[7] In this context, the principle of nationality must be subsumed

---

6. In another passage, he says: "The tie remains, what it has always been, not material but spiritual. It is the tie of a common political tradition, common political institutions and a common outlook on public affairs" (ibid.:100).
7. "Nationality is the great carrier of custom, of unreflecting habit and transmitted ideas that quench individuality. [...] Nationality has to be dealt with discriminatingly. It is not always liberal or constructive. It may be as dangerous when its boundary is outside that of the State as salutary when inside" (1917: 182).

to that of liberty. Hence, "nationality [is] an essential, but not a supreme element in determining the forms of the state" (1907).

The solution that Zimmern proposes to the incommensurability of liberty and nationality differs from Acton's, first because the principle of nationality seems to him to be unsuited to the political realm. From a theoretical point of view, it goes against the idea of equal justice among citizens, since the residents of a national territory who do not belong to the dominant nationality are *ipso facto* reduced to a position of civic inferiority. Here, one recognises Zimmern's political moralism, his belief in the moral progress of politics (Rich 2003: 89). From a practical point of view, he opines, the principle of nationality is contrary to the actual reality of national states, which are in no way homogeneous, thus weakening the correspondence between free institutions and national institutions (Zimmern 1934: 171-3). Such arguments are commonplace today and have been taken up by many critics of nationalism, too numerous to be cited here. What Zimmern proposes as a solution, however, is not a subordination of the political principle of nationality to that of liberty, as advocated by Lord Acton, but rather the straightforward depoliticisation of nationality and hence its exclusion from the political sphere (ibid.: 186).

Now, one must acknowledge that a nation depoliticised in this way is reduced to the status of a cultural community. If, on the one hand, the political realm rests on a system of law, a government and institutions, nationality, on the other hand, is of a cultural nature according to Zimmern. As a result, the two concepts occupy different ontological spaces: "The question of nationality raises a spiritual problem, or, if you like, a cultural problem. [...] It is perfectly possible for a group to be at once politically self-governing and culturally immature and even dependent" (ibid.: 175-6). This seemed to be the case in New Zealand, which at that time, as a dominion, possessed its own governmental institutions but a culture – white, of course – derived from England's. Conversely, Zimmern believes that "it is possible for a community under the British flag to be politically dependent and culturally independent" (ibid.: 176), as was India, then governed by London, but possessed of a rich culture peculiar to itself. On the basis of this fundamental distinction, Zimmern criticises the Durham report written in 1839 in the wake of the Rebellions of 1837 and generally construed by French Canadians as an example of ethnocentric English arrogance. In his view, Durham shows very well that he has grasped the political dimension of the problem in proposing an institutional reform in line with responsible government. Yet, he seems to have completely misjudged the problem of nationality in seeking to erase French Canadian culture in favour of English ways. He seems to have confused the political and cultural dimensions in attempting to resolve a problem that was strictly political. In this context, instead of invoking the cultural superiority of *Englishness* which, in his mind, is the product of a "reactionary philosophy" (ibid.: 178),[8] one merely has to apply the political and legal principles of *Britishness*.

In short, Zimmern's dialectic of unity and diversity corresponds to the relation between the single *political* state (including its laws, its government, its institutions) and the plurality of *cultural* communities in its midst. What the British Commonwealth stands for is precisely the harmony of these two planes, which can only be achieved by recognising that each has its own ontological space and its own sphere of activity. Problems arise, then, from the confusion of the two planes: "So far from associating and confusing government with nationality [the British Commonwealth] has recognized that the whole art of government consists in bringing different kinds of people, different nations, different groups, different religions, different cultures, under a single law, under what we call the 'Pax Britannica', under an international system – I stress the 'inter' – of justice" (Zimmern 1934: 174).

This passage and Zimmern's entire thought could be understood simply in terms of "world order", as many commentators of his work have done (cf. Miller 1979-80; Rich 2003). But the remainder of the text is quite telling with regard to the contexts in which the dialectic of political unity and cultural diversity can be applied. According to Zimmern, while referring to the right of different nationalities to exist within the state, "[i]t was on this principle that in the Act of 1867, French Canada and British Canada were included in a single confederation" (Zimmern 1934: 174). In other words, the dialectic of political unity and national diversity applies to the Canadian dominion insofar as a "dominion is a political entity" (ibid.: 175) that enables the subsumption of diverse nationalities, which Zimmern essentially construes as diverse cultures. He has conceived of nothing less than a multicultural Canada, whose model derived from the union of England, Scotland, Wales, and Ulster under the government of Great Britain. Moreover, it is significant, according to Zimmern, that three of the five dominions were at the time bilingual (i.e. Canada, South Africa, and Ireland). As a result, his idea of the union of nationalities or cultures under a political order translates not only an internationalist vision, but also an accomplished form of sub-state arrangement. In this sense, multiculturalism is internationalism writ small. To a great extent, that is what Britishness stands for in the Third Empire.

What should be underscored in Zimmern's sub-state multiculturalism, something which he thought he had already recognised in Canada's constitution itself, is his "strong" theory of cultural coexistence. In other words, for him it is not just a matter of *tolerating* cultural diversity, tolerance being far too passive a concept. One should rather seek actively to commit oneself to the other: "Tolerance is not

---

8. He applied this term to Dilke as well as Durham because of their Anglo-centric views.

enough. There is something further required – understanding and an effort to reach an equal relationship" (ibid.: 181). Indeed, on the basis of an equal dignity of cultures, one has not only to make sure that cultural communities are not perceived by others or by themselves as inferior or "colonial", but also that they attain self-respect: "the principle of nationality knows of no colonies; it knows only of equal, self-respecting communities" (ibid.: 184). Diversity is envisaged accordingly as a blessing for the benefit of all humanity that can even promote the peaceful resolution of many political disputes (ibid.: 185-6).

Of course, the idea of multiculturalism did not monopolise all of the normative space that existed during the Third Empire. Rather, it was engaged in a "competition of norms". This is why, from the start, Zimmern polemicised against the Anglo-centrists of his time. He recognises that there was a time when Britishness had an ethnic meaning, but he thinks that the term "Britishness" has shed this particular connotation by the time of the Third Empire. "Today [the term 'Britishness'] has no national significance whatsoever. If you are told today that a man is British or a Britisher, it does not convey anything at all as to his language or his culture. 'British' has become nationally colourless, in order to become politically significant" (ibid.: 180). Obviously, the descriptive formulation of this quote should not overshadow is normative tenor: according to Zimmern, the word "British" *should* be free from any national or ethnic meaning.

It seems that Zimmern may be recognised as one of the intellectual precursors of Canadian multiculturalism. But this thesis will be more convincing when it is shown in the next two sections that Zimmern's thought actually found articulate echoes in Canada.

The multiculturalism of the British Crown's representative in Canada, John Buchan

The idea of Britishness-qua-multiculturalism was more than a norm championed by English intellectuals during the interwar period. One could say that it was also, in a sense, a norm sanctioned by the Canadian state of the time, most notably in the person of its Governor General, representative of the British Crown and head of state, John Buchan, also known as Lord Tweedsmuir. This can be gathered from his addresses,[9] which allowed the idea of multiculturalism to flourish endogenously, as it were, in the Canadian public space of the 1930's. The dissemination of the idea of multiculturalism was quite successful in part because of the prestige and

---

9. I will rely principally on Buchan's addresses while he was Governor General of Canada, as they appear in Buchan 1940 and Gibbon 1938. For his non-published addresses, I will cite from Henshaw 2007.

dignity associated with the function of Governor General at the time, but also owing to the wide broadcasting of his addresses in the French as well as the English Canadian media. Indeed, many of these were radio broadcast throughout Canada and published in various newspapers of the country or in an anthology of addresses (Buchan 1940). This is not to say that multiculturalism was at that time a dominant idea nor that it constituted an official policy of the Canadian government. On the contrary, Buchan's multiculturalism seems to have been rather controversial, especially among Anglo-Canadians (Henshaw 2007: 201). Be that as it may, during Buchan's tenure, the idea of multiculturalism became firmly established in the normative landscape of Canadian public debate.

As the representative of the British Crown in Canada, Buchan most certainly had an acute sense of the Empire's dignity and virtues. His description of the British Empire echoes those of Zimmern and many other apologists. Interestingly, Buchan and Zimmern most probably knew each other and shared a similar vision of British imperialism. Both were members of what Carroll Quigley has called the "Milner Group" (1981: ix),[10] a group of Oxonians in Alfred Milner's entourage. Milner was a colonial administrator in South Africa at the beginning of the 20th century and Minister of War in David Lloyd George's cabinet during the First World War. He is known to have been a fervent imperialist and a champion of the idea of an imperial federation. According to Quigley, the members of the Milner Group, also known as "Milner's Kindergarten" or the "Round Table Group", among other designations, all knew each other "intimately" (ibid.). The members of this group also played an important role in David Lloyd George's cabinet during the First World War. More specifically, Alfred Zimmern was a leading figure of the Political Intelligence Department, a unit of the Department of Information, of which Buchan was the director (cf. Smith 1996: 120).

Like Zimmern, Buchan emphasises the dialectical play of unity and diversity characteristic of the British Commonwealth, with unity being ensured in Buchan's thought by the Crown:

> What is there in common between Canada, a white man's democracy, and, say, the Fiji Islands; or between India, which is now making its first trial of self-government, and Britain, which has been self governing for a thousand years? What is there in common between peoples who represent every race-stock on earth? Yet these differences are differences within a unity. The Throne binds the whole Empire together and gives cohesion to a vast growth whose ultimate destiny is unpredictable (1940: 99).

---

10. On Zimmern's association with this group, cf. ibid.: 52.

Again like Zimmern, Buchan believes that the British Empire constitutes a partnership of sorts between distinct peoples whose purpose is to maintain a Pax Britannica, not unlike the League of Nations. Expatiating on the Empire, he states shortly before his arrival on Canadian soil that "we are a living proof that peoples can dwell together in unity and peace, for have we not made in the Empire a league of nations of our own, and insured that over a great part of the earth's surface there can never be war?" (1940: 13). Diversity within the Empire constitutes in itself a virtue that ought to be celebrated. Thus, immediately upon his arrival in Canada, he claims that "it is the glory of our empire to embrace within its confines many races and traditions. It is in its variety that its strength lies" (from Henshaw 2007: 192).

Moreover, the British foundation of Buchan's multiculturalist thought is evident in the paradigmatic value he attributes to Scottishness within Britishness. Buchan was a Scot who made his career in the British Empire, and in his discourses, he rarely neglected to mention his native Scotland. It goes without saying that he asserted a strong Scottish identity coexisting with (or better yet: nested within) a strong British identity – coloured, one must add, by an Oxonian sense of elitism. In his mind, Scotland portrays doubly the dialectic of diversity and unity: internally, since it is the fruit of the union of diverse peoples, in particular of two groups that have often been at arms against each other, i.e. the Highland and Lowland Scots (Buchan 1940: 44; cf. Henshaw 2007: 199); but also in its relationship to England (Buchan 1940: 44). Great Britain was born of the union between Scotland (and other nations) and England, which leads Buchan to say: "We Scots have always been exponents of unity" (ibid.). With quasi-mystical fervour, he seems to attribute to the Scottish "race" a unifying power whose action should not be limited to Great Britain and the British Empire (cf. ibid.: 32), but should contribute to the ideal of "a unity in spirit of the nations of the world" (ibid.: 45). In the end, the entrenchment of Scottishness within Britishness is the primordial proof of the latter's capacity to integrate cultural diversity. It is this reality that one should strive to adapt to the Canadian context.

It is thus through the prism of a "British" Scotland, distinct but united, that Buchan sees Canada. As a result, "Canada, in one sense, is simply Scotland writ large" (ibid.: 39). In many passages, he reiterates that as a Scot, he has to insist on the culturally plural character of the Canadian nation. Accordingly, at the *Congrès de la langue française*, he states in 1937: "Any wise man, any Scot in particular, certainly believes that the mixing of races fortifies a nation" (ibid.: 243, my translation from French).

Buchan's addresses are telling in that one can discern in them different dimensions of Canadian multiculturalism. First, in general terms, one finds the attitudinal dimension of openness towards others, that is, towards individuals of different origins, religions, and cultures. As does Herder's nationalist humanism (and Charles

Taylor's in his wake), Buchan recognizes a certain intrinsic value in all foreign cultures. "It is our business in studying the mind of foreign peoples to look for the kernel of truth, the element of value which must be there" (Buchan 1940: 83). In this sense, diversity is valued in and for itself.

Now, if all cultures have an equal dignity, they can, and indeed must, all be celebrated equally. Anglo-conformity, insofar as it transgresses this principle, is thus *ipso facto* invalidated. For his part, Buchan often insists on the duty to remember incumbent upon all cultural communities in Canada and the importance of affirming one's roots. Here, one recognises the historical-identitary dimension of Canadian multiculturalism. This message is a leitmotif of Buchan's discourses, one which he regularly adapted according to the particular ethnic group that he happened to be addressing. To the members of the Icelandic community of Gimli, whom he congratulates as being "in the fullest sense good Canadians", he said: "I rejoice to think that you have never forgotten the traditions of your homeland" (ibid.: 27). To the Scots of Winnipeg gathered in honour of St. Andrew's Day, he declared: "We have a tradition to preserve, the full tradition. That is the first of our responsibilities." The task at hand for the Scots is then "to maintain a lively interest not only in their race, but in their fatherland" (ibid.: 42-43; cf. also ibid.: 32; Gibbon 1938: 307). In an address to a meeting of Ukrainians, whom he also recognises as "good Canadians", he said in lapidary prose: "You will all be better Canadians for being also good Ukrainians" (Gibbon 1938: 307). Likewise before the Francophone community in Quebec: "You have maintained your language, your rights, your religion and your culture, so rich in history and so invaluable for Canada as a whole" (Buchan 1940: 243; my translation). In such declarations, it must be granted, we are a long way from the Anglo-centrism generally attributed to the British of that time.

This historical-identitary dimension has consequences for the political-identitary or national dimension of Canadian multiculturalism. Indeed, it entails, on the one hand, at the level of the individual that a plurality of potential allegiances should contribute to the formation of individual national identity. Humans, though free, always have their roots in concrete forms of life from which they cannot escape: "[A free man] is one who is clothed in loyalties, loyalties to family and race and birthplace, to parish, and province and nation, and who is endowed with a multitude of cherished traditions" (ibid.: 158). It is then a matter of conciliating these loyalties or these narrow or local "patriotisms" with a large patriotism. In his own words: "[...] a man can never have too many loyalties. Therefore I want to see in the citizens of Canada a strong and continuing love of the district to which they belong, but at the same time a strong and continuing interest in the Dominion of which they are a part, the whole Canadian nation" (ibid.: 32). On the other hand, an attachment to diverse roots leads, at the level of the collectivity, to the celebration of diversity as a source of common national identity. The idea of diversity must then be incorporated into that of a Canadian identity. Thus is defined a national task of integration: "[Canada] has to join in a common patriotism citizens of many races" (ibid.: 189).

Nonetheless, it seems that his thought was not devoid of racist or ethnocentrist content, especially in his first years in Canada (Ipperciel 2012). Like other Victorian imperialist thinkers on diversity, such as Lord Acton (1907), he believed in a certain hierarchy of civilisations in which whites (especially Nordic ones) generally occupied the upper echelons, but where oriental civilisations could also theoretically have a place. In this sense, Buchan seems to have received favourably the idea of a self-governing India (1935: 283-286; 1940: 99). But there is no doubt in his mind as to a hierarchy of civilisations. As he notes in 1938 in a speech at Bishop's College in Lennoxville, those at the lower levels in the "scale of development" are in his view the "dark-skinned peoples in Asia and Africa and the isles of the sea government" (ibid.: 99-100). We need not be overly perplexed by such a position: not until after the Second World War, and especially after 1960 and 1970, will normative multiculturalism evolve to a more egalitarian and universal form.

Finally, it seems important, in order to avoid any confusion, to draw a sharp distinction between facts and norms. I believe that a normative multiculturalism established itself during the period of the British Commonwealth, gaining in importance in Canadian public discourse. However, this does not imply that it was commonly put into practice by the population or that it was adopted as public policy in Canada. Not until the 1970's did multiculturalism become public policy in Canada. As for its implementation in popular practice, one must see this as a work in progress.

Britishness and the French Canadian minority: The case of Édouard Montpetit

In *The Third British Empire*, Zimmern acknowledges that the Empire was founded on force and coercion. Yet, he argues, force in and of itself is insufficient to ensure the union of the Empire: "We conquered French Canada, we conquered India, and we conquered large parts of Africa, either directly or indirectly. But although we won our position there by force, we do not hold it by force" (Zimmern 1934: 101). Force has given way to what he terms "passive acquiescence", readily acquired, he believes, in French Canada thanks to a policy of prudence, tolerance, and appeasement, but also thanks to the prestige enjoyed by the Empire.

It is thus erroneous to construe French Canada solely as anti-British from the end of the 19th century. As noted by Phillip Buckner and R. Douglas Francis (2006:

3), although the French Canadians have never been as enthusiastic about the idea of British imperialism as English Canadians, the French Canadian elite never completely opposed it, in fact quite the reverse (cf. Thompson 2008: 91). This thought can be clarified with the help of a passage from the writings of Henri Bourassa. John Darwin, in the fourth tome of the monumental *Oxford History of the British Empire*, alludes to the characterisation of the British imperial system by Bourassa, a "French Canadian nationalist", as a "monstrous empire" (Darwin 1999: 70). These words can be traced back to the following passage in a letter written in 1916 by Bourassa:

> One point I did not develop in our conversation is the motive of my desire for the disruption of the British Empire. It is not because it is British, but because it is Imperial. All Empires are hateful. They stand in the way of human liberty, and true progress, intellectual and moral. [...] British nations have to choose between British ideals and British domination. I stand for ideals against domination. I may be hanged for it, in the name of British liberty, but that does not matter (Bourassa 2009).

Hence, it appears that Bourassa reprobates the specifically imperial tenor of the British Empire, leaving unscathed its British values. Imperialism is in essence hegemonic and coercive and as a result, it stands in opposition to the ideal of liberty. Britishness, for its part, harkens back to noble ideals, such as liberty and inclusion. It refers, as Bourassa noted in a previous text, to institutions that French Canadians have freely contributed to fashioning (Bourassa 1903: 9-10).[11]

In the remaining part of the text, I would like to bring to the fore the way in which this idea of Britishness-qua-multiculturalism was also present in French Canada. In discerning this idea in a particular French Canadian thinker, we have the confirmation that the ideals of Britishness were not confined solely to the English, but that they also found an echo among minorities in the Empire. This is why I would like to focus on a moderate figure of French Canadian interwar nationalism, namely Édouard Montpetit (1881-1954). Montpetit was a lawyer and economist, a public intellectual and founder of the École des sciences sociales, économiques et politiques of the Université de Montréal. Montpetit's nationalism was firmly rooted in the Quebec Zeitgeist of the 1920s and 1930s. It was heavily marked by the Catholic faith and by a sense of urgency with regard to the defence of the French language. It is well known that he collaborated on the clerical nationalist journal *L'Action française*, edited by Canon Lionel-Groulx, and later on the journal *L'Action nationale*, the organ of the very nationalist *Ligue d'action nationale*.

---

11. Bourassa has said, with a certain flair for controversy, that "French Canadians have been, in the Americas, the pioneers of English institutions" (Bourassa 1903: 21).

Though Montpetit was a staunch nationalist, an unwavering defender of the French language and French Canadian culture, he was nonetheless a federalist, open to English Canada, eager to contribute to the vitality of the Canadian federation. He believed in the importance of a rapprochement between English and French Canadians (1937: 37) with a view to consolidating a Canadian national unity (cf. ibid.: 49). In Montpetit's mind, there was no doubt that the two cultures mutually enriched each other. It should be noted that Montpetit explicitly defended a French and English biculturalism rather than multiculturalism. Yet, interestingly, he defends this biculturalism with the help of Zimmer's ideas on Britishness and the inherent value of diversity *per se*, thus opening the door to multiculturalism. Indeed, if one can justify the coexistence of two cultures through the idea of Britishness and diversity, on can do so for many. This is why we should be particularly interested in Montpetit.

One essay in particular should attract our attention, namely "Sommes-nous en pays britannique?" ["Are We in a British Country?"],[12] taken from his 1937 work entitled *D'azur à trois lys d'or*, which groups together a series of conferences presented to an English-speaking audience. An anecdote serves as the starting-point for Montpetit's remarks on the subject of Britishness. Montpetit tells the story of an English tourist lost in Montreal during the 1930s. After a number of fruitless encounters with Francophones who could not understand him, the tourist finally manages to make himself understood with a Scot, a colleague of Montpetit's at the Université de Montréal. At last in the company of a compatriot, the tourist takes the liberty of cursing French Canadians: they should be thrown into the sea! But the speaker's next words sparked Montpetit's reflection: "After all," the tourist said, "this is a British country" (Montpetit 2005: 120; 1937: 14; in English in original text).

Interestingly, according to Montpetit, the idea of Britishness has no connection with such chauvinism, far from it. In support of his thesis, he calls on Alfred Zimmern and his work *The Third Empire*.[13] In full agreement with Zimmern, Montpetit identifies two main characteristics of the British Empire: diversity and unity, which he also conceives of in a dialectical relationship. The true cohesive force of the Empire, according to Montpetit, is respect for diversity. He cites the coexistence of diverse cultures within the Empire and, like Zimmern and Buchan, he especially emphasises the existence of such diversity within Great Britain itself, where the Welsh, Scottish, Cockney, and other cultures happily coexist. Among the diverse

---

12. The text was also published in Montpetit 2005: 119-131. In this paper, references will be made to both editions.
13. Without explicitly citing *The Third Empire*, Montpetit refers specifically to this work when alluding to Zimmern's belief that the Empire lacked any guiding philosophy (Montpetit 2005: 121; 1937: 15), an opinion stated by Zimmern on page 13 of his work.

cultures of the Empire, he points out the many Indian cultures, marked themselves by a complex diversity, but also the Afrikaans and Québécois cultures (2005: 122; 1937: 17). Unity within diversity, argues Montpetit, is the result of the liberties and the equality that have been granted – in the wake of protracted struggles, certainly – to these national groups. This allows him to suggest that unity is "a phenomenon of emancipation" (ibid.: 123; 1937: 18-19). For Montpetit, it is this "unity of its mobile features" which is at the source of British imperial power.

One idea especially in Montpetit's short piece of writing on the meaning of Britishness is worthy of our attention here. He says that the British Empire, as a symbol of cultural diversity united by the principles of liberty and equality, ought to be a normative model for Canada itself:

> The problem of Canadian unity would be resolved if we applied to its full extent the principle of imperial power. The Commonwealth stands before us as an example. Canada is a British country in the sense that it is a country of diversity. To be a country of different civilizations, different languages, different cultures and religions, is, as we say today, synchronizing the Empire (Montpetit 2005: 124; 1937: 20).

This thought is not isolated in his work.[14] Canada should be on a small scale what the British Empire is on a large scale. It is "British" in a strong sense only inasmuch as it strives towards the ideal of cultural diversity.

For Montpetit, this formulation of Canadianness in normative terms at once points out the shortcoming of a Canadian nation not up to the standard of Britishness. Given that Montpetit is addressing an Anglophone audience in this text, it is quite obvious that the criticism of a chauvinistic state that does little to support the actual diversity in its midst is directed against English Canada. "Why, when it comes to Canada and no longer the Empire, to Canada as part of the Empire, do we spurn diversity, source of unity? Why be an imperialist in the Empire, and a nationalist – we know of which narrow nationalism – in Canada? Why praise imperial liberties if we are going to deprive our country of them?" (2005: 124; 1937: 19-20). Essentially, Montpetit criticises English Canadians for not being British enough. If Canada is to exist, it must be British, that is, multicultural in the sense that the diversity of free and equal cultures is celebrated.

Admittedly, when Montpetit sings the praises of multiculturalism, he likely has in mind the coexistence of the English and French cultures. In his idea of a multicultural Canada, he does not seem to envisage the participation of aboriginal cultures, the Ukrainian culture on the prairies, the Japanese culture on the West

---

14. Cf. "Les trois unités" (1937: 43): "Each group's genius enriches the Dominion as the greatness of each Dominion enriches the Empire. To deny this is to deny the Empire [...]".

Coast, and so on. Nonetheless, the normative idea pertaining to the coexistence of a plurality of cultures, languages, religions, ways of life, and to the rejection of "race egoism" (ibid.: 129; 1937: 26), is from then on introduced with force. The "is" – i.e. the "fact" – of a diversity more extensive than what Montpetit envisaged, changes nothing in the "ought" of the norm thus recognized.

Conclusion

As one can see, Canadian multiculturalism is not the simple product of recent history, as it were an *ex nihilo* creation. It is a way of viewing the world that was prepared some time ago. As has been shown here, one finds the seed of this worldview in the normative repository of the Third British Empire. In this sense, one could say that Canada's state multiculturalism is the fruit of Britishness-qua-multiculturalism as it was articulated in the interwar period. It appears as a postcolonial outgrowth. Of course, there is no question of arguing any actual fulfilment of the multicultural project at that time insofar as Anglo-centrism undoubtedly constituted the dominant model in the relationship between cultures in Canada, although the former seems to have subsequently prevailed over the latter in the norms competition that opposed them. Similarly, any claim of a full implementation of multiculturalism is all the more incongruous insofar as even today one could hardly declare multiculturalism a fait accompli. Conflicts between cultures still exist in Canada like elsewhere, but the ideal – i.e. the norm – of cultural coexistence, now dominant, presses the Canadian public to respond to them with vigour. Therein lies the crux of the matter, that is, the acknowledgement of multiculturalism – or interculturalism – as an established norm. In my view, this recognition took form during the period of the Third British Empire. In this sense, a certain Britishness has been maintained in Canada, at the very moment we thought we were rid of it.

■ References

Acton [John Emerich Edward Dalberg, Lord]. "Nationality." *The History of Freedom and Other Essays*. London: Macmillan, 1907.
Bourassa, H. *Les Canadiens-français et l'Empire britannique*, Québec: Imprimerie S.-A. Demers, 1903.
Bourassa, H. "Mr. Bourassa's Views on the Participation of Canada in the War – The Past and the Future." Quebec History Document, in *The Quebec History Encyclopedia*, ed. Claude Bélanger. Montreal: Marianapolis College, 2009.
Buchan, J. *The King's Grace, 1910-1935*. London: Hodder and Stoughton, 1935.
Buchan, J. (Lord Tweedsmuir) *Canadian Occasions*. Freeport, NY: Books for Libraries Press, 1940.
Buckner, P. and R. D. Francis. "Introduction." In *Canada and the British World: Culture Migration, and Identity*, P. Buckner and R.D. Francis, 1-28. Vancouver: UBC Press, 2006.

Darwin, J. "A Third British Empire? The Dominion Idea in Imperial Politics." In *Oxford History of the British Empire. Volume 4*, ed. Brown, J. M. and W. R. Louis, 64-87. Oxford: Oxford University Press, 1999.

Darwin, J. "Imperial Twilight, or When Did the Empire End?" In *Canada and the End of Empire*, ed. Philip Buckner, 15-24. Vancouver: UBC Press, 2005.

Day, R.J.F. *Multiculturalism and the History of Canadian Diversity*. Toronto: University of Toronto Press, 2000.

Dilke, C.W. *Problems of Greater Britain*. London: Macmillan, 1890.

Foster, K. A. *Our Canadian Mosaic*, Toronto: Dominion Council, Y.W.C.A., 1926

Gibbon, J.M. *Canadian Mosaic: The Making of a Northern Nation*. Toronto: McClelland & Stewart, 1938.

Hall, H.D. *The British Commonwealth of Nations*. London: Methuen & Co., 1920

Henshaw, P. "John Buchan and the British Imperial Origins of Canadian Multiculturalism." In *Canadas of the Mind: the Making and Unmaking of Canadian Nationalisms in the Twentieth Century*, ed. N. Hillmer and A. Chapnick, 191-213. Montreal: McGill's University Press, 2007.

Ipperciel, D. "Britannicité et multiculturalisme canadien." *International Journal of Canadian Studies*, 45-46 (2012): 277-306.

Kymlicka, W. *Multicultural Citizenship: a Liberal Theory of Minority Right*. Oxford: Clarendon Press, 1995.

Markwell, D. J. "Zimmern, Sir Alfred Eckhard (1879-1957)." In *Oxford Dictionary of National Biography*, ed. H. C. G. Matthew and B. Harrison. Oxford: Oxford University Press, 2004.

McIntyre, W. D. *The Britannic Vision*. Basingstoke: Palgrave MacMillan, 2009.

Miller, J. D. B. "The Commonwealth and World Order: the Zimmern Vision and After." *Journal of Imperial and Commonwealth History* 8 (1979-80): 159-74.

Montpetit, E. "Notre avenir." *La Revue trimestrielle canadienne*, 2ᵉ année, 8 (February 1917): 305-321.

Montpetit, E. *D'azur à trois lys d'or*. Montreal: Éditions de l'ACF, 1937.

Montpetit, E. *Réflexions sur la question nationale*. Saint-Laurent: Bibliothèque Québécoise, 2005.

Palmer, H. "Reluctant Hosts: Anglo-Canadian Views on Multiculturalism in the Twentieth Century." In *Readings in Canadian History, Post-Confederation*, ed. R. D. Francis and D. B. Smith, 192-209. Toronto: Holt, Rhinhart & Winston, 1990.

Quigley, C. *The Anglo-American Establishment*. New York: Books in Focus, 1981.

Rich, P. "Alfred Zimmern's Cautious Idealism: The League of Nations, International Education, and the Commonwealth." In *Thinkers of the Twenty Years' Crisis: Inter-War Idealism Reassessed*, ed. D. Long and P. Wilson, 79-99. Oxford: Clarendon Press, 2003.

Smith, A. *The New Statesman: Portrait of a Political Weekly, 1913-1931*. London: Frank Cass, 1996.

Thompson, J.H. "Canada and the 'Third British Empire,' 1901-1939". In *Canada and the British Empire*, ed. P. Buckner, 87-106. Oxford: Oxford University Press, 2008.

Wayland, S. "Immigration, Multiculturalism and National Identity in Canada." *International Journal on Group Rights*, 5 (1997): 33-58.

Zimmern, A. "German Culture and the British Commonwealth." In *Nationality and Government*, A. Zimmern, 1-31. London: Chatto & Windus, 1918 [1914].

Zimmern, A. "Nationalism and Internationalism". In *Prospects of Democracy and Other Essays*, A. Zimmern, 76-93. London: Chatto & Windus, 1929.

Zimmern, A. *The Third British Empire*. Oxford: Oxford University Press, 1934.

3 Misinterpreting Multiculturalism

Will Kymlicka

Since the late 1960s, a number of Western democracies have engaged in new experiments in the recognition and accommodation of ethnic diversity. These experiments include:

- recognizing land rights and self-government rights for indigenous peoples
- strengthening regional autonomy and official language status for substate national groups
- adopting more accommodationist policies for immigrant groups.

I will describe all of these as experiments in "liberal multiculturalism".[1]

Some of these policies have come under sustained attack in recent years, and multiculturalism is widely viewed as in retreat across the Western democracies. Multiculturalism policies in relation to immigrant groups, for example, are blamed for a wide variety of social ills, including:

- the residential ghettoization and social isolation of immigrants
- increased stereotyping, and hence prejudice, discrimination and distrust, between ethnic groups
- political radicalism, particularly amongst Muslim youth
- the perpetuation of illiberal practices amongst immigrant groups, often involving restricting the rights and liberties of girls and women.

Invoking these ills, a number of high-profile politicians – from Angela Merkel to Nicholas Sarkozy to David Cameron – have declared multiculturalism a "failure", as have a wide range of media commentators and academics from across the political spectrum.[2]

---

1. Keith Banting and I have attempted to measure the spread of these policies across the Western democracies in our "Multiculturalism Policy Index", available at: www.queensu.ca/mcp.
2. For an overview of the "failure" and "retreat" discourses, see Lentin and Titley 2011.

Yet these proclamations of failure are rarely if ever supported by any empirical evidence. It is not difficult to find evidence of social ills, but a quick look across the Western democracies makes it clear that these ills exist in all countries, to varying degrees, whether they have adopted multiculturalism policies or not. In order to determine the effect of adopting multiculturalism policies, we need to know whether these problems are worse in countries that embraced multiculturalism than in those that avoided multiculturalism, or whether these problems are worse after the adoption of multiculturalism than they were before. Perhaps problems are exacerbated when multiculturalism policies are adopted, but perhaps not – perhaps multiculturalism policies help ameliorate them. It is premature, indeed irresponsible, to make sweeping judgements without looking at the evidence.

Remarkably, in all of the voluminous literature proclaiming the failure of multiculturalism, virtually no one has attempted to actually look at this evidence. Even books that appear to be firmly grounded in social science research often fail the most minimal test of empirical adequacy. For example, in an influential book, Sniderman and Hagendoorn (2007) blame multiculturalism for the high levels of ethnic stereotyping between native Dutch and Muslim immigrants in the Netherlands. But of course ethnic stereotyping is a pervasive problem throughout history and around the world, whether or not multiculturalism policies exist, and the authors provide no evidence that this stereotyping became worse in the Netherlands after the adoption of multiculturalism than before; or that it is worse in the Netherlands than in countries that haven't adopted multiculturalism. In short, they make no effort to identify the *differential effect* that multiculturalism has on pre-existing dynamics of stereotyping.[3]

This is typical of work in the field, which generally lacks either longitudinal or comparative data needed to determine the differential effect of adopting multiculturalism. However, if we look at those few studies that do have a comparative or longitudinal dimension, and hence that attempt to isolate the differential effect of having multiculturalism policies, they generally suggest that multiculturalism policies have had beneficial effects. I have explored this evidence in more depth elsewhere (Kymlicka 2010: 2012), and will not review it in detail here. Let me just note that a series of cross-national studies have shown that multiculturalism policies promote political participation (Bloemraad 2007; Adams 2007), trust and social capital (Kesler and Bloemraad 2010; Harrell 2009; Kazemipur 2009), reduction in prejudice (Weldon 2006; Guimond et al. 2013), increase in solidarity (Banting and

---

3. As it happens, both the longitudinal and comparative data contradict the Sniderman-Hagendoorn claim. See my review in *Perspectives on Politics 6* (2008): 804-7.

Kymlicka 2006; Crepaz 2006), and psychological well-being (Berry et al. 2006).[4] I would not want to overstate this evidence: much more work needs to be done to confirm and refine these findings, which are fragmentary and preliminary. Yet there can be no doubt that the social science evidence to date offers little or no support for claims of "failure".

This raises a puzzle: why would so many commentators jump to the conclusion that multiculturalism is to blame for these social ills? In the case of right-wing politicians, we might think this is simply electoral politicking. Attacking multiculturalism may help mobilize the electoral base of conservative parties, no matter what the evidence says. One might expect that academics, who are professionally committed to norms of reasoned argumentation and evidence, would serve as a counter-weight to this partisan politics, testing politicians' claims against the available evidence. Instead, a surprising number of academics have engaged in their own forms of demonizing multiculturalism, equally unsupported by any actual evidence.

Why do so many academics feel entitled to blame multiculturalism for social ills without attending to the evidence? There are many factors at work, but in this paper I will explore one – namely, a misinterpretation of the origins of multiculturalism. Many academics have what we might call an "original sin" conception of multiculturalism. They believe that multiculturalism was conceived in sin – contaminated by some fundamental vice or error at its very birth – and is therefore destined to have pernicious effects. Those who endorse this conception rarely feel the need to examine the empirical evidence regarding the effects of multiculturalism policies in practice. Once we identify its original sin, then we can just deduce its pernicious effects.

Even if these original sin genealogies were sound, this is no excuse for ignoring the evidence. However, I will argue, these genealogies are mistaken. There are several contending original sin accounts of multiculturalism, and it would take a book to cover them all. I will focus on two such accounts – the "neoliberal" account and the "cultural determinist" account – and explain why they are mistaken. But before doing so, I will sketch my own account of the genealogy of multiculturalism, so that we can compare it with the original sin conceptions.

---

4. One exception to this generalisation is the work of Ruud Koopmans (2010; Ersanilli and Koopmans 2011), who argues that multiculturalism is responsible for some of the poorer outcomes of immigrants in Holland as compared to neighbouring countries without multiculturalism policies. For doubts about his analysis of the Dutch case, see Duyvendak and Scholten 2011. Even if his analysis holds up, it is an exception to a growing literature showing that multiculturalism policies have positive effects in cross-national and longitudinal studies.

Liberal multiculturalism: genealogy

In one sense, multiculturalism is as old as humanity – different cultures have always found ways of coexisting, and respect for diversity was a familiar feature of many historic empires, such as the Ottoman Empire. But the sort of multiculturalism that is said to have "failed" is a more specific historic phenomenon, emerging first in the Western democracies in the late 1960s. This timing is important, for it helps situate multiculturalism in relation to larger social transformations of the post-war era.

I believe that multiculturalism is best understood as part of a larger human rights revolution in relation to ethnic and racial diversity. Prior to World War II, ethnocultural and religious diversity in the West was characterized by a range of illiberal and undemocratic relationships of hierarchy, including relations of conqueror and conquered; colonizer and colonized; master and slave; settler and indigenous; racialized and unmarked; normalized and deviant; orthodox and heretic; civilized and primitive; and ally and enemy. These hierarchies were justified by racialist ideologies that explicitly propounded the superiority of some peoples and cultures, and their right to rule over others. These ideologies were widely accepted throughout the Western world, and underpinned both domestic laws (e.g., racially-biased immigration and citizenship policies) and foreign policies (e.g., in relation to overseas colonies). They created a political order in which some people were ruled, not by liberal-democratic principles of equality, consent and participation, but by illiberal principles of coercion and paternalism.

After WWII, however, the world recoiled against Hitler's fanatical and murderous use of such ideologies, and the UN repudiated them in favor of a new ideology of the equality of races and peoples. And this new assumption of human equality has generated a series of political movements designed to contest the lingering presence or enduring effects of older hierarchies. We can distinguish three waves of such movements: (a) the struggle for decolonization, in the period 1948 to 1965; (b) the struggle against racial segregation and discrimination, initiated and exemplified by the African-American civil rights movement from 1955 to 1965; and (c) the struggle for multiculturalism and minority rights, which emerged in the late 1960s.

Each of these movements draws upon the human rights revolution, and its ideology of the equality of races and peoples, to challenge the legacies of ethnic and racial hierarchies, and to replace inherited practices of coercion and paternalism with new practices of consent and participation. Indeed, the human rights revolution plays a double role here: not just as the inspiration for struggle, but also as a constraint on the permissible goals and means of that struggle. Insofar as historically excluded groups struggle against earlier hierarchies in the name of equality, they too have to renounce their own traditions of exclusion or oppression in the treatment of, say, women, gays, people of mixed race, religious dissenters, and so on. The framework of human rights, and of liberal-democratic constitutionalism more generally, provides the overarching framework within which these struggles are debated and addressed.

Each of these movements, therefore, can be seen as contributing to a process of democratic "citizenisation" – that is, turning the earlier catalogue of hierarchical relations into relationships of liberal-democratic citizenship, both in terms of the vertical relationship between the members of minorities and the state, and the horizontal relationships among the members of different groups. In the past, it was often assumed that the only way to engage in this process of citizenisation was to impose a single undifferentiated model of citizenship on all individuals. But the ideas and policies of multiculturalism that emerged from the 1960s start from the assumption that this complex history of ethnic relations inevitably and appropriately generates group-differentiated ethnopolitical claims. The key to citizenisation is not to suppress these differential claims, but to filter and frame them through the language of human rights, civil liberties and democratic accountability. And this is what multiculturalist movements have aimed to do.

The precise character of the resulting multicultural reforms varies from group to group, as befits the distinctive history that each has faced. They all start from the anti-discrimination principle that underpinned the second wave, but go beyond it to challenge other forms of exclusion or stigmatization. In most Western countries, explicit state-sponsored discrimination against ethnic, racial or religious minorities had largely ceased by the 1960s and 1970s, under the influence of the second wave of human rights struggles. Yet evidence of ethnic and racial hierarchies remained, and continues to be clearly visible in many societies, whether measured in terms of economic inequalities, political under-representation, social stigmatization or cultural invisibility. Various forms of multiculturalism have been developed to help overcome these lingering inequalities, including indigenous land rights, official language rights for national minorities, and accommodation rights for immigrant groups. All seek to convert older hierarchies into new relations of liberal democratic citizenship.

The result of this trajectory is a distinctly *liberal* multiculturalism (hereafter LMC). Both halves of that compound term are important. On the one hand, LMC is a distinctly *liberal-democratic* form of multiculturalism, grounded in core liberal values of freedom, equality, and democracy. It therefore differs from non-liberal or illiberal forms of multiculturalism, of which there are many historic examples, in which groups agree to terms of peaceful co-existence, while remaining indifferent to the freedoms or democratic rights of individuals within each group.

On the other hand, LMC is a distinctly *multicultural* form of liberal democracy, going beyond the familiar list of basic liberties contained in all liberal-democratic theories and constitutions to also include policies that recognise and accommodate ethnocultural minorities. Many features of a liberal democracy provide important protections to ethnocultural minorities – particularly guarantees of non-discrimination and guarantees of individual civil liberties (freedom of speech, association, religion, etc.). But a multicultural liberalism differs from other forms of liberal democracy by going beyond these generic guarantees to also adopt group-differentiated laws and policies that recognize various types of diversity, such as (i) indigenous land rights and self-government; (ii) regional autonomy and official language rights for national minorities; and (iii) accommodation rights for immigrant groups.[5]

In all of these contexts, I would argue that the experiments in recognition and accommodation adopted in the Western democracies over the past 40 years share this liberal multiculturalist character.[6] These policies have been framed to fit with liberal-democratic values, and their principles have been interpreted (e.g. by bureaucrats and courts) to preserve that fit.

This is my account of the genealogy of multiculturalism, emerging from the civil rights struggles of the 1950s, rooted in the human rights revolution and in struggles for citizenisation. Viewed this way, the rise of multiculturalism needs to be seen alongside other citizenisation struggles that emerged at the same time, including the claims of women, gays, and people with disabilities. They all have a similar trajectory, starting in the 1960s, responding to the same basic historic forces, seeking to replace earlier uncivil relations of domination, coercion, paternalism and intolerance with newer relations of democratic citizenship. All of these struggles borrowed arguments and strategies from each other, and understood themselves to be part of larger rainbow coalitions of citizenship struggles and social justice movements.

Of course, even if one accepts this story about the progressive impulses underlying multiculturalism, it does not follow that multiculturalism policies have been successful in practice. Public policies often have unintended, even perverse, effects. This is why it is important to pay attention to empirical evidence about policy outcomes, of the sort I listed earlier.

---

5. For a more comprehensive account of the group-differentiated policies related to these three types of diversity, see the Multiculturalism Policy Index (note 1), which distinguishes nine characteristic multiculturalism policies for indigenous peoples, six characteristic policies adopted in relation to national minorities, and eight such policies in relation to immigrant groups.
6. The motivations for adopting policies are complex, including the desire to win ethnic votes, or amoral bargaining amongst self-interested groups. But the policies adopted for these complex reasons are explicitly framed to fit with liberal-democratic values.

Original sin genealogies

Critics, however, offer a different picture of the origins of multiculturalism. According to these alternative stories, multiculturalism has nothing in common with the great human rights and civil rights struggles of the 1960s and 1970s, but is rooted in completely different impulses which preclude the very possibility of beneficial outcomes. I will consider two such alternative stories.

Multiculturalism as neoliberalism

One story is that multiculturalism is an offshoot of neoliberalism. Perhaps the best-known version of this argument is Slavoj Žižek, who famously stated that multiculturalism emerged as the "cultural logic of multinational capitalism" (Žižek 1997). Similar arguments have been made by other commentators, whether in relation to immigrants (Mitchell 2004), national minorities (Cardinal and Denault 2007) or indigenous peoples (Hale 2005). In each case, the central argument is that multiculturalism emerged as a technique of neoliberal governance, as a way of integrating minorities and minority cultural products into global markets.

I will dispute this genealogy below, but it is an important interpretation, and hence worth exploring in some depth. Neoliberalism is fundamentally about creating effective market actors and competitive economies, and so the overriding concern of neoliberals in the field of ethnic relations is with integrating minorities into global markets, and with the contribution they can make to economic competitiveness. It is important to note that this need not lead to support for multiculturalism policies. Indeed, in the past, the attachment of minorities to their languages and cultures was seen as a hindrance to effective market participation. But in the late 1980s and 1990s, some neoliberals came to believe that ethnic identities and attachments can be assets to market actors, and hence that they can legitimately be supported by the neoliberal state.

In some contexts, ethnicity is a market asset in the tangible form of cultural artefacts which can be marketed globally (music, art, and fashion). But in most cases, ethnicity is seen as a market asset because it is a source of social capital that successful market actors require. Consider the following description of the World Bank's commitment to "ethno-development" for indigenous peoples in Ecuador:

> Social exclusion, economic deprivation, and political marginalization are sometimes perceived as the predominant characteristic of Ecuador's indigenous peoples. But as they often remind outsiders, indigenous peoples are also characterized by strong positive attributes, particularly their high levels of social capital. Besides language and their own sense of ethnic identity, the distinctive features of indigenous peoples include solidarity and social unity (reflected

in strong social organizations), a well-defined geographical concentration and attachment to ancestral lands, a rich cultural patrimony, and other customs and practices distinct from those of Ecuador's national society...The [World Bank] project aims to mobilize this social capital, based on these characteristics, as a platform for ethnodevelopment (van Nieuwkoop and Uquillas 2000: 18).

Or consider this quote from Shelton Davis, one of the driving forces behind the World Bank's indigenous policy:

Until recently, a local culture has been seen as a hindrance to development, whereas today we must rather look upon culture as an asset, as a driving force for self-development... one might argue that more culture is more wealth, that having more know-how, more languages, and more centres of interest enriches indigenous peoples as well as enriching in the process the rest of a country's citizens and some segment of humanity as well (Davis and Ebbe 1993: 8).

In short, neoliberalism leads to multiculturalism because ethnicity is a source of social capital, social capital enables effective market participation, and governments can promote this market-enhancing social capital through multiculturalism policies.

The way in which ethnicity facilitates market participation varies from group to group. In the case of immigrants, social capital does not flow from "a well-defined geographical concentration and attachment to ancestral lands" – immigrants are precisely uprooted from their ancestral lands. But from a neoliberal perspective, this uprooting is itself a potential asset, since it enables transnational linkages that native-born citizens lack. Immigrant transnationalism, then, is an asset in an increasingly global market place – it facilitates global trade – exemplified by the commercial linkages in the Indian and Chinese diasporas. Insofar as multiculturalism legitimates the ethnic identities that underpin these transnational links, it can be seen as good for the economies of both sending and receiving countries.

So the neoliberal vision of transnational multiculturalism for immigrant groups is different from their vision of ethnodevelopment for indigenous peoples (which is different yet again from the neoliberal vision of the market role of substate national groups).[7] But in each case, neoliberals have found a way to legitimize ethnicity, and to justify multiculturalism policies that recognize ethnic identities, in line with neoliberalism's core ideas (enhancing economic competitiveness and innovation; shifting responsibility from the state to civil society; promoting decentralization;

---

7. Granting autonomy to groups like the Catalans and Scots has been supported by some neoliberals as a potential site for a more innovative and entrepreneurial culture, sustained by higher levels of social cohesion (Keating 2001).

de-emphasizing national solidarity in favour of local bonds or transnational ties; viewing cultural diversity as an economic asset/commodity in a global market).

This is a very different conception of multiculturalism than the one I offered in the previous section. In my interpretation, LMC is part of the human rights revolution, committed to fighting hierarchies and disadvantages and creating new forms of democratic citizenship. The neoliberal account of multiculturalism, by contrast, is not about social justice, but about creating cosmopolitan market actors who can compete effectively across state boundaries.

For those who believe that multiculturalism emerged out of neoliberalism, its pernicious effects can simply be deduced without examining the evidence. Žižek himself insists that multiculturalism is "impotent" to promote justice, not based on any empirical evidence, but simply as a deduction from his underlying genealogy. If multiculturalism originated in neoliberalism, then by definition it extends recognition to difference only insofar as it fits global capitalism's own scheme of values and priorities. The neoliberal conception of multiculturalism is therefore fundamentally indifferent to justice. In the case of immigrants, for example, while neoliberal multiculturalism affirms – even valorizes – ethnic immigrant entrepreneurship, strategic cosmopolitanism, and transnational commercial linkages and remittances, it silences debates on economic redistribution, racial inequality, unemployment, economic restructuring, and labour rights.

Similarly, in the case of indigenous peoples, neoliberal multiculturalism divides Indians into "safe" and "radical", and seeks to accommodate the former – the *indio permitido* ("permitted Indian"), in Hale's phrase – through a range of multicultural rights. These rights are deemed acceptable so long as 1) they do not contradict the long-term economic development model of moving towards free-market economies, and 2) the resulting level of political clout does not pass a certain line where existing authorities are seriously challenged. Neoliberal multiculturalism thereby gives state and business elites the "ability to restructure the arena of political contention, driving a wedge between cultural rights and the assertion of the control over resources necessary for those rights to be realized" (Hale 2005: 13). The "cultural project of neoliberalism" accords rights to indigenous peoples, but only "to help them compete in the rigors of globalised capitalism or, if this is deemed impossible, to relegate them to the sidelines, allowing the game to proceed unperturbed" (Hale and Millamen 2005: 301). And as McNeish notes, this cultural project is not just about limiting indigenous demands, but about restructuring indigenous subjectivities:

> Indians are recognized as citizens by governing elites as long as they do not question or threaten the integrity of the existing regime of productive relations, especially in the sectors most closely connected to the global markets. As such [...] the ultimate goal of neoliberalism

is not just radical individualism, but rather the creation of subjects who govern themselves in accordance with the logic of globalized capitalism (McNeish 2008: 34).[8]

Given these analyses of how multiculturalism is tied at birth to neoliberalism – of how multiculturalism just is "the logic of global capitalism" – there is little point looking for empirical evidence of its potential positive effects on democratic citizenship. Neoliberalism – and hence neoliberal multiculturalism – is seen as precisely an attempt to replace the logic of solidaristic citizenship with a logic of "radical individualism" and free markets (e.g. Somers 2008). So, by definition, multiculturalism is (at best) "impotent" in relation to struggles for equality and citizenship, if not actually corrosive of these struggles.

But is the neoliberal interpretation of multiculturalism correct? Is multiculturalism simply the logic of multinational capitalism? Clearly, neoliberal understandings of multiculturalism are articulated and promoted in public debate. But the idea that multiculturalism *emerged* as a tool of neoliberal governance is demonstrably incorrect. The timing is wrong. As we saw earlier, multiculturalism policies began to be adopted in the late 1960s, whereas neoliberalism only emerged in the 1980s. Moreover, neoliberals were initially quite hostile to multiculturalism, precisely because they viewed it as a manifestation of earlier activist forms of social democracy.

When neoliberalism emerged as a powerful force in the early 1980s, it emerged into societies that were already being transformed in a multicultural direction. And so, one of the first questions confronting neoliberal reformers was how to respond to this new social reality. Since multiculturalism at the time was clearly an outgrowth of 1960s progressive social movements, the initial reaction of most neoliberal actors was one of hostility. Indeed, the first wave of neoliberals in the US, UK, Canada, and Australia were critical of multiculturalism, which they viewed as a prime example of unjustified intervention in the market in response to "special interests", due to the capture of state power by ethnic entrepreneurs and their rent-seeking allies in the bureaucracy. The result, neoliberals argued, was both the distortion of the proper use of state power and the unhealthy dependence of civil society on government funds. Indeed, the close links between advocacy groups and the state built up under multiculturalism represented precisely the sort of "nanny state" they aimed to demolish. Neoliberals opposed on principle the idea of state support for ethnic projects, and opposed most of the reforms that followed in multiculturalism's trail, such as the employment equity laws which minorities demanded in the name of

---

8. On how neoliberal reforms aimed to reshape indigenous subjectivities, see Macdonald and Muldoon 2006: 218-19.

multiculturalism. In short, neoliberals viewed multiculturalism as embodying the sort of welfare state liberalism they opposed.[9]

This neoliberal attack on multiculturalism took both an institutional and a symbolic form. Institutionally, neoliberals severed the links between the state and progressive advocacy groups, slashing funding and political access for such groups. Symbolically, neoliberals delegitimised multiculturalism by contrasting the "ordinary" hard-working tax-paying citizen against the "special interests" represented by "ethnic lobbies". As James puts it, neoliberals invoked discourses that "valorized the so-called 'ordinary Canadian', figured as a taxpayer and consumer, to delegitimize group experiences and identities as positive considerations in civic deliberation and debate" (James 2013: 32).

It was only later that neoliberal actors learned to tolerate multiculturalism, and indeed to positively embrace it, and become agents for its diffusion. The idea that there was a neoliberal basis for multiculturalism was not obvious – it took time to emerge. If, at first glance, neoliberals saw multiculturalism as a pathology of the interventionist welfare state, on a sober second glance they saw certain elective affinities that could be built upon. They saw, in short, the potential for something like "neoliberal multiculturalism".[10]

As a result, for the past twenty years, we have seen the co-existence of two different conceptions of multiculturalism: the original progressive model of LMC, emerging in the 1960s, aiming to build fairer terms of democratic citizenship within nation-states, and a neoliberal model, emerging in the late 1980s, which views diversity as a competitive asset for cosmopolitan market actors, indifferent to issues of racial hierarchy and structural inequality. These two conceptions continue to shape public debates and polices, not just in the Western democracies, but around the world.

While some commentators assume that neoliberal multiculturalism has fully displaced progressive multiculturalism, I argue elsewhere that the story is much more complicated, and that in many contexts, what is striking is how unsuccessful neoliberals have been in rebranding multiculturalism (Kymlicka 2013). In many contexts, multiculturalism remains an effective vehicle for minorities to challenge hierarchies and to pursue new relations of democratic citizenship – as indeed one would expect given the evidence I cited earlier for its beneficial effects. Neoliberals may have hoped that their version of multiculturalism would lead to "the creation

---

9. See Kim 2010 on Thatcher's opposition to multiculturalism; Abu-Laban and Gabriel 2002 on neoliberal opposition in Canada.
10. We can trace this neoliberal rebranding of multiculturalism in Australia and Canada as neoliberal governments adopted the discourse of "productive multiculturalism", and organized conferences with titles like "Multiculturalism Means Business", and cities marketed themselves as the multicultural home of transnational entrepreneurs. See Murphy, O'Brien, and Watson 2003 on the neoliberal marketing of multicultural Sydney; Abu-Laban and Gabriel 1998 and Mitchell 2004 on Vancouver and Toronto.

of subjects who govern themselves in accordance with the logic of globalized capitalism", but ethnic, racial, and indigenous minorities continue to invoke multiculturalism in pursuit of projects of citizenisation.

Multiculturalism as cultural determinism

Despite their differences, the two interpretations I have discussed so far share the idea that multiculturalism is a profoundly modern phenomenon, rooted in either post-war human rights ideals or post-Keynesian neoliberal ideals. There is, however, a third reading of multiculturalism, which views it as rooted in premodern ideas of "cultures" as organic communities, and as a reaction against modernity. Multiculturalism, in this third view, did not emerge out of 1960s human rights struggles, nor out of 1980s neoliberal reforms, but out of earlier "culturalist" critiques of liberal modernity.

There are in fact different versions of this third story, offering slightly different genealogies. One traces multiculturalism back to 19th century German romanticism, and particularly the work of Herder and Spengler. This is the version told by Alain Finkelkraut (1988), Pascal Bruckner (2007), and Brian Barry (2001). Another version traces multiculturalism back to early 20th century American anthropology, particularly the work of Boas, Benedict, and Herskovitz. This is the version told by Jane Cowan (2001) and Frederik Stjernfelt (2012).

In both versions, multiculturalism is rooted in *cultural determinism*. What 19th century German romantics and early 20th century American anthropologists shared is the idea that people's identities are determined by their "culture", where "culture" is understood in terms of relatively discrete and internally homogenous groups, with fixed boundaries and static traditions. While some degree of cultural change is inevitable, both German romantics and pre-war American anthropologists believed that certain practices are vital to the "authenticity" or "integrity" of a culture, and must therefore be protected from change. These "authentic" practices are said to be essential to the identity of the group, and hence to the identity of its individual members. This link between culture and identity is thought to be particularly strong if the cultural practice is "traditional" – that is, deeply-rooted in a people's history, and not just the result of recent adaptations or outside influences.

Contemporary multiculturalism is said to be inspired by these cultural determinist ideas, and invokes them to claim cultural rights to protect "authentic" cultural practices from pressures to change. This pressure for change may come from without, through the exercise of the power of the larger society, or it may come from within, through calls for reform by women, youth, or other disaffected members of the group. In either case, multiculturalism is about protecting traditions from pressure for change.

Commentators who interpret multiculturalism this way argue that it is inherently oppressive. It enmeshes people in a logic that denies the fluidity of group boundaries, the hybridity of cultural practices, and the multiplicity of people's identities. While it promises to emancipate minorities and indigenous peoples from state-sponsored assimilation, multiculturalism in fact restricts people's choices and constrains their identities. Granting groups the right to protect their "culture" does not eliminate the problem of oppressive cultural homogenisation, but simply relocates it from the state to the group level. Group leaders use these "rights" to suppress individual choice and dissent in the name of protecting an "authentic" culture. Group rights therefore limit individual rights.

Indeed, early 20th century American anthropologists did object to the idea of universal rights developed by liberal political theorists and international lawyers. In 1947 the American Anthropological Association denounced the Universal Declaration of Human Rights as an assault on the integrity of cultures around the world. Since critics claim that contemporary multiculturalism rests on these very same anthropological theories, it is assumed to share their scepticism about human rights, and hence is inherently "anti-universalistic in [its] thrust" (Barry 2001: 5), "in its essence anti-European" (Huntington 2004: 171), or a "war against the West" (Kristol 1991: 15).

For those who endorse this cultural determinist interpretation, its pernicious effects can simply be deduced without examining the evidence. That multiculturalism is a threat to individual rights is not something to be empirically verified – it is true by definition. And, as one would expect, advocates for this interpretation rarely, if ever, provide any empirical evidence for their claims. One can find examples of, say, forced marriages or honour killings within a particular immigrant group, in which individual rights are violated in the name of some cultural tradition. But, to repeat a point made earlier, what matters for evaluating multiculturalism is whether adopting multiculturalism policies exacerbates or ameliorates this problem. Yet the critics who equate multiculturalism with cultural determinism never feel the need to examine the evidence on this question. Since multiculturalism is rooted in the original sin of cultural determinism, they simply deduce that it makes the problem worse.

But is the cultural determinist interpretation of multiculturalism correct? In the case of neoliberal multiculturalism, I argued that it is inaccurate as an account of the emergence of multiculturalism policies in the 1960s and 1970s, but that a form of neoliberal multiculturalism did subsequently arise as a powerful contender to LMC. Indeed, for at least a period of time in the 1990s, neoliberal multiculturalism was endorsed by some of the most powerful international organizations, such as the World Bank, the OECD and the EU.

By contrast, I do not believe that the cultural determinist account of multiculturalism has ever had any significant influence within the Western democracies.

While the cultural determinist interpretation is widely discussed in the academic literature, there is no credible evidence that it underpins any real-world multicultural policies. I have read literally hundreds of position papers and policy documents produced by the various participants in the policy networks on multiculturalism – governments, professional advocacy groups, philanthropic organizations – as well as the resulting laws and court cases, and I have yet to find a single discussion that expresses any sympathy for Spengler or Boas, either implicitly or explicitly.

On the contrary, contemporary multiculturalist claims are rooted in a language of human rights that is diametrically opposed to cultural determinist ideas. For example, all of the recent international declarations on cultural rights include safeguards to protect human rights, including principles of voluntary self-identification. UNESCO's 2001 Universal Declaration on Cultural Diversity states that "No one may invoke cultural diversity to infringe upon human rights guaranteed by international law, nor to limit their scope" (Article 4). Similarly, the UN's 1992 Declaration on the Rights of Persons Belonging to National or Ethnic, Religious and Linguistic Minorities states that any rights or duties recognized in the Declaration "shall not prejudice the enjoyment of all persons of universally recognized human rights and fundamental freedoms" (Article 8.2). The International Labour Organization's 1989 Convention on the rights of indigenous peoples says that the right of indigenous people to maintain their cultural practices should be respected "where these are not incompatible with fundamental rights defined by the national legal system and internationally recognized human rights" (Article 8.2). In all of these cases, the UN and its affiliated bodies endorse multiculturalism as a supplement to and expansion of universal human rights, not as an abandonment or abridgement of them.

The same is true of other international organizations. For example, the Council of Europe's 1995 Framework Convention for the Protection of National Minorities says that the Convention must be interpreted in a way that complies with the European Convention on Human Rights (Article 23). In fact, every international declaration and convention on these issues makes the same point – the rights of minorities and indigenous peoples are an inseparable part of a larger human rights framework, and operate within its limits. At the level of formal international law, therefore, the situation is clear: minority rights are endorsed because and insofar as they extend human rights, and are rejected insofar as they abridge human rights. Nor is this unique to international law. The same safeguards exist at the level of domestic laws and constitutions.

Authors such as Finkelkraut, Bruckner, Cowan, and Stjernfelt ignore these legal safeguards, since they do not fit within their narrative. But these safeguards are fundamental to the "logic" of real-world multiculturalism policies, and help to ensure that the legislative recognition of cultural rights has not created limitations on people's choices, whether it be the choice to leave a group, to question group authorities or practices, to adopt mixed or multiple identities, or to interact with members of other groups.

So the cultural determinist interpretation makes no legal sense. It also makes no political sense. How could cultural determinist ideas have become the official public policy of Western democracies, particularly in a forty-year era of wide-ranging liberalization and human rights reforms? How could a "winning coalition" be built in support of cultural determinist multiculturalism in Western democracies? How could it gain the support of the major political parties, or of a majority of members of the national legislature? It is difficult to make political sense of this scenario, and indeed most critics who discuss the adoption of multiculturalism treat it as a mystery (e.g. Barry 2001: 292), as if gremlins snuck into national parliaments and drafted multicultural policies while no one was watching. There is simply no credible genealogy that connects 19th century German romantics or early 20th century American anthropologists to public policy debates in the 1960s and 1970s.

If we look at the actual process by which multiculturalism policies were adopted, a different picture emerges. In reality, virtually everyone involved in adopting multicultural reforms in the West – from the political activists and civil society organizations that initially mobilised for these reforms, to the segment of the public that supported them, to the legislators who adopted them, to the bureaucrats who drafted and implemented them, to the judges who interpreted them – were inspired by the ideals of human rights and civil rights liberalism. These actors viewed multicultural reforms as part of a larger process of social and political liberalization, and embedded these reforms legally and institutionally within a liberal rights framework.

To be sure, once these policy structures were in place, conservative and patriarchal elites within various communities have attempted to gain control over them, or at least to influence their implementation and direction. This is a universal phenomenon: once new powers or resources are made available, competition will inevitably arise for control over them. For example, once multiculturalism funds were made available, and multiculturalism advisory councils established, conservative elites within immigrant/ethnic groups sought access to them. This sort of political contestation was inevitable. Indeed, it would violate every known law of political science if it didn't happen. It is even possible that these policies have sometimes, unintentionally, served to strengthen the hand of conservative elites against the forces of liberal reform within various communities.

So one important question we need to ask is whether conservative/patriarchal elites have been successful in capturing multiculturalism policies, and what safeguards are in place to ensure that the original emancipatory goals are not subverted. This is an important question, which I discuss elsewhere (Kymlicka 2015), but needless to say, we can only make headway on this question if we treat it as an empirical question, to be tested against the evidence. If we start instead from the presumption that multiculturalism policies are always already based on cultural determinist premises, then we blind ourselves to the political dynamics and legal processes at work.

Some critics acknowledge that patriarchal elites may not yet have succeeded in capturing multiculturalist policies, but they nonetheless insist that this is somehow destined to occur. Grillo calls this the "ticking culture scenario", which he relates to the widespread assumption amongst critics that "multiculturalism is always already 'unbridled'" (Grillo 2007: 987). In reality, contemporary multiculturalism in the Western democracies is always already bridled by liberal-democratic commitments. And how well it advances those commitments, and safeguards against their misuse, is something to be empirically investigated, not prejudged in advance.

I am cautiously confident that the empirical evidence will support the benefits of multiculturalism policies, at least in certain contexts, although I also believe there are many ways in which multiculturalism needs to be updated to deal with new challenges that were barely conceived of forty years ago. In facing up to the challenges of the 21st century, I would simply insist that liberal multiculturalism is to be judged on its merits, not dismissed on the basis of demonstrably false genealogies of original sin.

■ References

Abu-Laban, Y. and C. Gabriel. *Selling Diversity: Immigration, Multiculturalism, Employment Equity and Globalization*. Peterborough: Broadview, 2002.

Adams, M. *Unlikely Utopia: The Surprising Triumph of Canadian Pluralism*. Toronto: Viking, 2007.

Banting, K. and W. Kymlicka. *Multiculturalism and the Welfare State*. Oxford: Oxford University Press, 2006.

Barry, B. *Culture and Equality: An Egalitarian Critique of Multiculturalis*. Cambridge: Polity, 2000.

Berry, J. et al. *Immigrant Youth in Cultural Transition*. Mahwah: Lawrence Erlbaum, 2006.

Bloemraad, I. *Becoming a Citizen: Incorporating Immigrants and Refugees in the United States and Canada*. Berkeley: University of California Press, 2006.

Bruckner, P. "Enlightenment Fundamentalism or Racism of the Anti-Racists?" January 2007, www.signandsight.com/features/1146.html.

Cardinal, L. and A.-A. Denault. "Empowering Linguistic Minorities: Neo-liberal Governance and Language Policies in Canada and Wales." *Regional & Federal Studies* 17, 1 (2007): 137-56.

Cowan, J., ed. *Culture and Rights: Anthropological Perspectives*. Cambridge: Cambridge University Press, 2001.

Crepaz, M. "'If You Are My Brother, I May Give You a Dime!' Public Opinion on Multiculturalism, Trust and the Welfare State." In *Multiculturalism and the Welfare State*, ed. K. Banting and W. Kymlicka, 92-117. Oxford: Oxford University Press, 2006.

Davis, S. and K. Ebbe. "Traditional Knowledge and Sustainable Development: Environmentally Sustainable Development Proceedings Series No. 4." The World Bank, 1993.

Duyvendak, W.G.J. and P. Scholten. "The Invention of the Dutch Multicultural Model and Its Effects on Integration Discourses in the Netherlands." *Perspectives on Europe* 40, 2 (2011): 39-45.

Ersanilli, E. and R. Koopmans. "Do Immigrant Integration Policies Matter? A Three-Country Comparison among Turkish Immigrants." *West European Politics* 34, 2 (2011): 208-34.

Finkelkraut, A. *The Undoing of Thought*. London: Claridge, 1988.

Grillo, R. "An Excess of Alterity? Debating Difference in a Multicultural Society." *Ethnic and Racial Studies* 30, 6 (2007): 978-98.

Guimond, S., Crisp, R. J., de Oliveira, P., Kamiejski, R., et al. "Diversity Policy, Social Dominance, and Intergroup Relations: Predicting Prejudice in Changing Social and Political Contexts." *Journal of Personality and Social Psychology*, 104, 6 (2013): 941-58.

Hale, C. "Neoliberal Multiculturalism." *POLAR: Political and Legal Anthropology Review* 28, 1 (2005): 10-28.

Hale, C. and R. Millaman. "Cultural Agency and Political Struggle in the Era of *Indio Permitido*." In *Cultural Agency in the Americas*, ed. Doris Sommer, 281-304. Durham: Duke University Press, 2005.

Harell, A. "Minority-Majority Relations in Canada: The Rights Regime and the Adoption of Multicultural Values." Paper presented at the Canadian Political Science Association Annual Meeting 2009, Ottawa ON.

Huntington, S. *Who Are We? The Challenges to America's National Identity*. New York: Simon & Schuster, 2004.

James, M. "Neoliberal Heritage Redress." In *Reconciling Canada: Critical Perspectives on the Culture of Redress*, ed. J. Henderson and P. Wakeham, 31-46. Toronto: University of Toronto Press, 2013.

Kazemipur, A. *Social Capital and Diversity: Some Lessons from Canada*. Bern: Peter Lang, 2009.

Keating, M. *Nations against the State*. London: Palgrave, 2001.

Kesler, C. and I. Bloemraad. "Does Immigration Erode Social Capital?" *Canadian Journal of Political Science* 43, 2 (2010): 319-47.

Kim, N.-K. "Revisiting New Right Citizenship Discourse in Thatcher's Britain." *Ethnicities* 10, 2 (2010): 208-35.

Koopmans, R. "Trade-Offs Between Equality and Difference: Immigrant Integration, Multiculturalism and the Welfare State in Cross-National Perspective." *Journal of Ethnic and Migration Studies*, 1 (2010): 1-26.

Kristol, I. "The Tragedy of Multiculturalism." *Wall Street Journal*, July 31 (1991): 15.

Kymlicka, W. "Testing the Liberal Multiculturalist Hypothesis: Normative Theories and Social Science Evidence." *Canadian Journal of Political Science* 43, 2 (2010): 257-71.

Kymlicka, W. "Multiculturalism: Success, Failure, and the Future." In *Rethinking National Identity in the Age of Migration*, ed. Migration Policy Institute, 33-78. Berlin: Verlag Bertelsmann Stiftung, 2012.

Kymlicka, W. "Neoliberal Multiculturalism?" In *Social Resilience in the Neoliberal Era*, ed. P. Hall and M. Lamont, 99-125. Cambridge: Cambridge University Press, 2013.

Kymlicka, W. "The Essentialist Critique of Multiculturalism." In *Multiculturalism Rethought*, ed. V. Uberoi and T. Modood, 209-49 London: Palgrave, 2015.

Lentin, A. and G. Titley. *The Crises of Multiculturalism: Racism in a Neoliberal Age*. London: Zed Books, 2011.

Macdonald, L. and P. Muldoon. "Globalisation, Neo-Liberalism, and the Struggle for Indigenous Citizenship." *Australian Journal of Political Science* 41, 2 (2006): 209-23.

McNeish, J.-A. "Beyond the Permitted Indian? Bolivia and Guatemala in an Era of Neo-Liberal Developmentalism." *Latin American and Caribbean Ethnic Studies* 3 (2008): 33-59.

Mitchell, K. *Crossing the Neoliberal Line: Pacific Rim Migration and the Metropolis.* Philadelphia: Temple University Press, 2004.

Murphy, P., B. O'Brien, and S. Watson. "Selling Australia, Selling Sydney: The Ambivalent Politics of Entrepreneurial Multiculturalism." *Journal of International Migration and Immigration* 4 (2003): 471-98.

Sniderman, P. and L. Hagendoorn. *When Ways of Life Collide*. Princeton, NJ: Princeton University Press, 2007.

Somers, M. *Genealogies of Citizenship: Markets, Statelessness, and the Right to Have Rights*. Cambridge: Cambridge University Press, 2008.

Stjernfelt, F. "The Broken Cup: From Culturalism to Multiculturalism." In *The Democratic Contradictions of Multiculturalism*, ed. J.-M. Eriksen and F. Stjernfelt, 101-98. New York: Telos, 2012.

van Nieuwkoop, M. and J. Uquillas. *Defining Ethnodevelopment in Operational Terms: Lessons from the Ecuador Indigenous and Afro-Ecuadoran People's Project* (LCR Sustainable Development Working Paper No. 6, Environmentally and Socially Sustainable Development Sector Management Unit, Latin American and Caribbean Regional Office, World Bank). 2000.

Weldon, S. "The Institutional Context of Tolerance for Ethnic Minorities." *American Journal of Political Science* 50, 2 (2006): 331-49.

Žižek, S. "Multiculturalism, or the Cultural Logic of Multinational Capitalism." *New Left Review* 225 (1997): 28-51.

4. Too Little Culture – Too Much Culture: The Strange Coexistence of Two Opposite Notions of Culture

Frederik Stjernfelt

It is a remarkable fact that a wide range of very different notions of culture may be found in academic and political debates. Undoubtedly, this may be explained by the fact that, in itself, the concept of culture is complex (Williams 1983: 87) or even hypercomplex (Fink 1988), and that many particular variants of the notion make use of reduced or simplified versions of it.[1] As long as this takes place with the explicit recognition that such use is simplified for specific purposes, this is unproblematic. More problematic, however, are the many cases where such simplified versions are taken to be exhaustive and sufficient, maybe even identical to the concept of culture as such. Such uses lie behind the fact that very different, competing, even mutually exclusive notions of culture are circulating, causing problems which are not only conceptual.

This article critically isolates and compares two such simplified and deficient concepts of culture – they could be called "too much" and "too little" culture, respectively – and finally observes their strange coexistence, sometimes even in the same persons, currents, and conceptions. In the following, I shall introduce the two notions one by one. Current discussions of radicalization are chosen to illustrate different consequences springing from adopting each of the two notions. This also forms the basis for the final discussion of how and why the two notions may sometimes – even if contradictory – coexist.

The two conceptions – "too much" and "too little" – spring out of academic currents to which they, to some degree, remain allied – but what interests me here is not so much their current academic state but their function as *versunkenes Kulturgut* – disseminated culture – in the public sphere and politics. Sometimes, academic notions have the fate of surviving, even in simplified, strengthened ver-

---

1. Already Kroeber et al. 1952 thus list six different types of culture conceptions: descriptive, historical, normative, psychological, structural, and genetic.

sions in public and political discussions, and this is the case, to an eminent degree, with the two versions of the culture concept discussed here.

The former, the "too much" version, was traditionally a conservative notion, in the 20th century most often closely allied to nationalist positions claiming cultural inheritance and traditions to prevail over economic and social structures and thus form the deepest level of human behaviour and societies. Such a notion may be called "culturalism"[2]; an interesting fact is that the recent decades have seen a left wing version of such a viewpoint emerge and grow strong in many of the different versions of so-called "multiculturalism", claiming, like nationalism, that culture determines human individuals through and through and should, for that reason, enjoy center stage in policies regarding minorities, immigration, ethnicity, religion, etc. The broader notion of "communitarianism", claiming that certain pre-political, shared, traditional values are necessary for democratic societies, often also includes aspects of such culturalism. But even if nationalism and multiculturalism most often appear as hard opponents in actual Western politics, they thus share the same basic, anti-liberal anthropological notion of culture.

The other cultural version – the "too little" notion – has its roots particularly in sociology and social policies, reducing culture to an epiphenomenal surface level determined by deeper, social, and essentially non-cultural forces. A classic version of this notion, of course, is found in Marxism, where the basis-superstructure conception relegates culture to the level of superstructure, as a mere surface effect of real economical and political forces considered more basic. Such a view, however, is not found only in Marxism proper but also in many versions of modernization theories in sociology – and indeed in many political currents on the center-left inspired by that tradition. Interestingly, liberal, anti-Marxist versions of such a theory may also be found – liberalism and socialism often sharing a basic economism taking economical interests and regularities to form the basic level of human behaviour and politics from which other levels ultimately derive.

The two versions may be summed up, by simplification, as an anthropological (too much) versus a sociological (too little) notion of culture. It goes without saying that this is not to say that all of the respective disciplines of anthropology and sociology subscribe to the two versions of the concept – rather that the two versions have important roots in each of these two disciplines. Notions of culture are generally essentially contested, and many sociologists and anthropologists may hold reservations about such conceptions of culture.

---

2. In Eriksen and Stjernfelt 2012, we define culturalism, draw an outline over central parts of its intellectual history, especially its multiculturalist branch in the 20th century.

Too much

The "too much" notion of culture has been, in recent decades, in ascendancy as compared with the relative dominance of the "too little" approach in the West in mid-20th century, especially after WWII. In the "hard" versions of multiculturalism, particularly the "too much" idea appears in claims like "all cultures merit respect", that "culture forms the horizon of all human activity", that "all values are dependent upon culture", that "cultures should be given political protection", etc. Jens-Martin Eriksen and I have analyzed parts of the intellectual history of the "too much" version under the headline of "culturalism" (Eriksen and Stjernfelt 2012). Its general claim is that culture forms the ultimate horizon of human activity, thus making all of human behaviour, including economics, sociology, psychology, philosophy, etc. deeply, if not exclusively, dependent upon culture in the last resort. Thus, the main strategy of this concept is totalising – making the concept of culture so all-encompassing that it is taken to constitute the broadest characterisation of all human activity. Making concepts broader usually makes them more vague – not, however, in this case. Simultanously with the totalising strategy, culturalism makes of "culture" something very active: a force penetrating and determining all human activity in the minutest detail.

In a British context, a prominent source for this notion of culture is, of course, E.B. Tylor's famous definition of culture as "an entire way of life"[3]; on the Continent, an important intellectual root is Herder's conception of "the nation" as an irreducible whole, rooted in popular language, traditions, and customs and claimed to be specific to entities called "peoples". It is well known how Herder's originally tolerant, cosmopolitan version of the concept – envisaging an open plurality of "nations" – quickly yielded to the political use of the concept in liberal nationalisms in early 19th century Europe, only to form a bundle of general right wing positions in the European nation states which came out of the 19th and 20th centuries. According to this idea, the population of such a state must share a large amount of "culture" in order to count as politically viable. The further use of political nationalism in the totalitarianisms of the 20th century is well known in the right wing cases of Fascism and Nazism.[4] Herderian culturalism, thus, came in both more benign and more malign variants. A strange and often overlooked fact is that the very same ancestral

---

3. The famous first sentence of Tylor 1871: "Culture or civilization, taken in its wide ethnographic sense, is that complex whole which includes knowledge, belief, art, morals, law, custom, and any other capabilities and habits acquired by man as a member of society."
4. In a more general sense, it also influenced the two other large totalitarianisms originating in the 1910-20s, bolshevism and islamism. Even if these are, in different ways, internationalist by principle, they share the sharp culturalist distinction between insiders and outsiders. The four totalitarianisms emerged in the same period around WW1 and gained ground in similar contexts – the loss of empires – and were able to exchange ideas as to cultural

tree in intellectual history also gave rise to another culturalist doctrine, this time on the left wing, ultimately culminating in multiculturalism. This is based on the idea that also people without states might count as nations (Herder, living in imperial Europe with many state-aspiring groups suppressed by empires, realized this), and so could be taken to possess cultures in the same holistic sense as those politically equipped with their own states. This became central to early anthropology where the "culture" concept especially was developed in the American anthropology of the first half of the 20th century.

A influential book for the development of this anthropological notion of culture was Ruth Benedict's *Patterns of Culture* (1934). Benedict's argument has two main pillars. One is that cultures consist of infinitely variable sets of values; the other is that once a culture is articulated, it forms the indispensable horizon of all of its members. The process of "enculturation" ensures that all members share the basically same set of values and behaviours. These two ideas taken together thus result in the culturalist notion of "culture": cultures form large, integrated wholes which are closed off as against other cultures – self-sufficient, inward-turned bubbles at safe distance from each other, and fundamentally incapable of understanding one another. The same tradition interpreted this concept in terms of cultural relativism: as all values depend upon culture, there is no common measures enabling anybody to compare values and practices across cultures, because any measuring method will be, in itself, culture specific.[5]

Eriksen and Stjernfelt (2012) relate in more detail how this idea became part of the UN: in 1947, the American Association of Anthropologists protested against the universalism of the UN Declaration of Human Rights in the making. Through the inspiration and contribution by anthropologists like Lévi-Strauss, culturalism became part of the ideology of UNESCO, and came to form a constant and never resolved tension in the UN system between the universalism and individualism of human rights on the one hand and culturalism and group values on the other. Multiculturalism, in its many variants and guises, is the child of this tension. This implies that multiculti comes in many different versions, dependent upon which side – universalism and culturalism – are given preference and to which degree.

Eriksen and Stjernfelt (2012) propose the notions of "soft" versus "hard" multiculturalism to refer to the range of compromises between these two determinants. "Soft" multiculturalism, then, is freedom for individuals to live, choose, and change cultures, under the proviso that cultural traditions which are in contradiction to ba

---

homogenisation, aiming at total social shaping and control of the population of a polity, simultaneously boding ill for individuals in the population not sharing those features (Mozaffari 2006: 2013).

5. This claim obviously goes against the vast amount of international comparisons across nations of, e.g., health, education, economy, corruption, equality, liberty, and much more.

sic, liberal, democratic norms (such as human rights, rule of law, equality before the law, etc.) must be given up. "Hard" multiculturalism, on the other hand, will claim that liberal democracy is but one "culture" among many and that non-democratic cultures possess equal rights to thrive in modern societies, even to some degree at the expense of basic human rights of their members or of specific non-members. This soft-hard distinction is often not recognised, which is a source of much confusion. It seems as if many multiculti believers think that the liberal, democratic individualism and illiberal culturalism may easily find a stable compromise; some even think the two in some sense are basically one and the same thing – this seems to be the case with Kymlicka's much-discussed "liberal multiculturalism" (Kymlicka 1995; 2007), which claims that multiculti grows directly out of democratic liberalism as a sort of further extension.[6] It seems as if once you have admitted the equality of individuals, the extension to the equality of culture is an automatic outgrowth which needs not give rise to any conceptual tensions nor political problems. Dissident voices (Barry 2001; Eriksen and Stjernfelt 2012) claim that Kymlicka's position remains deeply culturalist and just glosses over deep conceptual tensions with universalist lingo.

The bottom line, then, is that the "too much" position is really "too much" in two different senses of the word. One is ontological. The claim for the role of culture is hypostasised in an erroneous manner. It is not true that cultures in reality form completely integrated, completely segregated wholes. Rather, cultures develop and change through futurist or traditionalist awakenings, they meet other cultures, merge, hybridise, vanish, often over surprisingly short periods. It is also not true that culture – inherited collective norms and practices – is the root of all human value and behaviour. Such values and behaviours have many different roots, causes, and purposes, some of them physical, biological, sociological, economic; some apriori, some empirical, some due to individual experience and invention. Only certain aspects of values and behaviour are cultural in the sense that they spring out of how young children experienced or were taught the traditions and ways of their parents and ancestors.

Another such sense is political. Giving culture too large a place in your ontology may prime you to give it too large a role in your policy as well. It is for this reason that the concrete politics of culturalism is generally of a conservative, even reactionary tendency.[7] If one believes that the most important in the life of individuals

---

6. Despite the fact that Kymlicka simultaneously clings to a culturalist definition of culture as that which provides the entire set of action options which an individual has to chose between.
7. Malik 2009 critically analyses multiculturalist policies of the Blair government: by allotting funding to "cultural" groups, the cultural representatives benefited proved, most often, to be clerics or other religious figures, favoring strongly conservative interpretations of each their "culture". This policy thereby pitted cultural groups against each other, rather than encouraging them to mutual tolerance.

is the mores and customs inherited from certain ancestors, then culturalist policy easily becomes one of preservation, one destined to rule out influences from other cultures, from science, from modernity, including liberal democracy. This fact is easily grasped in hard versions of nationalism, but exactly the same thing is at stake in multiculturalism. In some sense, multiculturalism as a political ideology is nothing but nationalism in the plural.[8]

Already Herder had this idea – and it becomes extremely clear in the actual version of far-right multiculti known as "ethnopluralism". Again, the central role of culture, its preservation and purity, is called for – with the conclusion that cultures should remain where they are (and, *a fortiori*, go back to where they were) – only territorial segregation will keep cultures pure. The only difference to received left-wing multiculturalism here is the notion of territory: hard multiculti claims that it is possible and realistic to preserve cultures within the same polity, in one and the same territory, particularly in modern, democratic states. But this immediately gives rise to tensions between illiberal features of "cultures" (such as different rights accorded to in-group and out-group, to men and women, to believers as well as non-believers, etc.). Hard multiculti either claims such illiberal features should be accepted as exceptions, or should even enjoy equal prominence with liberal principles.

The democratic, liberal counter argument is that cultural features should enjoy neither more nor less prominence than all other political claims – and that they, for that reason, should neither be allowed special status, nor legal exceptions.

Too little

While culturalism is deeply wedded to conservatism – despite its recent popularity on the left wing – the "too little" culture position comes out of a basically modernity-oriented current of intellectual history. In the universalist individualism coming out of the Enlightenment, culture was not seen as the horizon of all things human. Humanity was rather seen as something only partially realised as yet, rather, it was possible to develop it further in the future, cf. the ideas of man's perfectibility, of social engineering, of democratic politics as a process integrating the opinions of large masses of people and aiming at the improvement of their lot. This did not immediately imply, however, that cultures mattered little; rather, cultures were measured on their contribution to this overall future-oriented process of civiliza-

---

8. I owe this quip to Amartya Sen who calls multiculturalism "monoculturalism in plural", see Eriksen and Stjernfelt 2012, 306.

tion.[9] Thus, many early Enlightenment figures emphasised the contributions to that process not only of European antiquity, but also of ancient High Cultures of Eurasia, of China, of Muslim empires, and much else. Out of the Enlightenment tradition, however, certain currents tended to reduce culture to a very superficial, epiphenomenal status in human life. One particularly influential idea of this kind was the claim for reduction of all human intentions to economic purposes. This idea lay behind extreme articulations of both liberal and socialist social theories. It is well-known how Marx deemed religion to be but an "opium of the masses" which would cease to be necessary under future communist paradises – and it is well-known how liberal economists fashioned the idea of rational man, aware of all his preferences and able to judge any issue in life as one of rationally weighing different possibilities against each other in a cost-benefit analysis. In such ideologies, cultural motivations for human action shrink if not vanish completely.

The Marxist version can be expressed in this way:

> In the social production of their existence, men inevitably enter into definite relations, which are independent of their will, namely relations of production appropriate to a given stage in the development of their material forces of production. The totality of these relations of production constitutes the economic structure of society, the real foundation, on which arises a legal and political superstructure and to which correspond definite forms of social consciousness. The mode of production of material life conditions the general process of social, political and intellectual life. It is not the consciousness of men that determines their existence, but their social existence that determines their consciousness (Marx 1994 (1859): 211).

The Marxist dualism of base and superstructure relegates cultural notions – along with art, religion, ideas, etc. – to the superstructure which has the role of epiphenomenal side effects of economic relations at the level of production only. Such a theory, of course, necessarily comes with a supplementary theory of false consciousness. People who actually believe that art, religion, thought, ideas, etc. really matter are but deceived fools. They are even without any responsibility for their false beliefs because such beliefs stem, as a structural effect, from their social and economic positions in society. This is, then, the root of the "root cause" explanation: when people realize their real conditions, it is only possible because they are part of the proletariat avant garde (or, in any case, believe to be allied with it). When people believe in liberal principles, the root cause is really their adherence to the bourgeoisie in one of its guises. When people are strong believers, the root

---

9. The classic Enlightenment locus for this optimism as to progress, of course, is Condorcet 1988.

cause is really their supposedly poor social and economic situation. Today, Marxism hardly has the sway over large swathes of Western intellectuals and academics that it had in the middle of the 20th century, but the idea of "social root causes" seems to have taken root and to have acquired a life of its own beyond the confines of the Marxist tradition, namely in parts of the general theoretical current often called modernisation theory.

The theory is made of a bundle of different sociological conceptions kept together by their common assumption that a general development from "traditional" to "modern" social structures is active and even preferable in many if not all societies. Modernisation theory thus continues the general idea of "progress" of the Enlightenment, in for instance Condorcet, and counts Marx, Durkheim, Weber, Parsons, and many more in its ancestral tree. Modernisation is taken to involve a whole parcel consisting of economic growth, division of labor, development of technology, industrialisation, individualisation, rationalisation, massification, liberalisation, democratisation, secularisation, etc. Very often, but not necessarily, socio-economic development is taken to be the motor of modernisation – making modernisation theory prone to accept "social root cause" explanations. Traditional culture is supposed to perish to a large degree during modernisation processes, and cultural claims may thus be seen as vestiges, undercut by social evolution and most often effectively appearing as a displaced expression of social forces and demands which are not in themselves cultural.

Modernisation theory comes in many variants; in politics both liberal and socialist currents typically subscribe to versions of it, despite their disagreement on the role of the state, of social engineering and of economic redistribution. But common is the tendency to regard culture as a mere, superficial level without much, if any, causal effect, often consisting of behaviours and thoughts long since overtaken by "development" and without real influence on social and political structure. This "too little" theory of culture tends to see cultural claims and demands of nationalist parties or ethnic groups as a bit ridiculous, as effects of false consciousness which would be better addressed by economic growth and an increase in social and economic capabilities of the groups in question. The idea that certain old or new cultural ideas may seem to be very important to certain groups or forces – maybe so important as to trump utility, economy, and rational arguments – is regarded as preposterous to the "too little" school.

It probably goes without saying that this author rejects both the too much and the too little theories of culture, preferring a middle road of admitting culture as a force on a par with other basic human motivation types without neither totalising nor ignoring it.

Explaining extremism: radicalization theories as an example

Recent terrrorist attacks have brought the issue of radicalisation on the agenda. What makes certain persons – typically young men – prone to so extreme behaviour as to kill innocent civilians in order to further some political or religious conception, be it right wing ideas like radical nationalism and radical islamism or left wing ideas such as communism? Interestingly, the possible explanations differ with one's concept of culture. Classical sociological conceptualization of radicalization follows the modernist "too little" school. Ted Gurr's *Why Men Rebel* (1970) e.g., takes the reason to be "relative deprivation" (37). Thus, cultural or religious explanations of radicalisation are taken to be superficial as compared to deep economic roots. A current defence of a related position even claims as its title "Muslim radicalisation's socio-economic roots" (Abbas 2009). Abbas expects that "equal opportunities and equal outcomes" in society will serve to abate radicalisation. The obvious problem in such a theory is that most radicals are *not* poor, nor do they cite poverty grievances as the root of their activity. They typically cite cultural, ideological, or religious motivations rather than socio-economic ones. So, again, such a theory must be supplemented with root cause theories of false consciousness: such terrorists are simply completely mistaken as to the real motivations for their own actions. A further upshot of this theory is that they may be seen, for this reason, as completely irresponsible persons not really knowing what they are doing – because the violence they perpetrate evidently is an ill-chosen means to the supposedly economic end. Even if intended as an apology for their actions, such explanations categorize radicals in a way not far from racism: as persons without the same ability for rational thinking as the analyst.

Surprisingly, culturalists subscribing to versions of hard multiculturalism, defending the role of culture, rarely extend this framework to describe radicalists and terrorists. It is as if terrorists form an exception to their doctrine that culture has this deep determinative power – obviously because making radical acts the product of cultural backgrounds inevitably would taint that culture. Sometimes, they may even go so far as to adopt remnants of the "root cause" explanation which is better fit to exculpate culture for having caused the terrible acts which the perpetrators themselves may cite cultural reasons for doing. The culturalist theory here is rather adopted by the *opponents* of the specific terrorists. When e.g. the Norwegian extreme nationalist Breivik committed his infamous act of terror, many on the left wing blamed the culture he grew out of – namely the extremely nationalist, so-called islam-critical right wing blogosphere. Conversely, in case of Islamist attacks, right-wingers may easily ascribe the cause of such attacks to nothing less than "Islam" itself in all abstraction – claiming again that cultural factors are to be blamed for the actions of the terrorists. This, at first glance, strange structure – that culturalist explanations for radicalisations work only for your opponents – naturally comes from the fact that radicalisation is perceived as an evil to be explained (away), and no culturalist will like to see his own preferred culture appear as the guilty party behind atrocities. Culturalists typically *defend* cultures, which is probably why culturalist explanations of radicalisation are rare among academics, who strive for consistency. Only in public debate, where one may be culturalist about one's enemies and make exceptions for one's own culture, culturalist theories of radicalisation prevail.

Radicalisation theories ascribing a more moderate role to culture then seem to be preferable. Griffin (2012) provides such a theory, using Berger's 1967 description of cultures as "sacred canopies", granting the life of their members under their shelters. Modernity having eroded such shelters, spiritually homeless youngsters may choose to become terrorists. This gives rise to two different types of terror – oriented towards protecting or reconstructing a threatened canopy or towards constructing a better canopy from scratch in the future. In a certain sense, Griffin's explanation is culturalist – finding the explanation of terrorism in the painful modern erosion of traditional cultures. But he is not culturalist in the sense that he accepts the totalising assumption of culturalism: modernity, in his account, is no sacred canopy, and you can add that most of us who live in modern societies do not become terrorists for lack of protective canopies.

Another explanation claims that the sociological approach of modernisation theory misses the mark because it is too wide. Instead, it proposes micro-sociological explanations based on the small networks of youngsters looking for meaning in life. The ARTIS report, for instance, claims that the development of such "[…] networks, plots and attacks resembles more the development of a complex system, with inherently chaotic and unpredictable characteristics, which can nevertheless be evaluated for probabilistic and path-dependent developments" (2009: 4). The authors claim explicitly anti-culturalistically that "[i]nstead of viewing culture as a 'top-down' structure that imposes itself on individual beliefs and behaviours, we recommend focusing on modeling micro-processes at the level of individual beliefs and behaviors" (10). Instead, they point to a "cultural epidemiology" (ibid.) facilitated by the emergence of strong bonds between persons in a micro-social environment, leading to a willingness to sacrifice oneself for the fate and beliefs of one's close fellows, thus assuming a sacrality of values overriding other obligations and principles such as those of economic man. Only when active in such micro-networks, cultural representations may achieve a dangerous role, but the complexity of such networks makes it impossible to predict, in the single case, when the important threshold is crossed between "violent extremism" and "extremist violence".

The theories of Griffin and ARTIS may be said to give culture a moderate but non-negligible role and are thus quoted here to indicate positions in a middle ground between the "too much" and the "too little" schools.

Strange meetings of "too much" and "too little"

The strange thing, however, is that as much as the too much and the too little schools may compete in public debate, unexpected liaisons between them may occur. Strictly spoken, such combinations will be logically contradictory, but one should not expect politics and debate in all cases to follow logical principles. Thus, a possible version of the "too little" position may admit, to some degree, multiculturalist policies normally connected with the "too much" position – exactly for the reason that as culture is considered socially superficial and causally inert from the modernisation viewpoint, such policies are taken to be harmless, indifferent, inconsequential, and in any case temporary and provisional, because modernisation is believed to catch up with them and make them irrelevant, on a short notice anyway. Thus, the very same politician who asserts that "social conditions" are root causes responsible for cultural and religious claims made by certain immigrants may support illiberal multiculti special group rights demanded by those claims.

Such developments may give rise to baroque clashes of ideas. Let me take a current Danish example regarding Muslim immigration. Since the 1980s, a substantial part of immigration to Denmark has come from Islamic countries with the result that Denmark now has around 5% Muslims including a minority of Islamists.[10] These immigrants have a variegated background, from different countries involving many different Islamic currents – and often they have constructed local mosques in poor surroundings such as abandoned industrial buildings and storehouses. These conditions have given rise to a movement supported by left wing Danes, arguing in petitions and comments that Danish Muslims should have a "real grand mosque" (*en rigtig stormoské*) "where building of bridges and openness is the foundation and where democratic values are in focus".[11]

In the summer of 2014, a great mosque was indeed inaugurated in a Copenhagen suburb – the Hamad Bin Khalifa mosque in Rovsinggade in the Nørrebro area. The Danish mosque supporters, however, stayed away from the opening ceremony – the mosque is financed by the Emirate of Qatar, also supporting the Muslim Brotherhood as well as parts of the so-called IS armies in Syria and Iraq. One of the backers of the "real grand mosque", the leading Copenhagen politician Anna Mee Allerslev of a centre party (Det Radikale Venstre), used the occasion to once more market the idea of an even grander grand mosque, supposedly for all Danish Muslims, not only

---

10. How many among the Muslim constituency in the West support Islamist ideas is an open question as only a few investigations have been made. International and Danish surveys seem to point to the fact that a minority holds views associated with islamism, but not a small minority, cf. Eriksen and Stjernfelt 2013, 40; 399.
11. Allerslev 2014, my translations.

for the special Sunni interpretation reigning in the Qatar mosque. Her party has a long tradition as a modernisation party with little belief only in the values of traditional cultures. So why spend so much effort on a mosque? Probably the support for the "real grand mosque" is taken to be harmless – cultural values and norms are considered as having sparse effect and soon to be marginalised even further by the ongoing modernisation reforms undertaken in her party's government coalition with the social democrats.

The remarkable thing is that this traditional "too little" position hereby allied itself with the "too much" position when it came to describing the utopian "real grand mosque" to come. This mosque is supposed to be for all Danish Muslims. Such an idea is typically culturalist: Islam is taken to be one culture, all believers are taken to form a homogeneous whole which could, in fact, be represented by one large, grandiose ceremonial building. But as is the case with all real-world cultures, Islam is beset with internal strife and tension, movements, counter-movements, sects, and revivals ever since the Sunni-Shia schism of the 7th century. Such tensions, of course, also prevail among the small Danish constituency. Sunnis, Shias, Ahmadiyas, Alevites, etc. routinely consider each other unbelievers to be eradicated from the Islamic ideal state to come – and even within such currents, especially the large Sunni tradition, an enormous bundle of warring groups, from Sufists to Wahhabists, can be found, not to speak of the many "traditional" Muslims paying scant attention to theology.

It could only be because of the "too much" understanding of culture that these well-meaning Danes, spearheaded by Allerslev, the Copenhagen mayor of employment and integration, could really believe that all Muslims are actually sufficiently alike to accept to unite in one and the same congregation. To see the absurdity of the case, one might just imagine a parallel proposal of a "real grand cathedral" uniting all Christians, Orthodox, Catholics, and Protestants of all sorts, denominations and sects, from Jesuits to Pentecostalists. My guess is that such a degree of naivety is possible only because of the "too much" culture theory and its assumption that cultures are internally homogeneous and possess the power of defining their members through and through – combined with the "too little" assumption claiming that policies pertaining to culture remain, in all cases, a superficial circus for the masses.

Conclusion

Modernisation theory needs to be modified on a series of points. As Fukuyama has recently argued (2011), the different aspects of modern societies undoubtedly support each other, but this is not the same as claiming there is only one inviolable road to modernisation, driven by economic forces. Rather, modernisation may begin with very different parameters and proceed along very different paths, even if the force field of modernity may eventually attract all such pathways in the same overall direction. But modernisation must also admit that even its imagined end point in the future may not necessarily spell the end of all traditional culture with which the process is taken to have begun. The very notion of a completely homogeneous "traditional culture" is, in itself, but a conservative myth, and there has arguably never existed a society that did not include more or less entrepreneurial, experimental individuals, injecting novelty and tension despite the attempts of ubiquitous religious elders trying to contain such dangerous individuals.

Contrariwise, there is no reason to assume a society will ever appear which has completely dispensed with the irrational power sources of tradition and charisma – the most which can be hoped for would rather be a society keeping them in check. Given the high degree of liberty for which modern societies rightly praise themselves, there is no reason not to expect that significant fractions of the population will always use this liberty to embrace some degree of rigid, conservative, traditional values and behaviours, thereby liberating them from too much choice, deliberation, and rational speculation.

The goal of modernisation, hence, could never be the complete eradication of traditional culture and religion – the utopia of "too little". Rather, a more modest and modern secularist goal must be invoked: the idea that no such currents should be able to gain privileged access to political power and privilege. This implies, in terms of "culture" and "religion", that their adherents must be forced to accept basic modern, democratic principles and cease any attempt at curtailing democratic principles and rights with cultural arguments. To me, this would form a mediation of the "too little" and "too much" theories of culture. Each of those positions, of course, will despise it. The "too littlers" will hate that secularism will not, in itself, give rise to secularisation. But even more so, the "too muchers" will hate to see their political ambitions on behalf of culture, tradition, and religion framed by unnegotiable modern, democratic principles. For that reason, the price to pay is undoubtedly most expensive for the "too muchers", the culturalists. But my guess is they must be forced to pay that price for the sake, not only of all the utilities and advantages of modernity, but also for the sake of what the Enlightenment, not without pathos, called the dignity and liberty of man.

■ References

Abbas, T. "Muslim Radicalization's Socio-Economic Roots." *The Guardian*, 29 April 2009, http://www.theguardian.com/commentisfree/belief/2009/apr/29/islam-terrorism-radicalisation-recession.

ARTIS. *Theoretical Frames on Pathways to Violent Radicalization: Understanding the Evolution of Ideas and Behaviors, How They Interact and How They Describe Pathways to Violence in Marginalized Diaspora*, 2009, http://www.artisresearch.com/articles/ARTIS_Theoretical_Frames_August_2009.pdf.

Allerslev, A.M. "En dansk moské skal kunne rumme alle." *Jyllands-Posten*, 25 June 2014.

Benedict, R. *Patterns of Culture*. New York: Houghton Mifflin, 1934.

Condorcet, N. de. *Esquisse d'un tableau historique des progrès de l'esprit humain*. Paris: Flammarion, 1988 [1795].

Eriksen, J.-M. and F. Stjernfelt. *The Democratic Contradictions of Multiculturalism*. New York: Telos Press, 2012.

Eriksen, J.-M. and F. Stjernfelt. *De Anstændige*. Copenhagen: Gyldendal, 2013.

Fink, H. "Et hyperkomplekst begreb." In *Kulturbegrebets kulturhistorie*, ed. H. Hauge and H. Horstbøll, 9-23. Aarhus: Aarhus Universitetsforlag, 1988.

Fukuyama, F. *The Origins of Political Order*. London: Profile Books, 2011.

Griffin, R. *Terrorist's Creed: Fanatical Violence and the Human Need for Meaning*. London: Palgrave, 2012.

Gurr, T. *Why Men Rebel*. Princeton, NJ: Princeton University Press, 1970.

Kroeber, A.L., C. Kluckhohn, and W. Untereiner. *Culture: A Critical Review of Concepts and Definitions*. New York: Vintage, 1952.

Kymlicka, W. *Multicultural Citizenship: A Liberal Theory of Minority Rights*. Oxford: Oxford University Press, 1995.

Kymlicka, W. *Multicultural Odysseys: Navigating the New International Politics of Diversity*. Oxford: Oxford University Press, 2007a.

Kymlicka, W. "Disentangling the Debate." In Stein 2007, 137-56.

Malik, K. *From Fatwa to Jihad. The Rushdie Affair and its Legacy*. London: Atlantic Books, 2009.

Marx, K. "Preface to *A Contribution to the Critique of Political Economy*." In *Selected Writings*, ed. L. H. Simon, 209-213. Indianapolis: Hackett Publishing, 1994.

Mozaffari, M. "Islamisme og totalitarisme." *Kritik* 180 (2006): 22-30.

Mozaffari, M. *Islamisme. En orientalsk totalitarisme*. Copenhagen: Information, 2013.

Sen, A. *Identity and Violence. The Illusion of Destiny*. London: Allen Lane, 2006.

Stein, J. Gross et al. *Uneasy Partners. Multiculturalism and Rights in Canada*. Ontario: Wilfried Laurier University Press, 2007.

Tylor, E. B. *Primitive Culture*. London: J. Murray, 1871.

Williams, R. *Keywords: A Vocabulary of Culture and Society*. Oxford: Oxford University Press, 1983.

5 Community Conceptions and Social Cohesion: Theoretical, Empirical, and Normative Issues

Nils Holtug

Increases in ethnic and religious diversity are accompanied by worries about, for example, parallel societies, crime rates, terrorism, religious extremism, nationalism, xenophobia, the educational underachievement of (some groups of) immigrants, and whether diversity is compatible with redistribution in the form of a robust welfare state. And often, such worries are framed as concerns about *social cohesion*. Indeed, public policies and debates increasingly reflect a desire to promote social cohesion in response to challenges perceived to be due to diversity. More specifically, political responses have centred around the aim of preserving/fostering a sense of community, where *community conceptions* have tended to focus on notions of identity – something we need to have in common in order to live together in a peaceful welfare state. Former home secretary David Blunkett's (2001) call for a stronger sense of common British citizenship, following the riots in various towns in Northern England in 2001, is but one example of this. Blunkett specifically emphasized the need for shared British values to promote social cohesion.

Community conceptions, then, are ideas about what kinds of bonds between community members are conducive to social cohesion. Such conceptions may, for example, draw on elements of nationalism, republicanism, liberalism, or multiculturalism. In the present article, I first provide a more precise definition of the central concept of a community conception. Second, I develop a typology of different particular community conceptions, where these conceptions differ with regard to the values they consider conducive to social cohesion. Third, I present what I believe to be some of the main theoretical arguments for each of these different community conceptions. And finally since, at the end of the day, community conceptions are empirical claims about the effects of specific values on social cohesion, I briefly consider the (limited) available empirical evidence for thinking that particular community conceptions affect social cohesion in particular ways. The article can thus be seen as a contribution to a field of research that in many ways is still in its infancy and in particular, as a plea for an interdisciplinary approach to this field that involves both normative political theory, theoretical accounts of the relevant causalities, and empirical studies of the effects on social cohesion of policies and attitudes.

The particular aspects of social cohesion I focus on are generalized trust – trust in strangers – and solidarity. These two aspects have been of particular interest to political theorists because they are considered important preconditions for implementing social justice. The main idea is that in order for principles of social justice to be implemented, people need to have adequate levels of solidarity with others, that is, to be willing to contribute to them within the framework of a redistributive welfare state. This, again, requires a certain level of trust, including trust in other people to do their fair share in support of the welfare state, for example, to avoid tax evasion, not cheat with social benefits etc. (Miller 2004: 27; 2006: 328; Rawls 1971: 240; Rothstein 2014).

Before I turn to the analysis, let me say a few words about the location of the themes of the article in, respectively, contemporary political debates and social science research. At the level of politics, community conceptions are perhaps most explicit in efforts to determine national values, where these efforts explicitly aim to promote social cohesion, as in the case of Blunkett referred to above. Similar examples include the process initiated by Nicolas Sarkozy to define France's national identity (Crumley 2010), the former Liberal-Conservative Danish government's "Values Commission" set up in 2011 (Ministry of Culture 2012), and the proposal of Parti Québécois in 2013 of a Québec Charter of Values (Drainville 2013). But also the rejection of specific policies may harbour ideas about community conceptions; consider, for example, statements about the failure of multicultural policies by heads of state Angela Merkel, David Cameron, Nicolas Sarkozy, and in a report from the Committee of Ministers in the Council of Europe in 2008. The idea being conveyed here is that multicultural policies, aiming to accommodate difference, are likely to fracture and destabilise societies and that what is needed is rather the affirmation of a common identity, around which citizens can unite. This line of thought is also expressed in the UK Commission on Integration and Cohesion (CIC) 2007 report. Finally, in different ways various recent policies may be said to be influenced by community conceptions, including the Swiss vote to ban minarets, the introduction of tests on national history and culture as requirements for citizenship in various European countries, the ban of burqas in Belgium and France, and of judges wearing religious symbols in courts of law in Denmark.

In the social sciences, in recent years, researchers have investigated the relation between immigration and social cohesion.[1] This research has particularly focused on generalized trust, which is seen as a key component of both social capital and social cohesion. In social capital research, trust is considered conducive to a large number of economic, social, and political goods, including low transaction costs on markets, economic growth, health, education, low corruption, democracy, and even happiness (Halpern 2005; Putnam 2000; 2007; Svendsen and Svendsen 2009). Some studies indicate that ethnic diversity reduces trust (Alesina and La Ferrara 2002; Delhey and Newton 2005; Anderson and Paskeviciute 2006; Putnam 2007). Indeed, such studies are sometimes referred to in political discourses when justifying restrictive immigration policies and assimilationist approaches to integration (in a Danish context, see Jespersen and Pittelkow 2005; Støvring 2010). However, alternative accounts have been offered for the relation between ethnic diversity and social cohesion, suggesting that it is not ethnic diversity *per se* but rather residential segregation that drives down trust (Uslaner 2010; 2012). Furthermore, some recent studies in Europe seem to indicate that, here, there is in fact no negative effect of ethnic diversity on social cohesion (Gesthuizen et al. 2009; Hooghe et al. 2009; Lolle and Torpe 2011).

Thus, the evidence for suggesting that diversity brings down social cohesion is mixed, at best. And when we go from the impact of diversity to the impact of policies designed to promote social cohesion under conditions of diversity, the problem is not so much that the evidence is mixed, but rather there is too little evidence to begin with (Johnston et al. 2010: 353; Kymlicka 2010; 2011: 261).

What is a community conception?

I need to define more precisely what I mean by a 'community conception': a *community conception* is a set of (formal and informal) values regulating the conditions on which individuals interact in a group, including the distribution of political, social, and cultural advantages, with the aim of securing social goods within that group, such as trust, cooperation, stability, belonging, and solidarity (Holtug 2012: 197).

However, this definition still requires clarification in a number of respects. First, the concept is meant to be neutral between different competing community conceptions, that is, different specific ideas about what values are in fact conducive to social

---

1. Alesina and Glaeser 2004; Alesina and La Ferrara 2002; Banting and Kymlicka 2006; Gesthuizen et al. 2009; Holtug 2010; Hooghe 2007; Hooghe et al. 2009; Kumlin and Rothstein 2007; Leigh 2006; Lenard 2008; Lolle and Torpe 2011; Miller 2004; Newton 2007; Pevnick 2009; Putnam 2007; Sturgis et al. 2011; Torpe and Lolle 2010; Uslaner 2002, 2012; van Parijs 2004.

cohesion. Thus, for example, nationalists and liberals disagree about the values required for maintaining or fostering social cohesion, the former emphasizing the need for national identification, the latter the need for affirming a number of basic liberal principles. And so nationalists and liberals endorse different community conceptions. In this way, the concept of a community conception works like the concept of a political doctrine. Each ranges over a number of more specific accounts, committed to a particular set of values, but neither concept is itself committed to any of these more specific values.

Second, we need to distinguish between community conceptions and social cohesion. Each particular community conception identifies the means thought necessary to promote social cohesion, and so the assumed relation between such conceptions and social cohesion is a causal one. Nevertheless, the values thought to promote social cohesion may be reminiscent of the values in which social cohesion consists. For example, it is widely held that socio-economic equality tends to promote various aspects of social cohesion, including trust and solidarity (see, for example, Uslaner 2002: ch. 6, 8), and here the values of equality and solidarity are reminiscent of each other, especially if, as in the present article, solidarity is interpreted as support for redistribution. However, it is important to distinguish claims about the causes of social cohesion from claims about social cohesion itself.

Third, this also means that when I say that the concept of a community conception is neutral between different value-based conceptions of how to promote social cohesion, this does not imply that the concept is altogether value-free. By definition, a community conception will aim at promoting values such as trust, cooperation, stability, belonging, and solidarity. So the neutrality pertains to the values thought to promote social cohesion, not to the values in which social cohesion consists. This further means that the concept of a community conception differs from what may seem to be similar concepts, including that of "community cohesion" (Cantle 2001), where the latter encompasses both elements of social cohesion and of the values that may be thought to promote it. Thus, community cohesion consists in, among other things, equality, a common sense of belonging, a positive valuation of people's different backgrounds, and strong and positive relationships between people who have different backgrounds (Cantle 2013). Since, for example, a positive valuation of people's different backgrounds will be central to some, but hardly all accounts of how to promote social cohesion, the concept of a community conception should not include a reference to this or similar values.

Fourth, the definition refers to the distribution of political, social, and cultural advantages in a group to which a community conception will give rise, if implemented, where this distribution depends on the nature of the conception under consideration. To exemplify, consider again a nationalist conception. Often, nationalism involves privileging members of the dominant nationality in all three dimensions. Thus, nationalists may be hesitant to grant immigrants the right to vote until they have resided long enough to allow for assimilation to national values and for national identification. Furthermore, nationalist language policies may favour members of the dominant nationality over immigrants in access to jobs, education, and other social goods. And finally, nationalist policies may tend to favour the religion and cultural practices of the dominant nationality. These policies affirm a national identity seen by many nationalists as a condition for a high level of social cohesion. Liberals, on the other hand, may be less inclined to tie political, social, and cultural advantages too closely to nationality, emphasizing instead a more universal conception of citizenship to which rights are attached and which is seen as sufficient for promoting social cohesion. In other words, different community conceptions will give rise to different distributions of political, social, and cultural advantages.

Fifth, community conceptions can be found on different levels, so to speak. For example, they can be found in policies designed to promote social cohesion. Consider a couple of examples of diversity politics, such as citizenship tests and national curricula in schools. Where some citizenship tests focus mainly on political aspects of societal organization, others focus also on aspects of the national culture and history. For example, the Danish test has recently moved away from questions about national culture and history (Ministry of Justice 2013), whereas the UK test has moved in the opposite direction making it, in the words of Home Secretary Theresa May, a more "patriotic guide" for immigrants (Travis 2012; cf. Brooks 2013). As such, citizenship tests may be said to express expectations as regards the aspects of society that future citizens are to know about and, in some cases, ultimately identify with. Likewise, national curricula in schools will express expectations regarding a common basis for the value-orientations of children, and will differ in their focus on, for example, national culture, active citizenship, and multicultural accommodation. Such policies generally aim, implicitly or explicitly, to shape citizens on the basis of a common identity, but where that identity will take different forms, depending on the community conception on which it is built.

Community conceptions may also be found at the individual level, as beliefs about the values conducive to social cohesion. Such a belief is a cognitive state but will of course often be accompanied by a commitment to the values incorporated in the community conception in question, and so thought to promote social cohesion. Indeed, for many purposes it is the value commitment that is more important, not least because policies embedding community conceptions often aim to promote social cohesion by affecting that very commitment. More precisely, the aim of the policy may be to strengthen individual commitments to the values of the community conception on which it relies. For example, citizenship tests may aim to increase national identification among immigrants as a way of establishing the sort of bonds between citizens thought necessary for adequate levels of social cohesion.

Sixth, the list of social cohesion items included in the definition of a 'community conception' above – trust, cooperation, stability, belonging, and solidarity – need not be seen as fixed and might certainly have been longer. It is drawn from both social capital research, which tends to be quantitative and focus on trust, networks and reciprocity and research on social cohesion, which tends to be qualitative and to focus on stability, inter-group cooperation, a common identity, and solidarity (Hooghe 2007: 711; Holtug and Mason 2010: 409-10). However, as stated above, I am concerned only with trust and solidarity here.

A typology of community conceptions

Having now clarified the concept of a community conception, I shall proceed to develop a typology of such conceptions and the theoretical arguments that may be invoked in favour of them.

This, of course, is where different community conceptions differ, and the following may be considered an (incomplete) list of such conceptions:

- *Conservative nationalism*. Social cohesion is best (or adequately) promoted by sharing an entire, or at least large parts of a national culture.
- *Liberal nationalism*. Social cohesion is best (or adequately) promoted by sharing a commitment to liberal political structures and a national identity that is transformed over time, in part to accommodate the identities of immigrants.
- *Republicanism*. Social cohesion is best (or adequately) promoted by sharing a commitment to a set of rights and civic (democratic) virtues.
- *Liberalism*. Social cohesion is best (or adequately) promoted by sharing a commitment to a set of basic (liberal) principles of justice.
- *Polity patriotism*. Social cohesion is best (or adequately) promoted by sharing a commitment to a polity, identifying with its institutions and practices.
- *Multiculturalism*. Social cohesion is best (or adequately) promoted by a shared recognition of religious and cultural differences.

Each of these community conceptions is based on the idea that individuals need to share an identity to generate (adequate) social cohesion, but they differ regarding the thickness this identity is thought to be required to have, where "thickness" refers to how much individuals are thought to be required to share in order to generate (adequate) social cohesion. Here, these conceptions are listed in descending order of thickness, that is, with thick, cultural notions of identity at the top and thin notions at the bottom. I shall explain this way of ordering them as I elaborate on their content.

Consider, first, a traditional liberal conception, according to which social cohesion is best (or adequately) promoted by a shared commitment to values such as liberty, equality, tolerance, etc. The theoretical underpinnings for such an account can be found in the work of John Rawls (1971: Sections 69 and 76), who argues that a society in which his liberal principles of justice are widely shared and (known to be) implemented in its basic structure will generate its own support, that is, commitments to the principles and the basic structure will be preserved from one generation to the next. These principles and institutions will treat people as equals and indeed be justifiable to each citizen, and furthermore give them a sense of a common purpose in maintaining these institutions. In particular, the support of (even) the worst-off members of society for these principles and the basic structure is secured by the extent to which these principles and this structure work to their advantage. While Rawls does not explicitly speak of social cohesion, he emphasizes that a sense of justice and trust in one's fellow citizens will tend to mutually support each other (1971: 498), where trust in others to comply with the requirements of justice will tend to affirm one's commitment to this value and the institutions in which it is realized.

Indeed, Rawls advances two arguments for his theory of justice. According to the first, intrinsic argument, his principles of liberty and equality are justified because the distribution of advantages to which they give rise is a *fair* one. According to the second, instrumental argument (which should not be seen as independent), these principles are justified because they give rise to a *stable* society, that is, a society that generates its own support in the sense specified above. It is in this second argument that Rawls introduces a community conception. Indeed, his concern with the stability of his principles in diverse societies gained greater prominence over the years. Thus, in *Political Liberalism* (1993: ch. 4), he argues that an overlapping consensus can be reached on his principles between people who hold different religious, moral, and philosophical views (or, more precisely, what he calls 'reasonable comprehensive doctrines').

In fact, proponents of all the different community conceptions listed above are likely to rely on both intrinsic and instrumental arguments. For example, David Miller's (1995: ch. 4) case for liberal nationalism relies both on the intrinsic argument that we have stronger obligations towards co-nationals than non-nationals, simply in virtue of the nature of the relation of co-nationality, and on the instrumental argument that sharing a nationality increases trust and solidarity and so the conditions required for implementing social justice. And Will Kymlicka's (1995: ch. 6, 9) case for liberal multiculturalism relies both on the argument that group-differentiated rights are implied by plausible principles of liberty and equality and on the argument that such rights will stimulate social cohesion through stronger minority commitments to the political community and its institutions in virtue of these being accommodating of minority concerns.

Note, however, that the empirical claims made in an instrumental argument may turn out to be mistaken in a way that creates a tension with its intrinsic counterpart. Along such lines, it has been argued that multicultural policies tend not to promote social cohesion, but rather to fracture society and to undermine trust and redistribution (Barry 2001: 88; Uslaner 2012: 57-64) and so to also undermine the equality of opportunity they were supposed to bring about in the first place. If this is so, there is a sense in which multicultural policies, thus motivated, are indirectly self-defeating (cf. Parfit 1984: ch.1). However, as we shall see, there is little evidence for the claim that multicultural policies undermine trust and redistribution.

Liberal community conceptions have been criticized from both sides, that is, both for being too thick and for being too thin. Nationalists thus argue that a common sense of justice is too thin a basis for significant trust and solidarity and that, to a higher extent, people identify with each other on the basis of pre-political, cultural commonalities. Along such lines, Miller (1995: ch. 4) argues that national identity plays a dual role as a condition for justice. First, it generates a sense of sympathy and so motivates people to be willing to redistribute. Especially when it comes to redistribution that explicitly favours the poor, such as housing subsidies, income supplements, and long-term unemployment benefits, people need to "identify with the beneficiaries of the redistribution – an identification fostered by a sense of common national identity" (Miller 2006: 328). Second, national identity generates trust, where Miller considers trust a condition for acting on one's sympathy, for example by filling in one's tax returns honestly, because one will only be willing to do so if one expects others to reciprocate, that is, to do so as well (Miller 2004: 27). Thus, according to Miller, both trust and solidarity depends on national identification, and so will tend to be stronger between co-nationals than between non-nationals.

Liberal nationalists such as Miller (1995: ch. 5) nevertheless restrict policies to promote national identity in a number of ways, which may also be seen as a condition for such policies to maintain liberal credentials. First, national identities are not seen as fixed but in a flux, and basic liberal principles apply to the negotiation of what a particular identity is to involve in the future. This also means that national identities should be realistically open to immigrants and that immigrants may contribute to the negotiation of national identities on an equal footing. Furthermore, it means that policies to promote national identities, including immigration policies, are to respect basic liberal principles such as freedom of conscience, non-discrimination, and a right to privacy (Kymlicka 2001: 258). Second, according to liberal nationalism, a national identity is justified not by mere reference to traditions but also to the arguments put forward to motivate its different elements in the first place, and it should be continuously exposed to rational scrutiny.

These two points also allow us to distinguish liberal nationalists from conservative nationalists (Burke 1790; Scruton 1990; 2001), where the latter are likely to be more inclined to set aside liberal principles in cases of conflict with traditions and will tend to have more encompassing notions of national identity (Scruton 1990), rendering immigration problematic and pushes for assimilation more pressing in a larger range of cases (Scruton 1990: 62; 2011). As Scruton (1990: 310) puts it, the "real price of community [...] is sanctity, intolerance, exclusion, and a sense that life's meaning depends on obedience, and also on vigilance against the enemy". Furthermore, conservative nationalists will often be somewhat sceptical of the merits of rational scrutiny of the content of a national identity or indeed of rational political justification in general, giving tradition-based authority to the institutions in which this identity is expressed. In fact, resistance to liberalism is in part motivated by worries about the abstract, rational justification of liberal rights, based only on universal properties of human beings, where people's rights and duties in the nation state are thought to derive from the concrete history of the nation and the bonds developed over time between people therein (Burke 1790: 58-60; Scruton 1990: 327).

To exemplify such differences between liberal and conservative nationalists, liberal nationalists may be weary of including a particular religion in the national identity (Miller 1995: 92), whereas conservative nationalists may be more inclined to do so (Scruton 1990: 300; 315; 2001: 157-63; 2011; cf. Burke 1790: 90-105). So whereas liberal and conservative nationalists agree on the need for a pre-political identity to generate social cohesion and underpin the state, conservative nationalists consider liberal notions of the nation too thin and the basis of allegiance to them too shallow to achieve this goal.

Republicanism is a further community conception that considers a shared affirmation of liberal values insufficient for social cohesion. In particular, republicans find that liberal rights need to be supplemented with a form of active citizenship, where civic duties or virtues are needed in order to uphold (broadly) liberal political institutions, facilitate worthy political goals, and generate bonds of sympathy and toleration among citizens.[2] Solidarity is grounded neither in a sense of cultural

---

2. In my characterization of republicanism, I focus on civic virtues rather than on a specifically republican conception of freedom. Andrew Mason (2000: ch. 4) gives a similar description of the republican conception of community, highlighting the republican emphasis on active citizenship and special obligations to fellow citizens. For an account of the relation between civic virtues and the republican conception of freedom in contemporary political thought, see Laborde and Maynor (2008).

identity or simply in adherence to liberal principles, but in "a reflective acceptance of certain obligations and in practical engagement" (Honohan 2010: 94).

Following William Galston (1991: 221-4), civic virtues may involve general virtues (for example, law-abidingness), social virtues (for example, open-mindedness), economic virtues (for example, a strong work ethic) and political virtues (for example, respect for the rights of others). In particular, republicans have focused on democratic virtues, emphasizing a need for people to engage in political processes at various levels of society and for doing so in particular ways, for example in accordance with requirements of public reason, in order for a democracy to thrive. Such democratic participation may be justified either as an intrinsically important aspect of a good life, or instrumentally as an important vehicle for realizing social cohesion and (ultimately) justice (Mason 2000: 96-100). As regards diverse societies in particular, active citizenship may for example involve a duty not to justify political claims on the basis of religious beliefs in the public sphere (Rawls 1999) and securing a voice for minorities in political life (Laborde and Maynor 2008: 18). Furthermore, it may involve a duty to integrate (Mason 2012: ch. 7) – a duty that may have implications for both immigrants (for example, a duty to learn the language of the society they have joined) and prior citizens (for example, a duty not to avoid sending their children to schools that have high concentrations of immigrants).

In some republican models, active citizenship is furthermore combined with a particularly strong form of secularism, like in the French regulation of religion in the public sphere (Simon and Pala 2010; Villard and Sayegh 2012). For example, the banning of the Muslim veil in schools was motivated with an interpretation of *laïcité*, according to which citizens in the French republic are to appear religiously neutral in the public sphere, where such neutrality is again thought to express a norm of equality (Laborde 2005).

Republicanism focuses on a shared commitment to active participation in society and so goes beyond (mere) identification with certain liberal principles or with the nation, and there are at least a couple of reasons why such participation may be thought important for social cohesion. First, certain norms of civility may, when acted out, encourage trust and solidarity even with out-groups, for example treating other people, irrespective of their ethnic or religious affiliation, as equals. Second, participation in civic and political organizations and processes across ethnic and religious lines in pursuit of common goals and projects may likewise tend to increase trust and solidarity. More generally, Robert Putnam (2000: 136-7) suggests that civic engagement, trust, and solidarity are mutually reinforcing (cf. Svendsen and Svendsen 2006: ch. 3). The idea is that there is a spillover from membership in organizations to cooperative values. Furthermore, in order to explain the hypothesized causal impact of participation on social cohesion, we may appeal to contact theory. According to contact theory, contact between members of different groups will tend to eliminate negative stereotypes and increase toleration, especially if it is based on equal status, cooperation and common goals (Allport 1958: 252, 267; Pettigrew and Tropp 2006), suggesting that such contact may also facilitate trust and solidarity (Uslaner 2012).

Moving now to community conceptions that consider a shared commitment to basic liberal principles too thick rather than too thin a basis for social cohesion, it has been argued that what is required of citizens is only a sense of belonging to a polity, identifying with most of its institutions and practices (Mason 2010: 871). This is what I refer to as "polity patriotism" above. Note that polity patriotism involves less than sharing a commitment to a set of liberal principles, because institutions and practices may be justifiable on the basis of a variety of principles and so individuals may share a sense of belonging to a polity without sharing a specific set of principles on the basis of which they justify this commitment.[3] Note also that some liberals may be attracted to polity patriotism, holding that it is in a certain sense illiberal to expect individuals to hold specific liberal principles and even be willing to promote this aim in policies. Thus, it may be considered less invasive to require people to identify with the institutions that make liberal democracy work than with particular reasons for doing so, where it is after all in the institutions that a liberal society is realized. Andrew Mason (2000: 133-5) distinguishes between belonging to a polity and belonging together and argues that the former is more inclusive, gives rise to a sense of a common fate, and may therefore well be sufficient to bring about (adequate) trust and solidarity. Polity patriots, then, may argue that a polity-based identity is more likely to secure the allegiance of those who would not feel at home in the national identity or in a particular set of liberal values.

Finally, according to a multicultural community conception, a shared recognition of religious and cultural differences promotes or is at least compatible with (adequate) social cohesion, and in particular such recognition will tend to promote the allegiance of minorities who would otherwise feel that they receive insufficient opportunities to express their religious and cultural identities (Kymlicka 1995: 184-5; Parekh 2006: 203-4; Modood 2007: 146-44). This is so not least because liberal democracies tend to privilege the interests of the religious and cultural majority, for example, in terms of the language used in institutions, national holidays, dress codes, and opportunities for religious expression. So whereas recognition of difference is required by justice as a way of securing the liberty and equality of opportunity of minorities, it will also (and partly for this reason) promote a sense of being included in a political community on equal terms, which again tends to

---

3. Thus, polity patriotism differs from Habermas' (1998) constitutional patriotism, as the latter requires agreement on basic universal principles.

facilitate trust and solidarity. Recognition may here involve group-differentiated rights (for example, an exemption for Sikhs so that they can wear a turban rather than a safety helmet when working on construction sites) but also other forms of minority accommodation, such as a common multicultural curriculum in schools.[4]

The sense in which multiculturalism relies on a thinner identity than liberalism is that whereas liberalism proposes a set of liberal values for all to accept, multiculturalism proposes a shared recognition of the *different* identities possessed by individuals. Of course, the idea I am here labelling multiculturalism falls short of the value commitments multiculturalists typically have. For example, liberal multiculturalists will want to combine the recognition of difference with a range of more traditional liberal rights, including liberal constraints on permissible cultural practices and exit rights from cultural groups (Kymlicka 1995). Furthermore, many multiculturalists propose that multicultural accommodation should be combined with a shared commitment to an overarching national identity to adequately secure unity (Carens 2000: 107-39; Kymlicka 1995: 188-9; 2001; Modood 2007: 146-54; Parekh 2006: 199-206). Nevertheless, for conceptual and empirical reasons, it is important to distinguish these different value-commitments and to investigate the significance of each, which is why I have singled out a particular feature as definitive of a multicultural community conception.

In fact, this is a more general point in relation to the presentation of community conceptions above. They are by no means all mutually exclusive and we will often find political theorists endorsing more than one of them at the same time. For example, we may find nationalists, liberals, polity patriots, and multiculturalists expressing a need for active citizenship, although the precise content of that citizenship will differ. However, the community conceptions I have listed are conceptually distinct and it is important to distinguish them, not least to be able to investigate the extent to which policies that invoke them are in fact conducive to social cohesion. For example, liberal nationalists may be inclined to support active citizenship, but identifying with a set of national values and being active in democratic processes are distinct phenomena and they may have different impact on, for example, trust and solidarity.

Just as we may find political theorists combining different community conceptions, no state is likely to instantiate a pure form. Denmark is a case in point (Holtug 2012: 192-202). When guest workers began to arrive in the 1960s and 1970s, a pragmatic approach was adopted, where immigrants were expected to integrate on the labour market and religious and cultural issues were delegated to the private sphere. However, increasingly, such liberal policies have been supplemented with

---

4. For a longer list of explanations, given by multiculturalists, for why recognition may be expected to promote social cohesion, see Holtug (2016) and Murphy (2012: ch. 8).

nationalist policies, aiming at identification with "Danish" values, including citizenships tests, a Danish Cultural Canon to strengthen communal values by referring to a common Danish heritage, and recently a parliamentary majority reached a settlement on public schools that includes a National Knowledge Centre for History and Cultural Heritage. Furthermore, ideas about active citizenship have gained increasing importance in policies, for example in a government Action Plan on Ethnic Equal Treatment and Respect for Individuals from 2011, emphasizing the need for immigrants to become active citizens and supporting citizenship classes in schools to promote social cohesion. Thus, national policies may harbour a mosaic of different community conceptions, reflecting political compromises, ideas about multiple sources of social cohesion, a perceived need to take a firm stand, and probably also a sense of bewilderment concerning what might actually work.

Empirical evidence

In this final section, I briefly survey the (limited) empirical literature on the effects of different community conceptions on trust and solidarity. As pointed out above, community conceptions may be found at both the level of institutions/policies and at the level of individuals, and I shall invoke studies of both these levels.

Studies on nationalism seem to point in different directions. Shayo (2009) finds not only a negative correlation between national identification and support for redistribution at the individual level, but also a strong negative correlation between national identification and levels of actual redistribution on the country level. Hjerm and Schnabel (2012), on the other hand, find that a higher degree of ethnic individual identity slightly increases the acceptance of taxation. Likewise, Wright and Reeskens (2013) find that ethnic conceptions of national identity are linked to welfare state support, whereas civic and cultural conceptions are not, but also that all three forms of national conceptions are linked to welfare chauvinism and they conclude that national identity cannot sustain support for redistribution. However, Johnston et al. (2014) find that on an ethnic interpretation of national identification, such identification is correlated to lower levels of support for redistribution. Interestingly, some studies suggest that the effects of national identification on trust and solidarity depend on the content of the particular national identity in question (Johnston et al. 2010; 2014).

There is a general problem in many studies of nationalism, at least for present purposes, namely that national identification is typically measured as attachment to – or pride in – the nation, and where people may in fact feel attached to or take pride in the nation for a variety of different reasons. For example, an individual may feel proud of being French in virtue of French high culture, or in virtue of the

French republican model. In the latter case, she would seem to be expressing a commitment to a republican community conception, not a nationalist one. And, to the extent this is so, any correlation found between national identification and social cohesion would not tell us anything about the effects of nationalist community conceptions on the latter.

As regards republican community conceptions, it has turned out to be difficult to confirm the idea that, at the individual level, associational participation promotes generalized trust (Stolle 2003). A possible explanation of this could be that associations are by no means unique in promoting ideals of cooperation and equality and in establishing the sort of contact between members of different groups that may be conducive to social cohesion. For example, other relevant institutions may include educational institutions and the workplace. However, perhaps associations may play a more indirect role in generating trust. Thus, at the country level, there is a strong correlation between levels of associational membership and trust, which may perhaps be explained by the role of associations in facilitating cooperation with other associations and public institutions (Torpe 2013: 144-51). The positive impact may then in principle reach everyone who benefits from such cooperation, which is potentially every member of society, and so it may raise the trust level quite generally.

Turning now to liberal community conceptions, it is worth distinguishing between two different causal mechanisms. As we have seen, Rawls appeals to the fairness of liberal institutions as forming a basis for a sense of a common purpose in maintaining these institutions, where justice and trust tend to be mutually supportive. And indeed, there is evidence that socio-economic equality promotes trust (Uslaner 2002: chs. 6 and 8). In fact, according to Uslaner, "The Gini index has the greatest impact on trust of any independent variable" (Uslaner 2003: 181). Furthermore, institutional accounts of trust imply that the impartiality and perceived fairness of institutions is a foundation for high levels of trust (Rothstein and Stolle 2003: 192). Indeed, as emphasized by Rawls (1971: 240), in order for individuals to act on their concern for justice, they must trust others to reciprocate, and (generalized) trust will therefore tend to turn people's egalitarian inclinations into actual solidarity (or willingness to redistribute). Following this line of argument, and on the basis of studies suggesting that ethnic diversity has no negative impact on trust when people perceive the quality of government to be high, Rothstein (2014) concludes that negative effects of ethnic diversity on trust and solidarity can be offset by fairness in institutions.

Liberals may also argue that individuals who are committed to liberal values are particularly inclined to trust and exhibit solidarity. Indeed, Johnston et al. (2014) find that solidarity is positively correlated to a commitment to equal rights. Of course, it may be less surprising that individuals committed to the value of equality exhibit solidarity in terms of for example willingness to redistribute, but liberals may likewise argue that a commitment to values such as equality and toleration will tend to be accompanied by other positive attitudes towards other people, including trust. Along such lines, Uslaner (2002: 2-3) sees trust as "a fundamentally egalitarian ideal"; as part of a larger, inter-connected group of values that also include solidarity and a belief that other people are well-intentioned and are one's equals.

Roughly, studies of the effects of multicultural policies on trust and solidarity can be grouped into two main categories; those that conclude that such policies have no effects on these social goods and those that conclude that they have positive effects (cf. Kymlicka 2010; this volume).[5] Thus, Kesler and Bloemraad (2010) and Hooghe, Reeskens and Stolle (2007) find no statistically significant effects of multicultural policies on trust. Kesler and Bloemraad (2010), however, do find the combination of multicultural policies and low levels of income inequality to prevent the negative effects immigration would otherwise be expected to have on social cohesion. Furthermore, Banting et al. (2006) find that multicultural polices do not have a statistically significant effect on social spending.

Crepaz (2006: 113-15), on the other hand, finds that countries with stronger multicultural policies tend to generate more trust and higher levels of support for redistribution than countries with weaker such policies. And Torpe (2012: 162-65) finds a positive correlation between multicultural policies and trust in people with a different religious and national background than oneself. The bulk of the available evidence, then, suggests that multicultural policies either have no effect, or they increase trust, solidarity, and redistribution.

This concludes my brief summary of empirical studies on community conceptions. Clearly, more work needs to be done, both at the level of theory and empirical testing, in order to understand the mechanisms through which different community conceptions, or the values on which they rely, impact (different aspects of) social cohesion more fully. In particular, the effects of community conceptions in diverse societies may depend on a whole range of further factors, including the particular policies through which they are expressed, the place of these policies in the overall pattern of policies, the nature of the diversity in question, and the general cultural, religious, and political environment.

---

5. For a more elaborate account of the available evidence on multicultural community conceptions, see Holtug (2016).

■ References

Alesina, A., and E.L. Glaeser. *Fighting Poverty in the US and Europe. A World of Difference*, Oxford: Oxford University Press, 2004.

Alesina, A., and E. La Ferrara. "Who Trusts Others?" *Journal of Public Economics* 85, 2 (2002): 207-34.

Allport, G.W. *The Nature of Prejudice*. Garden City, NY: Doubleday Anchor, 1958.

Anderson, C.J. and A. Paskeviciute. "How Ethnic and Linguistic Heterogeneity Influence the Prospect for Civil Society: A Comparative Study of Citizenship Behavior." *The Journal of Politics* 68 (2006): 783-802.

Banting, K., and W. Kymlicka, eds. *Multiculturalism and the Welfare State. Recognition and Redistribution in Contemporary Democracies*. Oxford: Oxford University Press, 2006.

Banting, K. et al. "Do Multicultural Policies Erode the Welfare State? An Empirical Analysis." In *Multiculturalism and the Welfare State. Recognition and Redistribution in Contemporary Democracies*, ed. K. Banting and W. Kymlicka, Oxford: Oxford University Press, 2006.

Barry, B. *Culture and Equality. An Egalitarian Critique of Multiculturalism*. Cambridge: Polity Press, 2001.

Blunckett, D. Speech delivered in West Midlands to highlight the publication of reports into inner-city violence in 2001, http://www.guardian.co.uk/politics/2001/dec/11/immigrationpolicy.race.

Brooks, T. *The 'Life in the United Kingdom' Citizenship Test. Is It Unfit for Purpose?* Durham: Durham University, 2013.

Burke, E. *Reflections on the Revolution in France*. Oxford: Oxford University Press 1999 [1790].

Cantle, T. *Community Cohesion. A Report from the Independent Review Team*. Home Office, 2001.

Cantle, T. "About Community Cohesion," 2013, http://tedcantle.co.uk/?page_id=93.

Carens, J.H. *Culture, Citizenship, and Community. A Contextual Exploration of Justice as Evenhandedness*. Oxford: Oxford University Press, 2000.

Crepaz, M. "'If You Are My Brother, I May Give You a Dime!' Public Opinion on Multiculturalism, Trust, and the Welfare State." In *Multiculturalism and the Welfare State. Recognition and Redistribution in Contemporary Democracies*, ed. K. Banting and W. Kymlicka, 92-117. Oxford: Oxford University Press, 2006.

Crumley, B. "Why France's National Identity Debate Backfired," *Time*, 12 February 2010, http://content.time.com/time/world/article/0,8599,1963945,00.html.

Delhey, J. and K. Newton. "Predicting Cross-national Level of Social Trust: Global Pattern or Nordic Exceptionalism?" *European Sociological Review* 21, 3 (2005): 311-27.

Drainville, B. "Bill 60: Charter Affirming the Values of State Secularism and Religious Neutrality and of Equality Between Women and Men, and Providing a Framework for Accommodation Requests." National Assembly of Québec, Québec Official Publisher, 2013.

Galston, W. *Liberal Purposes. Goods, Virtues, and Diversity in the Liberal State*. Cambridge: Cambridge University Press, 1991.

Gesthuizen, M. et al. "Ethnic Diversity and Social Capital in Europe: Test of Putnam's Thesis in European Countries." *Scandinavian Political Studies* 32, 2 (2009): 121-42.

Habermas, J. *The Inclusion of the Other. Studies in Political Theory*. Cambridge, MA: MIT Press, 1998.

Halpern, D. *Social Capital*. Cambridge: Polity Press, 2005.

Hjerm, M. and A. Schnabel. "How Much Heterogeneity Can the Welfare State Endure?: The Influence of Heterogeneity on Attitudes to the Welfare State." *Nations and Nationalism* 18, 2 (2012): 346-69.

Holtug, N., "Immigration and the Politics of Social Cohesion." *Ethnicities* 10, 4 (2010): 435-51.

Holtug, N. "Danish Multiculturalism: Where Art Thou?" In *Challenging Multiculturalism. European Models of Diversity*, ed. R. Taras, 190-215. Edinburgh: Edinburgh University Press, 2012.

Holtug, N. "Multiculturalism and Social Cohesion." In *Migration and Integration: New Lessons From Diasporas and Difference*, ed. R. Hsu and C. Reinprecht. Vienna: Vienna University Press, 2016.

Holtug, N. and A. Mason. "Immigration, Diversity and Social Cohesion." *Ethnicities* 10, 4 (2010): 407-13.

Honohan, I. "Republican Requirements for Access to Citizenship." In *Citizenship Acquisition and National Belonging*, ed. G. Calder, P. Cole and J. Seglow, 91-104. Basingstoke: Palgrave Macmillan, 2010.

Hooghe, M. "Social Capital and Diversity. Generalized Trust, Social Cohesion and Regimes of Diversity." *Canadian Journal of Political Science* 40, 3 (2007): 709-32.

Hooghe, M., T. Reeskens and D. Stolle. "Diversity, Multiculturalism and Social Cohesion: Trust and Ethnocentrism in European Societies." In *Art of the State: Belonging, Diversity, Recognition and Shared Citizenship in Canada*, ed. K. Bantin, T.J. Courchene and L.F. Seidle, 1-24. Montreal: Institute for Research on Public Policy, 2007.

Hooghe, M. et al. "Ethnic Diversity and Generalized Trust in Europe. A Cross-National Multilevel Study." *Comparative Political Studies* 42, 2 (2009): 198-223.

Jespersen, K. and R. Pittelkow. *De lykkelige danskere. En bog om sammenhængskraft*. Copenhagen: Gyldendal, 2005.

Johnston, R. et al. "National Identity and Support for the Welfare State." *Canadian Journal of Political Science* 43, 2 (2010): 349-77.

Johnston, R. et al. "Diversity and Solidarity: New Evidence from Canada and the US." Unpublished, 2014.

Kesler, C. and I. Bloemraad. "Does Immigration Erode Social Capital? The Conditional Effects of Immigration Generated Diversity on Trust, Membership, and Participation across 19 Countries, 1981-2000." *Canadian Journal of Political Science* 43, 2 (2010): 319-47.

Kumlin, S., and B. Rothstein. "Minorities and Mistrust: The Cushioning Impact of Informal Social Contacts and Political-Institutional Fairness." Department of Political Science, Göteborg University. Unpublished, 2007.

Kymlicka, W. *Multicultural Citizenship*. Oxford: Clarendon Press, 1995.

Kymlicka, W. *Politics in the Vernacular. Nationalism, Multiculturalism, and Citizenship*. Oxford: Oxford University Press, 2001.

Kymlicka, W. "Testing the Liberal Multiculturalist Hypothesis: Normative Theories and Social Science Evidence." *Canadian Journal of Political Science* 43, 2 (2010): 257-71.

Kymlicka, W. "Multiculturalism in Normative Theory and in Social Science." *Ethnicities* 11, 1 (2011): 5-31.

Laborde, C. "Secular Philosophy and Muslim Headscarves in Schools." *Journal of Political Philosophy* 13, 3 (2005): 305-29.

Laborde, C. and J. Maynor, eds. *Republicanism and Political Theory*. Oxford: Blackwell, 2008.

Leigh, A. "Does Equality Lead to Fraternity?" *Economics Letters* 93 (2006): 121-25.

Lenard, P.T. "Trust Your Compatriots, but Count Your Change: The Roles of Trust, Mistrust and Distrust in Democracy." *Political Studies* 56 (2008): 312-32.

Lolle, H., and L. Torpe. "Growing Ethnic Diversity and Social Trust in European Cities." *Comparative European Politics* 9, 2 (2011): 191-216.

Mason, A. *Community, Solidarity and Belonging*. Cambridge: Cambridge University Press, 2002.

Mason, A. "Integration, Cohesion and National Identity: Theoretical Reflections on Recent British Policy." *British Journal of Political Science* 40 (2010): 857-74.

Mason, A. *Living Together as Equals: The Demands of Citizenship*. Oxford: Oxford University Press, 2012.

Miller, D. *On Nationality*. Oxford: Clarendon Press, 1995.

Miller, D. "Social Justice in Multicultural Societies." In *Cultural Diversity versus Economic Solidarity*, ed. P. van Parijs, 13-31. Brussels: De Boeck University Press, 2004.

Miller, D. "Multiculturalism and the Welfare State: Theoretical Reflections." In *Multiculturalism and the Welfare State*, ed. K. Banting and W. Kymlicka, 323-338. Oxford: Oxford University Press, 2006.

Ministry of Culture. "Værdikommissionen er nedsat," 2012, http://kum.dk/nyheder-og-presse/pressemeddelelser/2011/februar/vardikommissionen-er-nedsat/.

Ministry of Justice. "Aftale om indfødsret," 2013, http://www.justitsministeriet.dk/sites/default/files/media/Pressemeddelelser/pdf/2013/Aftaletekst_indfoedsret.pdf.

Modood, T. *Multiculturalism*. Cambridge: Polity, 2007.

Murphy, M. *Multiculturalism. A Critical Introduction*. London: Routledge, 2012.

Newton, K. "The New Liberal Dilemma: Social Trust in Mixed Societies." Unpublished, 2007.

Parekh, B. *Rethinking Multiculturalism. Cultural Diversity and Political Theory*. Basingstoke: Palgrave Macmillan, 2006.

Parfit, D. *Reasons and Persons*. Oxford: Clarendon Press, 1984.

Pettigrew, T.F. and L.R. Tropp. "A Meta-Analytic Test of Intergroup Contact Theory." *Journal of Personality and Social Psychology* 90 (2006): 751-83.

Pevnick, R. "Social Trust and the Ethics of Immigration Policy." *Journal of Political Philosophy* 17 (2009): 146-67.

Putnam, R.D. *Bowling Alone. The Collapse and Revival of American Community*. New York: Simon & Schuster, 2000.

Putnam, R.D. "*E Pluribus Unum*: Diversity and Community in the Twenty-first Century." *Scandinavian Political Studies* 30, 2 (2007): 137-74.

Rawls, J. *A Theory of Justice*. Oxford: Oxford University Press, 1971.

Rawls, J. *Political Liberalism*. New York: Columbia University Press, 1993.

Rawls, J. *The Law of Peoples*. Cambridge, MA: Harvard University Press, 1999.

Rothstein, B. "Solidarity, Diversity and the Quality of Government." Unpublished, 2014.

Scruton, R. "In Defence of the Nation." In *The Philosopher on Dover Beach*, R. Scruton. Manchester: Carcanet, 1999.

Scruton, R. *The Meaning of Conservatism*. Basingstoke: Palgrave Macmillan, 2001.

Scruton, R. "The Rebirth of Nations," *The America Spectator*, June 2011 Issue, http://spectator.org/articles/37503/rebirth-nations.

Shayo, M. "A Model of Social Identity with an Application to Political Economy: Nation, Class, and Redistribution." *American Political Science Review* 103 (2009): 147-74.

Simon, P. and V.S. Pala. "'We're Not All Multiculturalists Yet': France Swings between Hard Integration and Soft Anti-discrimination." In *The Multiculturalism Backlash*, ed. S. Vertovec and S. Wessendorf, 92-110. Abingdon, Oxon: Routledge, 2010.

Stolle, D. "The Sources of Social Capital." In *Generating Social Capital. Civil Society and Institutions in Comparative Perspective*, ed. M. Hooghe and D. Stolle, 19-42. London: Palgrave, 2003.

Sturgis, P. et al. "Does Ethnic Diversity Erode Trust?: Putnam's 'Hunkering-Down' Thesis Reconsidered." *British Journal of Political Science* 41, 1 (2011): 57-82.

Støvring, K. *Sammenhængskraft*. Copenhagen: Gyldendal, 2010.

Svendsen, G.T. and G.L.H. Svendsen, eds. *Handbook of Social Capital. The Troika of Sociology, Political Science and Economics*. London: Edward Elgar, 2009.

Torpe, L., and H. Lolle. "Ethnic Diversity and Social Trust in Denmark and Sweden." In *Diversity, Inclusion and Citizenship in Scandinavia*, ed. P. Bengtsson, P. Strömblad and A.H. Bay, 323-44. Newcastle upon Tyne: Cambridge Scholars Press, 2010.

Torpe, L. *De stærke samfund. Social kapital i Skandinavien*. Frederiksberg: Frydenlund Academic, 2013.

Travis, A. "UK Migrants to face 'Patriotic' Citizenship Test." *Guardian*, 1 July 2012, http://www.guardian.co.uk/uk/2012/jul/01/uk-migrants-patriotic-citizenship-test.

Uslaner, E. *The Moral Foundations of Trust*. New York: Cambridge University Press, 2002.

Uslaner, E. "Trust, Democracy and Governance: Can Government Policies Influence Generalized Trust?" In *Generating Social Capital. Civil Society and Institutions in Comparative Perspective*, ed. M. Hooghe and D. Stolle, 171-90. New York: Palgrave Macmillan, 2003.

Uslaner, E. "Segregation, Mistrust, and Minorities." *Ethnicities* 10, 4 (2010): 415-34.

Uslaner, E. *Segregation and Mistrust. Diversity, Isolation, and Social Cohesion*. Cambridge: Cambridge University Press, 2012.

van Parijs, P. ed. *Cultural Diversity versus Economic Solidarity*. Brussels: De Boeck University Press, 2004.

Villard, F. and P-Y. Sayegh. "Redefining a (Mono)Cultural Nation: Political Discourse Against Multiculturalism in Contemporary France." In *Challenging Multiculturalism. European Models of Diversity*, ed. R. Taras, 236-54. Edinburgh: Edinburgh University Press, 2012.

Wright, M. and T. Reeskens. "Of What Cloth are the Ties That Bind? National Identity and Support for the Welfare State across 29 European Countries." *Journal of European Policy* 20, 10 (2013): 1443-63.

6 The Normativity of Culture

Antje Gimmler

Cultural identity and cultural values have become key concepts for understanding the current political and social struggles characterising modern societies. These concepts remain important not only for internal value disputes within particular nation states but also for what has been coined 'the clash of civilizations' (Huntington 1993). Within this paradigm, Western and Arab cultures seem to remain locked in constant struggle without common ground in culture and religion. Multiculturalism is said to threaten societies and to put pressure on social cohesion, a cohesion that cannot be maintained in modern societies under conditions of cultural heterogeneity. Thus, the classical sociological and political question of 'what keeps societies together' has gained new gravity in the context of multiculturalism; empirical research, including Putnam's (2007) trust and diversity study, shows that high diversity leads to a loss in social capital and less cohesion within modern societies.

Multiculturalism poses severe problems to modern societies, both in the constitutional-political domain and at the societal level (Benhabib 2002; Kymlicka 1995; 2002; Taylor, Eriksen and Stjernfelt 2012). This article primarily focuses on the societal level without intending to downplay the constitutional dimension that is at stake. The article aims to investigate conceptual frameworks that deal with the complexity of cultural values and practices on the one hand, and the theoretical conceptualizations of "what keeps societies together" on the other. At first glance, culture and its practices seem to be the domain of the humanities, including descriptive perspectives from the fields of sociology, post-colonial studies, or anthropology. In the meantime, the question of "what keeps societies together" has an intrinsically normative meaning, and the answers provided by political philosophy and sociology are of a different epistemic nature. Normative theories are usually not interested in the richness, multiplicity, or variety of cultural practices, but aim towards a foundational framework for the empirical and actual understanding of "what keeps societies together". Concepts such as "trust", "recognition", or "solidarity" offer meta-narrations and overarching concepts in order to explain "what keeps societies together".

On the level of the constitution and institutions of democratic societies, "freedom", "equality", and "justice" are the formal principles that constitute and regulate democratic practices and the status of citizens with its interplay of rights, liberties and duties. However, these meta-narrations result from idealizations and theoretical reconstructions of a certain cultural understanding; the principles that govern institutions and citizens' legal status are affected by the contexts of culture, history and social relations. Social and cultural meaning form a complex background of how equality, justice and freedom are interpreted and performed (Cooke 2000). Thus, the formal normative principles are inscribed into social and cultural practices, and, at the same time, shape these practices.

Culture is not a mere "gloss" of democracy, and democratic institutions are not culture blind. Culture is inherently evaluative itself. Following a cultural practice involves the implicit appreciation of that particular culture. Culture allows for distinctions, playing the role of an "identity marker and differentiator" (Benhabib 2002: 1) in complex societies and nations. This role becomes apparent when cultural claims conflict with the basic rights of citizens. For example, the religious-cultural tradition of arranged marriages stands in conflict with the principle of autonomy for citizens. When arranged marriages occur, a certain culture is reaffirmed, but the fundamental norm of autonomy is violated and the possibilities of individuals to pursue their own life plans are impoverished. As culture often is a collective denominator, cultural claims can contradict the norms of liberal democracies, a problem that takes place on the constitutional and juridical levels; the lives of many second generation immigrants also attest to this very real contradiction (Kinnvall and Nesbitt-Larking 2011).

Normative political theory has not always acknowledged the complexity that is played out between the multiplicity and heterogeneity of cultural practices, its inherent normativity and the normative status of democratic principles. As Seyla Benhabib states: "This normative discussion, primarily about the duties of democratic citizenship and democratic theory, was carried out in a sociological vacuum. Political philosophers paid little attention to citizenship as a sociological category and as a social practice that inserts us into a complex network of privileges and duties, entitlements and obligations" (Benhabib 2002: 160-161). This amalgam of everyday practices and values with institutional normative claims can be illustrated with an anecdote from the 2010 election campaign for the Danish Parliament. The leader of the right-wing Danish People's Party, Pia Kjærsgaard, was asked how she would define "Danishness". She provided the following response: "The welfare state, of course, new potatoes and strawberries with cream" before adding, "It is an inner feeling, something you cannot explain" (Berlingske, 2010, author's translation). Besides the fact that people in other countries also enjoy new potatoes and strawberries with cream, the statement plays with this complex mixture of everyday values and goods on the one hand and the highly-organized and normatively-regulated institutions of the welfare state on the other. Strawberries and the welfare state are obviously situated on quite different levels, but both the everyday life goods and the democratic institutions are part of her feeling of being Danish.

In the following sections, I shall discuss this complex mixture of social and cultural practices while emphasizing that normative political and social philosophy should be careful not to over-philosophize and over-generalize particular social and cultural practices. I recommend what Michael Walzer called "the art of separation" (Walzer 1984) instead of generalising a particular cultural evaluation and reifying one cultural practice as a foundational value that keeps society together. Though Walzer's recommendation has its background in political liberalism, I think his heuristic advice sits well with the theory of deliberative democracy as developed most prominently by Jürgen Habermas (1992). Deliberative democracy formulates a normative theory of democracy and state of law without confounding these basic normative claims with specific cultural practices. Normativity plays a role on both the constitutional and societal levels, and in the following paragraphs, I will take up the question of the normativity of cultural practices, normativity from within so to speak.

In order to clarify my position, I will begin by briefly discussing the concept of culture as it is used in the discussion on multiculturalism before outlining a differentiated approach to culture. In the second part, Honneth's theory of recognition will be discussed as an example of a normative social theory that offers a way of understanding the inherent normativity of social relations. The third section will introduce the neo-pragmatic social theory of Laurent Thévenot. In Thévenot's theory, the network of practices, material things or artefacts, as well as the normativity of agents themselves are part of social practices. In the fourth section, I come back to the question of multiculturalism and suggest an understanding of cultural diversity that is neither normatively neutral nor overly determining in relation to the principles of modern Western democracies.

Culture and practices

In the discussion on multiculturalism, the notion of culture is obviously of central importance; the idea of multiculturalism builds upon the principle that different cultures can co-exist, but often in a constellation of conflict. In these debates, the term "culture" is used with rather different underlying presuppositions about what constitutes culture (Eriksen and Stjernfelt 2012). Aside from descriptive anthropological studies on culture and its practices, the discussion on culture in the multiculturalism debate has revolved primarily around two concepts: the relationship between individual identity and collective culture along with the possible tensions and contradictions between collective cultures and basic normative principles within Western liberal societies.

Seminal in this respect is an article by Charles Taylor entitled "The Politics of Recognition" (1994). For Taylor, individual identity is necessarily intertwined with collective culture, with group identity. The individual struggle for authentic selfhood is thought of as a harmonic realisation of collective values and ways of living. In this way, Taylor follows in the tradition of German philosopher J.G. von Herder who introduced culture as a holistic concept encompassing a people's distinct way of living, spirit and language. From here, Taylor takes a step towards a political theory of recognition that is rooted in collective identities that are preserved and renewed in the struggle for recognition. It is no accident that recognition and collective identity go hand in hand in Taylor's theory. However, as Benhabib outlines in her critique of Taylor's theory of recognition, it is questionable whether individuals use only one cultural background as a resource in their quest for living an authentic life; in addition, the underlying holism of collective cultures is problematic (Benhabib 2002: 58). For example, the holistic understanding of culture can neither account for dynamic and changing cultures nor for different cultural sub-groups and new hybrid forms. From Taylor's approach, it follows that there exists only one meaningful cultural framework serving as an interpretive resource for individuals and collectivities to express their identities. Collective culture is understood as the property of an ethnic group or race. In this version, culture has clear boundaries, distinguishes groups and acts as a "container" for a homogeneous group or nation.

Another advocate of the politics of multiculturalism is Will Kymlicka who developed a liberal version of multiculturalism. He also identifies cultures with specific nations or peoples who share a language and distinct history. However, in his definition of "societal cultures", he emphasizes that societal cultures rely more on shared language and institutions than on "common religious beliefs, family customs, or personal lifestyles" (Kymlicka 2002: 346). This definition seems to leave space for the diversity of different lifestyles and ethnic groups in modern liberal societies. However, the central point of Kymlicka's liberal multiculturalism is the territorial unity of the nation state that actively integrates its citizens into the societal culture by prioritizing one language over another, for instance. It is an open and empirical question how this integration by means of liberal policies would affect citizens' religious beliefs, family customs or lifestyles; it seems such policies would be counterproductive to the overall goal of enabling and affirming cultural diversity.

These conceptualizations of culture have been criticized for being holistic and oriented towards a totality of culture that provides a single language along with a shared set of values, habits and symbolic embodiment of practices (Reckwitz 2001; Benhabib 2002). The possibility of hybrid cultures and the existence of parallel cultural codes are only two possible counterexamples that contradict the totality concept of culture. This concept fails to take into account that individuals achieve authentic selfhood with a variety of simultaneous but differing cultural codes, which is particularly problematic in the context of globalization where cultural codes are proliferating and becoming more acute. For the following parts of this article, it will be useful to make some conceptual distinctions in order to understand culture in a more dynamic way. In this discussion, I will draw upon Seyla Benhabib's (2002) approach to cultures as narratively-contested accounts as well as anthropologist Ulf Hannerz's (1992) three dimensions of culture.

With culture, we usually identify "ideas and modes of thought" (Hannerz 1992: 7) that provide group concepts and values. These ideas and modes of thought, as Benhabib outlines, are not just instinctive or private ways of thinking about the world; instead, they are always already contested in relation to other people's ideas. We can account for our modes of thought by referring to others. These "first-order-narratives" (Benhabib 2002: 7) inform our actions, but as narratives, they don't determine them; they are constantly contested and negotiated. Hannerz (1992) also adds the dimension of "forms of externalization" (102, 7) of culture: visible and public representations of culture, such as symbols and material objects. As we have seen, even strawberries can become a cultural denominator for national identity. This material dimension is not addressed explicitly in Benhabib's approach, but could easily be linked to what she calls "second-order narratives" (Benhabib 2002: 7). The public and visible representations of culture include standards of evaluation, the way we interpret and value our actions, the narratives used or the material world. Benhabib's second-order narratives overlap with Hannerz's third dimension, the "social distribution" (Hannerz 1992: 7) of culture. External forms like institutions become meaningful, and work emerges as a distinguishing factor for groups and nations, forming the horizon for cultural practices. From this point of view, culture always forms an "evaluative universe" (Benhabib 2002: 7). As we will see later, the inherent evaluative stance – or normativity – of culture is important for understanding the function of culture from inside, from the perspective of a member of a culture.

Our actions and ways of thinking are put into focus by the lenses of the three dimensions of culture, the contested types of thinking about the world, the representations of these ways of thinking and the evaluative universes. They are not holistically closed. In all three dimensions, individuals contest their ways of thinking, adjust and negotiate what is culturally meaningful in relation to established cultural values and in relation to other members. Instead of a concept of culture that is oriented towards totality, this concept of culture emphasizes the meaningfulness of culture (Reckwitz 2001) in a given context with all its dynamics. Hybrid forms and parallel codes are not anomalies of cultures in decline but signs of vital and living cultures.

The normative culture of recognition

In his theory of recognition, Axel Honneth (1995a; 1995b; 2000) reformulates Hegel's notion of recognition as a renewal of critical theory with the reconstruction of the normative foundations of actual experiences of disrespect and social indignation. With the concept of recognition, he aims to formulate the normative expectations that members of modern societies legitimately hold in relation to each other and in relation to the institutions of modern democracies. From Honneth's point of view, the result is a phenomenologically rich understanding of moral indignation and a realistic description of social relations that links the normative foundation to the reality of societies in a way that allows for the diagnosis of social pathologies.

Recognition fulfils the task of capturing the inherent normative-evaluative stances that members of a society are competent to apply; moral standards govern both the social relations and the institutional outlook of modern democracies under the conditions of reflexive modernity (Honneth 1995a; 1995b; 2000). More precisely, recognition is actualized as the act of affirmation of positive characteristics and qualities of persons and groups. Candidates for qualities that are entitled to recognition have to be part of a plausible and reasonable set of values. People can be recognized for their achievements, their contributions to a group, for their character and the values they hold, as bearer of rights or simply as human beings. It is necessary to restrict recognition to a plausible and reasonable set of values in order to distinguish legitimate from illegitimate acts of affirmation. Racist groups, for example, would demand recognition for their values while remaining unwilling to reciprocate with the same recognition for other groups (Honneth 2010: 118). What counts as more or less plausible might differ in societies and subgroups. Honneth acknowledges this point by arguing for a cultural and historical contextualization of values while simultaneously dismissing value relativism. At this point, one might wonder whether the intended rich phenomenology of recognition is well-supported by the normative limitations inherent to Honneth's notion of recognition. Is the normatively-loaded notion of recognition able to capture all the contradictions and subtleties of acts of recognition and misrecognition?

The answer has to be found in his conceptualization of recognition. In his writings on this topic, Honneth aims at a social anthropology that substantiates the necessary conditions for a just society and for the 'good' lives of individuals (Honneth 2004: 360). This normative framework should enable us to understand social reality in terms of an idealization of inherent claims made by social actors. The starting point for this reconstruction of the normative framework are social experiences of injustice, experiences of humiliation and neglect. Ultimately, recognition theory is an "appropriate tool for categorically unlocking social experiences of injustice as a whole" (Honneth 2003b: 133). Recognition works both as a marker for injustice as well as a kind of anthropological indicator for what counts as a "good" life. Recognition, in Honneth's theory, is the fundamental form of relation and interaction as well as a necessary prerequisite for the development of individual identity.

Social relations and identity building depend on each other in the processes of recognition. Honneth (1995a) identifies three normative core principles as universal standards that have historically evolved as indicators of a good society: love or friendship in intimate relations, the equality principle that governs individual rights, and individual achievement in communities of solidarity. Honneth (2004) combines what could be called the culture of recognition with the institutionalization of recognition as a guiding principle for the democratic state. Recognition is, at the same time, a concept that governs social relations, identity development and cultural identity; it is also a principle that moulds political and legal institutions.

Honneth's overarching goal thus is to reconstruct the "bourgeois-capitalist society as an institutionalised recognition order" (Honneth 2003: 138). But is recognition really the core principle of the bourgeois-capitalist society? In his reconstruction of the bourgeois-capitalist society, Honneth focuses on private relations, institutionalized law and democratic procedures as well as civil society and communities. The bourgeois-capitalist society not only produces or fosters asymmetrical recognition but also symmetrical recognition in the form of human rights, for instance. If this phenomenon does not occur in the positive sense of fulfilment of recognition claims, then it emerges in the negative sense, marking a lack of recognition. However, Honneth (2003) himself admits that capitalism produces inequality foremost. Even if we accept the three principles of recognition as core normative principles that have the critical force to question the social order and exhibit immanent transcendence potential, the question will remain: can love, equality, and individual achievement tackle the structural inequality of capitalist market societies?

Nancy Fraser (2003) also takes up this problem in her critique of Honneth's theory. From her perspective, distributive justice is equally important to recognition; tearing them apart has the consequence of transforming recognition into a toothless instrument of lifestyle statements that fits neatly into the neo-liberal discourse. Without going into too much detail, it is worth mentioning that Honneth revised some of his overly-optimistic evaluations of the potential of recognition, and that he began to critically analyse its ideological uses (Honneth 2010).

The question of recognition as a lifestyle concept leads back to the issue of recognition as a governing principle for cultural practices. Based on the three dimensions of culture that have been introduced in the first part of this paper, recognition seems to be a fitting candidate for understanding the evaluative stances that compose the social interaction between members of a society and their self-understanding. To ask for recognition of one's own culture is another way of expressing and narrating one's own positive evaluation of what constitutes the identity of an individual or a group. Nonetheless, the quest for recognition often is directed against other groups, a case Honneth problematizes as illegitimate. On a cultural level, the struggle for recognition is much more diverse and blurred than the theoretical conceptualization allows. Hybrid identities also relate to this problem; such identities arise in groups that are most often themselves heterogeneous. For example, female Muslim immigrants in Denmark struggle against several frontiers at the same time: their struggle for recognition with a cultural and religious identity as a Muslim includes them into their ethnic group, while as Danish citizens, they are in the ambivalent position of exhibiting their equal rights while being suppressed by their own community for doing so. And furthermore, struggles for recognition can result in so-called "othering" (Yuval Davis 2006), a symbolic identification and distancing from those who are supposed to give recognition.

Recognition theory is thought to reconstruct a certain culture as the normative culture. The aim is to show the inherent normative claims or values that govern particular cultures, or even certain groups. It would not be too far of a stretch to interpret Honneth's theory of cultural recognition as meaning *the* culture of Western democracies. It also should be clear from this short presentation that Honneth does not reconstruct all dimensions of a culture, but that he aims to identify those background presuppositions that allow people to see a culture as meaningful, valuable and normatively regulated as well as to evaluate violations of the normative order. However, relations of recognition are far from harmonious, and often, the inherent normative claims of individuals and groups will not contribute to a solution for conflicts. Instead, the institutionalized norms of law and political procedures will have to decide. The question is whether or not it is possible to "theoretically" circumvent this tension between the particularity of cultural claims and the institutionalization of normative principles of democratic constitutions and procedures. Alternatively, this tension can be accepted. Both Habermas (1992) and Walzer (1984) recommend tackling it with the "art of separation".

Honneth chooses the first possibility of providing a theoretical circumvention of this crucial contradiction. In his latest book (2011), he attempts to unfold the inherent claims of culture as a coherent system of *Sittlichkeit* [ethical life], using Hegel's theory as a model for the reconstruction of a systematic normative order as well as a progressive evolution of normative order. The bottom-up approach was the underlying premise for the reconstruction of culture as normativity within the recognition theory. Whether it can be left in favour of a top-down model that subordinates cultural evaluations and narrations to the overall principles of autonomy and freedom is beyond the scope of this paper. However, this step towards a Hegelian *Sittlichkeit* indicates that the everyday life of culture and its inherent tensions and conflicts are downplayed; they might function as mere examples and illustrations. While Honneth's theory of recognition provides a model of understanding a preponderance of the inherent normativity of culture, one might ask why we should look for a single normative framework for Western cultures in the first place.

Engagements and the richness of the world

French sociologist Laurent Thévenot takes a different approach to the normativity of culture. Together with Luc Boltanski and Eve Chiapello, he belongs to what has been coined the New French Pragmatism in sociology. Developed in reaction to the more structurally oriented praxis theory of Pierre Bourdieu, this sociological pragmatism highlights social actors' plurality of normative orientations. Essential to Thévenot's approach is the Weberian argument that individuals need normative reasons, justifications and legitimations for their actions. Actors engage in society by attributing value to different realms and by testing these common values. Thévenot himself thinks of his approach as a combination of Bourdieu's structural sociology with Dewey's emphasis on the creativity of actors in relation to concrete situations (Thévenot 2011). The New French Pragmatism sits well in the overall social theory and philosophy movement, which has adopted the umbrella term "practice theory" (Schatzki et al. 2001). In practice theory, "the social is a field of embodied, materially interwoven practices centrally organized around shared practical understandings" (Schatzki 2001: 3). To the classical understanding of the social, as constituted by action and language, practice theory not only problematizes general structures of action and language use, but also adds the embodiment of actors and interaction with the material environment in the forms of architecture, objects, technologies to what counts as "the social".

In his recent work, Thévenot developed an analytical framework of forms of generalities towards which actors are oriented or reacting. Social actors test the reasons and arguments of commonalities – of values or things that have common worth – and, at the same time, they always negotiate these commonalities in order to justify their actions. Thévenot is interested in the "pragmatics of reflection" (Boltanski and Thévenot 2006: 348) that take place in actors' engagement with the world. *On Justification*, a book he co-wrote with Luc Boltanski, describes the construction of six different worlds (*cités*) of worth, forming different legitimate orientations for actors to use in their engagement with the world: the inspired world, the domestic world, the world of fame, the civic world, the market world, and the industrial world.

These different *cités* are constructed with the help of classical philosophical texts. For instance, the basic ideas for the inspired *cité* are taken from Augustine's *The City of God* as well as from a management handbook on creativity.

The regimes of these *cités* are conceptualized as realities that force the actor to engage and negotiate with the world, but also to criticize them. The inspired *cité*, for example, embodies creativity and spontaneity, contributing to the universal worth of uniqueness and geniality. Here, the originality of products and action opposes the routine and discipline of the industrial *cité*. The actor has to evaluate which *cité* is appropriate in relation to the concrete situation she or he is encountering. New social and political constellations would afford the construction of new *cités* of worth, such as the projective *cité*, which adopts the value of transition and temporary engagement in certain projects typical of the new organization of capitalism. As another example, a possible new cité might be green, merging ecology and sustainability as a decisive value. The focus of this paper is not on the specificities of the different *cités*, but already, at this point, it should be clear that a pluralism of orientations and values forms society, according to this new pragmatic sociology. The addition of new orientations indicates that society in this sociological pragmatism is conceptualized as a constant process of negotiating, attributing and testing what counts as worthy. Within this framework, social cohesion could be achieved within differing but overlapping regimes.

How does Thévenot conceptualize engagement with the world? He asserts that every engagement of actors plays out a tension "between some kind of good which governs the intervention and some sort of response that comes back to the agent from reality. I employ the term engagement precisely because it captures the link between these two orientations. When used in theories of practice, it usually signifies a material adjustment with the world, but it has a second acceptance, which points to a moral or political covenant" (Thévenot 2001: 60). Using Habermasian terminology, we might say that all interaction with the world contains instrumental and communicative actions at the same time. In contrast to Habermas, however, Thévenot is not interested in an overall normative framework of what "keeps societies together". Thévenot wants to understand social cohesion as something that emerges from the actor's engagement with the world; cohesion displays "modes of coordination commonly enforced" (Thevenot 2001: 66).

Social cohesion is not a general structure that explains how actors evaluate or behave in a certain situation. Actors engage with the world pragmatically in a dynamic confrontation, not mere adjustment. The dynamic confrontation between actor and world includes a moral element: actors have a conception of good, either on a private, functional or public level. One could rephrase this element of realism in Thévenot's theory as "reality bites", typical responsiveness in situations. Humanity is "equipped and furnished" (Thévenot 2001: 57) with the need to evaluate and to understand actions and beliefs in relation to a regime.

Public regimes, e.g., are justified and criticized when actors are engaged in a situation that includes the public, like entering a bus and not knowing which ticket to use. Pragmatic engagement also includes interaction with things. "Things" is meant in a very broad sense: nature, architecture and space, food and clothes, machines and technologies all play constitutive roles within these public regimes. From this perspective, it is not so surprising that Pia Kjærsgaard answers the question of what Danishness means to her with an amalgam of material things – strawberries and new potatoes – and structured and regulated actions within the institutions of the welfare state. Without stretching this example too far, I attempt here to outline that the problem with this type of statement lies not so much in the fact that certain cultural values, materialized cultural values, are used to identify the worth individuals or groups attribute to their way of living. The problem arises if such valued things and feelings are the sole signifier of a public regime, in this case of being Danish. It is the hegemony of specific values and regimes that constitute the problem.

What can be learned from the approach Thévenot uses to unfold the different pragmatic regimes and engagements of actors that constitute our social lives? First, social cohesion is not achieved by an overarching principle that governs all engagements with the world; rather, it results from the negotiations and attributions of different conceptions of good. Secondly, the material world is part of this engagement. From this perspective, it is not hard to see why wearing a scarf or burka has become a symbol for the struggles taking place in Western countries where Muslim religion and culture tend to be seen in opposition to the secular Western state. Another example might be the discussion about ghettos in Denmark. Non-ethnic Danes and their families (often second or even third generation immigrants) are commonly identified with a specific place that is characterized by dense housing and numerous antennas; in general, it is not as neat and decent as the ethnic Danish neighbourhoods. There are hard commonalities at stake that provoke dispute, dispute that is not easily solved or silenced with the principle of recognition.

From the discussion thus far, I will attempt to provide an initial conclusion: the combination of objective normativity – a normativity that is non-arbitrary and universal – and its contextualization within social practices remains problematic if the frame of reference for these social practices is too narrow. In this sense, Honneth's approach to justifying the normative framework of a good society with experiences of social discontent and disrespect over-philosophizes particular experiences. Thévenot's pragmatic sociology gives a richer description of both the moral capacities of actors and their entanglement in practical regimes. However, Thévenot does not seek to reconstruct a normative theory that would explain how all of these different regimes could co-exist. His point of view affirms the versatility afforded in modern societies with their social, political, cultural and technological dynamics. Social cohesion, in Thévenot's model, stems from the intrinsic double orientation exhibited by the engagement of actors. Actors are competent because they are able to agree, adjust, negotiate and criticize commonalities and rules within the different regimes. But what if dispute and conflict arises? Or to put it in a different way: how does the intrinsic normativity of social and cultural practices relate to the normativity that justifies democracy as a set of principles, laws, institutions and processes? This question is obviously highly relevant in heterogeneous societies and nation states with multicultural outlooks.

Multiculturalism

As it occurs in political philosophy, the media and everyday discourse, multiculturalism has a double meaning. On the one hand, it is a descriptive term. Due to migration, globalization and social differentiation, modern society consists of different cultures, often connected to different ethnic or lifestyle groups. On the other hand, the notion of multiculturalism also has a normative or prescriptive dimension: theorists, politicians or citizens commit themselves to the value of multiculturalism, thus presupposing that having different cultures is of intrinsic value. Factual multiculturalism is a reality in most countries, not just Western countries. The questions that arise for Western democratic states of law revolve around two – at least two – crucial distinctions: the differentiation between religion and state and the differentiation between the public sphere and the state. The role of the citizens, their rights, liberties and duties change according to the different forms of differentiation between religion and state and between the public sphere and the state. It is clear that, from a liberal perspective, the "art of separation" has to be used to safeguard most citizens' rights, thereby opening a broad variety of value orientations that are legal or legitimate so long as they don't harm the freedom of others, to refer to Kant's famous definition. The problem of multiculturalism could be rephrased as a problem of conflict between rights and principles – the right to wear a scarf in public for religious reasons and the principle of an egalitarian state where religious symbols are only legitimate within the religious and private spheres. As Seyla Benhabib also has shown, the problem of multiculturalism occurs in the conflict between rights and principles that are bound to the integrated national state and to the variety of social and cultural practices, and values that are either alien to, or at least differ from, the nation state in question.

These types of problems cannot be solved by finding a normative foundation that is rooted in shared social and cultural practices – even if the principle is as thin as the concept of recognition in Honneth's version of reconstruction. It is also not viable to merely separate the normative justification of citizen rights within democratic societies from the plurality of values without the acknowledgment that they influence each other. To connect my discussion of normativity and social practices to the open question of multiculturalism, I would like to use Walzer's art of separation: "The art of separation is not an illusory or fantastic enterprise; it is a morally and politically necessary adaptation to the complexities of modern life" (Walzer 1984: 6). This idea aligns with Thévenot's conceptualization of actors that are capable of learning how to vary their understanding of the common good in relation to different situations. The ability to orient oneself towards different regimes and to renegotiate is a necessary learning process that adds social skills to the otherwise thin concept of citizenship as a bearer of individual rights. I think it is important to emphasize that Walzer calls it the "art" of separation, indicating that it is something that has to be learned in relation to social realities. On the basis of Walzer's recommendation, I would like to propose two levels of normativity that influence each other without being foundational to one another: the normativity that defines and justifies citizenship rights and democratic procedures and the inherent normativity that actors exhibit in social and cultural practices. Neither the principles of citizenship nor cultural and social practices exist in a historical vacuum. They will change over time, but it is fundamental that the democratic framing of a multicultural society should be robust enough to regulate its own change. Solutions to conflicts that arise from what Honneth called the "struggle for recognition" must be found within the framework of democracy. Only by engaging in practices of cultural and social value will citizens be able to learn the art of separation themselves. The materiality of practices has meaning. A scarf or strawberries matter – they are not just of symbolic value. Only by engaging in such practices will citizens be able to contribute to the richness of the social and cultural world while allowing their engagement to assist in the ongoing endeavour of reinterpreting, adjusting and recreating democracy.

■ References

Benhabib, S. *The Claims of Culture. Equality and Diversity in the Global Era*, Princeton, NJ: Princeton University Press, 2002.
Berlingske. "Pia K.: Danskhed er kartofler og årstider", 2010, http://www.b.dk/politik/pia-k.-danskhed-er-kartofler-og-aarstider.
Boltanski, L. and L. Thévenot. *On Justification. Economies of Worth*. Princeton, NJ: Princeton University Press, 2006.
Cooke, M. "Between 'Objectivism' and 'Contextualism': The Normative Foundations of Social Philosophy." *Critical Horizons* 1, 2 (2000): 193-227.
Eriksen, J.M. and F. Stjernfelt. *The Democratic Contradictions of Multiculturalism*. New York: Telos Press.

Habermas, J. *Faktizität und Geltung. Beiträge zur Diskurstheorie des Rechts und des demokratischen Rechtsstaats*. Frankfurt: Suhrkamp, 1992.

Hannerz, U. *Cultural Meaning. Studies in the Social Organization of Meaning*. New York: Columbia University Press, 1992.

Honneth, A. *The Struggle for Recognition: The Moral Grammar of Social Conflicts*. Cambridge, MA/London: MIT Press, 1995a.

Honneth, A. *The fragmented World of the Social. Essays in Social and Political Philosophy*. Albany, NY: State University of New York Press, 1995b.

Honneth, A. *Das Andere der Gerechtigkeit. Aufsätze zur Praktischen Philosophie*. Frankfurt: Suhrkamp, 2000.

Honneth, A. "Redistribution as Recognition: A Response to Nancy Fraser." In *Redistribution or Recognition. A Political-Philosophical Exchange*, ed. N. Fraser and A. Honneth, 110-97. London/New York: Verso Books: 2003.

Honneth, A. (2004). "Recognition and Justice. Outline of a Plural Theory of Justice." *Acta Sociologica* 47, 4 (2004): 351-64.

Honneth, A. "Anerkennung als Ideologie." In *Das Ich im Wir*, A. Honneth. Frankfurt: Suhrkamp, 2010: 103-30.

Honneth, A. *Das Recht der Freiheit. Grundriß einer demokratischen Sittlichkeit*. Frankfurt: Suhrkamp, 2011.

Kinnvall, C. and P. Nesbitt-Larking. "Global Insecurity and Citizenship Strategies: Young Muslims in the West." *Scandinavian Journal of Social Theory* 12, 3 (2011): 271-90.

Kymlicka, W. *Multicultural Citizenship: A Liberal Theory of Minority Rights*. Oxford: Oxford University Press, 1995.

Kymlicka, W. *Contemporary Political Philosophy*. Oxford: Oxford University Press, 2002.

Putnam, R. "*E Pluribus Unum*: Diversity and Community in the Twenty-First Century." *Scandinavian Political Studies* 30, 2 (2007): 137-74.

Reckwitz, A. "Multikulturalismustheorien und der Kulturbegriff. Vom Homogenitätsmodell zum Modell kultureller Interferenzen." *Berliner Journal für Soziologie* 11 (2001): 179-200.

Schatzki, T. "Introduction: Practice Turn." In *The Practice Turn in Contemporary Theory*, ed. T. Schatzki et al., 1-14. London/New York: Routledge, 2001.

Taylor, C. "The Politics of Multiculturalism: Examining the Politics of Recognition." In *Multiculturalism*, ed. C. Taylor and A. Gutmann, 25-73. Princeton, NJ: Princeton University Press, 1994.

Thévenot, L. "Pragmatic Regimes Governing the Engagement With the World." In *The Practice Turn in Contemporary Theory*, ed. T. Schatzki et al., 56-73. London/New York: Routledge, 2001.

Thévenot, L. "Power and Oppression From the Perspective of the Sociology of Engagements: A Comparison With Bourdieu's and Dewey's Critical Approaches to Practical Activities." *Irish Journal of Sociology* 19, 1 (2011): 35-67.

UN Declaration of Human Rights, http://www.un.org/en/documents/udhr/.

Walzer, M. "Liberalism and the Art of Separation." *Political Theory* 12, 3 (1984): 313-50.

Yuval Davis, N. "Belonging and the Politics of Belonging." *Patterns of Predjudice* 40, 3 (2006): 197-214.

7 We Are All Authentic: Multicultural Strategies and Religious Constructions

Jørn Borup

Globalisation, transnationalism and the breakdown of meta-narratives are convincing arguments for relativising or downplaying the importance of culture and ethnicity. Hybridity seems to be the catchword for postmodern identity, in which particularisations (national, ethnic, cultural, religious) have a touch of pre-global or pre-modern identity.

However, globalisation is not monolithic, universal or irreversible, and it is sometimes redirected or even rejected by particular fields of religion, culture, or ethnicity. Due to globalisation, never before have so many religions, ethnicities, and cultures been both so distinct and close to each other as today. It is also an abstraction to assume the existence of a pre-multicultural reality in which there were monolithic, corresponding relations between ethnicity, religion, and culture. Historians can easily point to pre-globalised empirical evidence of hybrids, syncretisms, and interactions; and historians of religion can testify that the ideas of separate, coherent theologies are mainly modern inventions with a strong flavour of Western Protestantism.

While diversity has been a natural ingredient in Asian cultures, for most Western countries the transition between (mainly) mono to multi is a cultural and political challenge (Kühle et. al. forthcoming). Previous ideals of the American melting pot and almost automatic assimilation have mostly been abandoned (Hirshman 2003); and especially since the Immigration Act of 1965 and the massive immigration of "new immigrants", increasing focus has been placed on new social realities (Ebaugh and Chafetz 2000; Beyer 2011). In Europe, where one major religion has enjoyed privileged *default value* status due to historical and ideological reasons, multiculturalism and multireligiosity are a hotly debated political issue.[1] How does "culture

---

1. Thus, at EU level multiculturalism and religious diversity have been addressed at different levels. For instance the Report of the Group of Eminent Persons of the Council of Europe: 'Living together. Combining diversity and freedom in 21st century Europe' (http://hub.coe.int/event-files/our-events/the-group-of-eminent-persons).

Christianity" or secularisation fit with more or new kinds of cultural and religious diversity? To what extent do religion and a stronger presence of multiethnicities have an impact on "cultural values"? If it is true that multiculturalism triumphed because assimilation had failed, are we now *really* (almost) all multiculturalists (Kivisto 2012; Glazer 1997)?

In earlier social-science research into integration, the "soft" fields of religion and culture have often been ignored or explained away as dependent variables pointing to something more significant (economics, social class, etc.). Religion has "generally taken a backseat to other topics in the immigration field" (Foner and Alba 2008: 360), perhaps because it was considered to be an obstacle to assimilation, or perhaps because it was assumed that religion would "fade away" (through secularisation or individualisation) or be transformed into the religion of the host nation in question. However, years of study in recent years have shown that in the perspective of immigration and acculturation, religion does actually matter.

This paper addresses the complex relations between religion, ethnicity, and cultural identity formation in migration and multicultural settings. It is argued that although these concepts are not *sui generis*, they do in fact have an impact as living constructs and narratives on broader social and political spheres.

Religion and ethnicity in migration and acculturation

It is not coincidental that there has been a boom of migration research in recent years (Vertovec 2007: 962), and it is natural that most research on religion has been conducted in the fields of sociology and anthropology of religion, relating also to other concepts such as diaspora, transnationalism, pluralism, and acculturation.[2] Not least has the relation between religion and ethnicity "stimulated a substantial expansion of research agendas by both sociologists of religion and immigration studies scholars" (Kivisto 2007: 490).

Empirical evidence of close relations between religion and ethnicity[3] has been documented in many geographical and cultural fields. Religion can be an ethnic marker "used to boost ethnic identity" (Mitchell 2006: 1140), and ethnicity can be a religious marker, where the "ethnic category may also be filled up with religious or linguistic content" (ibid.: 1143). While religion in an immigration perspective is

---

2. Alba et al. 2008; Breton 2012; Carnes and Yang 2004; Cohen 1997; Ebaugh and Chafetz 2004; Kivisto 2007, 2014; Kumar 2006; McLoughlin 2005; Vertovec 2007.
3. Ethnicity is a complex and contested concept, but is understood here as a way of understanding identity with and belonging to a group, distinct from other groups, with a shared history and origin, and often with a particular cultural container of values and practices.

generally often part of a kind of "adaptive solidarity" (Breton 2012: 15), overlaps or different degrees of mutual interdependence and causality can be typologised, as Hammond and Warner did with the concepts of "ethnic fusion", "ethnic religion", and "religious ethnicity" (Hammond and Warner 1993).

Correspondingly, different religions and different ethnicities place different emphasis on the role of religious and ethnic significance and identity (Alba et al. 2009; Foner and Alba, Hirschman 2003; Min 2010; Yang 2008; Ebaugh 2001). In Denmark, the Danish Pluralism Project (Ahlin et al. 2012) and the two local projects of mapping religion in Aarhus[4] have clearly shown that ethnicity is an important factor as a general dividing line across religions and internally between religious groupings. Thus, migrant Muslims and Christians have their own congregational gatherings according to their country of origin, and the "Two Buddhisms" (ethnic Danes and immigrants from Asia) seldom have anything in common. So there has been an increase in multireligiosity, but not in interaction between the groups; there is a high(er) degree of diversity, but not pluralism.[5]

Diversity according to acculturation – how and to what extent different ethnic groups adjust to majority society – also seems to be generally significant. Chua and Rubenfelt (2014) have investigated how different ethnic groups according to "the triple package" (superiority, insecurity, and impulse control) have very different success stories in the acculturation process in America. A survey by a Danish think-tank concluded that ethnicity and the "culture hypothesis" was the single most important variable (overruling other social factors) in explaining differences of values and norms between the Danish ethnic majority and the ethnic minorities (Think Tank for Immigration and Integration 2007). My own research on immigrant Vietnamese and their descendants in Denmark showed significant differences between Catholics and Buddhists in terms of both religiosity and the importance of ethnicity, with a clear correlation between the two. The most religious individuals (measured in terms of belief, attendance, and attitude) are also the people with the highest level of ethnic consciousness (Borup 2014). It is also quite significant that even after five generations in Hawaii, Japanese-American immigrants still keep their main religion (Buddhism), framed by ethnicity (Borup 2013).

On the other hand, a high degree of assimilation and/or individualisation typically indicates that ethnicity (and transnationalism) are less important, with the younger generations in particular only enjoying "symbolic ethnicity" (Ganz 1979). So although Buddhism among Japanese-Americans in Hawaii is almost mono-ethnic and still celebrated at cultural displays, their Buddhism as a lived religion is also

---

4. http://samtidsreligion.au.dk/religion-i-aarhus-2013/.
5. This differentiation between diversity as a neutral term and pluralism as a normative term pointing to interaction between groups is taken from Beckford 2003, 73-81.

on the verge of dying out as the younger generations increasingly feel little identity and engagement with their "ancestors' religion" (Borup 2013). There is a logic in de-ethnifying religion if the context demands this, for instance owing to hostility towards an enemy during the war (Japanese descendants in USA), general ideals of secularism, "culture religiosity" (Europe), or what Breton calls "pristinization" (2012: 113): searching for universal truths behind ethnic and cultural restraints. In pluralist USA, religion typically counts more as symbolic and social capital, being regarded as the most important element of expressing ethnic identity (Casanova 1994). It is thus not surprising that there is a tendency for immigrants to become more religious the more American and engaged in society they get (Cadge and Ecklund 2007), even if "the general trend has been for ethnic churches to merge into larger bodies and by so doing, relegating the ethnic character of the church to the realm of nostalgia" (Kivisto 2014: 12). The fact that people in multicultural contexts are less happy and more isolated, have less trust in each other, and have less accumulated social capital might be a scenario that celebrators of multiculturalism can hope will be changed in the future (Putnam 2007).

Thus, throughout history and in contemporary time, the relations between religion, ethnicity, and migration and their relevance for and impact on society and transnational relations are evident. But the causality between the fields is complex. This is due not least to the different ways the concepts are used and the different ways the fields are managed in different contexts.

Managing and interpreting religious and ethnic diversities

Immigrants have different migrant histories and different ethnicities, cultures, religions, and types of capitals (economic, social, human) in their luggage upon arrival in new host countries. Their descendants have different contexts in which to create their identities, and receiving nations are as different as their ways of understanding and dealing with religious and ethnic diversities. Such diversities call for interpretation and, in political realities, *governance*[6], all being part of a practice field with different agents, interests, and power relations. Apart from national, political, and cultural differences, the implicit *understanding* of religion and culture itself has an impact on how diversities are managed and negotiated. Two ideal type models are often implicit in this field, each being entangled with the fields of investigation.

---

6. Governance is a concept often used interchangeably with accommodation or regulation, and often in a European context, where the real issue is the question of how to deal with Islam. Veit Bader defines it as "those mechanisms of action coordination that provide active intentional capacities to regulate, including co-regulating and self-regulating" (Bader 2009: 44).

a) Realism and essentialism

What could be called the "realist, essentialist model" is mainly used by ethnic and religious groups themselves, as well as by politicians, the media, and *vox populi*, as a common-sense way of understanding diversity. In this model, religions, cultures, and ethnic groups are understood as independents with a common core and origin, and with shared attributes and "genes", distinct from other groups and religions. Each individual represents the group, being a carrier of a more or less coherent "content". From an "outsider's" or *etic* perspective, the world out there is considered "real" with living people communicating by discourses and practices being part of a coherent whole that can (by careful transcription) be understood by the interpreter (or translator). This is the logic behind a so-called "religious dimension" in religious textbooks, and behind the governance of separate "faith communities" as units with legal rights and privileges in many Western countries.

According to this model, there is an underlying causal link between religion, culture, and ethnicity (and between text and practice), giving not only potentials for "clashes of civilizations" but also challenges in a migration perspective. In a European context, such essentialism is positively ascribed to Christianity as a cultural foundation myth explaining anything from democracy to women's rights, and negatively in ascribing an "Islamic essence" to particular expressions (actions or utterances) by Muslims or quotations from the Quran. When a young author with an immigrant (and Muslim) background writes poems about his childhood as an abused victim, it is mediatised as culture and religion; whereas his ethnic Danish colleagues' parallel stories of childhood abuse are addressed in quite different narratives.[7]

Post-colonial and post-Orientalist research have questioned such a Eurocentric gaze, often combining anthropologists' relativistic critique with alternative models in which the ideal of multiculturalism is normatively voiced. Anthropology was the academic discipline institutionalising the insight into cultural relativism and the legitimate criticism of monolithic worldviews, often forced upon the non-Western world as part of hegemonic regimes. The study of religion in the same sense has framed the understanding of diversity across history and geography, and a "difference paradigm" with incommensurability between different entities or positions is often the default approach in many religion and culture studies. The fact that culture and religion constitute a *habitus* which has to be learned and socialised is unquestionable, as is the idea that religions are transmitted and regenerated through socialisation differently according to historical and cultural context, with ethnicity being a framing identity factor. Many scholars have fought for rights and respect

---

7. This was the case in Denmark in 2013, when a young poet wrote a book accusing his immigrant family and environment of mistreating him, also in the name of religion.

for minorities and indigenous people, struggling for the co-existence of religions and cultures. And many multiculturalists have learned their ideological agendas from anthropologists or been inspired by postmodern criticism of particularised meta-narratives which are dressed as universal. In a post-colonial perspective, the very notion of "religion" has often been seen as an ethnocentric tool of power.

However, relativist and multiculturalist ideals are neither unproblematic nor less essentialist. In her book *Generous Betrayal* (Wikan 2001), anthropologist Unni Wikan describes cases in which young Muslim women in Norway are killed or harassed, actions which are implicitly accepted in the name of immigration and multiculturalism. She criticises the political system for legitimating such practices, as well as criticising her well-meaning anthropological colleagues ("if culture was the problem, then so were anthropologists", ibid.: 75), who with noble ideals end up moralising in wrong directions, essentialising cultures by using "an outdated model of culture" (77). This model and the official policy are "based on the premise that to each people there is one culture and one identity" (ibid.: 72), thus celebrating one specific kind of culture, and not the values and culture of the suppressed women or those promoting human rights (rather than the rights of groups). Accepting multiculturalism in this "culturalist" way also means approving cultural essentialism, reifying differentiation, segregation, and promoting "a kind of cultural determinism and cultural incommensurability", in which "culture-possessing groups, being the most authentic of groups, are taken not only to be real but to have rights, not the least of which are the rights of survival, institutionalization, and recognition" (Eller 1997: 252).

The criticism of such an essentialist model is not (necessarily) a matter of right or wrong culture (and religion), but involves understanding of what culture (and religion) *is* and not least how it is *used*. How much is part of the fields of "culture" and "religion", and who has the rights to represent them? When a group of Muslim leaders from Denmark went to Islamic countries to voice their protests over the Muhammed cartoons, and when a former editor-in-chief of a large Danish newspaper (*Politiken*) later excused for the publications to a delegation representing "descendants of Muhammed", whom did they represent, which "Islam"? In other words, "there is a shared assumption that multicultural claims are made on behalf of a collectivity of some kind, but there is disagreement about which collectivities count as multicultural and which do not" (Kivisto 2012: 5).

Although "pluralism represents a popular ideological ideal, especially for academic researchers and political liberals" (Beckford 2003: 101), multiculturalism and multireligiosity as political ideals are not necessarily in alignment with cultural studies, and differences between "multiculturalists" and "antimulticulturalists" (Eller 1997) are not explicitly part of scholarly debates. The concepts are not monolithic designations, and insisting on multireligiosity or multiethnicity is not necessarily the same as insisting on multiculturalism in the sense that different value systems are equally good in all societies. There are multiculturalist positions that are more or less "radical" or "soft", more or less "culturalist" and "essentialist" (see Kymlicka in this volume). And there are multiculturalist positions seeing the "essentialist model" mostly as a straw man for old-fashioned, normatively engaged religion- and diversity-celebrating scholarship, and who would rather subscribe to what they see as its opposite, the constructionist model.

b) Constructionism and perspectivism

Most mainstream scholarship on culture and religion more or less accepts some degree or version of what could be called the "constructivist paradigm".[8] In a broad sense, this is informed by a philosophical break with positivist or essentialist positions, but is perhaps more inspired by general postmodern scholarship within the humanities. Such a model deconstructs versions of culture and religion as coherent and separate units, and questions individual mono-identities as representatives of such units. Hybrids, complexities, diversities and power struggles are "essential" for post-essentialist studies; and a "practice turn", a "performative turn", and a "power relations turn" are ingredients in a general "constructivist turn" in which religion, culture, and ethnicity are deconstructed from any *sui generis* nature, and where traditions and identities are seen as both invented and negotiated as ongoing processes. Just as religion is not a "thing", ethnicity is also seen as a way of seeing the world, a perspective (Brubaker 2004), being a "highly variable and complex phenomenon subject to historical transmutations and transformations" (Kivisto 2007: 493). Whereas historical and structural constraints limit individual choice (race and ethnicity are also ascribed to and governed by hegemonic frames), they can also be negotiated, and "there is no more a one-to-one relationship between ethnicity and religion than there ever was between race and culture" (Breton 2012: 49).

Thus, what religious and cultural studies have also learned from the general constructivist model is to exchange nouns for verbs: objects of study are *processes* of ethnification, religionising, culturalising. Culture can be religionised, religion can be culturalised, ethnified, de-ethnified, politicised, or racialised when circumstances demand or necessitate this, or when it seems strategically appropriate. Apart from acknowledging theoretical insights from such a perspective, it becomes obvious that empirically such constructions have their own lives.

One significant gaze with which to see constructions at play is the paradigmatic ideal in contemporary times of authenticity. Whereas authority was previously at-

---

8. The literature in this broad field is too extensive to be mentioned here, but an excellent example of the sociology of religion and constructionism which also focuses on religious diversity is Beckford 2003.

tached to objective and genealogically related authenticity (Lindholm 2008: 2), the "age of authenticity" (Taylor 2007) is characterised by its focus on self-expression and expressive individualism in which authenticity has been democratised. Such individualised authenticity ideals are also negotiated collectively as group identity claims, performed as a sacralised ideal when appropriate in a resacralised world. Authenticity should thus also be understood in terms of power relations (Kivisto 2012: 19). In the same way that "culture" is a group's "seal of authenticity" and in identity politics a "fetish of a group-in-struggle" (Eller 1997: 252), "religion" has become fetishised as an approved badge of authenticity. What Gayatri Spivak called "strategic essentialism" (Spivak 1990) is a precise concept of what is often the strategy of representatives of religions as well as people who have an interest in describing them: couching a common identity in the motivation of achieving political goals, rhetorically neutralising actual differences of the groups claiming such essences.

Amartya Sen (2006) describes how ethnic and religious difference was often invented and constructed (rather than invigorated) in India, Yugoslavia, and Rwanda by being politicised as tools of differentiation, in a way similar to the strategic culturalism in the 1970s when "African values" were promoted by tyrannical leaders, and when "Asian values" were celebrated in the 1980s by successful Asian leaders as arguments against "Western" democratisation. The same kind of invention of tradition was rehearsed in the 1990s when religious identity was invoked by Hindus in UK universities to promote Hindu unity in a more cultural version of Hinduism (Mitchell 2006: 1146); or when the OIC (Organization of Islamic Cooperation) periodically claims particular Muslim rights across nations against "Western values" (such as democracy or equal rights).

Conflicts between different domains and systems are often invoked by claims of cultural and religious rights. Do religious rights overrule the rights to freedom of expression or basic laws of security? In public discourse or the politics of dress code, it does matter if we regard the head scarf (but not the soccer cap) as a symbol pointing to a cultural domain that needs special treatment; and it matters if we refer to the circumcision of girls as a cultural or religious issue instead of calling it child abuse. When should Native Americans be allowed to use peyote, and when should Sikhs be exempt from wearing a motorcycle helmet or allowed to carry a *kirpan* knife? When are arguments accepting creationism instead of science in schools more appropriate than denying the Holocaust? Can hate speech against homosexuals be legitimate if it occurs within the discourse of religion? Is a book on Hinduism with chapters on Tantrism defamation of religion?[9] Are cartoons of

---

9. In India, Hindu nationalists had Penguin withdraw a book by a highly praised scholar (Doniger 2009) because it hurt their feelings.

Muhammed an expression of Islamophobia? Is critique of Israel an expression of anti-semitism? Or are such claims of the right to religious immunity and authenticity themselves acts of power struggles, often fought by a minority of politically conscious individuals and groups?

Such individual issues and general discussions are often hijacked by populist political agendas, news media headlines, or religious groups. The arguments used are often based unreflectively on the realist/essentialist model. But they are challenges to academics doing "performative scholarship" when they are invited into courtrooms or appointed to advisory boards to help define what is and is not religion and/or culture (what Beckford 1999 calls the "politics of defining religion") when matters of recognition or privileges are dealt with. A constructionist understanding of culture and religion does not solve the political and ideological challenges of understanding and governing religious and cultural diversity. But it surely does provide a more comprehensive basis of negotiation.

Conclusion

Culture matters, ethnicity matters, and religion matters. They do so not in an essentialist, static way with a *sui generis* unchangeable and authentic core. They should primarily be seen as analytical concepts which can be applied usefully to domains of reality, and which are worth comparing with linguistic tools. As constructions they have their own empirically observable life. Religion, ethnicity, and culture are *real* both as discursive positions and as independent factors in their complex interactions with society and history. As such, the very use of such concepts and discourses is itself religious and cultural practice. In such practice fields, representation and authority claims are part of the game, not least when negotiating authenticity as truth claim.

Understanding cultural and religious diversity is an old endeavour of religious and cultural studies, but it has become even more relevant in a more or less globalised world with increased migration. It has been argued here that misgivings of ethnocentric conceptualisation and interpretation cannot be overcome by negating "Western scholarship" or by subscribing to a postmodern "difference paradigm". A constructionist view will transcend an essentialist model of understanding religion and culture, but not by necessitating a new essentialist, authenticity-claimed multi-paradigm. Critical scholarship does not need to be seduced by either culturalist or multiculturalist ideologies, but it does need to be aware of the discursive positions and formations that structure the two.

Entangled as they are by the necessity for "performative scholarship", scholars can help formulate more insightful questions to political challenges too. By which arguments is "religion" or "culture" used? When are so-called Western values exported as so-called universal values, and when are such arguments based on political rhetoric? To which extent are religious and cultural values and practices incommensurable with the values of the majority population? How does the majority's religion and culture position itself with claims of privileged positions? If the overall ambition is social cohesion, are multiethnicity and multireligiosity more negotiable than multiculturalism?

Clash metaphors are often the means by which politicians communicate. Many absurd claims of religious and cultural rights are announced on the news, with the result that the fields of multiculturalism and religious diversity as such are often represented by a discourse of strangeness and suspicion. In reality, most challenges of diversity are solved by pragmatic negotiation. As such, idealist and essentialist positions are often overruled by pragmatic practices. In one sense this illustrates and encapsulates the argument of this article that culture and religion are to be understood by a constructionist gaze as always dynamic and negotiable domains having their own life in interaction with diverse and equally negotiable contexts.

■ References

Ahlin, L., J. Borup, M. Qvortrup Fibiger, L. Kühle, V. Mortensen and R. Dybdal Pedersen. "Religious Diversity and Pluralism: Empirical Data and Theoretical Reflections from the Danish Pluralism Project." *Journal of Contemporary Religion* 27, 3 (2012): 403-18.

Alba, R., A.J. Raboteau and J. DeWind, eds. *Immigration and Religion in America. Comparative and Historical Perspectives*. New York/London: New York University Press, 2009.

Bader, V. "The Governance of Islam in Europe: The Perils of Modelling." *Journal of Ethnic and Migration Studies* 33, 6 (2009): 871-86.

Beckford, J. "The Politics of Defining Religion in Secular Society: From a Taken-For-Granted Institution to a Contested Resource." In *The Pragmatics of Defining Religion: Contexts, Concepts and Contests*, ed. J.G. Platvoet and A.L. Molendijk, 23-40. Leiden: Brill, 1999.

Beckford, J. *Social Theory & Religion*. Cambridge: Cambridge University Press, 2003.

Beyer, Peter. "Religious Diversity and Globalization." In *The Oxford Handbook of Religious Diversity*, ed. C.V. Meister, 185-200. New York: Oxford University 2011.

Borup, J. "Aloha Buddha – the Secularization of Ethnic Japanese-American Buddhism." *Journal of Global Buddhism* 14 (2013): 23-43.

Borup, J. "Religiosity and Ethnicity: Vietnamese Immigrant Religion in Denmark." In *The Changing Soul of Europe Religions and Migrations in Northern and Southern Europe*, ed. H. Vilaça, E. Pace, I. Furseth and P. Pettersson, 231-50. Surrey: Ashgate, 2014.

Breton, R. *Different Gods. Integrating Non-Christian Minorities into a Primarily Christian Society*. Montreal/Kingston: McGill-Queen's Press, 2012

Brubaker, R. *Ethnicity without Groups*. Cambridge, MA: Harvard University Press, 2004.

Cadge, W. and E.H. Ecklund. "Immigration and Religion." *Annual Review of Sociology* 33 (2007): 359-79.

Casanova, J. *Public Religion in the Modern World*. Chicago, IL: University of Chicago Press, 1994.

Christiano, K.J., W.H. Swatos, Jr. and P. Kivisto. *Sociology of Religion. Contemporary Developments*. Lanham, MD: Rowman & Littlefield Publishers, 2008.

Chua, A. and J. Rubenfeld. *The Triple Package: How Three Unlikely Traits Explain the Rise and Fall of Cultural Groups in America*. New York: Penguin, 2014.

Doniger, W. *The Hindu: An Alternative History*. New York: Penguin, 2009.

Ebaugh, H.R. and J.S. Chafetz. *Religion and the New Immigrants: Continuities and Adaptations in Immigrant Congregations*. Walnut Creek, CA: AltaMira Press, 2000.

Eller, J.D. "Anti-Anti Multiculturalism." *American Anthropologist* 99, 2 (1997): 249-60.

Foner, N. and R. Alba. "Immigrant Religion in the U.S. and Western Europe: Bridge or Barrier to Inclusion?" *International Migration Review* 42, 2 (2008): 360-92.

Glazer, N. *We Are All Multiculturalists Now*. Cambridge, MA: Harvard University Press, 1997.

Hammond, P.E. and K. Warner. "Religion and Ethnicity in Late-Twentieth-Century America." *The ANNALS of the American Academy of Political and Social Science* 527 (1993): 55-66.

Hirschman, C. "The Role of Religion in the Origins and Adaptations of Immigrant Groups in the United States." *International Migration Review* 38, 3 (2003): 1206-33.

Kivisto, P. "Rethinking the Relationship between Ethnicity and Religion." In *The Sage Handbook of the Sociology of Religion*, ed. J.A. Beckford and N.J. Demerath III, 474-94. Los Angeles: SAGE Publications, 2007.

Kivisto, P. "We Really Are All Multiculturalists Now." *The Sociological Quarterly* 53 (2012): 1-24.

Kivisto, P. "Reframing Immigrant Religious Organizations and Practices." *Nordic Journal of Religion and Society* 27, 1 (2014): 1-17.

Kühle, L., W. Hoverd, J. Borup and T. Jensen, eds. *Critical Analysis of Religious Diversity*. Oxford: Oxford University Press (forthcoming).

Kumar, P.P., ed. *Religious Pluralism in the Diaspora*. Leiden/Boston: Brill, 2006.

Lindholm, C. *Culture and Authenticity*. Malden: Blackwell Publishing, 2008.

McLoughlin, S. "Migration, Diaspora and Transnationalism: Transformations of Religion and Culture in a Globalizing Age." In *The Routledge Companion to the Study of Religion*, ed. J. Hinels: 526-49. London/New York: Routledge 2005.

Min, P.G. *Preserving Ethnicity Through Religion in America. Korean Protestants and Indian Hindus Across Generations*. New York/London: New York University Press, 2010.

Mitchell, C. "The Religious Content of Ethnic Identities." *Sociology* 40, 6 (2006): 1135-51.

Putnam, R.D. "*E Pluribus Unum:* Diversity and Community in the Twenty-first Century – The 2006 Johan Skytte Prize Lecture." *Scandinavian Political Studies* 30, 2 (2007): 137-74.

Sen, A. *Identity and Violence; the Illusion of Destiny*. New York: W. W. Norton, 2006.

Spivak, C. G. *The Post-Colonial Critic: Interviews, Strategies, Dialogues*. New York: Routledge, 1990.

Taylor, C. *A Secular Age*, Cambridge, MA/London: Harvard University Press, 2007.

Think Tank on Immigration and Integration in Denmark (Tænketanken om udfordringer for integrationsindsatsen i Danmark). *Værdier og normer – blandt udlændinge og danskere*. Copenhagen, 2007.

Vertovec, S. "New Directions in the Anthropology of Migration and Multiculturalism." *Ethnic and Racial Studies* 29, 6 (2007): 961-78.

Wikan, U. *Generous Betrayal. Politics of Culture in the New Europe*. Chicago, IL: University of Chicago Press, 2001.

Yang, F. and H.R. Ebaugh. "Religion and Ethnicity among New Immigrants: The Impact of Majority/Minority Status in Home and Host Countries." *Journal for the Scientific Study of Religion* 40, 3 (2001): 367-78.

Internet

Center for Contemporary Religion, http://samtidsreligion.au.dk/religion-i-aarhus-2013/
 Report of the Group of Eminent Persons of the Council of Europe: "Living together. Combining diversity and Freedom in 21st century Europe", http://hub.coe.int/event-files/our-events/the-group-of-eminent-persons

PART 2

CULTURE, CONFLICT, AND WORLD ORDER

8 Cultural Challenges to the Liberal World Order

Georg Sørensen

Liberals have always been hopeful about the future; their optimism is based on the process of societal modernization. That process began in the West unleashed by the scientific revolution which led to improved technologies and thus more efficient ways of producing goods and mastering nature. This was reinforced by the liberal intellectual revolution, which had great faith in human reason and rationality; the liberal economic and political system would lead to "the greatest happiness of the greatest number", so Jeremy Bentham. Further, modernization would not be limited to the West; it would eventually come to traditional or backward countries as well, sooner rather than later because the Western experience can help accelerate the process of change.

The end of the Cold War would appear to confirm this liberal optimism, especially when combined with the mood, spirits, and changes of the 1990s. The number of democracies in the world doubled, from 43 in the early seventies to 88 by the late nineties (Sørensen 2008). Nearly all countries, democratic or not, committed themselves to liberal market economies based on private property. Most countries wanted to participate in international cooperation through international institutions. The Millennium Declaration, adopted by UN member states, confirmed universal allegiance to liberal principles.

In the new century, things went the other way. The years between 2000 and 2010 were labeled "a decade from hell" by *Time Magazine*: "The most dispiriting and disillusioning decade Americans have lived through in the post-World War II era" (*Time*, 7 December 2009). 9-11 conjured a different set of security threats; "democratization" turned out to be frail political openings rather than real transitions to democracy; many countries remained semi-democratic or semi-authoritarian. The financial crisis was the most serious economic slump since the 1930s. And the commitment to liberal values frequently turned out to be skin-deep, a set of rhetorical gestures with no real substance behind them.

It is against this more sinister background that we must contemplate current cultural challenges to liberal world order. Cultural challenges are those that have to do with the value basis of liberal world order. A core question for many contemporary observers is whether the "decade from hell" is really that significant in the larger scheme of things, or it can be considered a mere bump in the road, a temporary setback in a larger process of uninhibited liberal progress (Ikenberry 2009). The optimists subscribe to the "bump in the road view". They most often support an idealist view – popularized by Francis Fukuyama (1989) – according to which liberal modernity is a fixed ideal, discovered in its final form several hundred years ago, and slowly rolled out across the world (including bumps and setbacks) ever since. But the idealist view is wrong. Liberalism is not a fixed and unchanging entity. Liberalism is a complex set of values, of principles and propositions that have been contested and discussed, modified and developed, from the very beginning to this day.

The relevant question, then, is this: the liberal project currently faces a new set of cultural and other challenges. How serious are these challenges and is the liberal project ready to give convincing answers to them? My assessment is that the challenges are very serious and the liberal answers so far have been glaringly insufficient. That bodes ill for any quick return to easy liberal progress. In cultural terms, we must prepare for a world where liberal values are increasingly contested and may far from always win the day. Specifically, I seek to make three points:

- The traditional liberal view that the process of modernization will with a high degree of certainty lead to a society which adopts the entire liberal package, including liberal democracy, must be rejected. In the long run, modernization might not bring democracy. Culture matters and modernization and westernization are not the same.
- Liberal progress creates its own set of problems. It can lead to liberal hubris ("we can do anything we want in the world and our values are true for everyone") which will be received as liberal imperialism. In that way, liberal strength may in itself undercut liberal advance.
- Liberal democracies have not been able to develop good answers to the political, economic, institutional, and value challenges that they face. In the medium/long run, this will threaten a dramatic loss of liberal soft power.

Modernization and democracy

Seymour Martin Lipset famously claimed that "the more well-to-do a nation, the greater the chances that it will sustain democracy" (Lipset 1959: 75). To be sure, modernisation and wealth generate factors conducive to democracy: higher rates of literacy and education, urbanization, and the presence of mass media. Moreover, wealth provides the resources needed to mitigate the tensions produced by political conflict. The Lipset hypothesis received much empirical support. In 1971, Robert Dahl considered it "pretty much beyond dispute" that the higher the socioeconomic level of a country, the more likely it was to be a democracy (Dahl 1971: 65).

But the expectation far from always holds true. Argentina had many years of authoritarian rule despite a relatively high level of per capita income, as did Taiwan and South Korea. In his analysis of the major South American cases, Guillermo O'Donnell developed an argument that turns the Lipset thesis on its head: Authoritarianism, not democracy, seems to be the more likely concomitant of the highest levels of modernization. That is because the process of industrial modernization that took place in South America in the 1960s and 1970s had little to offer the majority of people. In order to pursue this model in the face of popular resistance, the ruling elite needed an authoritarian system (O'Donnell 1973).

These early South American cases, together with current processes of modernization in China, the Middle East, and elsewhere, bear witness to an insight which runs counter to the liberal idea of a uniform, Western package of modernity that will inexorably unfold everywhere. Recall William McNeill's argument in his masterly work on the rise of the West: "even if non-Westerners should happen to hold supreme controls of world-wide political-military authority" he wrote, "they could only do so by utilizing such originally Western traits as industrialism, science, and the public palliation of power through advocacy of one or the other of the democratic political faiths. Hence 'The Rise of the West' may serve as a shorthand description of the upshot of the history of the human community to date" (McNeill 1963: 806n).

McNeill was wrong. The paths to modernity followed by today's rising powers are not copies of the West with its early constitutional rule, nascent bourgeoisies, and religious reformations. The rising powers are "each following unique paths towards modernity based on their own political, demographic, topographic and socioeconomic conditions. Accordingly, they are developing versions of modernity divergent from the West's" (Kupchan 2012: 87n). Kupchan's analysis covers a large number of non-Western paths to modernity. They include variants of autocracy on one extreme and more democratic cases on the other (China, Russia, Persian Gulf sheikdoms, African strongmen, Latin American populists, and India).

For present purposes, I briefly focus on China, the allegedly most prominent of the current non-Western models. In economic terms, China is a capitalist market system, albeit one where the hand of the state is heavier than in many market systems. The political dominance of the Communist Party is based on three elements: co-optation, legitimacy, and repression. Co-optation involves the integration of the economic and intellectual elite into the party system. On the one hand, party cadres have moved into the business community as managers or private entrepreneurs. On the other hand, businessmen have been able to become members of the Chinese Communist Party (CCP) since 2001. That is to say, capitalists are welcome in the ranks of the CCP; so are intellectuals, including university students, and the post-1989 generation of students who consider Tiananmen "a riot" have joined the party in vast numbers.

Second, party legitimacy flows from economic and social achievements. Annual growth rates in the area of 10+ per cent for almost thirty years have lifted more than 600 million people out of poverty, a stunning accomplishment. Not all is well of course. Some 170 million remain under the $1.25-a-day international poverty line; environmental sustainability, inequality, and external imbalances are other major challenges (World Bank 2012). Yet 82 per cent of the population are satisfied with their lives, and 92 per cent report that they enjoy a higher standard of living than did their parents at a similar age. But there is also growing concern about corruption, pollution, food safety, and the gap between rich and poor (Pew Research Center 2013).

The third element in the CCP's power is repression. Most well-known in the West are the crackdowns on prominent opposition figures, such as Al Weiwei and Liu Xiaobo and the attempts to control the Internet. But the Chinese repression system is a vast and complex machinery. China now spends in the excess of 700 billion dollars annually on "domestic security"; that is a higher amount than the regular defense budget. The U.S. State Department reported a "negative trend" concerning the Chinese human rights record in the spring of 2011, with growing restrictions on freedom of speech, crackdowns on government critics, and "severe repression" (State Department 2012) in some regions, including Tibet and Xinjiang.

The Chinese model of autocratic capitalism does contain some of the same elements as the Western model, including industrial growth, social transformation, education, and higher levels of welfare for most people. But it is abundantly clear that the model is qualitatively different from the Western model. That difference is exacerbated by substantial cultural dissimilarities. "Chinese society has long privileged stability, solidarity, and communal welfare over personal gain – in contrast to Western traditions of liberalism and the autonomy of the individual" (Kupchan 2012: 94). This difference in cultural context needs to be drawn in when considering a variety of protest movements in China. In the West, social protest is based on the liberties connected with individual rights. In China, social protest is concerned with the duty of the state to provide for well-recognized rights to a decent livelihood for citizens. That is to say, to Westerners, "*liberty* rather than *livelihood* is the foundation of political morality" (Perry 2008: 44). In China, it is typically the other way round. It follows that social protest in China is most often *not* transcending the established political system by demanding individual rights and liberties. Protests are sooner conformist in relation to the system; they require the state to live up to its obligations in terms of providing secure livelihood for its citizens (Perry 2008); the intention is not to change the system in a more democratic direction.

In short, there are a number of rather successful processes of modernization going on in the world but they are distinctly different from the Western model. At the same time, differences in terms of cultural setting provide for a context with its own peculiar challenges in terms of socio-political change. Nothing of this can be framed in terms of a law-like statement that democracy will never happen in China or anywhere else. In China, the problems of corruption and the environmental challenges will probably amount to an increasing pressure on the system and the leadership still needs to convincingly demonstrate that the problems can be effectively confronted. But it is a good guess that any process of democratization will be long and arduous and that communal autocracy will persist for some considerable time; the end of history is nowhere in sight.

In contrast to the Cold War, the liberal world order now has global reach. Most countries subscribe to a policy of involvement in economic globalization and participation in international institutions. But China and other non-liberal powers will surely also be less enthusiastic members of the international society, viewing international politics as a struggle for position, power, and relative advantage (Lampton 2008; Ross and Feng 2008). Leading liberal countries, including the United States, will want to accommodate China. Any support for liberal values, including human rights in China or Tibetan secession or autonomy, will take second place to the strategic issues of partnership (Clinton 2009).

The emerging liberal order will not have a common value foundation that includes freedom, democracy, and human rights. Non-democratic great powers will be major stakeholders in the system. They will emphasize traditional values of sovereignty, nonintervention, and fundamental differences of national interest. That will further discourage any developments toward a universal compact of "Responsibility to Protect" which looks after basic human rights in fragile states. China's current activism in Africa runs in a different direction: it is ready to support full-blown dictatorships insofar as the bargains meet traditional Chinese national interests by providing access to raw materials, energy, and agricultural products (Malone 2008).

There is a further tension in the inclusion of non-democratic states in a liberal world order. The development of economic globalization leads to intensified interdependence. That increases the demand for regulation across borders. Instead of negative regulation (i.e. regulations that prohibit states from taking certain measures), there is an emphasis on positive regulation (i.e. regulations that require states to take certain measures). Furthermore, focus is increasingly on "behind-the-border-issues" (i.e. regulations that do not concern tariffs or quotas but product standards, investment regulations, competition policies, transparency measures, etc.) According to Michael Zürn, economic globalization tends to change the character of international institutions; "increasingly, their aim is to regulate not only the action of state actors but also those of societal actors, and not only at the border, but also behind-the-border issues. In doing so, positive regulations have gained importance relative to negative regulations. The extent and the objects of international governance no longer easily match the notion of a sovereign state in the Westphalian system" (Zürn 2002: 247). But it is exactly this traditional notion of sovereignty and non-intervention that China and other non-democratic players want to emphasize.

In sum, it is a major cultural or value challenge to liberal world order that currently successful modernizing countries are not moving in a liberal direction. They combine their own peculiar versions of capitalism with political and social systems which are in many ways fundamentally different from the liberal West. China is perhaps the most prominent example of this but the tendency applies to other modernizers as well. As a result, the emerging "liberal" world order will be much less liberal than the successful post-World War II Bretton Woods order which involved democracies dedicated to liberal values. The emerging order can perhaps be committed to some values in the liberal package, such as autonomy, sovereignty, and non-intervention, but it cannot be fully committed to democracy, openness, and liberty. The question is whether a stable liberal world order can be built on such a truncated foundation.

Liberal strength and activism undercutting liberal values

The end of the Cold War created a new, and rather unique, situation in global balance of power terms. In the earlier period two superpowers, each with a coalition behind them had faced each other in a bipolar standoff. The dissolution of the Soviet Union left one global power on the scene; unipolarity had replaced bipolarity (Sørensen 2009). A unipolar power is in a rather exceptional situation because it is relatively unconstrained by other states in the system. The United States now indeed dominated the world in the sense that it was "unchecked by any rival and with decisive reach in every corner of the globe" (Krauthammer 2004). An unconstrained power can basically do anything it wants; this can lead in all kinds of directions of course. On the one hand, it can embark on ambitious expansionist policies, making its influence felt everywhere; on the other hand, it may become introverted and isolationist, preoccupied with its own domestic agenda. Any combination of those extremes is of course also possible (some of what follows draws on Sørensen 2011).

Both of these elements, expansionism and introversion, have been present in the case of the United States after the end of the Cold War. A particularly virulent form of expansionism came to characterize the George W. Bush presidency. This was surely amplified by the terrorist attacks of September 11, 2001, but it began sometime before that. By June that year, Charles Krauthammer could claim that the United States had embarked on a foreign policy that "seeks to strengthen American power and unashamedly deploy it on behalf of *self-defined* global ends". The President confirmed these intentions in a West Point commencement address: "America has, and intends to keep, military strengths beyond challenges – thereby making the destabilizing arms races of other periods pointless, and limiting rivalries to trade and other pursuits of peace" (Bush 2002).

These statements were combined with a high-profile US activism in the wake of 9-11. The US National Security Strategy of 2002 vows to "defend liberty and justice, because these principles are right and true for people everywhere" (NSS 2002). It also emphasized that the United States must be unconstrained in responding to threats and this must include preemptive use of force; the wars in Afghanistan and Iraq followed. The Iraq war was particularly controversial because it was not sanctioned by the international community; the UN Security Council would not support it. The US had to make do with a "coalition of the willing" which included the UK and a string of lesser powers, including Denmark. A further aspect of American unilateralism was the retreat from international institutions and agreements: the abolishment of the 1972 Anti-Ballistic Missile Treaty with the Soviet Union, the rejection of the Kyoto Protocol of global warming, of the Biological Weapons Convention, and of the International Criminal Court.

In sum, an overwhelming power position can lead towards unilateralist arrogance where the unipolar power requires the world to subject itself to an order that leaves the United States entirely unconstrained while requiring commitments to rules and regulations from everybody else. This is a form of liberal imperialism, that is, "a neoimperial vision in which the United States arrogates to itself the global role of setting standards, determining threats, and meeting out justice" (Ikenberry 2002: 44). It is not a coherent and stable recipe for a post-Cold War liberal world order. Several close allies of the US (Germany, France) would not accept it, nor would other great powers such as China, Russia, and India. In other words, an unconstrained liberal power may adopt policies that undercut a stable liberal world order because it will not itself comply with the principles and values that it demands from others.

The Barack Obama administration has gone to work on these problems in a way that promises a more cooperative multilateralism on the part of the United States. I have argued elsewhere (Sørensen 2011) that the creation of a stable liberal world order in the post-Cold War world remains a complicated and tenuous project. In the present context, however, I want to focus on the ongoing war in Afghanistan and the ways in which it has tended to undercut rather than promote and strengthen liberal values in that country.

The United States and its supporting coalition came to Afghanistan in pursuit of operation "Enduring Freedom" which was part of the war on terror. The Afghan regime harbored terrorists so the intervention wanted to defeat Al Qaeda as well as the Taliban regime. This was accomplished quickly; the goal then shifted towards a long term promotion democracy, state-building and development in Afghanistan; that project is not completed and has run into serious setbacks. What is the problem?

First, even hegemonic powers face limitations. Intervention involves material as well as human cost. Domestic public opinion will be skeptical towards great involvement. That will most always lead to smaller interventions than seen as necessary by experts. The American Defense Science Board recommended 20 troops per 1,000 inhabitants in Afghanistan; the actual number was about 0.5 soldiers per 1,000 inhabitants (Logan and Prebble 2006). It's lower today. Second, intervention is not a replay of colonial takeover; outsiders are under pressure to get out quickly and declare the mission completed. This leads towards "imperialism in a hurry" (Ignatieff 2003); long term projects are played down in favor of short-term achievement.

Third, when the aim of intervention is not takeover but the creation of a self-sustaining state that is effective as well as democratic, then local conditions in the subject society become crucial. Locals must carry out the long-term undertaking of state-building; outsiders cannot do it for them. Externally imposed institutions will have little legitimacy and sustainability unless supported by major groups in domestic society. State institutions "cannot simply be imposed by external actors, but need to grow out of indigenous realities" (Papagianni 2007: 254). It follows that state-building and democratization projects crucially depend on prior conditions in the subject societies and the local demand for reform.

Afghanistan has been a country at civil war for more than thirty years. During all that time, interventions by outsiders have intensified and prolonged the bloodshed and the hardships of the population. International forces thus tend to confront a skeptical population from early on. In particular, any state-building and democratization effort requires the support of local elites. But substantial groups among these elites are "spoilers" because an effective and responsive state is a threat to their self-seeking orientation toward power and wealth. Contending elite groups must simultaneously be pacified and neutralized while also included in the process of state building and democratization. This is, to put it mildly, easier said than done.

Finally, the creation of a democratic basis for legitimacy is impeded by the lack of support from citizens and groups who fear that democracy is a zero-sum game of politics between winners and losers where they will end up on the losing side. Citizens are further disillusioned by the holding of elections that are accompanied by serious democratic deficits and poor institutional performance. Liberal outsiders play a core role in this. When liberals insist on the universal validity of their values, they also pose a power challenge and an identity challenge to others that risk undermining liberal ambitions; instead of the inclusion of others, the gulf between insiders and outsiders opens up even more.

The grand assembly of traditional Afghan leaders, the Loya Jirga, voted by a two-third majority in favor of making the aging King Zaher Shah the interim head of state in 2002. It took comprehensive US interference behind the scenes, including "bribes, secret deals, and arm twisting" (Johnson and Mason 2009), to nominate the US candidate, Hamid Karzai, instead. The result was a strong reaction against the United States. Thomas Johnson and Chris Mason (2009) explain why:

> An American cannot declare himself king and be seen as legitimate: monarchy is not a source of legitimacy of governance in America. Similarly, a man cannot be voted president in Afghanistan and be perceived as legitimate. Systems of government normally grow from existing traditions, as they did in the U.S. after the Revolutionary War, for example. In Afghanistan, they were imposed externally. Representative democracy is simply not a source of legitimacy in Afghanistan at this point in its development. This explains in no small measure why a religious source of legitimacy in the form of the hated Taliban is making such a powerful comeback.

In short, the United States was able to project power anywhere in the world after the end of the Cold War, but it cannot install democracy and conduct effective state-building in a fragile state unless local elites and popular groups are willing to move in that direction. The power challenge and the identity challenge posed by liberal outsiders strongly contribute to the fact that they are unwilling rather than willing. Outsiders must then face charges of liberal imperialism.

The general lesson from this is that liberal power has led to liberal hubris which has undercut liberal advance. In spite of R2P and other measures, Western democracies will not easily be able to promote democracy and effective state-building in fragile states. Tony Blair (2007) recently argued in favor of the universal validity of liberal values and claimed that "given the chance" all people want democracy. He is wrong; people will want democracy when they are convinced that it is a sensible way forward for themselves and the groups to which they belong. Their demand for democracy is conditional. Those conditions deteriorate when powerful outsiders attempt to coerce them in a liberal direction in ways which directly contradict the liberal principles that they formally advocate.

Liberal economic and political order: still an attractive model?

Liberal values have advanced in the world because they represent economic and political models that most people find attractive. Liberal democracies have usually been vastly superior when it comes to soft power (Nye 2005), that is, the power to attract and to persuade rather than the power to coerce. This was due to attractive models; we had something that others also wanted for themselves. The question today is whether the consolidated liberal systems in North America, Western Europe, and Japan can continue to boast economic and political models that are hugely attractive around the world? The short answer is that there are serious problems which must be confronted if the attraction of liberal values and thus liberal dominance in terms of soft power is to be sustained in the future.

At the core of the liberal model is a society built around a well-to-do and successful middle class with good jobs, secure incomes, comfortable life-styles, and ability to provide for the future of their children. It is this middle class model which is in a crisis. In the United States, the top one percent now takes home close to 25 percent of the total income; that is up from nine percent in 1974. At the bottom, 15 percent are below the official poverty line and another 15 percent are scarcely above it. That is to say, a small group of super-rich, one-third at the bottom, and a middle class which has not seen substantial improvement for about three decades (Fukuyama 2012). This is a new level of inequality in comparison with the inter-war New Deal model and the post-world-war-II consolidation-of-the-middle-class model. It has been pushed by dramatic tax cuts for the wealthy in combination with intensified globalization which has eliminated what used to be secure middle class jobs.

Since 2008, these developments have been combined with a financial and economic crisis for the neoliberal model of capitalism, which has dominated the old capitalist centers in recent decades, Europe, North America, and Japan. The model is too heavily tilted towards securitization and financial speculation, it is too deregulated, and it is too unequal because it does not have enough to offer the large middle classes and the less skilled groups in our societies in terms of income and employment.

A reform of that model is surely necessary. A reformed model needs to emphasize the production of real goods and services, gainful employment, and sound finance; in short, a more robust and less speculative capitalism. But basic reform is not forthcoming. In the US, it is blocked by vested interests, including Wall Street. In EU-Europe, focus is on short-term stabilization of debt-ridden countries via austerity measures. More middle- and working-class despair in these countries is the unavoidable result. The EU does not appear to be moving towards basic reform either. It has been keen on bailing out banks, but much less keen on bailing out people.

Behind the European problems are Southern European member states that are fragile, ineffective, have serious corruption problems, weak capacities for adopting and implementing rules and regulations, and are excessively dominated by vested interests that have been successful in taking care of themselves on behalf of the state. Euro zone membership handed such states an almost unlimited access to cheap credit. The results, when ample funds flowed into fragile states, ought to have been predictably disastrous.

Second, the vast differences between member countries of the euro-zone were played down, and perhaps expected to disappear very soon. They didn't and in retrospect the euro was not an economically sound project; it made more sense in terms of political prestige, i.e. "driving integration forward". Third, to the extent that rules were in place, no member of the euro-zone was particularly interested in respecting them and enforcing them when things looked better. The economic crisis will risk exacerbating a legitimacy crisis for the EU. Anonymous bureaucrats take far-reaching decisions behind closed doors and people suffer. It is no help that national politicians are talking European co-operation down rather than up. They blame the EU for every problem and take personal credit for every success, and sometimes people believe them.

The basic liberal value challenge here concerns the formulation of revised liberal economic and political models which will secure a continued strong attraction of the liberal model in its heartlands and in the world. I have indicated that not much is happening in the liberal core countries as regards a reform of the economic model. What the advanced liberal states continue to recommend to the rest of the world are the neo-liberal principles which are in crisis at home: public sector cutbacks, removal of industrial and agricultural protectionism, and lifting of trade and currency regulations.

But the advanced countries had not themselves relied on neo-liberal principles in their own process of development. They instead turned to mercantilist policies of support for domestic industry and regulation of trade and foreign investment. Only when their domestic industries were robustly competitive did they begin to strongly support economic openness and free trade. The current imposition of neo-liberal standards on latecomers "kicks away the ladder" (Chang 2002) under them as they are denied certain ways forward. This is behind the fact that successful latecomers are instead pursuing models which are in basic ways non-liberal, as mentioned earlier.

The economic crisis in the liberal heartlands is accompanied by a political crisis which plays out on several levels. At the national level, the democratic process has lost vigor and dynamism in the liberal heartlands. One aspect of this is the loss of "social capital" (Putnam 1995) connected with the increasing fragmentation of late modern societies. Another aspect is the dominance of vested elite interests of the political process impeding possibilities for comprehensive reform. On the left side of the political spectrum, social democratic parties have not so far been able to formulate new, comprehensive political projects that simultaneously tackle the challenges of run-away-globalization, socio-economic inequality, and interest group domination (Fukuyama 2012).

The greatest challenge to established forms of liberal democracy is economic globalization. Globalization may undermine democracy because national governments have less and less control over what happens within their own borders. One way to confront this is via regional integration, as in the case of the EU. But it is clear that the EU's supranational governance structures are in several ways less democratic than those of national parliaments and governments (Sørensen 2008) because of distance to the people, lack of public debate, and lack of transparency. When it comes to global structures of governance, such as the UN system, these problems are amplified. Liberal democracy was always designed for the nation state. It has not been sufficiently thought through when it comes to governance across borders. This is a more serious problem today than earlier, because the progress of globalization has increased the demand for political cooperation and regulation across borders. In this situation, liberal politics is plagued by "institutional competition, overlapping jurisdictions, the excessive cost of inaction, and the failures of accountability" (Held 2007: 249).

In sum, an attractive liberal economic and political model must be able to confront the major challenges of a globalized world. There are serious indications that liberal democracies have not (yet) risen to these challenges. Observing current political processes in the liberal heartlands does not make one optimistic that this will change for the better sometime soon. That will make the liberal model less attractive; in that sense liberal values may be increasingly challenged.

Conclusion

There has surely been liberal progress in the world: more democracies, commitment to liberal market economies, and cooperation through international institutions. But liberal progress is never guaranteed; liberal values must always be able to successfully confront new challenges. I have discussed three areas where liberal values are increasingly challenged: (a) there are a number of successful modernizing countries in the world today, but their social and political models contain features that are distinctly non-liberal and it is not likely that these features will disappear; (b) the increase of liberal power in the world has led to liberal *hubris* which has undercut liberal advance. Recent cases of liberal imperialism will not help increase the standing of liberal values in the world; (c) liberal soft power is endangered because the liberal economic and political model has not been fully able to confront the challenges of a globalized world. An attractive and successful political and economic model is the foundation for liberal soft power.

All this does not mean that the liberal world order is on the verge of breaking down or that chaos and anarchy are in the cards. It does mean that history never guarantees progress in a liberal direction. Each historical phase of liberal development must be able to confront the important challenges that emerge in a given historical period. So far, liberal democracies have not at all been able to convincingly confront the post-Cold War challenges to continued liberal progress.

■ References

Blair, T. "A Battle for Global Values." *Foreign Affairs* 86, 1 (2007): 79-90.
Bush, G.W. Graduation speech at West Point, 2002. http://georgewbush-whitehouse.archives.gov/news/releases/2002/06/20020601-3.html.
Chang, H. *Kicking Away the Ladder: Development Strategy in Historical Perspective*. London: Anthem Press, 2002.
Clinton, H. "Chinese Human Rights Can't Interfere with Other Crises," 2009, http://edition.cnn.com/2009/POLITICS/02/21/clinton.china.asia/.
Dahl, R. *Polyarchy: Participation and Opposition*. New Haven: Yale University Press, 1971.
Fukuyama, F. "The End of History." *The National Interest* 6 (1989): 3-18.
Held, D. "Reframing Global Governance: Apocalypse Soon or Reform." In *Globalization Theory. Approaches and Controversies*, ed. D. Held and A. McGrew, 240-61. Cambridge: Polity Press, 2007.
Ignatieff, M. *Empire Lite: Nation-Building in Bosnia, Kosovo, and Afghanistan*. London: Vintage, 2003.
Ikenberry, G.J. "America's Imperial Ambition." *Foreign Affairs* 81, 5 (2002): 44-60.
Ikenberry, G.J. "Liberal Internationalism 3.0: America and the Dilemmas of Liberal World Order." *Perspectives on Politics* 7, 1 (2009): 23-37.
Johnson, T.H. and M.C. Mason. "Democracy in Afghanistan is Wishful Thinking," 2009, http://www.csmonitor.com/Commentary/Opinion/2009/0820/p09s01-coop.html.
Krauthammer, C. *Democratic Realism: An American Foreign Policy for a Unipolar World*. Washington, D.C.: AEI Press, 2004.
Kupchan, C.A. *No One's World. The West, the Rising Rest, and the Coming Global Turn*. Oxford: Oxford University Press, 2012.
Lampton, D.M. *The Three Faces of Chinese Power: Might, Money, and Minds*. Berkeley: University of California Press, 2008.
Lipset, S.M. "Some Social Requisites of Democracy: Economic Development and Political Legitimacy." *American Political Science Review* 53, 1 (1959): 69-105.
Logan, J. and C. Preble. "Failed States and Flawed Logic. The Case against a Standing Nation-Building Office." *Policy Analysis*, 560, CATO Institute, 2006.
Malone, A. "How China is Taking over Africa," 2008, http://www.dailymail.co.uk/news/article-1036105/How-Chinas-taking-Africa-West-VERY-worried.html.
McNeill, W.H. *The Rise of the West: A History of Human Community*. Chicago: University of Chicago Press, 1963.
NSS. "The National Security Strategy of the United States of America." Washington: The White House, Office of the President of the United States, 2002.
Nye, J.S. Jr. *Soft Power: The Means to Success in World Politics*. Washington: PublicAffairs, 2005.
O'Donnell, G. *Modernization and Bureaucratic-Authoritarianism: Studies in South American Politics*. Berkeley: University of California, Institute of International Studies, 1973.

Papagianni, K. "State Building and Transitional Politics in Iraq: The Perils of a Top-down Transition." *International Studies Perspectives* 8, 3 (2007): 253-71.

Perry, E. "Chinese Conception of 'Rights': From Mencius to Mao – and Now." *Perspectives on Politics* 6, 1 (2008): 37-50.

Pew Research Center, 2013, http://www.pewglobal.org/2013/03/13/what-chinese-are-worried-about/.

Putnam, R.D. "Bowling Alone: America's Declining Social Capital." *Journal of Democracy* 5, 1 (1995): 65-78.

Ross, R.S. and Z. Feng, eds. *China's Ascent: Power, Security, and the Future of International Politics*. Ithaca: Cornell University Press, 2008.

State Department, 2012, http://factsanddetails.com/china.php?itemid=297#300.

State Department, U.S., 2012, China. Country Report on Human Rights Practices, http://www.state.gov/documents/organization/204405.pdf.

Sørensen, G. *Democracy and Democratization. Processes and Prospects in a Changing World*, 3rd. ed. Boulder: Westview, 2008.

Sørensen, G. "'Big and Important Things' in IR: Structural Realism and the Neglect of Changes in Statehood." *International Relations* 23, 2 (2009): 223-39.

Sørensen, G. *A Liberal World Order in Crisis. Choosing Between Imposition and Restraint*, Ithaca: Cornell University Press, 2011.

Time Magazine. "Person of the Year," 2007, http://www.time.com/time/specials/2007/personoftheyear/0,28757,1690753,00.html

Time Magazine. "A Decade from Hell," 2009, http://www.time.com/time/covers/0,16641,20091207,00.html.

World Bank, 2012, http://www.worldbank.org/en/country/china/overview.

Zürn, M. "From Interdependence to Globalisation." In *Handbook of International Relations*, ed. W. Carlsnaes et al., 23-51. London: SAGE Publications, 2002.

9 Culture and Conflict in Global Perspective

Uwe Wagschal

Cultural conflicts have become of special interest for the public and in social sciences after Samuel Huntington's *Clash of Civilizations* was first published in 1993. Huntington was convinced that, after the collapse of the Soviet Union, culture would become the driving force behind future international tensions. He was particularly concerned with the conflict lines running between the Western and the Islamic world. Several prominent wars have been interpreted in line with his argument, including U.S. military action in Iraq and Afghanistan as well as the Israel-Palestine conflict. This article aims to analyze the empirical evidence of cultural conflicts, for example how often they occur, where they occur, and how they are interrelated to other conflict items. Furthermore, it raises the point that other factors, especially demographic factors, are more relevant to conflicts.

The understanding of culture varies among scientific disciplines. Ethnicity, religion, and historicity (tradition) are the main characteristics of culture as it concerns the definition of cultural conflicts (see also Croissant, Wagschal, Trinn, and Schwank 2009; 2010). Conflicts can also be defined in several ways. In conflict research there are several empirical approaches, including the Correlates of War project (COW, Singer and Small 1972; Small and Singer 1982; Sarkees 2000) and the Uppsala Conflict Data Project (UCDP, Wallensteen and Sollenberg 2001; Harbom and Wallensteen 2007) which both use the number of deaths in a specific conflict to assess intensity. The CONIS conflict database, which covers all forms of political conflict around the globe since 1945 and is not limited to individual regions or violent conflicts, uses a wider concept (5 levels), circumventing the problem of data validity. The first level ("*dispute*") denotes the articulation of opposing interests, with the second level ("*non-violent crisis*") representing the threat of violence. The third level ("*violent crisis*") denotes a selective, limited use of violence. On the fourth level ("*limited war*") violence is used in a planned manner without the goal of completely vanquishing the opposing side, but rather causing the opposition to capitulate instead. The fifth level ("*war*") is the systematic use of violence with the goal of defeating the opposing side and forcing it to submit to the victor's will (Schwank 2012). Section 2 shows the descriptive data for global and cultural conflicts.

In general, cultural conflicts are political conflicts in which culture serves as the conflict issue. In designating a conflict as "cultural", the focus is thus not on the causes of the conflict or the motives of the actors, but on the issues that the actors refer to over the course of the conflict through their statements or actions, and the meaning they assign to them. In a cultural conflict, cultural factors such as religious or "ethnic" differences are thus not necessarily the cause of the conflict.

Two different perspectives on culture conflicts are possible: (1) where culture is the dependent variable (see section 3). In this respect, cultural conflicts are defined as political conflicts in which culture is the main conflict issue, i.e. language or religion. This type of cultural conflict is measured by the issues to which the actors make reference through their statements and actions over the course of the conflict, and the way in which those statements and actions are conceived. Cultural factors such as religious or ethnic differences thus need not serve as the cause of the conflict. (2) cultural factors can also be independent or explanatory factors (see section 4). In this perspective, cultural factors have a direct influence on a conflict. Culture is therefore a possible causal factor of a conflict. In this respect, culture explains a conflict, i.e. it can be assumed that the cultural variables impact the probability that a conflict will take place. This is - more or less - the Huntington perspective.

Conflicts can also be classified in respect to their geographical extensions:

- Conflicts between non-state actors within a nation-state or between a nation-state and a non-state actor seen as belonging to it (*domestic conflicts*)
- Conflicts between nation-states (*interstate conflicts*)
- Conflicts between non-state actors of different national backgrounds or between a nation-state and non-state actors associated with another state (*transnational conflicts*).

Global and cultural conflicts

The global conflict picture (see figure 1) reveals a steady increase of conflicts which can partly be attributed to better measurement and media coverage in a globalized world. Especially low level conflicts are now detected more easily compared to the 1950s and 1960s. Figure 1 shows the development of medium (= level 3) and high intensity conflicts (= level 4 and 5) (HIIK 2009: 2), which displays an increase of the total conflicts over the past 62 years. However, high intensity wars remain rather stable and have even decreased, if one looks at the data on interstate conflicts. It is mainly intrastate conflicts which have grown over the past decades.

Figure 1: Global Conflicts (1945-2009)

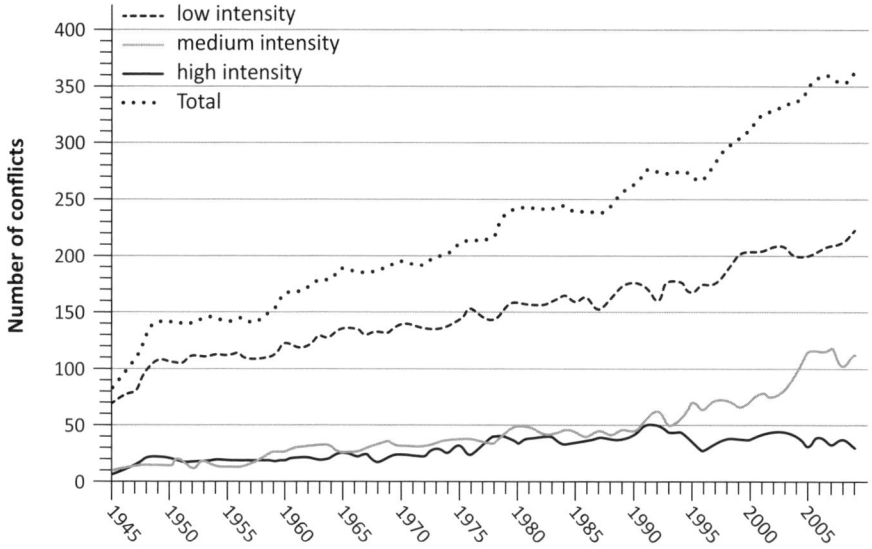

Note: Data from the CONIS Database (see hiik.de).

Cultural conflicts are a subgroup of these political conflicts. The central empirical question is: How does one measure whether a conflict is cultural? One is able to differentiate cultural clashes from other types of non-cultural conflict through conceptualizing cultural conflicts and understanding culture as a social phenomenon in light of the three factors of language, religion, and historicity. Cultural conflicts are measured by the verbal or active violation of religious, linguistic, and historical symbols. In addition to killings, the bodily harm of persons or destruction of objects is used as further indicators. For example, a religious conflict can be the controversial visit to a temple by a head of government or an attempt to assassinate a religious leader. A language conflict is the prohibition for a group to use its own language. A historical conflict can be identified through the celebration of historical defeats or battles (e.g. the Battle of Boyne in Northern Ireland). The scaling of the conflict is the same as the original CONIS-scale (1 to 5). The categorization of non-cultural and cultural conflicts is dichotomous, i.e., the question at hand is whether a cultural area was affected or not, resulting in the following possible conflict types (see table 1):

Table 1: Possible conflict types

Conflict Type	Religion	Language	Historicity	Examples
Non-cultural conflict	0	0	0	East Timor vs. Australia and resource conflicts
Religious conflict	1	0	0	Israel (Palestine)
Linguistic conflict	0	1	0	Belgium (Flemings vs. Walloons)
Historical conflict	0	0	1	United Kingdom (Scotland vs. England)
Religious-linguistic conflict	1	1	0	Sri Lanka (Tamils vs. Singhalese)

Note: All other combinations of religion, language, and historicity (0/1/1, 1/0/1 and 1/1/1) are coded either as religion or language conflict. The decisive criterion is the most relevant component vis-à-vis historicity.

In summary, a cultural conflict as a dependent variable is categorized on the basis of the three dimensions of religion, language, and historicity. Hybrid forms are possible, although they are assigned to either the main dimensions of religion or language, or the mixed religious-linguistic conflict group. It should be noted that this concept of cultural conflict differs from other definitions commonly used in this area of research. Usually "ethnic conflicts" are political conflicts between ethnic groups or conflicts which involve at least one such group. In that case, the actors are an ethnic conflict's defining characteristic.

Cultural conflicts, i.e. those conflicts in which culture is an issue, make up a considerable share of the conflicts taking place around the globe. Since the mid-1980s, the total number of cultural conflicts (i.e. the sum of all forms of cultural conflict around the globe) has surpassed the number of non-cultural conflicts. In 2007 (the latest year for which data is available), the number of cultural conflicts reached a historic high (see figure 2).

The descriptive overview shows that of the 762 political conflicts found in the CONIS database (between 1945 and 2007), a total of 334 or almost 44 percent can be classified as "cultural". When looking exclusively at the violent conflicts (levels 3 to 5), this share climbs to 50 percent (268 out of 534 conflicts). Figure 2 reveals that the number of cultural conflicts surpasses the number of non-cultural conflicts in 1986 and peaks in 2007, which is the end of our period of investigation. It is important to note that the data in figures 1 and 2 are collected on an annual basis, but that conflicts usually last several years. Conflicts which last more than one year are therefore included in each year's count.

Looking at the basic descriptive information on cultural conflicts, one can see that 81 percent of all cultural conflicts are intrastate. This figure rises to 86 percent when looking at particular violent conflicts. Another aspect is the distribution of the different conflict types in the groups of intrastate and interstate conflicts. Within the group of intrastate conflicts, 56.3 percent are cultural conflicts whereas

Figure 2: Number of non-violent and violent cultural and non-cultural conflicts over time (1945 to 2007)

Source: Data calculated by Croissant/Wagschal/Trinn/Schwank (2009) using the CONIS Database.

within the interstate conflicts only 22.2 percent are cultural. Both angles show a clear dominance of domestic cultural conflicts in contrast to international ones.

The 334 cultural conflicts can be divided into four categories:

- 49.4 percent of all cultural conflicts are historicity conflicts (n =165);
- 25.7 percent of all cultural conflicts are religious conflicts (n − 86);
- 13.2 percent of all cultural conflicts all are religious-linguistic conflict (n = 44);
- 11.7 percent of all cultural conflicts all are linguistic conflicts (n = 39).

Going into more detail, one observes that historicity conflicts are the most frequent sort of cultural conflict for both domestic (or intrastate) and interstate categories. However, for interstate conflicts – as noted above – cultural conflicts are not frequent, only historicity conflicts (12.9%) have a share of more than 5 percent. Linguistic conflicts, as seen in figure 3, have the lowest share in both subgroups.

Figure 3: Number of non-violent and violent cultural and non-cultural conflicts over time (1945 to 2007)

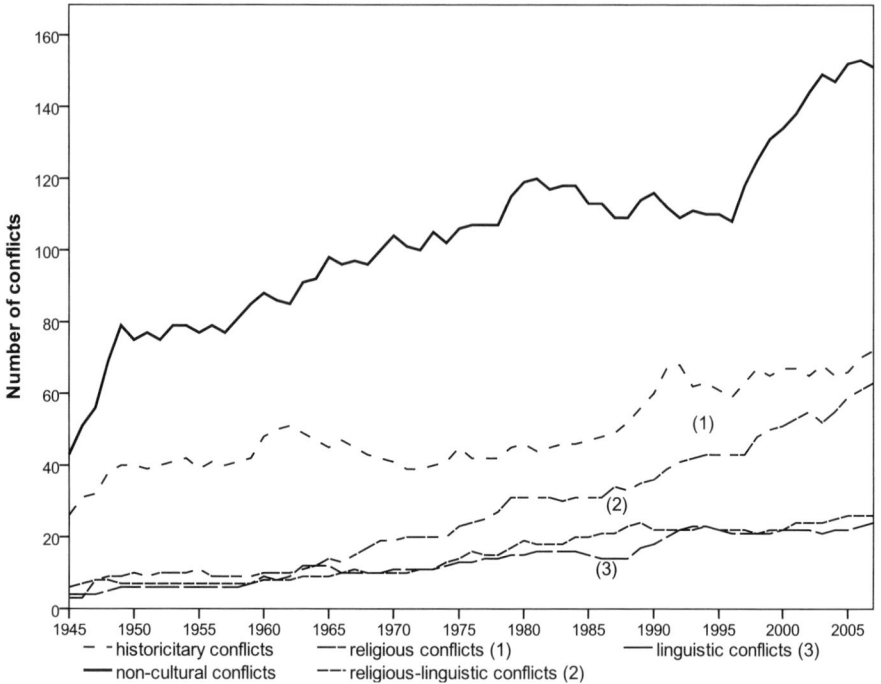

Source: Data calculated by Croissant/Wagschal/Trinn/Schwank (2009) using the CONIS Database.

It is clear that especially cultural conflicts have been brutal, cruel, and resulted in mass murder in the past centuries (see Heinsohn 1998; Goldhagen 2009). The genocide of the Jewish people in the Holocaust and other attempts to eliminate Jews over the past centuries are the most terrible examples. Genocides, defined as systematic destructions of an ethnic, racial, religious, or national group, result in huge losses of population. Since 1945, many other genocides have been observed, for example, the Rwanda genocide (where Hutus killed approximately 75 percent of the Tutsi minority), the Balkan genocide (where Serbs killed thousands of Muslims in Srebrenica), or the Armenian genocide (where Turks killed millions of Armenian people).

It is possible to identify a relationship between the level of conflict intensity (i.e., level of violence) and the type of conflict using the CONIS database. While non-cultural conflicts predominate at the lower intensity levels, cultural conflicts are most present in the categories of "limited war" and "war." It can also be seen (see figure 4) that the share of non-cultural conflicts declines progressively as the

Figure 4: Number of non-violent and violent cultural and non-cultural conflicts over time (1945 to 2007)

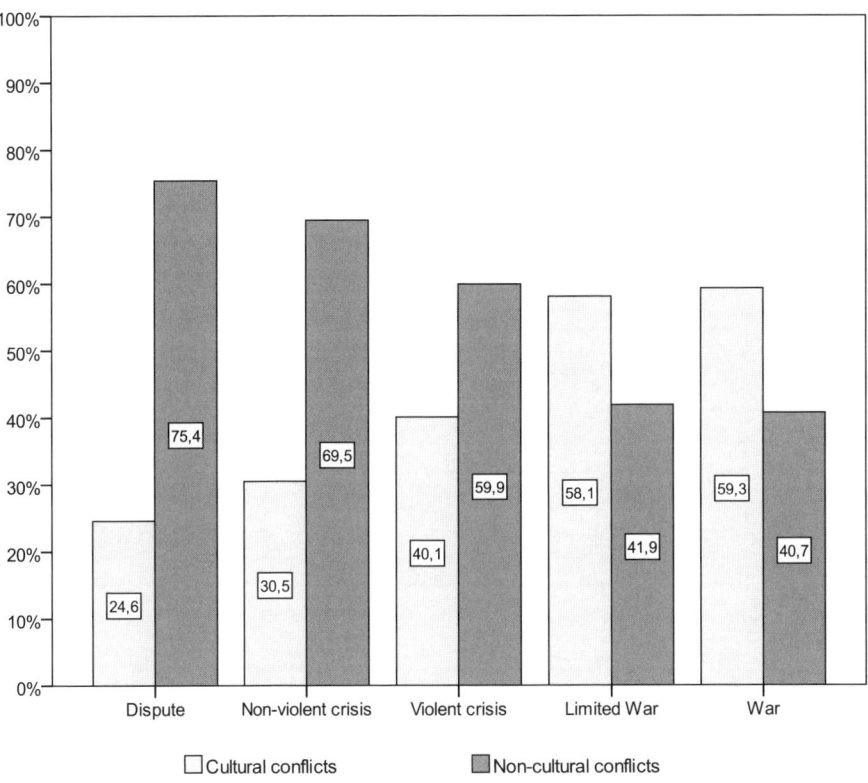

Source: Data calculated by Croissant/Wagschal/Trinn/Schwank (2009) using the CONIS Database.

level of intensity increases, while the share of cultural conflicts rises progressively. This holds true especially for interstate conflicts.

Cultural conflicts are generally intrastate (domestic) conflicts. Just by reading the newspaper one can see that some world regions are more affected than others. Asia has the largest number of intrastate conflicts with medium intensity. High intensity conflicts (i.e. wars and limited wars – see classification above) are also the most numerous in Asia, but are closely followed by Africa and the Middle East. Another perspective shows the distribution of each conflict type within world regions (see figure 5, only domestic conflicts). The distribution of the different conflict types across five global regions shows that non-cultural conflicts are predominant in the Americas. Cultural conflicts are of less importance in North and South America, only historicity conflicts reach a share of more than 10 percent. Furthermore, the Western hemisphere completely lacks religious-linguistic strife.

169

Figure 5: Share of conflict types (domestic) by region (1945 to 2007)

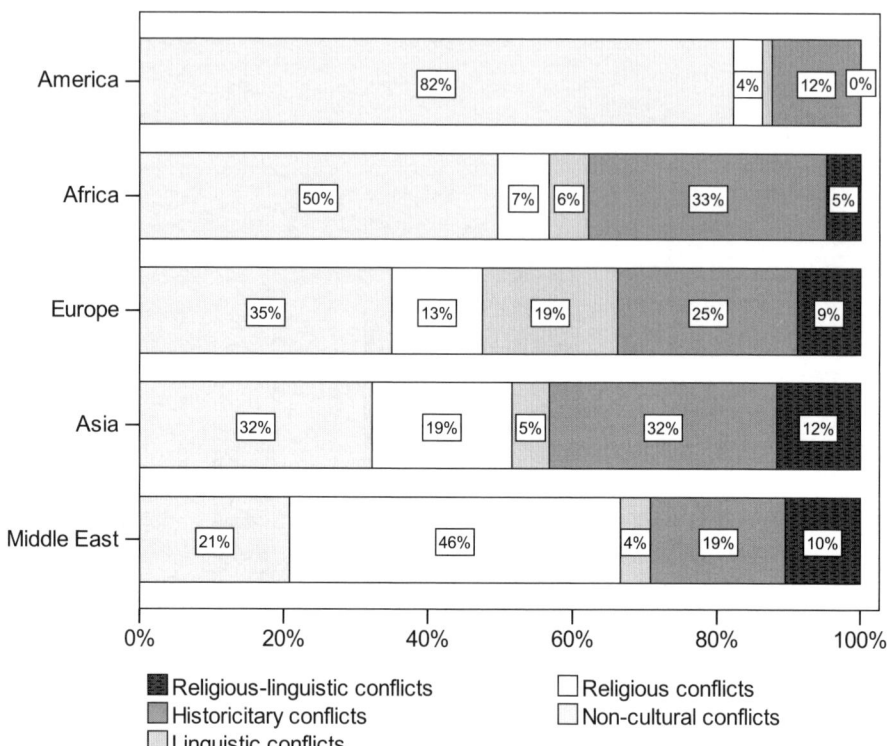

Source: Data calculated by Croissant/Wagschal/Trinn/Schwank (2009) and the CONIS Database.

Europe displays a rather "equal" distribution with medium to large shares of non-cultural and historicity conflicts. Notably, linguistic conflicts are relatively common in Europe: for comparison, Europe holds the highest share of all other regions (19 percent). Historicity conflicts, in turn, are typical of Asia and Africa. However, in Africa we also observe a high share of non-cultural conflicts (50 percent). In the Middle East, religious conflicts are by far the largest category. Together with the religious-linguistic conflicts they make up more than 56 percent of all conflicts in this region. Non-cultural conflicts (e.g. over resources) or historicity conflicts are less important, though both are around 20 percent. Language conflicts are of no importance in the Middle East.

In the interstate category (not graphically displayed) the spread of conflicts looks similar to the domestic category: the Americas are primarily home to non-cultural conflicts. Again, religious conflicts are typical of the Middle East, while linguistic conflicts predominate in Europe and historicity conflicts are common in both Europe and the Middle East. Religious-linguistic conflicts do not exhibit a dominant regional pattern. In terms of conflicts between states, it must be noted that the number of interstate conflicts, especially interstate cultural conflicts, is very small.

Causes of cultural conflicts

This section takes the analytical view on the determinants of cultural conflicts, i.e. when cultural conflicts are the dependent variable. In the next section (4) we turn to the "Huntington view", where we focus more on the impact of cultural factors in determining conflicts, i.e. when culture is the independent variable. The main objective of this section is to present the findings of multivariate analysis on the determinants of conflicts. Our research design for this chapter depends on two different perspectives, as mentioned in the introduction.

For the following analysis a longitudinal and cross-sectional design is used. Due to missing data for other variables, we cover the time period 1950-2005 for 197 countries, which creates 11032 cases for one variable over time and all countries. How can the consequences of political, socio-economic, and cultural factors within a country's conflict situation be empirically and theoretically modeled? The CONIS data provides an ordinal variable with six possible values for different intensities of conflict, starting with "0" for no conflicts. The characteristic of this variable therefore requires a different test method than the classic ordinary least squares method in regression analysis. The basic problem is the reduction of this prognosis variable across the value range of 0 to 5 and respectively in cases of dichotomous variables from 0 to 1. We can use different procedures within the general category of GLM (Generalized Linear Models) depending on whether we are dealing with a binary or categorical dependent variable and which assumptions we make with respect to the distribution of these values. These methods include LOGIT regression, PROBIT regression, and logistic regression, to name but the most important procedures (Backhaus et al. 2003; Andreß et al. 1997; Liao 1994; Greene 1993; Cohen et al. 2003).

A fundamental difference of OLS-Regression is the different interpretation of the regression coefficients, as these coefficients cannot be as directly and clearly interpreted in the logistic regression procedure as in a linear model. It is simplest to compute the results as odds (probability), which, however, necessitates a conversion of the coefficients of the regression output. In table 2, the corresponding conflict intensities have been encoded into a binary variable, in which the attribute values 3, 4, and 5 become 1 and the values 0, 1, and 2 become 0. Moreover, computations were carried out for three modes of conflict: (a) intrastate, (b) interstate, as well as (c) both intra- and interstate, which encompasses all conflicts. Due to the fact that intrastate conflicts are the most prominent and most frequent, only the findings for the domestic (intrastate) conflicts are presented.

These different levels of analysis are also theoretically important in that we expect different causalities. For domestic conflicts, our first hypothesis stipulates that a higher degree of cultural (linguistic and religious) fragmentation increases the likelihood that a country will experience domestic conflict. For interstate conflicts our hypothesis is different – we expect that a high degree of cultural (linguistic and religious) fragmentation will have no impact on the likelihood of an interstate conflict.

We assess the cultural heterogeneity of the various countries and compare them across national borders by using quantitative indicators to measure their linguistic and religious diversity. On the basis of Croissant et al. (2009) we use three indices of cultural fragmentation:

- An index of linguistic fragmentation, which measures a country's linguistic diversity
- An index of religious fragmentation, which measures a country's religious diversity
- An index of cultural fragmentation, calculated as a composite of the first two indices and representing the degree of cultural (i.e., linguistic-religious) fragmentation present in a given country

The linguistic fragmentation is based on the SIL Ethnologue dataset, which supplies a value for each country's linguistic heterogeneity based on Joseph Greenberg's diversity indices (Greenberg 1956). The Encyclopedia Britannica, in turn, serves as the source for creating the religious fragmentation index, calculated using also the Rae index. Each country's cultural fragmentation was then derived from the arithmetic mean of its linguistic and religious indices.

Clear regional differences are visible among countries in terms of their linguistic fragmentation. It becomes evident, for example, that countries located in the eastern Middle East, such as Oman, Iraq, Iran, and Afghanistan, and in Central Asia and South Asia, form a cultural zone which has a high degree of linguistic fragmentation. Similarly, sub-Saharan Africa is almost exclusively characterized by high levels of linguistic diversity.

In addition to the possible impact of cultural factors, the research literature offers a comprehensive range of explanatory variables which go beyond cultural structures and influences. It is not possible to assess here the derivation of all these variables or approaches. It must be noted instead that the current study's findings are based on a logistical regression model that contains a number of standard factors for explaining the probability of conflict. Additionally, cultural context simultaneously checks for countervailing causalities among these factors (cf. Croissant et al. 2009; Wagschal et al. 2010).

Table 2: Determinant factors for probability of intrastate cultural conflicts (1950 to 2005; binary logistical regression)

	(1) CONIS (3,4,5)	(2) CONIS (3,4,5)	(3) CONIS (3,4,5)
Constant	-9,533 (0,589)***	-10,128 (0,586)***	-10,243 (0,593)***
Population (log)	0,733 (0,038)***	0,812 (0,038)***	0,767 (0,038)***
Infant mortality (per 1000 births, UNWPP)	0,002 (0,001)	0,009 (0,001)***	0,005 (0,001)***
Cultivable land (hectare per person, WDI)	-0,289 (0,138)**	-0,182 (0,140)	-0,246 (0,133)*
Growth rate GDP/person, int. US$, PPP, const. prices (Penn World Tables)	-0,005 (0,007)	-0,008 (0,007)	-0,007 (0,007)
Export of commodities and trade (in percent of GDP, WDI)	0,008 (0,003)**	0,021 (0,003)***	0,014 (0,003)***
Degree of democracy (Polity IV: -10 to +10)	0,038 (0,008)***	0,042 (0,008)***	0,042 (0,008)***
Degree of democracy (Polity IV, squared)	-0,004 (0,002)**	-0,004 (0,002)***	-0,004 (0,002)**
Gross migration per 1000 inhabitants (positive value = immigration)	-0,010 (0,008)	0,001 (0,007)	-0,002 (0,008)
Youth Bulge: proportion of 15-24 year old men to men over 14 years old	0,006 (0,010)	0,012 (0,010)	0,019 (0,010)*
Index of language fractionalization	1,645 (0,171)***		
Index of religious fractionalization		-1,118 (0,225)***	
Index of cultural fractionalization			0,979 (0,229)***
Pseudo-R² according to Nagelkerke	0,265	0,245	0,243
Applicable cases (N)	4427	4421	4421

Notes: The method used is binary logistic regression, the dependent variable is a dichotomous compilation of conflict intensity (0 – low or no conflict; 1 – high conflict intensity). The numbers in parentheses next to the dependent variable give the aggregated conflict intensities of the CONIS Database. Displayed are the logistic regression coefficients (first value) as well as the standard deviation (in parentheses) with: * = significant on the 10% level, ** = significant on the 5% level, *** = significant on the 1% level (two-tailed hypothesis test).

The basic model in applying these "control variables" focuses on comparative studies taken from the research literature (Fearon and Laitin 2003; Collier and

Hoeffler 2004; Hegre and Sambanis 2006). The variables used account for a country's level of development and democratization as well as its social fragmentation, international economic interdependence, arable land mass, level of migration and migration flows, and economic growth. In other words, these explanatory factors are generally considered relevant in quantitative empirical conflict research (cf. Croissant et al. 2009). This standard model has been augmented by an additional variable that can be seen as a significant challenge to culture-driven hypotheses: the youth bulge (Huntington 1997; Heinsohn 2003; Urdal 2004, 2006). The youth bulge is measured as the number of males between the ages of 15 and 24 as a percentage of the overall male population over 15 years of age. This factor has become prominent in many recent cultural and political conflicts. The Arab revolutions in many countries such as Tunisia, Egypt, Syria, Libya, and Yemen among others seem to be strongly related to a large youth bulge. These young people without economic prospects are struggling for higher participation, less unemployment, and more political rights.

We have several different hypotheses as to the impact of the control variables on the intrastate cultural conflicts:

- Population size directly increases the probability of conflict.
- Infant mortality (used to gauge a country's underdevelopment) increases the likelihood of conflict, especially in the domestic context.
- Scarce resources, especially of cultivable land (i.e. arable land mass), increases the probability of conflicts.
- A high level of economic growth reduces the likelihood of conflict, especially in the domestic context.
- Countries that trade do not fight. Therefore we expect a lower conflict probability for those countries who are more involved in the world market.
- More developed democracies are less likely to experience conflict. However, we model a non-linear relationship (see Polity IV squared), as one can observe that autocracies can suppress conflicts in their countries. On the other hand, transition countries are particularly in danger of conflicts as incumbents and elites struggle to maintain their privileges. Moreover, different actors often try to take over power in such transition phases.
- Migration to other countries should reduce the likelihood of internal conflicts.
- The high percentage of young males between the ages of 15 and 24 compared to the overall male population over 15 (a large youth bulge) increases the probability of conflict.

The results of table 2 reveal that most variables have the hypothesized impact. However, the economic growth variable as well as the migration variable in all three models is insignificant. A large youth bulge is significant in only one equation. For cultural conflicts, the degree to which a country is integrated into the global economy has the wrong sign, i.e. the notion that "those who trade don't wage war" does not hold true.

The analysis of cultural conflicts at the domestic level shows that the probability of a cultural conflict taking place increases significantly with the degree of linguistic fragmentation. This result holds true no matter whether we use level 3, 4, or 5 of the CONIS data for the cultural conflicts (violent crises) or only level 4 or 5 intensities. In translating the results into probabilities, one finds that countries with a high degree of linguistic fragmentation have a conflict probability that is twice as high as countries with only moderate or low fragmentation. Such a relationship between fragmentation and conflict propensity is not evident in cases of religious diversity. In contrast, the higher the religious fragmentation the lower the likelihood of domestic wars and conflicts. The details (see below) reveal that the impact of religious fragmentation on cultural as well as non-cultural conflicts is at its highest in countries that exhibit a moderate level of religious fragmentation.

The second perspective is on cultural conflicts between states. Here the findings are only summarized in comparison to the domestic conflicts. Both linguistic and cultural fragmentation increases the likelihood of interstate conflicts while religious fragmentation reduces it. In other words, a higher degree of linguistic and cultural diversity brings a higher probability of interstate conflict. Religious fragmentation reduces this probability. In contrast to all conflicts, the combined index of cultural fragmentation proves highly significant for cultural conflicts, in that a higher level of combined linguistic-religious fragmentation leads to a higher propensity for conflict, regardless of whether all violent cultural conflicts are considered or only those with the highest intensity of violence.

The findings on the correlation between religious fragmentation and the occurrence of cultural and non-cultural conflict both between and within countries need clarification given that they run counter to the standard presumption that higher levels of religious diversity result in higher levels of conflict. This is expressed through popularized notions of Huntington's clash of civilizations as a "battle" between different religions. In addition to substantive explanations, i.e., those illuminating the causality between religious factors and conflicts, other more mundane reasons can also be suggested that have to do with data quality and the systematic skewing which results when data on religious structures are collected within a given society.

The quality and reliability of the statistics on the religious characteristics of the countries examined here are quite varied. While most industrialized countries have a range of detailed methods for collecting data, developing nations, which may or may not be venues for conflict in addition to their other challenges, often have only rudimentary estimates at their disposal. Given the ensuing inaccuracy, it is plausible that more religious groups are accounted for in the more well-off industrialized countries (which tend to experience less conflict) than in developing nations. The index could thus produce results which are too low for developing nations by showing a lower level of fragmentation than is actually the case. In addition, it is feasible that certain religious communities might not be accounted for in countries ruled by dictatorships (Alesina et al. 2003: 167).

The arguments above are predicated on the assumption that as a country's cultural fragmentation rises, so does the number of its cultural actors, reflecting the change in its cultural structures. As the number of actors increases, the probability of misunderstanding among actors also increases, something that would ostensibly lead to a greater risk of conflict. This assumption of linear causality between cultural fragmentation and the risk of conflict (the more fragmented a society, the greater the probability of conflict) is, however, not necessarily plausible. While growing diversity does imply a greater number of actors, it is possible this would not result in an increased risk of conflict, as diversity for example may also promote tolerance between different groups. The prevailing assumption must therefore be further examined to see, for example, whether the connection between religious, linguistic, and cultural fragmentation and the probability of conflict might in fact be non-linear.

The Causes of all conflicts

The findings of this chapter refer to all violent conflicts and do not distinguish between cultural and non-cultural political conflicts, meaning a broader concept of conflicts is employed. The results for all domestic conflicts (see table 3) are similar to those for domestic cultural conflicts. Table 3 shows that most of the control variables are highly significant. Globalization is an exception: the degree to which a country is integrated into the global economy (i.e. exports), is irrelevant for all types of conflicts examined here. Large countries (i.e. with high population) have more conflicts than small countries. Migration is once again not a significant control variable. The main difference is the relevance of the highly significant youth bulge factor (see below). Additionally, the findings for migration flows are dichotomous: In the case of domestic conflicts (both for cultural conflicts in particular and all conflicts in general), immigrant influx diminishes the likelihood of conflict, whereas influx in an interstate context increases the probability of conflict. In order to correctly interpret the signs in table 3, a positive sign means an increasing effect of the respective variable, while a negative sign shows dampening effects. High economic growth, arable land, and the degree of democracy are such variables.

Table 3: Determinant factors for probability of intrastate conflict 1950 to 2005 (all conflicts; binary logistic regression)

	(1) CONIS (3,4,5)	(2) CONIS (3,4,5)	(3) CONIS (3,4,5)
Constants	-7,909 (0,511)***	-8,066 (0,514)***	-8,326 (0,515)***
Population (log)	0,577 (0,032)***	0,628 (0,033)***	0,610 (0,033)***
Infant mortality (per 1000 births, UNWPP)	0,001 (0,001)	0,004 (0,001)***	0,003 (0,001)***
Cultivable land (hectare per person, WDI)	-0,629 (0,141)***	-0,576 (0,148)***	-0,584 (0,141)***
Growth rate GDP/person, int. US$, PPP, const. prices (Penn World Tables)	-0,015 (0,006)**	-0,016 (0,006)***	-0,017 (0,006)***
Export of commodities and trade (percent of GDP, WDI)	-0,003 (0,003)	0,004 (0,003)	0,002 (0,003)
Degree of democracy (Polity IV: -10 to +10)	0,050 (0,007)***	0,052 (0,007)***	0,052 (0,007)***
Degree of democracy (Polity IV, squared)	-0,008 (0,001)***	-0,008 (0,001)***	-0,007 (0,001)***
Gross migration per 1000 inhabitants (positive values = immigration)	-0,014 (0,006)**	-0,012 (0,006)*	-0,010 (0,006)
Youth Bulge: proportion of 15-24 year old men to men over 14 years old	0,060 (0,008)***	0,057 (0,009)***	0,063 (0,009)***
Index of language fractionalization	0,500 (0,137)***		
Index of religious fractionalization		-1,453 (0,195)***	
Index of cultural fractionalization			-0,249 (0,192)
Pseudo-R² according to Nagelkerke	0,242	0,256	0,241
Applicable cases (N)	4427	4421	4421

Notes: see table 2.

Demographic variables, particularly male youth bulge, have been long neglected in attempts to better understand wars and conflicts. The results in table 3 clearly show an important impact. The fundamental premise of the youth bulge (Heinsohn 2003; Urdal 2006) thesis concerns the unbalanced age composition, and therefore the form rather than the size of a population pyramid. The assumption is that the relatively high proportion of young men, a group especially fixed on the acquisition of societal status, considerably codetermines the risk of conflict.

Surprisingly religious fragmentation seems to dampen the risk of conflict. However, this finding is only one part of the story, since high religious fragmentation means many religious groups balancing each other. Further examination of countries with moderate religious fragmentation brings greater clarity to the findings. According to these findings, such countries are more often affected by conflict than those with lower or higher levels of religious diversity. Initial assumptions about religion are thus cast in a new light: Increasing religious diversity is not the core problem facing fragmented societies; rather, when a limited number of religious groups of roughly equivalent size is present, the probability of conflict rises, for all conflicts in general and for cultural conflicts in particular.

The findings for the impact of cultural factors on all conflicts – as well as for domestic and intrastate conflicts – are summarized in table 4. We start with the hypothesis that cultural factors (i.e., religious or linguistic) lead to a greater propensity for conflict. For illustrative purposes, shaded areas and symbols are used to depict the level of causality. A plus sign (+) denotes a statistically positive association and a minus sign (-) signals a statistically negative association, with a "0" representing an insignificant association.

White is used to show the cases where no correlation was found. Light gray is used to show the cases where higher levels of cultural fragmentation correlate significantly to a higher probability of conflict. Dark gray shows the cases with negative correlation, where a high level of religious-linguistic or cultural fragmentation correlates to a low probability of conflict. The dark gray fields represent instances that run counter to the presumed correlation.

The findings for all (cultural and non-cultural) domestic conflicts in columns I and II of table 4 provide a differentiated picture of how cultural factors impact conflict. First, linguistic fragmentation seems to have the expected effect in that a country's frequency of violence rises along with its degree of linguistic fragmentation. Second, counter to expectation, the index of religious fragmentation does not positively correlate to the level of conflict (cf. Croissant et al. 2009), as the more religiously fragmented a country is, the lower the probability of conflict in domestic contexts. Third and finally, the combined index of cultural fragmentation shows no correlation with domestic conflict. Evidently the countervailing impacts of religious and linguistic fragmentation negate each other.

An examination of how cultural factors impact interstate conflicts (columns III and IV) shows that language and culture, in the form of the aggregate index, have a significant effect, as does religion, at least to some extent. This means that greater linguistic heterogeneity and cultural diversity increase a country's prospect of entering into violent conflict (cultural *and* non-cultural) with another nation-state. In terms of religious fragmentation, this same propensity for conflict is found when conflicts of all levels of intensity are considered. When comparing the indices' regression coefficients (not shown here), it becomes apparent that cultural fragmentation in its various guises plays a lesser role in interstate conflicts than

Table 4: How cultural variables impact domestic and interstate conflicts (1950-2005)

	All Conflicts			
	Domestic Conflicts		Interstate Conflicts	
	(I) CONIS (3, 4, 5)*	(II) CONIS (4, 5)**	(III) CONIS (3, 4, 5)*	(IV) CONIS (4, 5)**
Language	+	+	+	+
Religion	–	–	+	0
Culture (aggregate)	0	0	+	+

Note: + = positive coefficient at 5% significance level; 0 = not significant; – = negative coefficient at 5% significance level. Based on the empirical findings in Croissant et al. (2009: 161 ff.). White signifies a lack of correlation, light gray signifies confirmation of the expected correlation, and dark gray signifies findings that run counter to the expected correlation. * = dichotomous dependent variable: CONIS conflict intensity at levels 1 and 2 =0, levels 3, 4 and 5 = 1; ** = dichotomous dependent variable: CONIS conflict intensity at levels 1, 2 and 3 = 0, levels 4 and 5 =1. For both analyses of the probability of domestic conflict, CONIS levels 3, 4 and 5 and CONIS levels 4 and 5 are assigned a value of "1", respectively.

in domestic conflicts. This is probably due to a number of reasons, including the fact that conflict issues between states are usually different from those within any given country. In general, the approach used here has considerably greater power to explain domestic conflicts than interstate conflicts.

Conclusions

The main descriptive findings include the following: Cultural conflicts make up a high and increasingly large share of all conflicts. Furthermore, cultural conflicts are mainly domestic (intrastate) conflicts and not interstate conflicts. The majority of cultural conflicts are historicity and religious conflicts, and cultural conflicts are particularly violent. Finally, there are major differences between regions, e.g. religious conflicts are predominant in the Middle East, while historicity conflicts occur mainly in Africa and Asia. Linguistic conflicts are most prevalent in Europe, and in the Americas there are few cultural conflicts. There, non cultural conflicts are more important.

Looking at the cultural dimensions of global conflicts from 1950 to 2005, our analysis of "cultural conflicts" has two perspectives. First, they are examined as a "dependent" variable, that is, as a phenomenon to be explained. Second, cultural factors are investigated as causal agents (as "independent" variables). Cultural conflicts are thus defined as political conflicts that focus on language, religious, or historical contexts. In cultural conflicts, culture is not necessarily the cause of a conflict, but the issue around which it revolves.

The quantitative analysis revealed that the probability of domestic cultural conflict and of all types of intrastate conflict increases the higher a country's cultural and, in particular, linguistic fragmentation is. If one looks at the relevance of cause of conflict, language plays a key role and is more significant than religious fragmentation in that the degree of linguistic fragmentation more readily increases the probability of conflicts both within and between states.

It can also be seen that, in addition to cultural variables, several other factors influence the likelihood of conflict taking place. Cultural variables cannot therefore be seen as "master variables," since conflicts are also more likely to coincide with a country's larger population, the higher the share of young men it is home to, the less arable land it has at its disposal, and the lower its economic growth. In contrast to the assumption that a direct causality exists between religious fragmentation and the likelihood of conflict, a much more compelling explanation for domestic conflict is the interaction of moderate levels of religious fragmentation with demographic factors such as a youth bulge (i.e., a large number of young males as a percentage of the overall population).

Overall, cultural structures are significant factors in explaining conflicts. A more telling factor, however, is a non-cultural phenomenon: the youth bulge. This factor becomes even more relevant when it interacts with cultural factors. Ultimately, evidence exists to suggest a non-linear relationship between cultural factors and conflicts. Countries with a low or moderate level of linguistic and religious fragmentation exhibit a higher probability of conflict, which in turn is reinforced by the presence of a greater share of young men within the general population.

■ References

Alesina, A., A. Devleeschauwer, W. Easterly, S. Kurlat, and R. Wacziarg. "Fractionalization." *Journal of Economic Growth* 8, 2 (2003): 155-94.

Andreß, H.J., J.A. Hagenaars, and S. Kühnel. *Analyse von Tabellen und kategorialen Daten*. Berlin: Springer, 1997.

Backhaus, K., J. Büschken, and M. Voeth. *Internationales Marketing*. Stuttgart: Schäffer-Poeschel, 2003.

Cohen, J., P. Cohen, S.G. West, and L.S. Aiken. *Applied Multiple Regression/correlation Analysis for the Behavioral Sciences*. Mahwah, NJ: Lawrence Erlbaum Associates, 2003.

Collier, P. and A. Hoeffler. "Greed and Grievance in Civil War." *Oxford Economic Papers* 56, 4 (2004): 563-96.

Croissant, A., U. Wagschal, N. Schwank, and C. Trinn. *Culture and Conflict in Global Perspective. The Cultural Dimensions of Conflicts from 1945 to 2007*. Gütersloh: Verlag Bertelsmann Stiftung, 2009.

Eller, C. and P. Nawrotzki. "Dynamische Stabilitätsanalyse eines Dreigelenkstabwerks unter Verwendung numerischer Nachweiskonzepte." *ZAMM – Journal of Applied Mathematics and Mechanics* 78 (1998): 483-93.

Encyclopaedia Britannica. Britannica Book of the Year. Chicago: Encyclopedia Britannica, Inc., 2007.

Fearon, J. and D. Laitin. "Ethnicity, Insurgency, and Civil War." *American Political Science Review* 97, 1 (2003): 75-90.

Freud, S. *Group Psychology and Analysis of the Ego*. Leipzig/Vienna/Zürich: Internationaler Psychoanalytischer Verlag, 1921.

Freud, S. *Civilization and Its Discontents*. Leipzig/Vienna/Zurich: Internationaler Psychoanalytischer Verlag, 1930.

Fukuyama, F. *The End of History and the Last Man*. New York: Free Press, 1992.

Goldhagen, D.J. *Worse Than War: Genocide, Eliminationism, and the Ongoing Assault on Humanity*. New York: Public Affairs, 2009.

Greenberg, J., "The Measurement of Linguistic Diversity." *Language* 32 (1956): 109-15.

Greene, W. *Econometric Analysis*. New York: Macmillan, 1993.

Hansen, K. *Kultur und Kulturwissenschaft. Eine Einführung*. Basel: Uni-Taschenbücher, 2003.

Harbom, L. and P. Wallensteen. "Armed Conflict, 1989-2006." *Journal of Peace Research* 44, 5 (2007), 621-32.

Hegre, H. and N. Sambanis. "Sensitivity Analysis of Empirical Results on Civil War Onset." *Journal of Conflict Resolution* 50, 4 (2006): 508-35.

Heinsohn, G. *Lexikon der Völkermorde*. Reinbek: Rowohlt. 1998.

Heinsohn, G. *Söhne und Weltmacht. Terror im Aufstieg und Fall der Nationen*. Zurich: Orell Füssli, 2003.

HIIK. "Conflict Barometer, 2009." Heidelberg Institute for International Conflict Research: 2, http://www.hiik.de/en/konfliktbarometer/pdf/ConflictBarometer_2009.pdf.

Huntington, S. "The Clash of Civilizations." *Foreign Affairs* 72, 3 (1993): 22-50.

Huntington, S. *Kampf der Kulturen. Die Neugestaltung der Weltpolitik im 21. Jahrhundert*. Munich: Europaverlag, 1997.

Liao, T. *Interpreting Probability Models: Logit, Probit, and Other Generalized Linear Models*. Thousand Oaks: SAGE Publications, 1994.

Luhmann, N. *Soziale Systeme: Grundriß einer allgemeinen Theorie*. Frankfurt: Suhrkamp, 1984.

Münch, R. and N. Smelser. *Theory of Culture*. Berkeley: University of California Press, 1992.

Sarkees, M. "The Correlates of War Data on War: An Update to 1997." *Conflict Management and Peace Science* 18, 1 (2000): 123-44.

Schwank, N. *Konflikte, Krisen, Kriege: Die Entwicklungsdynamiken politischer Konflikte seit 1945*. Baden-Baden: Nomos, 2012.

Singer, J. D. and M. Small. *The Wages of War, 1816-1965: A Statistical Handbook*. New York: John Wiley, 1972.

Small, M. and J.D. Singer. *Resort to Arms: International and Civil Wars, 1816-1980*. Beverly Hills: SAGE Publications, 1982.

Tajfel, H. and J. Turner. "An Integrative Theory of Intergroup Conflict." In *The Social Psychology of Intergroup Relations*, ed. W. Austin and S. Worchel, 94-109. Monterey: Brooks-Cole, 1979.

Tajfel, H. and J.C. Turner. "The Social Identity Theory of Intergroup Behavior." In *Psychology of Intergroup Relations*, ed. S. Worchel and W.G. Austin, 7-24. Chicago: Nelson-Hall, 1986.

Urdal, H. "The Devil in the Demographics. The Effect of Youth Bulges on Domestic Armed Conflict, 1950-2000." The World Bank, Social Development Working Paper 14 2004.

Urdal, H. "A Clash of Generations? Youth Bulges and Political Violence." *International Studies Quarterly* 50, 3 (2006): 607-629.

Wagschal, U., A. Croissant, T. Metz, C. Trinn, and N. Schwank. "Kulturkonflikte in inner- und zwischenstaatlicher Perspektive." *Zeitschrift für Internationale Beziehungen* 17, 1 (2010): 5-37.

Wallensteen, P. and M. Sollenberg. "Armed Conflict, 1989-2000." *Journal of Peace Research* 38, 5 (2001): 629-44.

10 The Impact of Human Security on Social Trust and Tolerance

Pippa Norris and Ronald Inglehart

Social scientists have long viewed social trust and tolerance as important in solving problems of societal cooperation, to strengthen governance, and to make markets work. An extensive body of research has demonstrated the importance of these phenomena. Hence Fukuyama (1997) argues that social trust is essential to prosperity, through sustaining open market, commerce, and trade relationships. Putnam (2000) has emphasized the links between social capital in American states and the provision of collective goods such as education, health, and happiness. Ever since *The Civic Culture*, many theorists have regarded trust as a basis for stable democracy (Almond and Verba 1963). In general, people who see others as trustworthy are thought more willing to work together and thereby achieve collective solutions to achieve common goals. Co-operation can be achieved through alternative mechanisms, notably the carrot of individualized incentives and the stick of legal regulations and penalties. But collaboration is regarded as less efficient without the lubricant of generalized trust. At individual and societal level, a host of things which are normatively desirable appear to be connected with social trust (Rothstein and Uslaner 2005).

Despite widespread recognition of the value of social trust and tolerance, however, no broad consensus exists concerning the conditions most conducive to strengthening them. Debate continues between several schools of thought: those that focus on the social-psychological characteristics of individuals, such as the experience of participating actively in community associations, and the role of education and the mass media; and those that concentrate on the risky environment facing individuals, communities, and states. The first part of this study examines this debate in the literature and proposes an explanation based on existential security, hypothesizing that feelings of *subjective* security (as measured by a new battery of items in the World Values Survey) are even more conducive to social trust than is associational membership, educational level, religiosity, or exposure to television or the Internet.

This implies that vulnerable populations with a low sense of security – ironically, the groups most in need of cooperative solutions to improve their lives – are least likely to trust other people. Part II describes how these propositions are tested in a wide range of societies by using the World Values Survey. Our earlier preliminary analysis examined some of these ideas, but data analysis was limited to only seven societies (Norris and Inglehart 2012). In this study, however, the range of countries is expanded to three dozen diverse societies worldwide, involving interviews with 50,551 respondents, increasing confidence in the robustness of the generalizations. Data is derived from a new battery of items monitoring human security, included in the 6th wave of the World Values Survey 2011-2013. Factor analysis demonstrates that people distinguish three dimensions of human security, at national, community, and personal levels. Models are run for alternative objects of particularized and generalized trust. Part III presents the results of the analysis of the predicted relationships. Models control for several social psychological factors associated with trust, including education, media use, and associational activism. The conclusion in Part IV summarises the core findings and considers their broader implications.

I: Theories of social trust

Human security strengthens social trust and tolerance

We argue that a sense of vulnerability to existential threats undermines social trust and tolerance. This vulnerability can arise from a wide range of causes: disease, poverty and hunger, environmental degradation, climate change and natural disasters, exposure to drug dealers and crime, failing states, terrorism, and armed conflict. When people perceive threats to their survival and well-being, it is rational to be cautious about trusting strangers. Indeed to behave otherwise would be irrational, by leading the gullible and credulous into danger. Living near the subsistence level, one's margin for survival is narrow and even one mistake can be fatal. By contrast, trust and tolerance are more likely to flourish in relatively safe environments, such as those of prosperous professional middle class families living in smaller European cradle-to-grave welfare states, with effective states, low crime rates, and little active armed engagement in international conflict.

To understand threats to well-being, security scholars, backed by international organizations and a growing number of national governments, have developed the concept of Human Security. This focuses on the welfare of ordinary people facing a broad range of dangers, including national defence against external military threats but extending well beyond it. Human Security recognizes the complex links between "freedom from fear" and "freedom from want", anticipated decades earlier in Franklin D. Roosevelt's 1941 State of the Union speech. Thus feelings of vulnerability to risk and threat are expected to be stronger among those experiencing poverty, major wars or natural disasters, growing up in risky neighbourhoods, and among the more susceptible sectors of the population, such as the elderly, the poor, women, and those with lower levels of skills and education. Security perceptions are also shaped by the social safety nets provided by the family, community, and welfare state, which can mitigate risks; and by the dangers depicted in mass communications (the "mean world" effect). In turn, security perceptions are predicted to shape a wide range of cultural values, including feelings of social trust and tolerance.

Figure 1: Heuristic Model of Human Security

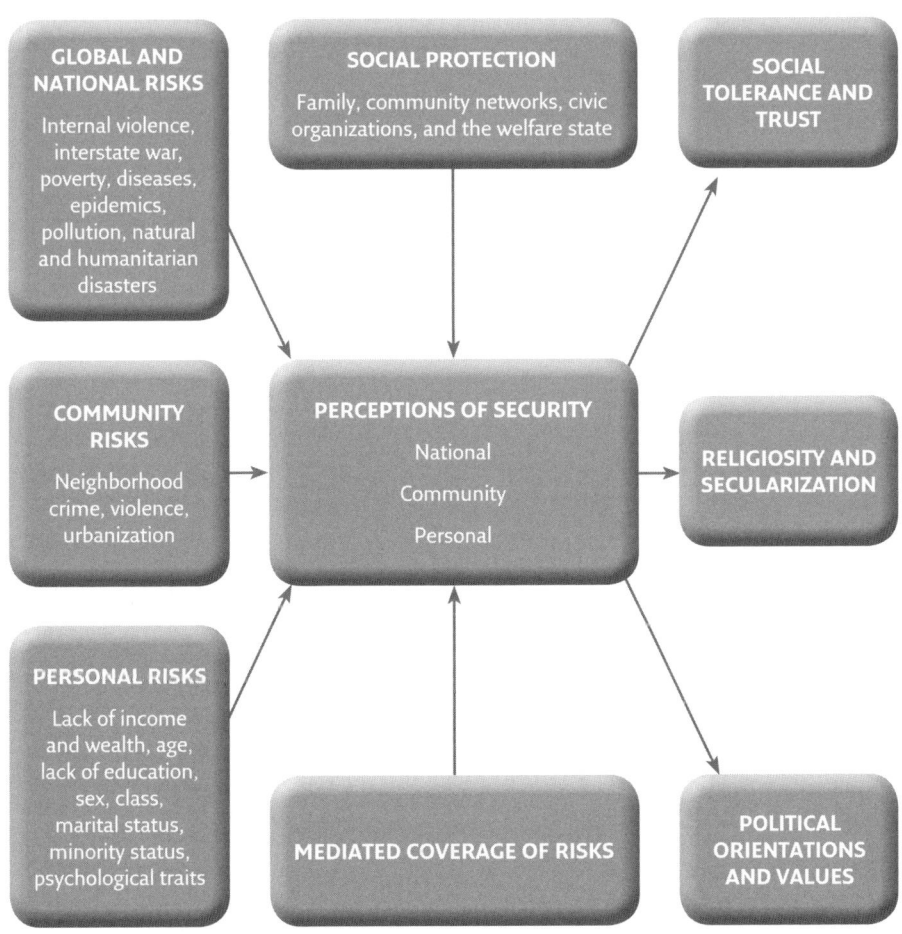

The heuristic model presented in figure 1 can be used to understand how perceptions of Human Security shape feelings of social trust. The core components are only sketched here although the logic can be briefly described. Our theory predicts that perceptions of Human Security will reflect experience with 'objective' structural conditions, at global and national (macro), community (meso), and personal (micro) levels. Thus perceptions of insecurity will be stronger among those living through major wars or natural disasters, growing up in risky neighbourhoods, and among the more vulnerable sectors of the population, such as the elderly, the poor, women, and the less educated. Over the years many studies have found that threat perceptions are strongly related to levels of political tolerance (Sullivan et al 1982, 1985; Gibson 1987; Marcus et al. 1995; Sullivan and Transue 1999). The exact weight and influence of personal, community, and national threats remain to be determined, however, for example which of these risk perceptions have the strongest impact on tolerance of minorities or other outgroups.

It should also be noted that the risk of insecurity can be expected to rise in societies with marked economic inequality and poor equality of opportunities – the explanation of generalized trust which is advocated by Rothstein and Uslaner (2005), among others. Nevertheless, Human Security cannot be reduced simply to economic or social inequality. Today, affluent societies such as the United States and Japan have grown increasingly immune to life-threatening risks due to starvation, contagious diseases, and armed violence. Emerging economies such as Brazil and Russia have raised their national GDP. But a country's wealth is not a guarantee of feelings of insecurity; even the richest societies are not safe from natural and manmade disasters. Risks cut across social cleavages; disasters such as cyclones, floods, tsunami, and hurricanes decimate coastal populations in poorer developing cities in Bangladesh and Thailand – but even relatively-affluent populations living in Fukushima and the Jersey Shore are not immune.

What do we know about public perceptions of human security? Drawing upon the public health literature, a large body of research has studied the relationship between objective indices of risks and subjective assessments of threats. Security perceptions seem to be conditioned by the social safety nets provided by the family, community, and the welfare state, which can mitigate risks. Informal networks function as the first form of support, mitigating care of the elderly or children, and coping with natural disasters. Philanthropic and religious organizations, trade unions, and other cooperative associations and local networks can also provide help in time of need. Security perceptions are also expected to be affected by the depiction of threats and dangers conveyed in mass communications (the "mean world" effect). In turn, security perceptions are predicted to shape a wide range of cultural values, including feelings of social trust and tolerance. In a risky world, it is rational to be wary of strangers.

Psychological accounts

The theory of human security can be tested from new survey data, controlling for a range of factors considered to be important in several alternative accounts. An extensive literature has long speculated about the roots of social trust. Early psychological theorists treated trust and institutional confidence (or distrust and lack of confidence) as basic aspects of personality types. According to Erikson (1950), feelings of inner goodness, trust in others and oneself, and optimism form a "basic trust" personality trait that is formed in the first stages of psychological development as a result of the mother-baby feeding experience. Core personality traits, it is argued, are enduring and general, influencing many aspects of behaviour (see Allport 1961; Cattell 1965). Similarly, the seminal work of social psychologist Morris Rosenberg (1956; 1957) argues that alienation, trust in people, and beliefs that people are fundamentally cooperative and inclined to help others combine to form a single "trust in people" scale. Because of their psychological history and make-up, some individuals have an optimistic view of life and are willing to help others, cooperate, and trust. Because of their own early life experiences, others are more pessimistic and misanthropic. They are thus inclined to be guarded or alienated, more distrustful and cautious of others, and pessimistic about social and political affairs and about people and politicians in general. In other words, there are trusters and there are cynics who carry their political perceptions around with them without much reference to their adult life experiences. In this regard, trust is an affective orientation that forms part of our basic personality and it is largely independent of our adult experience of the external political world.

More recent revisions of this view by social psychological theorists hold that the ability to trust others and sustain cooperative relations is the product of early socialization *and* adult social experiences, rather than due to inherent personality types. Social capital theories emphasize that social trust is closely related to the experiences acquired from active engagement in the sorts of voluntary associations of modern society that bring different social types together to achieve common goals. The theory goes back to Alexis de Tocqueville and John Stuart Mill, both of whom emphasized the importance of voluntary associations and social engagement as training grounds for democracy. Many contemporary writers pursue the same theme, discussing society's ability to inculcate "habits of the heart" such as trust, reciprocity, and co-operation (Bellah et al. 1985), emphasizing the importance of civil society in generating cooperative social relations (Coleman 1990; Inglehart and Abramson 1994; Sztompka 1996).

The social capital model argues that individual life situations and experiences – especially participation in a community with a cooperative culture, and involvement in voluntary activities (Geertz 1962; Ardener 1964; Williams 1988; Putnam 2000) – create social trust and cooperation, civic-mindedness, and reciprocity between individuals. This in turn helps create strong, effective, and successful social organizations and institutions, including political groups and governmental institutions in which people can invest their confidence. Such organizations and institutions, in turn, help build trust, cooperation, and reciprocity among citizens. In short, this school argues that there is a direct and mutually reinforcing relationship between the types of people who express trust in other people, on the one hand, and engagement in social organizations and institutions, on the other. Nevertheless this claim remains contentious and it has not stood up well to systematic cross-national empirical tests (Delhey and Newton 2003).

Moreover, it has also been argued that exposure to television entertainment is the primary culprit for a generational decline in social capital in America (Putnam 2000), with the privatization of leisure thought to erode older forms of engagement in the public space. The Internet is regarded by Putnam (2000) more cautiously as a potential creative and destructive force for social connections, both simultaneously widening potential networks whilst also probably attenuating many linkages. The subsequent literature has generated many studies which have sought to determine the impact of social media and experience of the Internet on social trust, but the results remain mixed and indeterminate.

Finally, the role of education, especially the cognitive reasoning skills acquired through higher education, has often been seen as particularly important to social trust and tolerance (Doring 1992). Numerous empirical studies over the years have demonstrated that schooling is consistently one of the strongest predictors of these values. But the reasons for this phenomenon remain unclear. Does the correlation between education, on one hand, and trust and tolerance on the other hand, reflect higher levels of cognitive skills – or does it simply reflect the fact that more educated people tend to be economically and socially more secure?

If social psychological accounts are true, then we would expect to find that people who express attitudes of generalized trust toward others are likely to be highly educated and also well integrated into voluntary associations and other forms of cooperative social activity. Heavy television watching is predicted to depress social trust, while similar hours spent online is regarded more agnostically. These factors will be included in models as controls when analyzing the survey data.

II: Measures and evidence

Although it seems plausible to predict that trust of other people may be rooted in basic feelings of human security, to date little empirical work has sought to measure subjective perceptions of Human Security among ordinary people, to compare these perceptions among and within diverse societies worldwide, and to identify the core drivers of this phenomenon, still less to analyse the consequences for cultural values.

Measuring perceptions of Human Security

In the previous literature, Human Security has been measured at the national level. The most ambitious attempts to create a composite Human Security Index have sought to compare national-level inequalities worldwide based on internationally-standardized official statistics (Hastings 2011). Werthes, Heaven and Vollnhals (2011) constructed a measures with threshold estimates (to gauge the severity of threats) using indices in each society, such as poverty (GDP per capita), food (the proportion of under-nourishment), health (child mortality rates), environment (access to water), personal security (the political terror scale), and political security (press freedom).

This approach is useful but it is also limited, since mean and median scores can disguise substantial disparities within societies, and the existence of marked inequalities in security among vulnerable populations. There are no clear principles to select and weigh neither the component parts nor the appropriate threshold. The measures are therefore constructed on an *ad hoc* basis, selecting variables arbitrarily, often based on data availability, without monitoring to what extent they actually impact on a given people's sense of risks and threats. It also remains unclear what value the composite measures add for public policymakers. Saying that a country such as Somalia or Haiti ranks low in overall Human Security (which seems intuitively obvious) tells us nothing about whether donor aid should be spent strategically on, say, training the police force, funding water wells, or supporting clinics. The macro-level composite measures are also conceptually flawed, since they reflect a state-centric perspective. It is well-known that micro-level perceptions of risk, for example evaluations of the personal risks of cancer or strokes, may also differ substantially from objective indices and probability estimates for the general population.

To develop more specific and policy-relevant insights, measures of Human Security ideally need to be analysed at the individual level. The measure used in this study therefore compares *how ordinary people perceive risks*. This strategy allows the analysts to then re-aggregate the data, for example to monitor how far perceptions of Human Security vary among women and men, rich and poor households, those living in the rural periphery and those in the urban center, different ethno-religious or ethno-linguistic communities, and to measure the drivers of peoples' sense of security. This measure also facilitates comparisons of what shapes a sense of security across countries, types of societies or regimes, and global regions.

Evidence is drawn from a new battery of survey items designed to monitor perceptions of Human Security, included for the first time in the 6th wave of the

World Values Survey (with fieldwork conducted in 2010-2012). The data which is available allows us to compare three dozen diverse nations, including rich societies and long-established democracies, such as Sweden and the United States, as well as several middle-income and poorer developing societies from different global regions. Dimensions of perceived Human Security are measured and compared across and within societies.

Table 1: Public perceptions of security threats

	Dimensions		
	Community	National	Personal
COMMUNITY SECURITY: *How frequently do the following things occur in your neighborhood?*			
Drug sale in streets	.762		
Robberies	.737		
Alcohol consumed in the streets	.702		
Racist behavior	.677		
Police or military interfere with people's private lives	.670		
Do you live in a secure neighborhood?	-.491		
NATIONAL SECURITY: *To what degree are you worried about the following situations?*			
A civil war		.880	
A war involving my country		.869	
A terrorist attack		.865	
PERSONAL SECURITY: *In the last 12 months, how often have you or your family...?*			
Gone without enough food to eat			.829
Gone without medicine or treatment			.827
Gone without cash income.			.804
Felt unsafe from crime in one's home.			.549
Percentage of variance	**28.2%**	**17.6%**	**11.3%**

Note: Extraction Method: Principal component factor analysis with varimax rotation and Kaiser normalization. See the Technical Appendix for details about all survey items.
Source: The World Values Survey 2010-11 (6th Wave): Release, 17 January 2013 (36 countries N. 50,551).

The battery of survey items were subjected to factor analysis with the results presented in table 1. The analysis suggests that the public distinguishes between three components or dimensions: *national security* (the broadest level, in terms of threats from armed conflict), *community security* (including threats from the surrounding neighbourhood), and *personal security* (involving risks and threats to the self and family). Thus the *object* of the security risks appears to be as important to most people as the cause of the threat. The results suggest, as traditionalists emphasize, that concern about the risks to the nation-state arising from internal violence, interstate war, and terrorism remains an important and distinct dimension of public perceptions of Human Security, focused on "freedom from fear". Nevertheless the findings also lend some support to the revisionist perspective, by emphasizing that perceptions of Human Security also encompass and recognize other important types of threat and risk, such as those arising from crime and illicit drugs, and personal insecurity from lack of food or income, emphasizing 'freedom from want'.

Following the results of the factor analysis, three normalized scales were developed by adding each of the items, standardized to a 100-point scale for ease of comparison across each dimension. Each of the scales was reversed for analysis so as to focus upon determining some structural causes of insecurity and perceptions of risk.

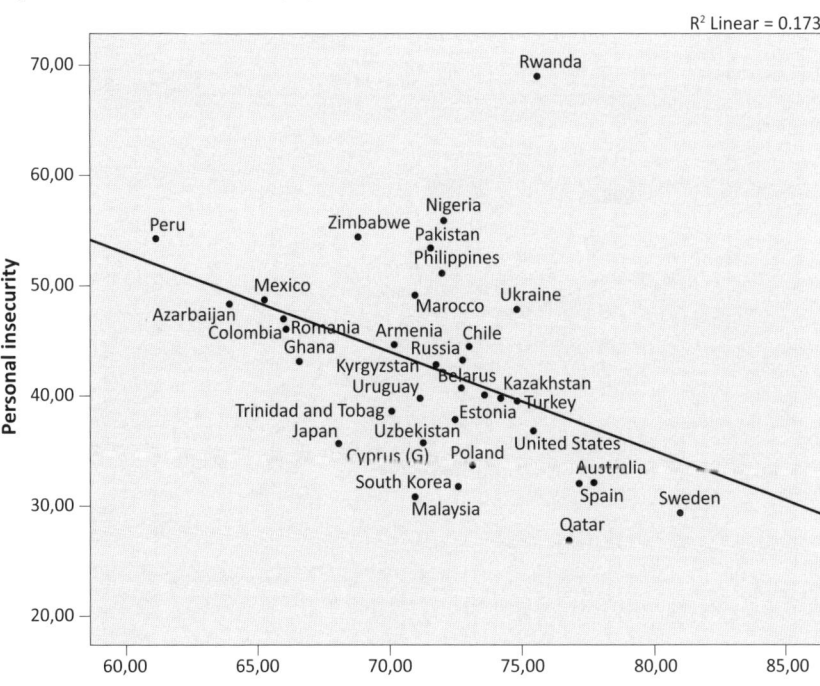

Figure 2: Insecure societies display minimal social trust

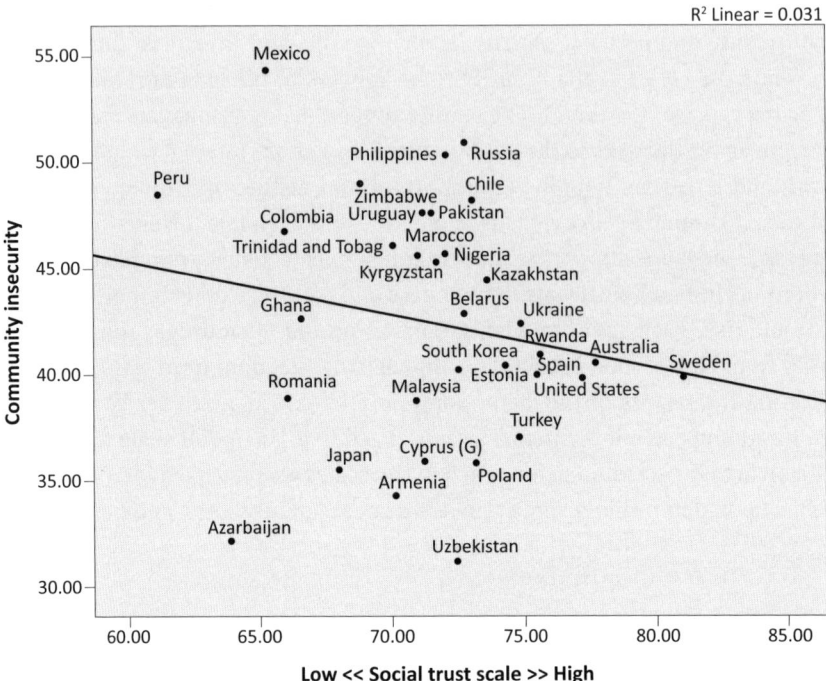

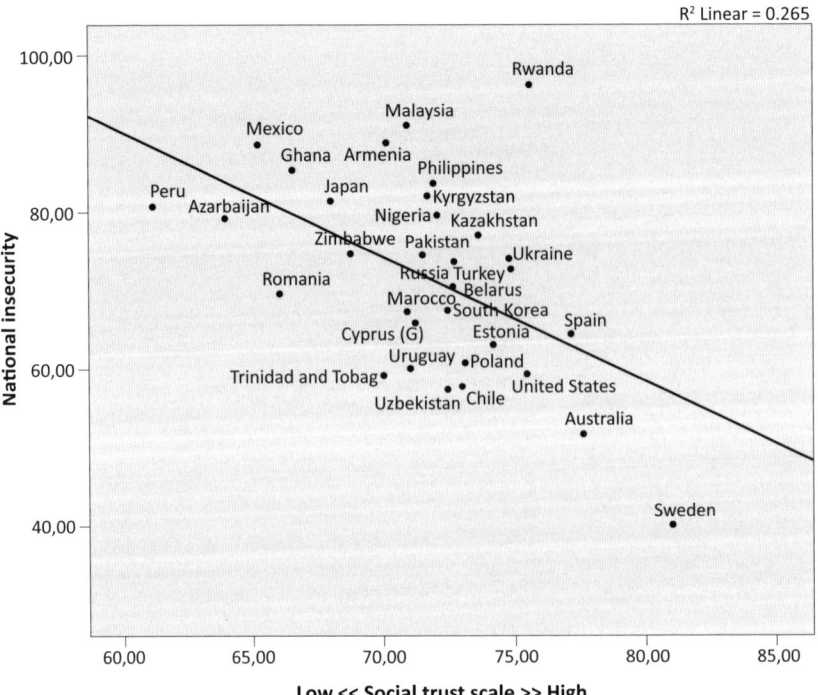

Source: The World Values Survey 2010-11 (6th Wave): Release, 17 January 2013 (36 countries N. 50,551).

Figure 2 illustrates the main contrasts in mean scores in insecurity perceptions on the 100-point scales by society. As might be expected, in terms of personal threats, Sweden emerged as consistently the most secure nation, followed by other post-industrial nations such as Australia and Spain. At the opposite pole, Morocco, Peru, and Azerbaijan ranked among the least secure. On average, people felt that personal insecurity was almost twice as great in Peru as in Sweden. Perceptions of community insecurity were strongest in Mexico, possibly due to the effects of the violent "drug-wars" in this country.

Measuring social trust and tolerance

The World Values Survey also included a wide range of items designed to measure social trust and tolerance. As shown in the technical appendix, respondents were asked: *"I'd like to ask you how much you trust people from various groups. Could you tell me for each group, whether you trust people from this group completely, somewhat, not very much or not at all?"* A battery of six items was designed to monitor both *particularized* trust (in family, neighbours, and people known personally) as well *generalized* trust (in strangers, and in people of another religion and nationality). Reliability tests confirmed that these items could be combined into a single Personal Trust Scale (Cronbach's Alpha .718), used for the main model. Subsequent models also tested the effects of both particularized and generalized trust as well, to see if the results differed.

To check the robustness of the analysis, the main model was also run using the standard dichotomous measure of social trust which has commonly been used in the older literature, asking respondents *"Generally speaking, would you say that most people can be trusted or that you need to be very careful in dealing with people?"* Substitution of this measure did not substantially alter the results of the analysis, strengthening confidence in the association found regardless of which measure of social trust was used.

To measure social tolerance, a series of eight items were selected concerning tolerance of several social groups who often experience discrimination against them, including women, immigrants, other religions, and homosexuals. These items were checked using reliability analysis and a scale was generated by combining them. For ease of interpretation, all dependent variables were standardized to 100-points, for comparison across separate models.

III: Results and analysis

The links between human security and social trust

Turning to the results, figure 3 illustrates the relationship between perceptions of security and trust (using the composite measures described in the appendix), without any controls. Figure 3 suggests that perceptions of personal and community insecurity are strongly related to social trust; as predicted, the most secure populations are also the most trusting. Nevertheless the descriptive results could be spurious and due to other factors, such as the fact that secure societies are also often the most affluent and highly educated, so that properly-specified multivariate models are required to test the association.

Figure 3: Greater insecurity drives down social trust

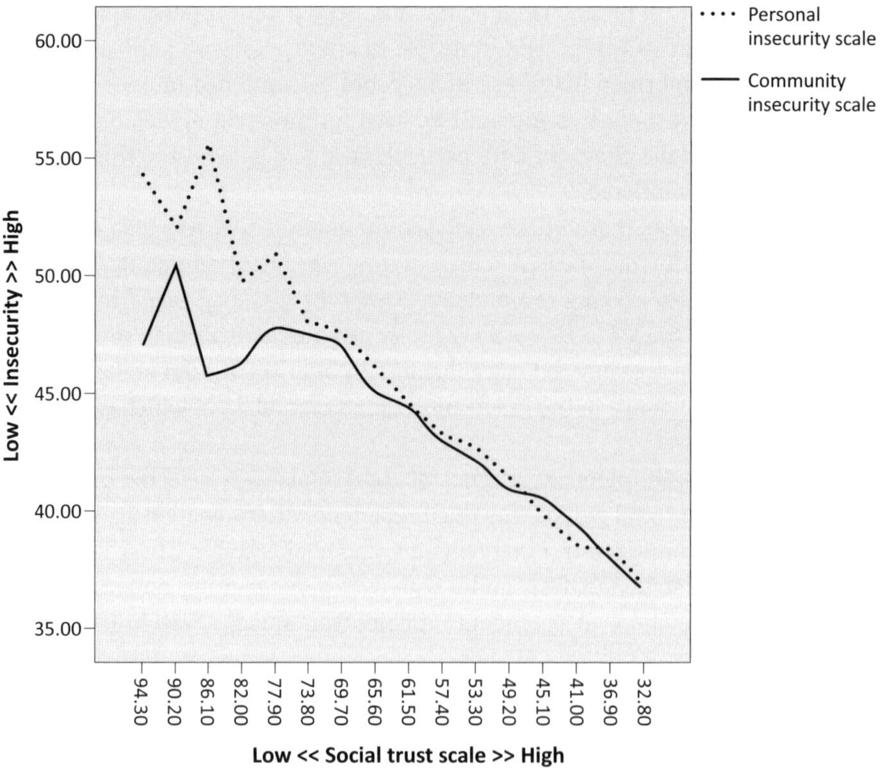

Source: The World Values Survey 2010-11 (6th Wave): Release, 17 January 2013 (36 countries N. 50,551).

Table 2 presents the main regression models used to test the core propositions, using the pooled World Values Survey data. The results confirm that personal insecurity, community insecurity, and national insecurity are all significantly associated with lower levels of social trust, as predicted. Moreover among all variables included in the models, feelings of threats to one's neighbourhood prove to have the strongest association with social trust.

Table 2: Factors explaining social trust and tolerance

	Social trust scale				Social tolerance scale			
	b	s.e.	Beta	Sig	b	s.e.	Beta	Sig
HUMAN SECURITY								
Personal insecurity scale	-.059	.004	-.093	***	-.025	.002	-.095	***
Community insecurity	-.095	.005	-.117	***	.044	.002	.131	***
National insecurity	-.025	.003	-.055	***	-.034	.001	-.182	***
SOCIAL CAPITAL								
Associational activism scale	.059	.004	.083	***	.036	.002	.122	***
Frequency watching TV news	-.307	.070	-.027	***	-.053	.026	-.011	*
Frequency of using Internet	.329	.048	.043	***	.154	.018	.049	***
SOCIAL CONTROLS								
Age (years)	.068	.004	.097	***	.005	.002	.016	***
Sex (male)	-.045	.135	-.002	N/s	-1.49	.050	-.154	***
Education	.255	.031	.050	***	.261	.012	.124	***
Strength of religiosity	-.286	.025	-.069	***	-.373	.009	-.222	***
Constant	77.3							
Adjusted R2	**.074**				**.198**			

Note: OLS regression models where the Social Trust and Social Tolerance standardized 100-point scales are the dependent variables. All models were checked with tolerance statistics to be free of multicollinearity. The columns represent the unstandardized beta coefficients (b), the Standard Error (s.e.), the Standardized Beta (B) and the statistical significance of the coefficients (P). *=>.05 **=>.01 ***=>.001 N/s = not significant.
Source: The World Values Survey 2010-11 (6th Wave): Release, 17 January 2013 (36 countries N. 50,551).

One important qualification needs to be discussed. Since data are only available from a single cross-national survey, we cannot lag effects over time, and the direction of causality is not clear and needs to be considered. The security items were designed to monitor perceptions of a range of risks, such as whether respondents or their family had gone without enough food to eat or without medicine, whether robberies or drug sales occurred in the neighbourhood, and whether they were concerned about wars or a terrorist attack. The models assume that perceptions of these sorts of threats would encourage people to mistrust others – particularly strangers and foreigners. Nevertheless it remains possible that minimal levels of generalized trust could also strengthen perceptions of risks – for example, in Rwanda, fear of armed conflict spilling over borders in the Great Lakes region, and memories of the bloody civil war between Hutus and Tutsis, could well be expected to colour mistrust of strangers and "foreigners". It is also possible that lack of social trust could affect experience of personal security, for example those who mistrust their family, neighbours, and acquaintances may thereby lack the informal social networks which help to sustain the poor through bad times as well as good, such as where local communities help to provide food, or where neighbourhood watch schemes deter home crime. It remains difficult to disentangle the causal links in these relationships through cross-national survey data, just as it does between joining voluntary associations, or use of the mass media, and feelings of social trust. Other types of research designs, such as field experiments and panel surveys, are required to establish the direction of causality with any degree of confidence. Nevertheless the descriptive data enable us to examine the strength of the association between reported experience and perceptions of security and social trust and tolerance, in comparison with several rival explanations of these phenomena.

The results suggest that alternative theories cannot be wholly ruled out as these also receive some support from the models. Thus theories of social capital predict that associational membership and activism help to encourage trust, while total hours watching television has a negative effect by privatizing leisure, and our models support these claims – though they indicate that subjective human security has an even *stronger* effect on trust and tolerance than does associational membership. Internet usage, however, has the opposite sign, suggesting that online engagement through social media may have more positive effects on trust than the relatively passive activity of watching television. The social controls behave much as expected, with trust proving higher among the well-educated, as commonly observed, as well as among the older generation – except for the fact that trust is relatively *low* among the most religious populations.

The links between human security and social tolerance

A further test of the evidence is to compare the results of analyzing social trust and social tolerance. Comparable findings would increase confidence in their robustness, given different dependent variables and measures. In terms of social tolerance, the results in table 1 show many similarities, although the strength of the coefficients varies. Thus personal and national insecurity are both associated with significantly less tolerance of outgroups, although at the same time community insecurity has the opposite effect. Associational activism and use of the Internet are both associated positively with more tolerant attitudes, while TV use is linked with less tolerant orientations. As the research literature has repeatedly reported, education and the cognitive skills and knowledge which come from schooling are positively associated with social tolerance. The rapid expansion of schooling and higher education is one of the main factors driving processes of cultural change, such as the greater acceptance of homosexuality and gender equality among the younger generation in post-industrial societies, as exemplified by public opinion towards acceptance of gay marriage. Another factor pulling in the opposite direction is the strength of religiosity, associated with intolerance of outgroups, although again long-term trends towards secular values have contributed to rising levels of tolerance (Norris and Inglehart 2012). Overall the comparison of the strength of the standardized Beta coefficients for all these factors suggests that feelings of national and personal security are linked with social tolerance – although other factors, including education, religiosity, and social networks through community activism, also play a role in shaping these attitudes and values.

Types of particularized and generalized trust

One further way to examine the evidence is to consider the effect of different types of social trust; after all, feelings of national security associated with the occurrence of wars or terrorist attacks can be expected to be strong predictors of trust in people from other countries, but not necessarily to have any effect on trust in one's immediate family. Similarly personal insecurities, such as lack of money, medicine, or food, may increase dependence and trust in informal networks of friends, neighbours, and relatives, but this may have little effect on perceptions of military threats arising from armed conflict.

Table 3 runs the main models broken down by the type of trust. Generalized trust is defined by trust in people one has met for the first time, people from other religions, and people from other nations. Particularized trust is constructed from trust in family, neighbours, and people known personally. These items are each summed and standardized. The results show that personal and national insecurity are negatively related to both particularized and generalized forms of social trust. These effects are statistically significant and indeed the link between national insecurity risks and generalized social trust is particularly strong. Community insecurity is negatively linked to particularized trust, but positively related to generalized social trust, for reasons that remain unclear. The other variables in the models behave as

Table 3: Factors explaining particularized and generalized social trust

	Particularized social trust scale				Generalized social trust scale			
	b	s.e.	Beta	Sig	b	s.e.	Beta	Sig
HUMAN SECURITY								
Personal insecurity scale	-.064	.005	-.086	***	-.056	.005	-.079	***
Community insecurity	-.142	.006	-.149	***	-.051	.006	-.056	***
National insecurity	-.010	.003	-.019	***	-.041	.003	-.080	***
SOCIAL CAPITAL								
Associational activism scale	.024	.005	.029	***	.095	.005	.121	***
Frequency watching TV news	.056	.083	.004	N/s	-.679	.078	-.053	***
Frequency of using Internet	.306	.057	.034	***	.362	.053	.043	***
SOCIAL CONTROLS								
Age (years)	.072	.005	.088	***	.066	.005	.085	***
Sex (male)	.071	.159	.003	N/s	-.162	.150	-.006	N/s
Education	.135	.037	.023	***	.384	.035	.068	***
Strength of religiosity	-.215	.030	-.044	***	-.366	.028	-.079	***
Constant	84.7				72.2			
Adjusted R2	**.06**				**.07**			

Note: OLS regression models where the Generalized and Particularized Social Trust standardized 100-point scales are the dependent variables. Generalized trust is constructed from trust in people met for the first time, people from other religions, and people from other nations. Particularized trust is constructed from trust in family, neighbors and people known personally. All models were checked with tolerance statistics to be free of multicollineamity. The columns represent the unstandardized Beta coefficients (b), the Standard Error (s.e.), the Standardized Beta (B) and the statistical significance of the coefficients (P). *=>.05 **=>.01 ***=>.001 N/s = not significant. Source: The World Values Survey 2010-11 (6th Wave): Release, 17 January 2013 (36 countries N. 50,551).

expected, with both types of trust proving significantly strong among those who are active in voluntary associations and Internet users, older populations, and the well-educated, and negative among TV watchers and the most religious populations. Thus, with the exception of community insecurity, the type of particularized or generalized social trust does not fundamentally alter the picture already depicted from the analysis of the overall trust scale.

Conclusions and implications

The importance of interpersonal trust and social tolerance is a recurring theme in attempts to identify the cultural underpinnings of democracy. Thus, in the 19th century, de Tocqueville described these values as a critical ingredient of the American attempts at democracy. This tradition has been reinforced by Almond and Verba (1963) and subsequently by the work of Putnam (1993; 2000). Nevertheless the specific links connecting perceptions of threats to human security and these democratic values have been poorly demonstrated. Attempts to document the macro-level links between human security and proxy indicators of economic development or inequality in different countries are far from convincing, not least because so many other factors vary among rich and poor societies worldwide. By documenting the micro-level evidence based on new survey data, this study has reinforced the argument that trust and tolerance flourish best under conditions where people feel safe and secure, whether against threats to personal well-being, risks of crime and drugs in one's neighbourhood, or conflict within or between nation states. Security is not the only factor that affects trust and tolerance, but it plays an important role.

Technical Appendix A

1. Personal security index

In the last 12 month, how often have you or your family	Often	Sometimes	Rarely	Never	DK/NA
V188. Gone without enough food to eat	1	2	3	4	-1
V189. Felt unsafe from crime in your home	1	2	3	4	-1
V190. Gone without medicine or medical treatment that you needed	1	2	3	4	-1
V191. Gone without a cash income	1	2	3	4	-1

2. Community security index

How frequently do the following things occur in your neighborhood?	Very frequently	Quite frequently	Not frequently	Not at all frequently	DK/NA
V171. Robberies	1	2	3	4	-1
V172. Alcohol consumption in the streets	1	2	3	4	-1
V173. Police or military interfere with people's private life	1	2	3	4	-1
V174. Racist behaviour	1	2	3	4	-1
V175. Drug sale in streets	1	2	3	4	-1

V170. Could you tell me how secure do you feel these days in your neighborhood?

Very secure	1
Quite secure	2
Not very secure	3
Not at all secure	4
DK/NA	-1

3. National security index

To what degree are you worried about the following situations?	Very much	A good deal	Not much	Not at all	DK/NA
V183. A war involving my country	1	2	3	4	-1
V184. A terrorist attack	1	2	3	4	-1
V185. A civil war	1	2	3	4	-1
V191. Gone without a cash income	1	2	3	4	-1

4. Social tolerance scale

Do men make better political leaders than women?

When jobs are scarce, do men have more right to a job than women?

Is a university education more important for a boy than for a girl?

When jobs are scarce, should employers give preference to people of (your nationality) over foreigners?

Would you be willing to have a foreign worker/immigrant as a neighbor?

Would you be willing to have someone of another religion as a neighbor?

Would you be willing to have a homosexual as a neighbor?

Is homosexuality ever acceptable?

5. Social trust scale

Composite scale based by summing the following items and standardizing the resulting scale to 100-points.
"I'd like to ask you how much you trust people from various groups. Could you tell me for each whether you trust people from this group completely, somewhat, not very much or not at all?"

- *"Your family,*
- *Your neighborhood,*
- *People you know personally*
- *People you meet for the first time*
- *People of another religion*
- *People of another nationality."*

6. Social controls

	Coding
Sex	Male=1, female=0
Age	In years (18-95)
Household income	Categorized scale from low income (1) to high (10)
Family savings during past year	From spent savings and borrowed money (1) to save money (4)
Education	Highest qualification: No qualification (1) to university degree (9)

■ References

Almond, G. and S. Verba. *The Civil Culture*. Princeton, NJ: Princeton University Press, 1963.
Allport, G. W. *Pattern and Growth in Personality*. New York: Holt, Rinehart and Winston, 1961.
Bellah, R.N. et al. *Habits of the Heart*. Berkeley: University of California Press, 1985.
Cattell, R.B. *The Scientific Analysis of Personality*. Baltimore: Penguin Books, 1965.
Coleman, J.S. *Foundations of Social Theory*, Cambridge: Belknap, 1990.
Craig, S.C. *The Malevolent Leaders: Popular Discontent in America*. Boulder: Westview Press, 1993.
Crozier, M., S.P. Huntington, and J. Watanuki. *The Crisis of Democracy*. New York: New York University Press, 1975.
Dalton, R.J. *Citizen Politics*. Chatham, NJ: Chatham House, 1996.
Dalton, R.J. "Political Support in Advanced Industrial Countries." In *Critical Citizens: Global Support for Democratic Government*, ed. P. Norris. Oxford: Oxford University Press, 1999.
Delhey, J. and K. Newton. "Who Trusts? The Origins of Social Trust in Seven Societies." *European Societies* 5, 2 (2003): 93-137.
Dogan, M. (1994) "The Pendulum between Theory and Substance: Testing the Concepts of Legitimacy and Trust." In *Comparing Nations*, ed. M. Dogan and A. Kazancigil, 296-313. Oxford: Blackwell, 1994.
Doring, H. "Higher Education and Confidence in Institutions." *West European Politics* 15 (1992): 126-46.
Dunn, J. "The Concept of 'Trust' in the Politics of John Locke." In *Philosophy in History*, ed. R. Rorty et al., 638-45. Cambridge: Cambridge University Press, 1984.
Dunn, J. "Trust and Political Agency." In *Trust: Making and Breaking Cooperative Relations*, ed. Diego Gambetta, 73-93. Oxford: Blackwell, 1988.
Easton, D. *A Systems Analysis of Political Life*. New York: John Wiley, 1965
Erikson, E. H. *Childhood and Society*. New York: Norton, 1950.
Fukuyama, F. *Trust: The Social Virtues and the Creation of Prosperity*. New York: Free Press, 1997.
Gabriel, O.W. "Political Efficacy and Trust." In *The Impact of Values*, ed. J.v. Deth and E. Scarbrough. Oxford: Oxford University Press, 1995.
Gamson, W.A. *Power and Discontent*. Homewood, Ill.: Dorsey, 1968.
Geertz, C. "The Rotating Credit Associations: A 'Middle Rung' in Development." *Economic Development and Cultural Change* 10 (April 1962): 241-63.
Giddens, A. *Consequences of Modernity*. Stanford: Stanford University Press, 1990.
Hardin, R. "Trustworthiness." *Ethics* 107 (1996): 26-42.
Inglehart, R. *Culture Shift in Advanced Industrial Societies*. Princeton, NJ: Princeton University Press, 1990.
Inglehart, R. and P. Abramson. "Economic Security and Value Change." *American Political Science Review* 88 (1994): 336-54.
Inglehart, R. *Modernization and Postmodernization*. Princeton, NJ: Princeton University Press, 1997a.
Inglehart, R. "The Erosion of Institutional Authority and Post-Materialist Values." In *Why Americans Mistrust Government*, ed. J.S. Nye, P.D. Zelikow, and D. C. King. Cambridge, MA: Harvard University Press, 1997b.
Inglehart, R. "Postmoderization, Authority and Democracy." In *Critical Citizens: Global Support for Democratic Governmen*, ed. P. Norris. Oxford: Oxford University Press, 1999.
Kaase, M. "Trust and Participation in Contemporary Democracies." Unpublished, WZB, Berlin, 1997.

Klingemann, H.-D. "Mapping Political Support in the 1990s: A Gobal Analysis." In *Critical Citizens: Global Support for Democratic Government*, ed. P. Norris. Oxford: Oxford University Press, 1999.

Ladd, E.C. and K.H. Bowman. *What's Wrong: A Survey of American Satisfaction and Complaint*. Washington, D.C.: The AEI Press, 1998.

Lipset, S.M. and W. Schneider. *The Confidence Gap*. Baltimore: John Hopkins University Press, 1983.

Listhaug, O. "The Dynamics of Trust in Politicians." In *Citizens and the State*, ed. H.-D. Klingemann and D. Fuchs. Oxford: Oxford University Press, 1995.

Listhaug, O. and M. Wiberg. "Confidence in Political and Private Institutions." In *Citizens and the State*, ed. H.-D. Klingemann and D. Fuchs, 298-322. Oxford: Oxford University Press, 1995.

Luhmann, N. "Familiarity, Confidence, Trust: Problems and Perspectives." in *Trust: Making and Breaking of Cooperative Relations*, ed. D. Gambetta. Oxford: Basil Blackwell, 1988.

Mischler, W. and R. Rose. "Trust, Distrust, and Scepticism: Popular Evaluations of Civil and Political Institutions in Post-Communist Societies." *Journal of Politics* 59, 2 (1997): 418-51.

Misztal, B.A. *Trust in Modern Societies*, Oxford: Blackwell, 1996.

Newton, K. "Social Capital and Democracy." *American Behavioral Scientist* 40, 5 (1997): 575-86.

Newton, K. "Social and Political Trust." In *Critical Citizens: Global Support for Democratic Government*, ed. P. Norris. Oxford: Oxford University Press, 1999.

Niemi, R.G., J. Mueller, and T.W. Smith. *Trends in Public Opinion*. New York: Greenwood, 1989.

Norris, P., ed. *Critical Citizens: Global Support for Democratic Government*. Oxford: Oxford University Press, 1999.

Norris, P. and R. Inglehart. "Four Horsemen of the Apocalypse: Understanding Human Security." *Scandinavian Political Studies* 3, 1 (2012): 71-96.

Norris, P. and R. Inglehart. *Sacred and Secular: Politics and Religion Worldwide*. New York: Cambridge University Press, 2011.

Nye, J. S. "Introduction: The Decline of Confidence in Government." In *Why Americans Mistrust Government*, ed. J.S. Nye, P.D. Zelikow, and D.C. King. Cambridge, MA: Harvard University Press, 1997.

Nye, J.S. and P.D. Zelikow, (1997). "Reflections, Conjectures and Puzzles." In *Why Americans Mistrust Government*, ed. J.S. Nye, P.D. Zelikow, and D. C. King. Cambridge, MA: Harvard University Press, 1997.

Ostrom, E. *Governing the Commons: The Evolution of Institutions for Collective Action*. New York: Cambridge University Press, 1990.

Putnam, R.D. *Making Democracy Work: Civic Traditions in Modern Italy*. Princeton, NJ: Princeton University Press, 1993.

Putnam, R.D. "Bowling Alone; America's Decline of Social Capital." *Journal of Democracy* 6, 1 (1995a): 65-78.

Putnam. R.D. "Tuning In, Tuning Out: the Strange Disappearance of Social Capital in America." *PS: Politics and Political Science* 28, 4 (1995b): 664-83.

Rose, R. "Postcommunism and the Problem of Trust." *Journal of Democracy* July (1994): 18-30.

Rose, R., W. Mischler and C. Haerpfer. "Social Capital in Civic and Stressful Societies." *Studies in International Comparative Development* 32 (1998): 85-111.

Rosenberg, M. "Misanthropy and Political Ideology." *American Sociological Review* 21 (1956): 690-95.

Rosenberg, M. "Misanthropy and Attitudes Towards International Affairs." *Journal of Conflict Resolution* 1, 4 (1957): 340-45.

Rothstein, B. and E. Uslaner. "All for All: Equality, Corruption, and Social Trust." *World Politics* 58, 1 (2006): 41-72.

Seligman, A.B. *The Problem of Trust*. Princeton, NJ: Princeton University Press, 1997.

Sztompka, P. "Trust and Emerging Democracy." *International Sociology* 11, 1 (1996): 37-62.

Sullivan, J.L. and J.E. Transue. "The Psychological Underpinnings of Democracy: A Selective Review of Research on Political Tolerance, Interpersonal Trust, and Social Capital." *Annual Review of Psychology* 50 (1999): 625-50.

Williams, B. "Formal Structures and Social Reality." In *Trust; Making and Breaking Cooperative Relations*, ed. D. Gambetta. Oxford: Blackwell, 1988.

Wright, J.D. *The Dissent of the Governed*. New York: Academic Press, 1976.

Hastings, D.A. 2011. "The Human Security Index: An Update and a New Release," http://www.HumanSecurityIndex.org.

Werthes, S., C. Heaven and S. Vollnhals. *Assessing Human Security Worldwide: The Way To A Human (In)Security Index*. University of Essen: Institut fur Entwickland und Frieden (INEF) Report 102, 2011.

PART 3

DIVERSITY AND THE NATION STATE

11 Globalisation, Civilisations, and Capitalism

Jan-Erik Lane

The emergence of globalisation theory looking upon Planet Earth as a whole in terms of politics, economics and culture makes civilisation analysis relevant again, although this field of study could use other methods and starting-points than those of for instance Spengler (1918) and Toynbee (1934-54) focussing upon the life cycle of civilisations or van Sloan with his notion of civilisation leadership as well as Huntington with his somewhat narrow focus upon conflict or clashes between civilisations (1996).

Although the historical study of civilisations received new stimuli from the evolutionary perspective of Diamond (1999) or Morris (2009), the basic concepts in civilisation enquiry of birth, life span and death as well as leadership of or conflict among civilisations are value loaded. A civilisation is a mere statistical concept, aggregating first and foremost country similarities or differences. The categories of civilisations are immense aggregations in the world population, collecting groups of the somewhat 200 countries of the world into a parsimonious set of super groups. Several attempts have been made, but they have all been criticised for either too much simplification or some inherent bias.

It is necessary to reflect upon the value-loaded notion of a civilisation. Alternative lists of civilisations have been suggested (Toynbee 1934-54), but here we concentrate upon the present vibrant civilisations with important economic activities in both the real and the financial economies. Here, a new scheme for the analysis of the civilisations in the period of globalisation is outlined. And the different civilisations of the world today are further evaluated from the point of view of institutional economics or economic sociology, attempting to grasp the meaning and significance of the global market economy, called "modern capitalism".

The interconnectedness in the global economy has become so large that any major shock would hurt almost all economies in the world. The amount of interaction in the global economy is typically measured with the IMPEX indicator, which divides imports plus exports with the GDP. Diagram 1 shows the constantly growing IMPEX scores for the global economy, which follows closely the expansive trend for global

Figure 1: Interconnectedness: IMPEX scores, Trade and Global GDP

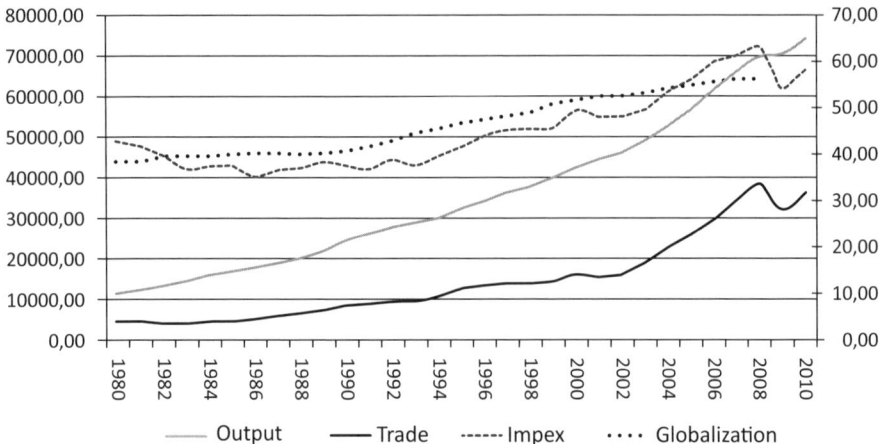

Note: Output = Gross domestic product based on purchasing-power-parity (PPP) valuation of country GDP;
Current international dollar; Billions (left axis)
Trade = Imports and exports of goods and services; Current dollars; Billions (left axis)
Impex = Trade / Gross domestic product, current prices; Current dollars; Billions (right axis)
Globalization = Means for KOF index (Dreher 2006) for 174 constant countries (right axis)

Sources: IMF (2010) World Economic Outlook Database; available via: http://www.imf.org/external/pubs/ft/weo/2010/02/weodata/index.aspx
Dreher, Axel (2006): Does Globalization Affect Growth?
Evidence from a new Index of Globalization, Applied Economics 38, 10: 1091-1110; data available via: http://globalization.kof.ethz.ch/

output and world trade. The so-called KOF index measuring a wide variety of indicators on the occurrence of globalisation in many countries is clearly up since 1980.

The close match between the trends in Diagram 1 confirms the basic insight in market economics that only free trade can deliver affluence. Global trade and foreign direct investments remain the engines that power global economic expansion, or as it is typically called: capitalism.

Typical of the civilisations of the world today is that they are connected through the global market economy, i.e. both aspects of it, namely the real economy on the one hand and the financial economy on the other hand. This *ONE* market economy is often called "capitalism", by both people on the Right (with approval) and people on the Left (with critique). Faced with several civilisations and capitalism, one may enquire into whether the various civilisations on Earth display different relationships to capitalism. But how to approach this notoriously value-loaded concept?

The two meanings of "modern capitalism"

This is not the place to comment upon the longish discussion surrounding the phenomenon of what we label "capitalism", from Karl Marx to Milton Friedman (1962) and Kenneth Galbraith (1982) over W. Sombart (1927) and J.A. Schumpeter (1989), it is enough to make a few key distinctions.

First, one may identify capitalism as a dynamic economic process, characterized by swing between expansion and depression, and measured in rates of economic growth – an outcome definition. In this sense, China is a capitalist country, or perhaps the most capitalist in the world. Capitalism is this approach driven by the search for profits, short-term or long-run, and it could also include *capitalisme sauvage*. This is "capitalism" as the acquisitive spirit (Tawney 1920), a universal phenomenon. "Capitalism" referring to economic exploitation includes all forms of activities where the remuneration is often excessive, such as tax farming and share cropping (e.g. *the Zamindari* system) or *Commenda* trading with for instance Venice merchants.

Second, one could mean by "capitalism" *modern capitalism*, i.e. link capitalism with a specific set of institutions, outlined in the school of *Law and Economics* (Coter and Ulen 2011), which makes it different from Ancient (slavery) or Feudal Capitalism (serfdom). Crucial here is not only the limited liability organisation – *Aktiengesellschaft* – or the *Bourses*, but a high degree of economic freedom for both capital and labour, including full private property. Modern or organised capitalism involves several of the rights and duties that enter the concept of rule of law, in the World Bank framework for analysing good governance (World Bank 2009). According to this meaning, China is hardly a fully modern or organised capitalist country, especially when taking its high level of corruption into account also.

To Marxists, "capitalism" stands for a determinate period in the evolution of the social systems of mankind, namely the *industrial epoch* when the employment of large scale physical capital in huge factories permitted the appropriation of immense surplus value from the proletariat. Today many Marxists speak of our time period of the dominance of financial capital, i.e. currencies, bonds and stocks. Sombart spoke of three stages in the emergence of capitalism, viz. *Early, High and Late Capitalism*. Yet, the distinction between the general concept of capitalism and the specific concept of modern capitalism was clearly spelled out in the early 20th century by Max Weber in his analysis of economic history (2003) as well as in his painstaking enquiries into the economic ethics of world religions. They actually broke the established racist perspective upon civilisations, typical of late 19th century thinking. Whereas both Sombart and Schumpeter predicted wrongly the coming end of capitalism, Weber argued that capitalism as exploitation (meaning I) is inerasable and capitalism as institutionalised capitalism (modern capitalism, meaning II) is the most rational form of economic activity that also socialist countries have to acknowledge and adopt.

Weber rejected any biological basis for the classification of civilisations, very similar in tone to his disbelief in primordialist ethnicity (Weber 1978). What separates men and women is their belief, and not races, he argued with emphasis against for instance his famous competitor in the modern enquiry into capitalism, namely Werner Sombart (Langer 2012). And, according to Weber, here religion constitutes the most powerful source of belief-systems in the form of articulated dogmas of faith.

Weber focussed upon the economic effects of the world religions, searching for the origins of modern capitalism, which he equated with the requirements of rationality or modernisation. Of the link he suggested in 1904-05 – Protestantism and the market economy – there remains nothing today, as other civilisations or economic centres display presently as much if not more economic dynamism than the Western one. The institutions of modern capitalism, as Weber spelled them out, can be exported to other civilisations than the Western one and they may learn how to put them to work vibrantly.

Let us instead search for civilisation effects outside of the global economic system, within politics. I will argue that the countries of the world today display difference in the respect for rule of law as well as that this variation has a civilisation background. The crucial importance of the rule of law institutions become intelligible when put into the principal-agent framework for analysing politics and political rulership, derived from the new economics of information.

How to identify civilisations: cultural items to use?

Culture is employed to single out a set of civilisations, but culture covers a huge variety of items, such as behaviour, beliefs and artefacts. One may consider a number of criteria with which to classify countries into a set of civilisations, *inter alia*: 1) Language families; 2) Religion; 3) Values; 4) Legacies; 5) Economic mode of production; 6) Geography. Since civilisations are constructed by the scholar, the choice between 1 and 6 depends upon what one intends to illuminate or show. Given the sharply increasing relevance of religion in the period of globalisation, I will employ the criterion b) above. Again, one may debate what a fruitful classification of the religions in the world today would amount to. A number of criteria have been used (Glasenap 2000), *inter alia*:

- Monotheistic – polytheistic;
- Animism;
- Magic;

- Salvation: Inner worldly – outer worldly;
- Asceticism: World-rejecting – world mastering;
- Ethical – prophetical;
- Western – Eastern;
- Eschatological – fatalist;
- Finite – infinite;
- Dualistic – monistic.

If we accept Weber's idea that religion has had a pervasive impact upon social organisation and politics, then it seems most convenient to focus upon the world religions, i.e. the largest of them: Catholicism, Protestantism, Orthodox, Islam, Hinduism, Buddhism and Confucianism as well as Shintoism. However, the growing number of atheists or agnostics should be taken into account, as these groups are of considerable size in both Western Europe and Eastern Europe, in Russia as well as China. Thus, strong Communism is to be found in Far East Asia, where religion is barely tolerated.

One could, of course, have included several other religions or sects, but they are seldom predominant in a country, with the exception of the *Shias* in Iran. Using countries as the basis for an enquiry into religion, one may suggest a parsimonious list of ten civilisations:

- Western: Protestantism + Catholicism;
- Latin America: Catholicism with some Protestantism;
- Orthodox: Greek and Russian Orthodox;
- Arab Islam;
- Non-Arab Islam;
- Sub-Saharan Africa: animism, Christianity, Islam;
- Hindu;
- Buddhism, Confucianism/Taoism, Shintoism;
- Communist;
- Pacific: animism, Christianity.

One may point out that these groups of countries are not compact in terms of culture, not even when the criterion is world religion or atheism. Thus, religious minorities are to be found in most countries.

Yet, the theory that the world religions have had strong social implications implies that they have formed parts of legacies, or historical traditions that linger on even if the religious ferment may have subsided. In the case of Communism, it is the atheist legacy that counts, leading often to the suppression of religion, as in China at times.

Historical traditions

Neo-institutionalism and economic sociology have emphasized the importance of long lasting practices, or customs for social, economic and political outcomes. Such legacies may comprise patterns of behaviour, clusters of attitudes as well as long lasting institutions. Civilisations are historical traditions, but historical traditions could be smaller in scope and range than entire civilisations. Historical traditions could be based upon other kinds of culture than religion, such as ethnicity and political history. One may argue that the civilisation categories above harbour such a number of historical traditions, like for instance the following tentative but not exhaustive listing:

- Latin America: Spanish and Portugal legacies, Catholicism; Indian legacies, the *latifundia* mode of production, *caudillos*, etc;
- Sub-Saharan Africa: Colonialism, tribal society, ethnic heterogeneity;
- Orthodox legacy: Hierarchy in state, society and church; tsarism and *caesaropapism*; the patriarch legacy, serfdom;
- Islam: Submission to religion, religious jurisprudence, gender inequality, oriental despotism; the *madhi*;
- Hindu legacies: Re-incarnation and magic, oriental despotism, castes and gurus, *bhakti*;
- East and Far East Asian traditions: The *sangha* organisations or monasteries, oriental despotism, *tantrism*, spiritism.
- Pacific countries: Clans, tribes, *ratu*, colonialism, animism;
- Western traditions: secularisation; individualism; institutionalisation of the sciences;
- Communist legacy: planned economy, atheism, state control over society.

One may wish to add numerous other traditions to the list above, as it would be difficult to be exhaustive here. Historical developments tend to be complex, meaning that various traditions may coexist with each other with more or less tensions. When different traditions occur, it may be almost impossible to tell which is most important. Important to what? One could examine present day outcomes.

Capitalism today

Weber saw modern capitalism, or the institutions of the market economy, as the giant difference maker among the civilisations of the world, resulting in economic rationality meaning affluence and power. If capitalism is merely a motivation force, then it has always existed as the incessant search for economic advantages, profits and success. However, if "capitalism" stands for a set of institutions, or rules, then one may wish to enumerate a number of different types of capitalisms: ancient, state, feudal, modern, etc. Weber summed up his position as follows:

> It is only in the modern Western world that rational capitalistic enterprises with fixed capital, free labor, the rational specialization and combination of functions, and the allocation of productive functions on the basis of capitalistic enterprises, bound together in a market economy, are to be found (Weber 1978: 165).

But the institutions of modern capitalism can be exported and adopted by other civilisations, learned and refined, which is exactly what occurred in the 20th century. Thus, even if Protestantism, or Protestant ethics, had something to do with the origins of modern capitalism in the West, which is an essentially contested matter, it could never guarantee any persisting advantage. Today, modern capitalism, at least when measured in terms of output, is perhaps stronger in East and South East Asia, with a few strongholds also within Islam.

Modern capitalism is not a difference maker in the world today. All civilisations practice it. If Weber perhaps led us in the wrong direction by focussing upon the amorphous phenomena labelled "capitalism", then we must ask: Why did he not enquire into the civilisation sources of his famous ideal-types of political power, or legitimate authority? I will show below that the civilisation variation remains as large today as it was in 1900, when it comes to legal-rational authority, interpreted as the rule of law.

Capitalism as economic dynamism

One may raise the question whether we are witnessing the definitive eclipse of what Weber theorized as the dominance of modern Western capitalism, as we do not find European or American countries among the top most dynamic countries in the world today. Table 1 shows economic growth among the G20 countries, for 2000-2006 (a) and 2007-2011 (b), where the economic success of the BRIC is obvious.

Table 1: Average economic growth in G20 countries

		(a)	(b)
Argentina	ARG	3,75	6,16
Australia	AUS	3,23	2,32
Brazil	BRA	3,36	3,67
Canada	CAN	2,50	0,87
China	CHN	10,25	9,19
France	FRA	1,81	0,01
Germany	DEU	1,40	0,60
India	IND	7,28	6,87
Indonesia	IDN	4,94	5,66
Italy	ITA	1,25	-1,15
Japan	JPN	1,40	-0,77
Korea, Republic of	KOR	4,57	3,07
Mexico	MEX	2,48	0,99
Russia	RUS	6,54	1,34
Saudi Arabia	SAU	3,39	3,83
South Africa	ZAF	4,24	1,98
Turkey	TUR	4,78	3,15
United Kingdom	GBR	2,88	-0,71
United States	USA	2,34	0,18
The European Union	EUU	2,00	-0,20
Euro Area	EMU	2,39	-0,08

Note: Economic growth = ((natural logarithm (GDP year n) - natural logarithm (GDP year 1))/n-1) * 100.
Sources: USDA-ERS: http://www.ers.usda.gov/data-products/international-macroeconomic-dataset.aspx;
World Bank: http://databank.worldbank.org/data/home.aspx.

Consider also the basic economic growth data in table 2, covering the 67 largest country economies in the world. Over a rather long time span of 12 years, the Nafta and EU countries have performed much worse than the dynamic economies in Latin America, Asia, and Africa.

Table 2: Summary of economic growth per year in total GDP 2000-12 in the largest country economies in the world today

Groups	Mean	Std.Dev.	Freq.
1	2.3	.84	3
2	4.3	1.1	7
3	3.1	1.0	21
4	3.8	1.8	14
5	5.6	2.1	22
Average	4.1	1.9	67

Note: Groups: (1) Nafta; (2) Latin America; (3) The EU; (4) Asia: East, South East and South; (5) Others.

If Japan with chronic economic stagnation is deleted from Group 4, then only the NAFTA and the EU countries would score below the global growth average. The relative decline of the NAFTA and the EU has no doubt been painful.

Research in the 20th century had to ask: Did Weber get it right when he argued in several painstaking enquiries into the world religions that other civilisations than the Western could not bring forward the market economy, or modern capitalism (Weber 1988)? The debate concerning his portraits of some of the chief world religions has not ended today, as scholars ask: Did Weber harbour an occidental bias, i.e. *orientalism*? Here I will underline not his omission of Catholicism and Orthodoxy, or his brief as well as rather negative remarks upon Islam due to its social effects. But instead I will emphasize that he concentrated exclusively upon economic outcomes in his civilization enquiry.

What is legal-rational authority?

Weber identified four types of political regimes: naked power, traditional, charismatic and legal-rational authority. However, he was not clear about the nature of the last type, linking wrongly – I wish to argue – legal-rational authority with his ideal-type model of bureaucracy. Typical of legal-rational authority is, I would wish to emphasize, government based upon rule of law. Let us first state the definition of "legal authority" from Weber: The validity of the claims to legitimacy may be based on: 1. Rational grounds – resting on a belief in the legitimacy of enacted rules and the rights of those elevated to authority under such rules to issue commands (legal authority) (Weber 1978: 215). The key terms in this general definition is rules or institutions. Yet, he moves on to equate legal-rational authority with bureaucracy: "The purest type of exercise of legal authority is that which employs a bureaucratic administrative staff" (Weber 1978: 220).

Yet, bureaucracy as a mechanism for carrying out the policies of rulers has, historically speaking, never operated according to the Weberian ideal-type. Bureaucracies have been invaded by affective ties, tribal loyalties and opportunistic selfishness. 20th century research into the bureaucratic phenomenon has resulted in numerous findings that question the applicability of Weber's bureaucracy model. As a matter of fact, bureaucracies can support traditional domination, as within Chinese Empires or the Ottoman rulership. It may also figure prominently in charismatic rulership, like in The Third Reich or the Soviet State.

Legal-rational authority emerges in a state that honours rule of law. This involves the employment of LAW, both in high politics and in low politics. It differs from all other forms in terms of the exercise of political power by complying with norms and by offering ways to correct abuses of these norms. Thus, this regime is not only legal, but also rational in the meaning of the introduction and observation of a set of norms that are secular in nature, protecting the common best of the political community.

This legal-rational dispensation, ranging from constitutional norms at the top to legality and reasonable principles for day-to-day interaction at the bottom, does not have to harbour the democratic polity. What legal-rational authority entails is the following (Raz 2009):

- Legality: regulations are sanctioned by laws that are sanctioned by a constitution, or *lex superior*;
- Predictability of law enforcement: laws and regulations meet with effective enforcement and wide-spread respect;
- Equality under the law;
- Autonomy of the judiciary;
- Natural reason: no torture, no arbitrary seizure or arrests, no prison sentence without court procedures, property rights.

The occurrence of legal-rational authority, i.e. rule of law, may be mapped using the governance indicators from the World Bank Governance project.

Rule of law indicators

Rule of law – in German *Rechsstaat* – includes both low politics – the predictable institutionalisation of transparent norms in everyday life – and high politics – the weight of constitutional law in government and administrative law in public services.

In the World Bank Governance project, one encounters the following definition of "rule of law":

> Rule of Law (RL) capturing perceptions of the extent to which agents have confidence in and abide by the rules of society and in particular the quality of contract enforcement, property rights, the police, and the courts, as well as the likelihood of crime and violence (Kaufmann, Kraay and Mastruzzi 2010: 4).

RL is explicitly separated from "voice and accountability", which is defined as follows in the WB project:

> Voice and Accountability (VA) = capturing perceptions of the extent to which a country's citizens are able to participate in selecting their government, as well as freedom of expression, freedom of association, and a free media (Kaufmann, Kraay and Mastruzzi, 2010: 4).

The WB Governance project suggests four additional dimensions of good governance (political stability, government effectiveness, regulatory quality and the control of corruption), but we will only enquire into RL here. The WB Governance project employs a host of indicators in order to measure the occurrence of RL around the globe, which results in a scale from -2 to +2.

Rule of law with the WB is a complex index, composed of the addition of many often used indicators, such as:

- Fairness of judicial process
- Occurrence of political violence
- Confidence in courts and police forces
- Security of persons and goods
- Independence of judiciary
- Property rights

It is true that many countries are so-called constitutional democracies, meaning that they score high on both these two composite indices in the WB Governance Project, rule of law on the one hand and voice and accountability on the other hand. However, the two concepts are distinguishable. From an historical point of view, it must be emphasized that rule of law developed much earlier than the democratic polity.

One may wish to go beyond this conventional classification of political regimes, based upon the Western concept of democracy, and enquire into the relevance of rule of law for any country, whether liberal, illiberal or anarchic. In whatever political regime a human being may live, he/she would value institutions that promote: Transparency of norms in low politics or daily life, constitutionality of high politics, court independence from politics and religion, immunities: a list of rights like *habeas corpus*.

Thus, one may advocate rule of law reforms in all kinds of political regimes without the accusation that one wants to force countries to adopt Western type democracy. Several countries score low on democracy, according to the WB Governance indices, but they achieve a moderate level of rule of law. Let us look at the global variation in rule of law, as measured by the WB. Here, we will employ the notion of a civilisation, as it offers a high level set of aggregates, suitable for globalisation analysis.

Cultural outcomes: civilisations matter

Approaching political culture as a set of legacies, the question that this interpretation of civilisations raises is what the more specific social and political impact has been for the present. Broadly speaking, one may search for cultural effects in either the economy – affluence – or in politics – democracy. The former approach is distinctly Weberian, whereas the latter perspective figures prominently in the theory of civic culture.

Here, I will target the rule of law, which is not identical to either the standard economic outcomes or the occurrence of the democratic regime. Concerning affluence and culture – the Weber thesis, it has little relevance to the world today, as other civilisations than the Western have adopted the institutions of capitalism with considerable success. With regard to the democratic political system, it can be argued that it is too much of a dichotomy. One cannot expect that the ideal-type of competitive democracy with party governance could be introduced in each and every country, at least not in the short run.

Let me focus upon a variable that allows for a large variation and that is related to both the market economy and democracy, to some extent, namely the rule of law. The rules inherent in the notion of rule of law date far back into political history and philosophy.

The Governance Project of the World Bank has made a tremendous effort at quantifying the occurrence of rule of law, employing all the indices in the literature. The findings are presented in a scale ranging from +2 to -2. Table 1 presents the aggregated scores for the civilisations, introduced above.

Table 2: Civilisations and Rule of Law 2009

	Mean	Std. Dev.	Freq.
Communist	-.755	.383	6
Hindu	-.533	.643	2
Muslem NONARAB	-.724	.656	21
Africa	-.801	.622	38
Arab	-.304	.715	18
Asia	.475	.963	9
Latin America	-.185	.788	34
Orthodox	-.507	.355	8
Pacific	-.187	.630	16
Western	1.20	.668	38
Total	**-.107**	**.984**	**190**

The eta squared statistic from ANOVA -.54 - suggests that civilisation is indeed highly relevant for understanding the country variation in the respect for rule of law. Some of the civilisations display negative overall scoring, although the high standard deviation should be taken into account. Thus, the Communist, Muslim NON-Arab and African civilisations score negative, which is also true of the Orthodox civilisation. We also find negative scores for the Hindu civilisation, but it only comprises two countries: India and Nepal. One may perhaps have expected a more negative score for the Arab civilisation, but the scores for several of the countries in this group is slightly positive: the UAE, Kuweit, Qatar for example. Both Hong Kong and Singapore score strongly positive, like Japan and South Korea.

It should perhaps be pointed out that poverty accounts to some extent for the disrespect for due process of law - see Diagram 2.

However, culture also matters in the form of civilisations. The Latin American civilisation has still some way to go before the overall ranking is positive. But compared with the 1980s, major improvement has been accomplished.

The importance of rule of law

One may discuss the relevance of rule of law from two different angles, the micro on the one hand and the macro on the other hand. Thus, rule of law may matter for single individuals, or ordinary men and women. Or it has a clear impact upon the political system and the structuring of political institutions.

Figure 2: Rule of law and affluence (GDP per capita)

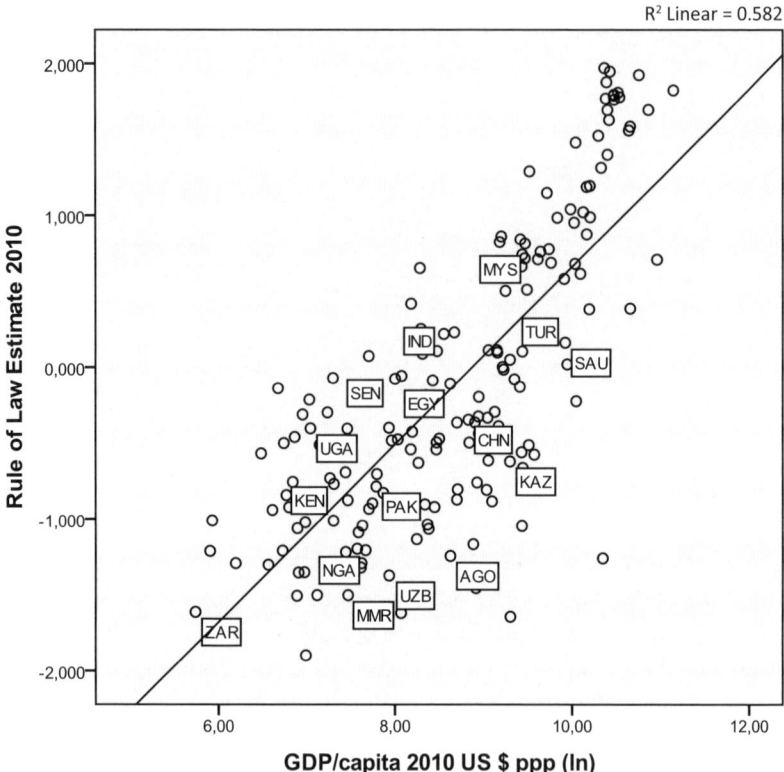

Micro or low politics

For the individual person, the implementation of some form of rule of law regime, or set of institutions would affect daily life considerably. Thus, the single individual would cherish:

- *Predictability*: Public law when properly implemented makes it possible for people to increase the rationality of behaviour. They know what rules apply, how they read as well as how they are applied consistently. This is very important for the making of strategies over a set of alternatives of action.
- *Transparency*: Societies operate on the basis of norms prohibiting, obligating or permitting certain actions in specific situations. Rule of law entails that these norms are common knowledge as well as that they are not sidestepped by other implicit or tacit norms, known only to certain actors.

- *Due Process of Law*: When conflicts occur either between individuals or between persons and the state, then certain procedures are to be followed concerning the prosecution, litigation and sentencing/incarceration. Thus, the police forces and the army are strictly regulated under the supervision of courts with rules about investigations, seizure, detainment and prison sentencing. No one person or agency can take the law into their own hands.
- *Fairness*: Rule of law establishes a number of mechanisms that promote not only the legal order, or the law, but also justice, or the right. For ordinary citizens, the principle of complaint and redress is vital, providing them with an avenue to test each and every decision by government, in both high and low politics. Here one may emphasize the existence of the Ombudsman, as the access to fairness for simple people. People have certain minimum rights against the state, meaning that government faces definitive duties concerning the protection of life and personal integrity. Thus, when there is due process of law – procedural or substantive – one finds e.g. the *habeas corpus* rights.

One could dare suggest that a majority of individuals in almost each and every country would wish to live under these principles.

Macro or high politics

Rule of law at the macro level is conducive to constitutionalism in high politics. Constitutionalism was identified already in Roman political thought as the best regime, with Cicero. It comprises:

- *Lex superior:* If the making of single decisions by the authorities is regulated by agency rules, and agency rules by administrative law, and administrative law by ordinary legislation, then what regulates legislation? Ultimately one arrives at a Kelsen's Basic Norm that both legitimates and restrains the rule of law regime, in the form of a constitution.
- *Secularism*: In terms of religion, it adheres to a secular state based upon religious tolerance. When a state is identified with some religion or religious sect, then it cannot maintain *neutrality* and *anonymity* in relation to all groups in society. The idea of *multiculturalism* is as relevant for ethnically divided societies as for countries with high religious heterogeneity.
- *Separation of Powers*: In order to have respect for the law as the key instrument for governing society and regulating the state, legislation, policy-making and implementation as well as law adjudication must somehow be separated. Under rule of law, this separation of powers targets the political elite active in the state,

with the claim that it has to be divided into three different elites: legislators, governors or governments and courts.
- *Counter-weighing Powers*: Under the rule of law regime there could be no single source of political power, or a hierarchical order of command. Instead, it favours multiple centres of power, or pluralism. Separation of powers enhances *checks and balances* in the state.
- *Court Independence and Judicial Integrity*: Government under the laws is not feasible unless the judicial branch of government rests upon the interpretation of law as *impartiality*, with regard to both government and civil society.

Constitutionalism, harbouring the rule of law regime, is today combined with the democratic polity in almost 50 per cent of the states of the world. However, it is also relevant for non-democratic polities.

Conclusion: Solving the principal-agent problematic in politics

The significance of the rule of law regime derives from the omnipresent principal-agent problematic in the state, both with regard to policy-making and policy implementation. Political elites – whether they be politicians, royal family, religious leaders, bureaucrats or professionals – must be seen as the agents of the population. How are they to be selected, monitored, remunerated and evaluated as well as held accountable, given the omnipresence of asymmetric information (Rasmusen 2006)? The rule of law regime solves this problem by two mechanisms:

- Government under the laws;
- Checks and balances within the state among elites with counter-weighing powers.

The respect for rule of law today occurs unevenly in the major civilisations of the world. Where the enforcement of its principles is weak, like in several countries in the Muslim civilisations, in many states in Sub-Saharan Africa as well as in parts of the Orthodox civilisation, people suffer from politics. The so-called West still enjoys a comfortable advantage in terms of due process of law, both procedural and substantive, which should be emphasized when scholars speak of the decline of the West (Ferguson 2012).

References

Coter, R.B. and T. Ulen. *Law and Economics*. New York: Pearson, 2011.
Diamond, J. *Guns, Germs, and Steel: The Fates of Human Societies*. New York: Norton, 1999.
Ferguson, N. *The Great Degeneration*. London: Penguin, 2012.
Friedman, M. *Capitalism and Freedom*. Chicago: University of Chicago Press, 1962.
Galbraith, K. *The Affluent Society*. New York: Houghton Mifflin Harcourt, 1988.
Glasenap, H. v. *Die Fünf Weltreligionen*. Jena: Diederichs, 2001.
Huntington, S. *The Clash of Civilisations*. New York: Simon & Schuster, 1996.
Kaufmann, D., A. Kraay and M. Mastruzzi. *Governance Matters VIII: Aggregate and Individual Governance Indicators 1996-2008*. Washington, D.C: World Bank Development Research Group, Macroeconomics and Growth Team, 2010.
Langer, F. *Werner Sombart, 1863-1941*. Munich: C.H. Beck, 2012.
Morris, I. *Why the West Rules – for Now: The Patterns of History, and What They Reveal About the Future*. New York: Picador, 2011.
Rasmussen, E. *Games and Information*. Oxford: Blackwell, 2006.
Raz, J. *The Authority of Law*. Oxford: Oxford University Press, 2009.
Schumpeter, J. *Essays: On Entrepreneurs, Innovations, Business Cycles, and the Evolution of Capitalism*. Piscataway, NY: Transaction Publishers, 1989.
Sombart, W. *Der Moderne Kapitalismus* III. Munich, 1987 [1927].
Spengler, O. *Der Untergang des Abendlandes*. Wien: Braumüller. 1918.
Tawney, R.H. *The Acquisitive Spirit*. New York: Harcourt, Brace and Howe, 1920.
Toynbee, A. *A Study of History* I-X, London, 1934-1954.
Weber, M. *Economy and Society*. Berkeley: University of California Press, 1978.
Weber, M. *Gesammelte Aufsätze zur Religionssoziologie* I-III. Tübingen: J C B. Mohr, 1988.
Weber, M. *The Protestant Ethic and the Spirit of Capitalism*. London: Routledge, 2001.
Weber, M. *General Economic History*. London: Dover, 2003.
World Bank. "Governance Matters 2009: Worldwide Governance Indicators 1996-2008." Washington: World Bank, 2009.

12 *Gemeinschaft* and *Gesellschaft* or the Life and Death of Proselytising Organisations

Margit Warburg

Proselytising groups and organisations are as modern as they have been since the emergence of the myriad of new religions in Hellenistic and Roman Antiquity. With the rise of political liberties and freedom of speech in the West in the 18th and 19th centuries it became common to proselytise for other ideas than religious beliefs, notably political programmes and civil liberties, such as the abolition of slavery and later women's right to vote.

Religious groups and organisations rise and fall with their ability to attract and mobilise adherents in tension and in competition with other non-governmental organisations and social movements of civil society. This also holds for the state-supported majority churches in many European countries. Today, the established churches cannot anymore take their membership for granted, but must compete with other groups and organisations to ensure active participation in church life. In other words, for all kinds of religious groups proselytising has become increasingly topical.

In many ways the organisational challenges facing proselytising religious groups are parallel to the challenges facing political parties, political interest groups, social movements, and organisations doing voluntary social work (Beckford 2001). Unless all these types of organisations can mobilise resources to advance their goals while maintaining organisational integrity, they will be short-lived phenomena.

The pertinent issue of resource mobilisation

The scholarly interest in resource mobilisation emerged with studies of social movements (McCarthy and Zald 1977; Gamson 1988). The resource mobilisation approach has gradually proved to be fruitful in studies in many types of civil society organisations and has influenced organisational studies in general (McCarthy and Zald 2001; de Bakker et al. 2013). Within sociology of religion, the resource mobilisation approach has been important when examining different types of religious organisations and their different methods for raising money, encouraging member participation, and mobilising voluntary labour (Bruce 1992). For example, when Billy Graham began to preach on television, his surprising success in expanding and maintaining his campaigns, called Crusades, was based on a strategic mobilisation of a large number of local churches. Up to ten months before a planned Crusade, the Billy Graham organisation arranged with ministers and other leaders of the local churches to mobilise their congregations for a systematic and active preparation of and a broad involvement in the mass events of the Crusade (Johnson, Choate, and Bunis 1984).

In my own study of the Baha'i religion I also addressed the issue of resources and the Baha's' ability to mobilise the resources necessary for expanding their membership base and for the construction of their remarkable pieces of religious architecture around the world (Warburg 2006: 374-423). In my analyses of the Baha'is' proselytising methods I further found it fruitful to combine the resource mobilisation approach with Ferdinand Tönnies' paired concepts of *Gemeinschaft* and *Gesellschaft* (Warburg 2006: 374-376). This gave a general insight in the organisational dynamics of a proselytising organisation and the crucial balance of resource allocation between maintenance and expansion. I believe that this insight is of wider interest, in terms of the sociology of religion and beyond.

Gemeinschaft and *Gesellschaft* in brief

Ferdinand Tönnies' book *Gemeinschaft* and *Gesellschaft* is a classic in the social sciences. Originally written in 1887 it was re-issued and reprinted several times in German and translated into English twice (Tönnies 1970; 1974; 2001). As with other classic concepts, interest in the meaning, implications, and use of *Gemeinschaft* and *Gesellschaft* has also waxed and waned over time. I should here mention that at least in Scandinavia the German terms are preferred, because they have certain connotations which are lost in the translation to English as *community* and *society*, respectively.

In much of the literature referring to Tönnies, *Gemeinschaft* and *Gesellschaft* has been seen primarily as an evolutionist historical transformation of human relations from the rural close community to the modern impersonal society. To some extent Tönnies himself was to blame for this, because he also idealised the development of European society from its traditional medieval form to its modern form as a development from *Gemeinschaft* to *Gesellschaft* (Tönnies 1970: 245-256; Schachinger 1991). As a consequence Tönnies' general and time-independent ideal-type use of the paired concepts of *Gemeinschaft* and *Gesellschaft* has often been neglected

(Schachinger 1991). The partial understanding of *Gemeinschaft* and *Gesellschaft* also seems to be based on Émile Durkheim's early, biased reading of Tönnies, and it has been perpetuated in later literature (Tribe 2004). This may explain why Tönnies is often mentioned in a sentence or two, but not used further in a more in-depth analysis.

An example of such a passing reference to Tönnies appears in Jan-Erik Lane's and Uwe Wagschal's foreword to their book *Culture and Politics*:

> In the first decade of the new century, the social sciences must come to grips with the anti-Tönnies predicament of the growing relevance of culture for politics. Predicting that associations would trump communities in terms of social and political saliency, Tönnies's *Community and Society* [...] seemed a correct analysis of industrial society. However, in the postmodern society culture seems to be at least as important as economic relationships (Lane and Wagschal 2012: xv).

It is not my intention with this quotation to engage in a discussion of whether or not this diagnosis of modern industrial society versus postmodern society is correct. My point is only to illustrate that on the one hand Tönnies' work is regarded as significant and relevant, also today; on the other hand it is also dismissed as an outdated analysis of a historical transition from pre-modern communities into modern industrial societies.

However, Tönnies' juxtaposition of *Gemeinschaft* and *Gesellschaft* runs deeper than a simple prediction of the societal development of advanced industrial countries. By reading Tönnies carefully it is clear that he goes beyond his idealisation of European societal development and conceives of *Gemeinschaft* and *Gesellschaft* as ideal types (*Normalbegriffe*) independent of both space and time (Tönnies 1931; Heberle 1973; Schachinger 1991). The paired concepts of *Gemeinschaft* and *Gesellschaft* are ideal types of structural relations within a given social entity (a business, a religious group, a nation, etc.).[1] These relations are created and sustained by two different types of willed actions: *Gemeinschaft* relations are created and sustained by *natural* will (*Wesenwille*); they are unspecific mutual bonds of obligations, rather than means to an end, and the people involved share a common fate. *Gesellschaft* relations are created and sustained by *rational* will (*Kürwille*); *Gesellschaft* relationships depend upon agreements and contracts, and obligations are limited and specified (Tönnies 1931; Heberle 1973).

Gemeinschaft is based on the sentiments of kinship, neighbourhood, and friendship; *Gesellschaft* is based on rationality and calculation. This, however, should not

---

1. The following exposition of *Gemeinschaft* and *Gesellschaft* as ideal types is a condensed summary of my earlier discussion of this topic (Warburg 2006: 111-117).

lead to the misunderstanding that, for example, natural will is irrational (Heberle 1973). Nor should one make the mistake to equate *Gemeinschaft* with informal groups and *Gesellschaft* with formal groups (Cahnman 1973). The fact that a group of people know each other well and are bound together by sentiments of loyalty does not exclude that formal rules play a role. On the contrary, *Gemeinschaft* relations are often best served when people in a group also obey formal rules and where the practical needs of the group are managed in a rational way. Any mother has realised this when trying to gather a family with two or three adolescents around the dinner table at a specified time! This need for formal rules is obviously more important for larger groups than it is for a family.

A study in rural areas of Canada of the working conditions for nurses, doctors, social workers, lawyers, and pastors illustrates the difference between *Gemeinschaft* and *Gesellschaft* in the social relations between these often isolated professionals and their patients/clients/parishioners (Mellow 2005). Mellow stresses that *Gemeinschaft* and *Gesellschaft* are ideal types of social relations, and she argues that professional relations obey characteristics of *Gesellschaft* relations by harbouring ideals of being rational, objectified, and without regard to personal preferences or to favouritism. Through reviews of earlier studies supplemented with interviews of pastors, Mellow could clearly identify how working in a rural area represented a challenge to the usual *Gesellschaft*-oriented professional standards, in particular those dictating that personal involvement with those seeking professional service should be limited. However, to do their work effectively, these rural professionals often had to rely more on personal, informal meetings and networks than their urban peers had to, and in communities where everybody knew everybody this balancing between *Gesellschaft*-oriented and *Gemeinschaft*-oriented conduct often necessitated a considerable readjustment of professional procedures and work habits – a readjustment which for some professionals could be stressful.

Gemeinschaft and *Gesellschaft* as two complementary ideal types

Nearly all social relations have both a *Gemeinschaft* aspect and a *Gesellschaft* aspect, as emphasised by Tönnies:

> I call all kinds of association in which natural will predominates Gemeinschaft, all those which are formed and fundamentally conditioned by rational will, Gesellschaft. Thus these concepts signify the model qualities of the essence and the tendencies of being bound together. Thus both names are in the present context stripped of their connotation as designating social entities or groups, or even collective or artificial persons; the essence of

both Gemeinschaft and Gesellschaft is found interwoven in all kinds of associations, as will be shown (Tönnies 2001: 17-18).

Following this lead I have proposed that *Gemeinschaft* and *Gesellschaft* should be seen as *complementary* ideal types of social relations, rather than as two *contrary* ideal types (Warburg 2006: 115-118). The difference between contrary and complementary ideal types is illustrated by the two graphic models shown in figure 1.

Figure 1: Models of *Gemeinschaft* and *Gesellschaft*: contrary or complementary ideal types?

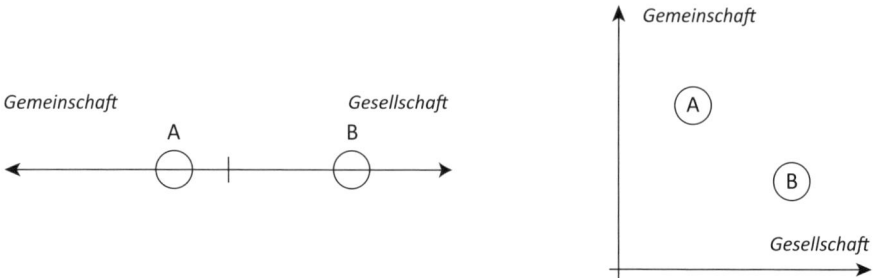

Source: Warburg 2006: 117-118; © Margit Warburg.

The first model to the left places *Gemeinschaft* and *Gesellschaft* at the opposite ends of a straight line, indicating them to be contrary or even antagonistic principles. An organisation, for example a religious group, which is mainly *Gemeinschaft*-oriented in its outlook and activities, could be placed on the line to the left of the centre point, like the circle A. Another group, which is largely *Gesellschaft*-oriented in its outlook and activities, could be represented by the circle B to the right of the centre point. None of the two groups are placed at the extreme ends of the opposing axes, which indicates that in their daily activities group A also cares for *Gesellschaft* and that group B also emphasises *Gemeinschaft*. Among religious groups and organisations, group A could be a convent or a religious hippie commune, while group B could be Scientology.

The alternative, complementary view on *Gemeinschaft*-oriented versus *Gesellschaft*-oriented groups is illustrated in the model to the right. Here, a *Gemeinschaft* axis is drawn perpendicularly to a *Gesellschaft* axis. The position of group A is closer to the *Gemeinschaft* axis than to the *Gesellschaft* axis, and it symbolises a group that is predominantly *Gemeinschaft*-oriented in its outlook and emphasises *Gemeinschaft*-oriented activities more than *Gesellschaft*-oriented activities. The reverse is the case with group B: this group is closer to the *Gesellschaft* axis than to the *Gemeinschaft* axis, which means that with respect to outlook and activities it is more *Gesellschaft*-oriented than *Gemeinschaft*-oriented.

The advantage of the model to the right is that it illustrates that *Gemeinschaft*-oriented activities and *Gesellschaft*-oriented activities are both present in a concrete case and are not opposing principles – their complementary relation is clearly communicated by the model.

Both kinds of activities are important to any kind of group or community – at least all those based on voluntary participation. The group must fulfil the members' expectations of *Gemeinschaft* – otherwise, in the long run they will become passive or even resign. However, the functioning of the organisation must not be jeopardised by neglecting the need for administrative efficiency and management of resources, and this is a *Gesellschaft*-oriented activity. Disregarding *Gemeinschaft* or *Gesellschaft* is ultimately a question of life or death of the group.

The sociology of religion is a ready purveyor of illustrative death stories of religious groups which disregarded *Gesellschaft*, but went on in a happy-go-lucky cultivation of *Gemeinschaft*. An example is a religious hippie commune formed in 1968 and based in Seattle, the *Love Family* (Balch 1988). The group had grown successfully for fifteen years to become a prosperous community of more than 350 members, and they owned several houses, a middle-sized farm and other real estate. The members shared a utopian worldview of being one people in Jesus Christ, and they lived in a style modelled after the kingdom of Judah, including Old Testament dress codes, full beards, Hebrew names, and polygamy. Drugs, in particularly marijuana and LSD, were part of the life-style. The leader, who called himself Love, effectively controlled the economy and few bothered to complain, as long as their modest needs were cared for in a communal *Gemeinschaft* with Love exercising absolute authority. However, Love's personal lifestyle gradually became a severe burden with his luxurious habits and a massive cocaine abuse. He also forced most of the members to take outside paid work to provide more income, and this *Gesellschaft*-oriented activity, more than anything else, was detrimental to group *Gemeinschaft*. Love's impulsive buying and selling of property furthermore led to severe debts, and in 1983, the majority of his most trusted followers left the commune, leaving it in poverty and a shadow of its former style. In 1986 there were only 45 adult members left (Balch 1988).

In a classification of activities as mainly *Gemeinschaft*-oriented or mainly *Gesellschaft*-oriented, one should also consider that 'beauty is in the eye of the beholder'. What at a first glance might seem a *Gesellschaft*-oriented activity may carry so much symbolic value to the group members that it would be better to classify it as *Gemeinschaft*-oriented (Warburg 2006: 275). An illustrative example of this is from the conservative Protestant group Old Order Amish (ibid.). They live in scattered rural communities, mainly in Pennsylvania and Ohio, and for religious reasons they turn against modern inventions such as electricity and automobiles. Old Order Amish people are also famous for their communal barn raisings. All male community members participate in the work of raising the barn, so that instead of paying professional carpenters to do the job, advantage is taken of an abundant resource among the Amish, namely free labour provided by neighbours. Superficially seen, the barn raising could be called a *Gesellschaft*-oriented activity, because it is a rational way of saving scarce economic resources. However, the raising of a barn is also an important ritual which shows the mutual obligations and solidarity of Amish community, and it might therefore also be classified as *Gemeinschaft*-oriented. The barn raising exemplifies that no act is purely *Gemeinschaft*-oriented or *Gesellschaft*-oriented – most transactions between people have an element of *Gemeinschaft* as well as of *Gesellschaft*.

The dilemma in resource allocation for proselytising groups

To strike the 'right' balance between activities that strengthen *Gemeinschaft* and those that strengthen *Gesellschaft* is a challenge to any community, and thus it is a strategic issue for the leadership to determine how to mobilise resources most effectively and allocate them for different tasks (Richardson 1988).

It should be stressed that resources are not just pecuniary in nature. For any voluntary organisation, not only for proselytising religious groups, I have suggested there are at least three different kinds of resources to be considered: time, labour, and money (Warburg 2006: 376-378). *Time* represents the members' participation in communal activities in the group, for example attending church service, prayer meetings, and other social events which strengthen *Gemeinschaft*. *Labour* is voluntary work for the organisation, for example mailing the internal newsletter to the members or preparing food and coffee for different social events. Finally, there is, of course, *money* without which any voluntary organisation soon would come to a halt in its activities.

To a limited extent the different kinds of resources can substitute for each other; for example, some of the voluntary labour can be substituted with money used to hire professionals, thus saving some of the time resources of the community (McCarthy and Zald 2001). Members' time in a religious commune can also be converted into money by taking paid work outside the commune and handing over the salaries for collective use, such as was the case for the Love Family presented above. In general, however, the different types of resources cannot be reduced to the one variable of money.

Mission as a more permanent activity requires not only mobilisation of people engaging in mission work but also rational planning, organisation, and money to be efficient. In other words, it requires resources of all three different kinds – time, labour, and money (Warburg 2006: 397-400). Although the proselytising activities may strengthen *Gemeinschaft* among those adherents involved in a certain mission activity together, a lot of their attention is directed towards people who at least initially have no close ties to the religious community that the missionaries represent. This makes mission a predominantly *Gesellschaft*-oriented activity.

Mission implies the creation of new social connections, and this may illustrate the distinction between bonding and bridging, as forwarded originally by Pamela Paxton and Robert Putnam (Patulny and Svendsen 2007; Geys and Murdoch 2010). The initial contact with a potential convert is *bridging*, which is to establish social connections with somebody who does not belong to the proselytising group. An example of bridging is to invite an outsider individual to the next church service held by the group. At the same time the mission activities may strengthen *bonding* among those engaged in a collective mission campaign. Ultimately, the aim with proselytising is to recruit new members to the group, so that *bridging* eventually is converted into a situation where the new members are socialised into the group and participate in the internal *bonding* of the group.

While the bridging-bonding typology can illustrate the social transformation of potential proselytes into fully-fledged members, the typology cannot substitute the distinction between *Gemeinschaft* and *Gesellschaft* in general. *Gemeinschaft*-oriented activities usually sustain bonding within the group, but *Gesellschaft*-oriented activities do not always involve bridging. Internal administration is an evident example that does not involve bridging.

For a proselytising organisation a dilemma is how much of its resources should be allocated for *Gesellschaft*-oriented mission, and how much for other activities that keep the community going. Resources are always limited, and meagre resources are never a trivial problem – 'resources matter' as concluded by McCarthy and Zald (2001). So, when a group increases its mission activities, it will usually have to reduce other activities. Unfortunately, the time spent on other *Gesellschaft*-oriented activities, typically administration and management, can rarely be reduced sufficiently to compensate fully for the extra time spent on mission. The consequence is that when a religious community decides to put emphasis on mission, it will usually be, at least partly, at the expense of activities that strengthen *Gemeinschaft*.

For a limited period of course, the required additional resources for increased mission efforts might be mobilised among the present members. Generally, however, the safest option for the religious organisation is to economise with the existing resources rather than attempt to increase them by demanding more from the members. The latter strategy carries the risk that, after some time, members might feel over-exploited, burned-out, and become distinctly passive (Barker 1984: 258).

Consequently, the launching of a mission campaign usually demands a reallocation of the existing resources. This can be illustrated by the model of the complementary *Gemeinschaft-Gesellschaft* relation, see figure 1.

The model is made more sophisticated if the distance of the circles from the zero point represents the amount of available resources, see figure 2. The number of members at the beginning of a mission campaign is a convenient measure of available resources (Warburg 2006: 403).This number is constant as long as new members are not recruited, so the amount of resources do not increase in the beginning of the campaign. Therefore, when a mission campaign is launched and more resources are spent on this *Gesellschaft*-oriented activity, the position of the community moves downward to the right, keeping the same distance from the zero point (path A).

Figure 2: Mission campaign and change in the balance between *Gemeinschaft* and *Gesellschaft*

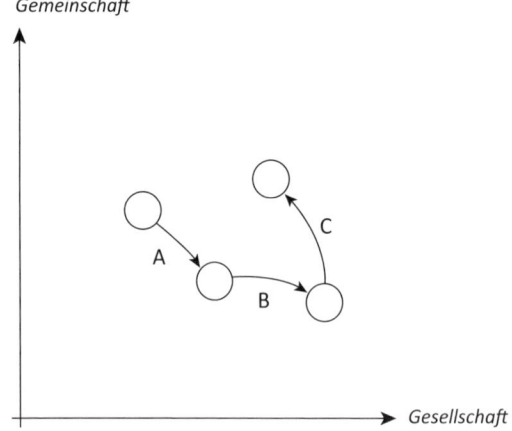

Source: Warburg 2006: 399; © Margit Warburg.

If the mission campaign succeeds, new members will be enrolled. The new members are gradually socialised into the religious community and they should thereby be able to contribute to the community with their personal resources. However, the socialisation of the new members draws upon resources from the older members, so it takes some time before the organisation experiences a net gain in available resources after the enrolment of new members. Furthermore, in the beginning, the new members can mainly contribute with *Gesellschaft*-oriented activities, because the skills required to work on strengthening *Gemeinschaft* are only gradually learnt during the socialisation process. On the graph, this means that the circle moves further towards the *Gesellschaft* axis while its distance from the zero point increases (path B).

The result of a successful mission campaign thus represents a movement along path A and path B, which means that the amount of available resources increases. However, the resources devoted to strengthening *Gemeinschaft* are less than before, even though there are more members than before, and it can be assumed that the members' demand for *Gemeinschaft*-oriented activities is not adequately fulfilled. To remedy this, the organisation will have to allocate more resources to the strengthening of *Gemeinschaft* – or to use Putnam's typology, the organisation must strengthen bonding. The circle now moves along path C at a constant distance from the zero point, until a new and more optimal ratio of *Gemeinschaft* and *Gesellschaft* is reached.

The changing strategy in Baha'i mission plans

A concrete example of the use of the model in figure 2 is taken from my study of the Baha'is. The Baha'i religion is an off-spring from a schism in Shi'i Islam in the middle of the 19th century. Late in the 19th century the religion spread outside its Middle Eastern setting through active and coordinated mission, and today the Baha'i religion attracts adherents in virtually all countries around the world. The number of enrolled adherents is repeatedly stated as "more than five million" in the official Baha'i year book series, *The Bahá'í World* (Warburg 2006: 215), making the Baha'i religion one of the larger and more permanent of the many new religions which mushroomed during the 20th century.

The Baha'is have a tradition of formulating mission plans which span several years. These year plans for each national Baha'i community typically contain about ten specified goals and activities, of which some concern proselytising and others concern activities that are directed towards internal training and strengthening of the religious communal life of the Baha'is.

The model in figure 2 can be used to analyse the dynamics of resource allocation in four consecutive year plans for the Danish Baha'i community (Warburg 2006: 400-403). All goals involving proselytising are counted as *Gesellschaft*-oriented, while the goals and activities that are directed towards those who are already Baha'is are counted as *Gemeinschaft*-oriented. The ratio between these two numbers determines the horizontal position of the particular year plan in the *Gemeinschaft*-*Gesellschaft* diagram, as shown in figure 3. For example, in the 7-year plan 9 out of 11 goals and activities are *Gesellschaft*-oriented – that is 82 pct., and the circle is therefore closest to the *Gesellschaft* axis. In contrast, in the subsequent 6-year plan, only 3 out of 8 goals, or 38 pct. of the activities involve the *Gesellschaft*-oriented proselytising, and the circle is therefore placed closer to the *Gemeinschaft* axis than to the *Gesellschaft* axis.

Figure 3: Balance between *Gemeinschaft* and *Gesellschaft* in the goals of the year plans for the Danish Baha'i community, 1974-1996

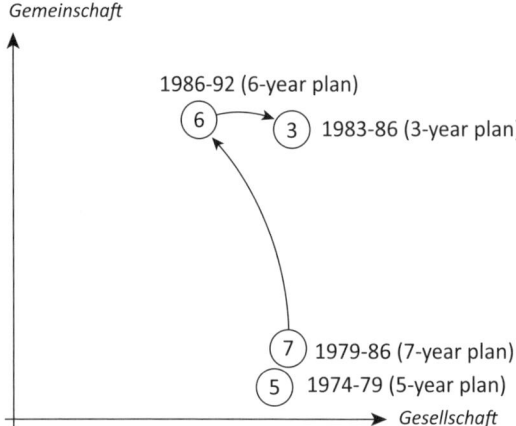

Note: The number of members at the beginning of each year plan are: 162 (1974), 171 (1979), 206 (1986), 240 (1993).

Source: Warburg 2006: 404; © Margit Warburg.

In the model the distance from the zero point to each of the circles is a measure of the resources available for reaching the different goals of the Baha'i year plans. As mentioned before, these resources are taken as being proportional to the number of members at the start of the plan, and these numbers I know from other sources (Warburg 2006: 254-257). Looking at the figure it is clear that this distance has grown through the successive year-plan periods, illustrating that the mission campaigns gave a significant gain in the membership base of the Danish Baha'i community. In the period of 19 years altogether, the number of Danish Baha'is grew from 162 to 240, which is a relative increase of 48 pct.

The graph also illustrates that there is a distinct change in strategy in 1986 between the 7-year plan and the subsequent 6-year plan, which emphasised internal goals much more than in the two previous plans. This is probably due to a successful enrolment of new Baha'is in the 1970s and early 1980s, which stressed the need for consolidation of these gains. From my scrutiny of available statistics for other Baha'i communities around the world it seems that the failure to do so led to a high degree of passivity among the Baha'is, in particular in India, Africa and Latin America. The Baha'i leadership on all levels has obviously learnt from this lesson, and the goals set up in the plans over the subsequent years put much more emphasis on strengthening *Gemeinschaft* among the Baha'is. But the consequence has also been that growth in membership since the 1990s has been much more modest. In resource management, there is no such thing as a free meal – what you lose on the swings you can only hope to gain on the roundabouts.

Perspectives

My approach for analysing the internal dynamics of proselytising religious organisations is to link *Gemeinschaft* and *Gesellschaft* with a resource mobilisation view. This can be generalised to other organisations which share the characteristics that they need to mobilise people voluntarily in order to achieve the goals set by the organisation.

In politics, the obvious parallel to a proselytising religious organisation is a political party. It is essential to a party that active party members spend time developing and discussing the political platform of the party. But the party also needs money for running the party organisation and reaching the public in a professional way, and money is nearly always in short supply. The party therefore also must rely on the unpaid labour of for example the younger members who are mobilised before a general election to put up party billboards on the lamp posts. This is a trivial task which could be paid for, but it could also be argued that the joint work strengthens *Gemeinschaft* within in the youth organisation of the party.

In fact, a lot of party work deals with the goal of promulgating the political mission of the party and attract new voters and new members, and this is a *Gesellschaft*-oriented activity. Like the eagerly proselytising religious groups, also the party organisation must attend the issue of balancing the resources spent on the *Gesellschaft*-oriented promotion of party politics against the necessary strengthening of *Gemeinschaft* among the party members. Time must be spent on a detailed and sober discussion of the party platform before the election campaigns begin, and this is a *Gesellschaft*-oriented activity which in principle is based on rationality and calculations. However, this cannot stand alone – the party cadres also need wild parties and free beer. Without at least a little bit of *Gemeinschaft* the footmen of the political parties will not engage in the campaigns, press door bells, write on Facebook, and rally at the open-air meetings, where the leading politicians speak.

Politics may be created by *rational* will but those who *do* politics are also part of a group where the people involved share a common fate, and where *natural* will creates and sustains *Gemeinschaft*.

■ References

de Bakker, F.G.A, F.d. Hond, B. King, and K. Weber. "Social Movements, Civil Society and Corporations: Taking Stock and Looking Ahead." *Organization Studies* 34 (2013): 573-93.

Balch, R. "Money and Power in Utopia: An Economic History of the Love Family." In *Money and Power in the New Religions*, ed. J.T. Richardson, 185-221. Lewiston, NY: The Edwin Mellen Press, 1988.

Barker, E. *The Making of a Moonie. Choice or Brainwashing?* Oxford: Basil Blackwell, 1984.

Beckford, J.A. "Social Movements as Free-floating Phenomena." In *The Blackwell Companion to Sociology of Religion*, ed. R.K. Fenn, 229-48. Oxford: Blackwell, 2001.

Bruce, S. "Funding the Lord's Work: A Typology of Religious Resourcing." *Social Compass* 39 (1992): 93-101.

Cahnman, W.J. "Introduction." In *Ferdinand Tönnies. A New Evaluation. Essays and Documents*, ed. W.J. Cahnman, 1-27. Leiden: Brill, 1973.

Gamson, W.A. "Introduction." In *Social Movements in an Organizational Society. Collected Essays*, ed. M.N. Zald and J.D. McCarthy, 1-7. New Brunswick: Transaction Books, 1987.

Geys, B. and Z. Murdoch. "Measuring the 'Bridging' versus 'Bonding' Nature of Social Networks: A Proposal for Integrating Existing Measures." *Sociology* 44 (2004): 523-40.

Heberle, R. "The Sociological System of Ferdinand Tönnies: An Introduction." In *Ferdinand Tönnies. A New Evaluation. Essays and Documents*, ed. W.J. Cahnman. 47-69. Leiden: Brill, 1973.

Johnson, N.R., D.A. Choate, and W. Bunis. "Attendance at a Billy Graham Crusade: A Resource Mobilization Approach." *Sociological Analysis* 45 (1984): 383-92.

Lane, J.-E. and U. Wagschal. *Culture and Politics*. London: Routledge, 2012.

McCarthy, J.D. and M.N. Zald. "Resource Mobilization and Social Movements: A Partial Theory." *American Journal of Sociology*, 82 (1977): 1212-41.

McCarthy, J.D. and M.N. Zald. "The Enduring Vitality of the Resource Mobilization Theory of Social Movements." In *Handbook of Sociological Theory*, ed. J.H. Turner, 533-65. New York: Kluwer Academic, 2001.

Mellow, M. "The Work of Rural Professionals: Doing the *Gemeinschaft-Gesellschaft* Gavotte." *Rural Sociology* 70 (2005): 50-69.

Patulny, R.V. and G.L.H. Svendsen. "Exploring the Social Grid: Bonding, Bridging, Qualitative, Quantitative." *International Journal of Sociology and Social Policy* 27 (2007): 32-51.

Richardson, J.T. (1988). "An Introduction." In *Money and Power in the New Religions*, ed. J. and T. Richardson, 1-20. Lewiston, NY: The Edwin Mellen Press, 1988.

Tönnies, F. "Gemeinschaft und Gesellschaft." In *Handwörterbuch der Soziologie*, ed. A. Vierkandt. Stuttgart: Ferdinand Enke Verlag, 1931.

Tönnies, F. *Gemeinschaft und Gesellschaft. Grundbegriffe der reinen Soziologie*. Darmstadt: Wissenschaftliche Buchgesellschaft, 1970.

Tönnies, F. *Community and Association (Gemeinschaft und Gesellschaft)*, ed. and transl. C. P. Loomis. London: Routledge and Kegan Paul, 1974.

Tönnies, F. *Community and Civil Society*. Ed. J. Harris, translated by J. Harris and M. Hollis. Cambridge: Cambridge University Press, 2001.

Tribe, K. "Book Review: *Community and Civil Society*." *German History* 22, 3 (2001): 478-479.

Warburg, M. *Citizens of the World. A History and Sociology of the Baha'is from a Globalisation Perspective*. Leiden: E.J. Brill, 2006.

13 Why not Become Multicultural? Second Generation of Intellectual Sri Lankan Tamil Hindus in Denmark

Marianne Q. Fibiger

Over the last twenty years, the number of academic studies on immigrant groups' settling patterns and place-making methods has increased significantly; some of the more recent studies also focus on the many groups of South Asians, represented in most parts of the world, who have settled and assimilated to the way of life of their new societies (Jacobsen and Kumar 2004). This growing number of local studies on immigrant groups of South Asian origin not only gives us an insight into the complexity and plurality of these traditions as such, it also provides us with new knowledge about how these traditions adapt to a new context and whether this process varies across immigrant groups with different traditional and cultural backgrounds.[1] This is not only interesting in relation to South Asian traditions in general – or, in the case of this chapter, the Hindu tradition in particular – it is also interesting in terms of a comparative analysis of whether and how traditions and cultures (including religion), as reservoirs of meaning, behavioural patterns and normative frameworks, provide groups with different life-views, world-views, paradigms or symbolic resources that, in turn, affect their adaption process into new societies.

---

1. The notions of culture, religion, and tradition overlap in many ways and are used differently in research within sociology, anthropology and religious studies. In this chapter, culture refers to a particular world- and life-view, behavioural pattern (good and bad conduct), shared symbols and concepts that ascribe values to certain things, and attitudes toward gender, nature, the human and art, which are understood as so important that they are transferred from generation to generation (socialisation) and from place to place (place-making). Religion as a shared meaning system is often an important part of culture and, with its reference to a transcendental world, it is not only given special authority but can also be transplanted from one cultural setting to another, thereby giving meaning to and constituting the anchoring point for identity (social, cultural) for the individual as well as the group in a cultural disorientation when establishing itself in a new cultural environment. Tradition is used to underline that culture as well as religion are constructed in a local setting (geographically, socially, historically) and therefore plural in its forms. With the use of tradition, the process of transfer (orally, textually, behaviour-patterns, symbols) from generation to generation is emphasised.

This question does not imply that culture is not constructed (individuals are not passive recipients); however, it does suggest that such a construction is based on at least two aspects. Firstly, it is based on a particular socialisation within a family that is affiliated to a particular group – be it ethnic, cultural, religious or connected through shared values – to which the individual is introduced and with which he/she has to act accordingly (either by partially adopting, fully adopting or rejecting). Secondly, it is based on the receiving society's overall *a priori* understanding of a given group or culture as either a threat or an asset to its own existence. Although the first of these factors is often considered in secondary literature, the second has received little scholarly attention. In this chapter, I argue that both of these factors should be seen as part of one dialectical process.

In this chapter, I do not intend to perform a comparative analysis of different immigrant groups, their identity formation or their ability to adapt to different cultural and social settings. Instead, I wish to present part of a case study of second generation Sri Lankan Tamil Hindus in Denmark. Here, there is a clear tension between being part of a shared culture or tradition and wishing to adapt this tradition in response to the receiving society's positive and negative understanding of it. This tension is playing an obvious role in their identity formation.

I wish to examine how the desire to keep alive a sense of cultural belonging in an immigrant situation – despite continual internal and external critique – can lead to particular in-group social relations (a topic that undoubtedly relates to the theme of this book as a whole). In trying to maintain a sense of cultural belonging, the notion of being part of a special group is articulated and specific aspects of the tradition are identified as particularly important. At the same time, this also leads to varying degrees of intentional compartmentalisation strategies, where the differentiation between the in-group and the out-group's relations[2] become more apparent, both in relation to behavioural patterns and what is understood as good conduct in different situations. This process results in a form of cultural hybridity (Bhabha 1994) or multiculturality, which, as I will claim in this chapter, is more easily coped with or even understood as a privilege among bearers of cultures that not only have a universal and inclusive meaning system as part of the normative framework but also have an appeal to Western societies as a whole, which makes the relation between in- and out-groups differ from other immigration groups.

This situation describes the basic condition for most South Asian traditions, not only because Eastern notions and Eastern world-views and life-views seem to appeal to many Westerners, but also because they have become part of the Western meaning system; for example, yoga, karma, reincarnation, the individualistic

---

2. The out-group is understood as other circulation spheres, such as leisure, work, education, community associations or political parties.

soteriology and spirituality now offer an alternative to institutionalised religion (Campbell 2007; Heelas and Woodhead 2005; Singleton 2010). In other words, I will argue that, when transplanting a tradition into a new setting, the process of cultural adaptation has two basic conditions; not only that the tradition is met with a generally positive attitude in the receiving society but that elements of the tradition have already become a part of that society, albeit under new conditions and interpreted through a Western lens, so they fit Western life-styles but are also given new meaning. Or, as Campbell states in his book on the Easternization of the West:

> Rather the East – or at least, to make an important qualification, the West's image of the East – exerts a powerful *influence* over the West. It is this influence, when coupled with the process of internal evolution that has occurred within the culture of the West itself that largely explains why Easternization has happened (Campbell 2007: 40).

This does not necessarily make the adaptation process easier, but it makes it different, because the whole framework for negotiation between being part of a particular group with a shared history and affiliation to a particular local tradition (in-group association) and being part of a meaning system that is somehow shared with the surrounding society (out-group association) becomes more blurred.

This chapter will focus on which types of negotiations seem to be at play for the second generation of intellectual Sri Lankan Tamil Hindus in Denmark during this process. It will also examine to what extent or through which filter these Sri Lankan Tamil Hindus understand themselves as multicultural (understood as having both in-group and out-group relations). It is in this context that the title of this chapter, *Why not become multicultural?*, should be read as a rhetorical question, where the answer provided is shaped or constructed in a way that suits the young Sri Lankan Tamils' life in Denmark but does not threaten the link to a shared idea of belonging to a culture or tradition they share with their parents.

As an example of how in-group and out-group relations are dialectical, I will refer to an internal discussion of a problem raised by the second generation of intellectual Sri Lankan Tamil Hindu women who now live in university cities in Denmark. These women are trying to balance their desire to obtain a university education and a subsequent career in civilian life with the in-group demand for caste based arranged marriages.

What I find particularly interesting in this example is not only that the young Tamil women openly articulate how difficult it is in Denmark to find a suitable young Tamil man to equal their education level and ambitions, but that they appeal to an in-group articulation of education as a religiously justified (and not a secularly justified) endeavour as an argument for overruling another in-group parameter for finding the right match, namely caste. In their own way, they have begun to speak out, criticising matters within the Tamil Hindu tradition that they believe contradict their lives in a modern Danish society, both as Tamil Hindus and as women; however, they continue to adhere to these practices – presumably from an insider perspective – when viewing Hinduism as an encompassing global religion. The tendency for Hindus to inadvertently and intentionally modify their beliefs and practices towards a unitary Hinduism in which the local- or caste-based divisions are abandoned in favour of a more homogenised and essentially text-based Brahmanic tradition can also be witnessed in other parts of the world, such as Canada (Breton 2012: 113).

Members of the second generation of young Sri Lankan Tamil Hindus do this in such a way that they combine their ambition to be a modern, young person in Denmark with their relation to the Tamil Hindu tradition, which they still perceive as an important norm-giver as well as an important factor in their quest to feel as though they belong; a feeling that they, to a certain extent, wish to pass on to their children. Breton (2012) claims that immigrants have to fit in as individuals but also as a distinct group. He writes, "[immigrants] need to gain social acceptance as members of a group who identify themselves and are identified by others as different. Thus the challenge is not only their own individual social standing but also that of their group" (Breton 2012: 24). For the second generation of immigrants, this means that, even if they prefer not to be related to their background, it nevertheless remains present in their lives.

Introduction: The Sri Lankan Tamil Hindus in Denmark

In Denmark, there are approximately 11,000 people of Sri Lankan origin out of which approximately 10,000 are Hindus.[3] The first Sri Lankan Tamil Hindus came to Denmark in 1983 because of the escalating conflict in Sri Lanka. They were mostly men, and they were categorised as *ipso facto* refugees. During the 1990s, those who had left families behind in Sri Lanka were reunited with their families in Demark; the others married Sri Lankan Tamil women in Denmark and began to settle down.

Today, more than 8,000 of the Sri Lankan Tamils living in Denmark have become Danish citizens. This demonstrates their sincere wish to settle down for good in Denmark. However, although they wish to stay in Denmark, they do not wish to lose their relation to Sri Lanka, which they still understand as a kind of homeland. They are also reluctant to lose their connection to Tamil Hinduism, which they

---

3. Since Statistics Denmark, who register all newcomers to Denmark, do not take religious but only geographical affiliation into account, it is difficult to provide an exact figure when it comes to religious grouping.

continue to understand as an important identity-marker in Denmark. The six Sri Lankan Hindu temples in Denmark are a testament to this.[4] The second generation of Sri Lankan Tamils in Denmark, who were either born in Denmark or came to Denmark as small children, also feel this way, but they are struggling with how to connect to their homeland and religion, as expressed by the following 25-year-old woman (when asked *Where do you feel you belong?*):

> It really depends on where I am. When I am asked at home [Denmark], I answer either Sri Lanka or Struer [city in Denmark]. When asked abroad, I tell them I am from Denmark (Sri Lankan Tamil Hindu, female, 25 years).

Compared to most of the other refugee and immigrant groups in Denmark, the Sri Lankan Tamils are very well integrated in Danish society. Approximately 67 per cent of all Tamils in Denmark are fully employed, which means that, together with the Indians and the Vietnamese, they have the largest number of employees among all immigrant (and refugee) groups. The education level among the young Tamils is also high compared to other groups (Source: www.danmarksstatistics.dk 2012). One reason for this is the very strong work ethic implicit in the Hindu tradition, which means that Hindu children are raised in an atmosphere in which education matters. Moreover, it becomes clear that education is not only understood as a secular indicator for success in society, but also as a kind of token or offering to God, as formulated by a 55-year-old first generation Sri Lankan Tamil Hindu father:

> I have raised my children to understand the importance of education. They have possibilities in Denmark for education that I myself didn't have in Sri Lanka. They just have to fulfil these – from my point of view – God-given possibilities.

When it comes to cultural adaptation, an increasing number of Sri Lankan Tamils are adopting selected Danish traditions (for example, Christmas Eve) but on their own terms. A Sri Lankan Tamil Hindu father remarked:

> We do celebrate Christmas with presents and a Christmas tree, decorated with things our children make at school, in our living room, but we don't sing Christmas Carols or go to church. Some of our Tamil friends in Germany go to church, but we have decided not to.

---

4. The scope of this article unfortunately cannot encompass a discussion of the role of religious organisations as tradition keepers and in the social integration of immigrants. Regarding the latter, Breton identifies at least four ways in which religion can assist; it can: a) provide practical services and social opportunities; b) foster social and civic participation; c) make available cultural tools to cope with the moral challenges encountered in the new cultural milieu; and d) offer a paradigm by which the new society is defined by members of the group (Breton 2012: 97).

> We think it is important that our children get a relation to our temple instead. It's not that they are not allowed in the church – they go there with the school – but just for them to get an idea of where our tradition comes from or belongs to.

This inclusion of elements from the Danish tradition and culture also makes Tamil Hindus more aware of the important hallmarks associated with being Hindu and Tamil, and it provides us with an interesting example of how inclusiveness and exclusiveness in relation to tradition or culture can mutually affect each other. This is true even if the motivation for adapting to westernised and Christian-like forms is to achieve greater respectability among the majority, as observed by Vertovec while investigating Hindus in Trinidad (Vertovec 1990: 232).

Collective memory

This common source of idea or reference that forms a culture or group identity is what Jan Assmann (2006) and Danièle Hervieu-Léger (2000: 124-125) call cultural or collective memory. Both these authors emphasise that memory is culturally transmitted, that it is not only located within the individual but is somehow stored in institutions or texts. I would like to add that, in relation to the Hindu tradition, memory is also found in rituals, behavioral patterns, and ethical conduct and is shared among a group of beings. From this point of view, the young Sri Lankan Tamil Hindus use collective memory as a central point of departure for the choices they make in life.[5]

Using the idea of collective memory as a theoretical framework does not imply that I disagree with constructionist viewpoints; in fact, I wish to emphasise that the presumed normativity anchored in the collective memory is under negotiation or is interpreted and connected to other identity-markers in such a way that it still provides meaning for those who relate to it; in other words, it is negotiated, interpreted and used in such a way that it gives meaning to those who relate to it

---

5. I have also used this perspective in the article "Young Tamil Hindus in Denmark and Their Relationship to Tradition and Collective Memory" (2010). Assmann's point of departure is an elaboration of culture and evolution, but I think his statements can also be applied to religion in diaspora and how elements from the collective memory are not moved diachronically in time but synchronically in space, despite the fact that it is still the diachronic or historical linking to a shared heritage that seems to necessitate the retention of shared identity markers, but in a new setting and under new circumstances. Jan Assmann (2006), who is inspired by Maurice Halbwachs' (1952) work with social memory, claims that memory is fundamentally a social phenomenon. And, with reference to Aleida Assmann (1999), he defines tradition as a special case of communication in which information is not exchanged reciprocally and horizontally but is transmitted vertically through the generations and can be recalled regardless of place and space because it is stored (ibid. 8).

as something they share. And, as Raymond Breton remarks, "individuals are not passive recipients of identities or cultural attributes but active agents in their construction" (2012: 35); or, as Paul Connerton (1989) claims in his book *How Societies Remember*, the collective memory is always shaped or conceived by the individual.

What is of interest here is Connerton's differentiation between three different forms of memories that together constitute the collective memory: the personal memory, the cognitive memory, and the habitual memory. It is important that these three memories coincide. This means that the individual can perceive collective memory as something he/she shares with others but that this perception is always read through the individual filter which is again formed by the other two forms of memory.

The shared tradition as part of a hybrid identity

The shared tradition is particularly open to negotiation among second- or third-generation immigrants who are struggling with their identity; for example, an identity as both Danish and Tamil or an identity as a Hindu on new terms. While a permanent re-interpretation process is currently occurring for the whole group, there is also an important generation gap when comparing first- and second-generations. Like their parents, second-generation immigrants understand themselves as Hindus, but they appear to assign different aspects to this category. First-generation immigrants generally try to uphold the tradition as they know it from Sri Lanka, whereas second-generation immigrants do not (Fibiger 2010).

As an overall pattern in Denmark, it seems as though the majority of second-generation Sri Lankan Tamil Hindus withdraw from many of the local or family-based rituals, which they categorise as a form of disbelief. But at the same time, as can be seen below, they do not completely reject the tradition they are socialised to; however, they feel strongly that it is important to understand the logic behind or to understand how different part of the tradition can contribute the their lives in Denmark before agreeing to keep them as a part of their new meaning-system.

> I will take the good things from both the Danish and the Tamil culture, and, in relation to Hinduism, I would like to understand it more before I choose what to give my children from it (Sri Lankan Tamil Hindu, Male, 25 years of age).

> I guess the Tamil culture is important to me, but it is difficult to define when it stirs inside me. It definitely has something to do with the language and the way I am raised. This doesn't mean that there isn't a lot from the Tamil Culture in Denmark I dislike; for example, shame

> and honour in relation to marriage, sexuality and gossip. I just want to get rid of these things! (Sri Lankan Tamil Hindu, female, 27 years of age).

These statements touch upon the relation between preservation and adaptation, but they also refer to the wish for change as second-generation Sri Lankan Tamil Hindus try to find new ways of constructing meaning in a Danish setting. This is an on-going process of negotiation during which their understandings of identity and belonging are redefined. Such a negotiation between being Hindu and Tamil, as well as being a Danish citizen is constantly present, and shapes their particular understanding of who they are. What I find interesting is that the second generation do not seem keen to relinquish any of these anchoring points; they clearly appreciate this form of cultural hybridity, but in a form that links them to a sense of belonging they share with their parents. At the same time, I argue that this form of multicultural blend is not arbitrary but is formed in relation to upbringing and a cultural heritage with a specific world- and life-view that informs their selection. Or, as Brahmadat writes while investigating immigrant-groups in Canada, "this recreation happens neither *in toto* nor *ex nihilo* - rather newcomers remake Islam, Buddhism, Hinduism, etc....out of a combination of old and new building resources" (Brahmadat 2005: 13-14).

Culture and gender issues

A double-bond of linking and de-linking is something the second generation of Sri Lankan Tamil Hindus share with all young immigrants living as minorities in a diaspora situation; however, I argue that the difficulty of deciphering the Hindu tradition gives rise to arguments that both support belonging to a specific tradition and support living as a modern second-generation intellectual Tamil Hindu in Denmark. This is particularly relevant when it comes to gender matters. The question of which arguments or duties should be excluded and which should be retained, reinterpreted or emphasised in relation to stree-dharma ("stree = woman, dharma = duty") has prompted debate, especially among young Tamil intellectual women. This debate relates to both their self-understanding and the question of how to find the right spouse here in Denmark (a suitable partner for a modern woman in Denmark but with a Tamil Hindu background). This is expressed in the following quotation:

> For me it is about the balance between our Tamil background and our Danish upbringing. I try to combine the good things from both cultures. I would like to have a husband who thinks the same also in relation to the upbringing of children, in relation to education, values, religion, boys/girls, alcohol, etc. (Sri Lankan Tamil Hindu, female 24 years of age).

These women are part of an open conflict between following traditional marriage patterns (in relation to caste or kin) and finding an equally educated husband, without losing the possibility to link their children to the tradition that they understand as an important identity-marker and an important resource in many matters of life. And, despite their open-minded criticism of their own upbringing and certain aspects of the Tamil Hindu tradition – which they understand as disbelief – most of them emphasise their role and duty as caretakers and transmitters of tradition. This could be the main reason for their reluctance to marry ethnic Danes,[6] as the following statements given by second-generation Sri Lankan Tamil Hindu women indicate:

> Hinduism doesn't take up much space in my daily life, but it is still part of my identity and it is part of my wish to keep up traditions; for example, in relation to marriage and raising my children. I feel I have a duty (as a result of my respect for the tradition) to keep up the relation to Tamilness and to Hinduism, but this is due to loyalty, not a forced duty (27 years of age).

> I don't want my children to become rootless. I do have roots here, but anyway. The Tamil language, but also the Hindu temple, must play a role (24 years of age).

These statements make it clear that tradition matters. However, what is of particular interest to the theme of this chapter – and for me as a scholar in Hindu religion – is to understand why or which elements of the tradition seem to be of such importance to the young Tamil Hindu women that they both wish to preserve them, pass them on to the next generation, and relate to them in their self-understanding and quest for what they view as the "ideal life".

As I mentioned previously, the members of this particular group face many of the same challenges that other young second and third generation of women in Denmark or in diaspora in general face (for example, identity constructions, double belonging, generation conflicts, gender conflicts, cultural hybridisation, relation to tradition, and multiple identities). However, I would like to claim that their status as Sri Lankan Tamil Hindu women in Denmark shapes these processes in a particular way. It is interesting that they seem reluctant to relinquish their anchoring points and that they appreciate their form of cultural hybridity. They understand such factors as important resources, which appear to be the main reason for wishing to marry a Sri Lankan Tamil Hindu man – a man who shares the same relations

---

6. Various surveys and research on Hindu Women's role in diaspora emphasise how Hindu women play an important role as cultural/religious caretakers and transmitters (Hole 2001; Knott 1996; 2000; Lourenco 2011; Rayaprol 1995; 1997).

to the aforementioned elements of belonging. Or, as expressed by a 26-year-old second-generation Sri Lankan Tamil Hindu woman:

> I would like to get married to a Tamil Hindu who lives and has been raised here in Denmark. The reason for this wish is that we would understand each other; for example, in relation to lifestyle (relationships between men and women, independence, work) and interests (concerts, dancing, drink a cold beer, travel). At the same time, we would share a common idea of belonging as both being Tamil and Hindu. I think that would help us when raising our children.

In the following section, I provide an example of how this schism of being a modern Danish woman (out-group relations) and a Tamil Hindu woman (in-group relations) has initiated a discussion on how to find the right husband; a husband who can live up to their ideals as independent and aspirational women and balance this with their need to maintain a tradition that links them to their social upbringing, their families, Sri Lanka, Tamil-ness and to Hinduism. What is of particular interest for the dialectic between in-group and out-group relation is how the young women find arguments or interpret elements within their tradition in such a way that fits their new way of life in the society of which they are now a part. In this strategy formation, they attempt to balance deals from both inside and outside.

How to find the right spouse?

> Tamil women beat every record when it comes to educational level and integration in Denmark. But the following question arises: are we able to find enough well-educated Tamil men for all these Tamil women when they wish to find a husband?

This was the main statement and question on a poster that invited young Tamils (and other interested people) for a debate event on 18th April 2009 (International Women's Day) in Aarhus, Denmark. The debate was arranged by the individuals behind the Internet chat forums *Nizhal.dk* and *Tamilgirls.dk* and the Tamil Magazine *The Bridge-builder* (in Danish: Brobyggeren).

The title of the poster was *Challenges Tamil Women Meet when Choosing a Partner* and, aside from the main question stated above, this issue was explored further with the following questions:

- What kind of possibilities do Tamil women find on the marriage market?
- Do freedom and independence have an impact on Tamil women when choosing a partner?
- In which way do parents, society and unwritten rules have an impact on Tamil women's lives?
- Does the fact that women are better educated than men affect gender patterns?
- Which expectations and demands do modern, independent and well-educated Tamil women have in terms of their future husband?

Unfortunately, the event was cancelled at short notice due to problems in Sri Lanka – the flow of refugees from Jaffna to various refugee camps gave rise to new political tensions on the island – but the invitation was published on the Internet and further elaborated with questions such as:

> Have Tamil women found a new social status to replace their parents' patriarchal values? Why is it more common for a Tamil woman to marry a Danish man than for a Tamil man to marry a Danish woman? Do we see a pattern in which young Tamil women are increasingly breaking with their parents' values and socioeconomic relations and marrying for love? Has the concept of love changed? (Tamilgirl.dk, Nizhal.dk, 18.4. 2009).

This initiated a long and continuing debate in the Internet chat rooms and in the magazine *Bridge Builder*, and it also caused people to reflect more widely on what it is to be a Tamil Hindu woman with a Danish twist. For some, it appears that the situation in Denmark differs from other Sri Lankan Tamil Hindu groups living in diaspora, as the following comment from an anonymous woman writing on Tamilgirl.dk (triggered by the above call) indicates. This could be the reason why the above debate seemed important to second-generation intellectual Tamil Hindu women in Denmark:

> Dear all,
> I write this comment as a person who has followed the development of the arrangements from the sideline. I have noticed two different groups of critics [...] One group argues that the problem does not exist, and criticizes the arrangers for making up a problem. The other group argues that the arrangers are making the problem too vague. They want an even more critical announcement. I think that things are changing quicker in Denmark in comparison with, for example, England and Canada. It is not because the Tamils in Denmark are more "humane", but because we are a small community. It is more difficult for a small community to reproduce and keep up values in their original form. In England and in Canada Tamils mostly marry within the same caste and they mostly interrelate with Tamils within

the same caste. At the same time they also marry within their own educational level. Both are possible in big communities.

In 2005, around 16% of all the Tamil marriages were mixed marriages between a Tamil (mostly women) and an ethnic Dane (source: the Ministry for Integration).[7] I have been told by some of the Tamil women that it was because they never met any Tamil boy while studying [...] (www.Tamilgirl.dk, April 2009).

This writer claims that, in large communities – such as those found in England and Canada – it is possible to find the right match in terms of caste and educational level; however, she doesn't believe this is possible in Denmark. At the same time, by using the word "humane", she implicitly criticises the way things are done in Canada and England without explicitly claiming that the Danish model is the accomplished ideal. This is also expressed in the concluding paragraph, when she notes that the reason for marrying ethnic Danes may not be because they are the ideal match, but because it is difficult to meet Tamil men on the same educational level while studying.

In relation to mixed marriages, most of the second-generation Sri Lankan Tamil Hindu women I have interviewed are divided on the issue. One the one hand, they are attracted to the idea, but, on the other hand, they doubt it will succeed in the long term. They are particularly concerned about their children, whom they do not wish to become 'rootless', and the relation to the tradition they share with their parents (as expressed by one of the Sri Lankan Tamil women, 26 years of age, I had interviewed: 'It has formed me to become the person I am today...'). This emphasises the fact that linking to the tradition matters; however, when it comes to de-linking, it becomes clear that most of the second-generation Tamils would like to eliminate caste as a parameter for whom to marry. This is also what the implicit criticism of Canada and England is hinting at. Instead, second-generation Sri Lankan Tamil Hindu women would like a new hierarchical system to be taken into account; namely, educational level. Considering their relation to tradition and collective memory, it is interesting that young Sri Lankan Tamil Hindus seem to find arguments within the tradition itself to align educational level with caste. They refer – at least indirectly – to *purusha-artha*, the four goals in life, which are part of the Hindu ethic and stress the need for engaging in life. These four goals are *dharma* (ethics, morality), *artha* (wealth, political power), *kama* (erotic and aesthetic enjoyment) and *moksha* (liberation from reincarnation). They are all related to each other and to the four life stages (ashramas). *Artha* in particular is used to legitimise engagement in a modern society, because it is interpreted as

---

7. The young woman refers to the following research by Statistics Denmark: Table 2: Education among 16–29-year-old women and men from Sri Lanka in 2007.

valuing education and prestigious work as a means to its fulfillment. So, in this way, their negotiating is not a question of dismantling tradition but of making it fit their lives in Denmark.

Cultural hybridisation

The concept cultural hybridisation has been employed by many post- or late-modern theorists (Homi Bhabha, Stuart Hall) as a way of transcending the essentialising tendencies in identity discourse, suggesting that identity and culture are generated by a cross-cultural or multi-dimensional communication or better mutual impact. This constructed meeting-point both contains elements of and differs from the "original" cultures. This meeting point is never fixed but comprises heterogeneous elements with shifting points of views. In this way, cultural hybridity is continuously constructed in new ways and is a product of an on-going process of negotiations and identifications formed in relation to context. However, I wish to argue that the point of departure is not completely constructed; or, to be more precise, I contend that it is constructed within certain patterns, so that it forms a kind of recognisable and meaningful framework for the communication or dialogue. That is what I have referred to in this chapter as cultural memory.

This corresponds to what Mikhail Bakhtin conceptualises as the *dialogical self*, which is understood as autonomous positions within an individual; however, I interpret this (along with Connerton's reading) in relation to collective memory, where the inner communication in the dialogical self is shaped by upbringing, circumstances, context and that which has triggered the inner dialogue. As Breton writes, "Cultural entrepreneurs, however, need symbolic resources for such an undertaking" (Breton 2012: 117).

Bhatia and Ram apply Bakhtin's idea of the dialogical self to what they call "the immigrant self" and, from this, they use it to understand how immigrant groups "constantly negotiate their multiple and often conflicting, dialogical voices, histories and subject positions...challenging the linear, static, universal models of acculturations" (2004: 229).

The dialogical self can also be used effectively to understand the multiple identities of the second generation in general and, therefore, to understand the identities of the second generation of Sri Lankan Tamil Hindus in Denmark. This group clearly wishes to become multicultural, but they wish to do so on certain premises and without delinking from the collective memory, which they simultaneously attempt to qualify so it fits (and will continue to fit) their new setting. They are generally critical toward their parents' relation to tradition, which they interpret as being unreflective and superstitious.

In general, the second generation of Sri Lankan Tamil Hindus in Denmark do not wish to relinquish the collective memory that connects them to their family and kin, but they reinterpret it or select the parts of it that suit their daily living in Danish society. Firstly, they often require proof or textual authority to support a given view or embedded behavioural pattern before they accept it as part of their meaning system. Secondly, this process is shaped by the Danes' relation to certain elements within the Hindu-tradition, which approves of yoga, meditation, the idea behind karma and reincarnation, and the personal striving for resurrection, and disapproves of the caste system and arranged marriage.

This demonstrates that the role of culture is not only to define and sustain existing world- or life-views, but also to devise and support new ones. In this way, culture (as well as religion) becomes a tool kit of symbolic resources interpreted in such a way that it helps them to cope with the ambiguities they experience in their new social environment and the various conflictive situations they face in relation to their parents, gender, and other groups.

This double-bond of linking and de-linking is something the second generation of Sri Lankan Tamil Hindus share with all young immigrants living as minorities in a diaspora situation. However, as I argued above, the fact that the Hindu tradition is so difficult to decipher means it can contribute arguments for both belonging to a specific tradition and living as a modern second-generation Sri Lankan Tamil Hindu in Denmark. This was expressed very profoundly by a young Sri Lankan Tamil Hindu woman:

> I don't think that Hinduism limits my possibilities to play an active role in Danish society. I am pleased that I am a Hindu, because our religion – compared to Islam – is not a limitation for integration. Our religion teaches us to use the oppotunities we have got in this life; that means to get a good education and to work hard...And when it comes to God, despite the name he is given, he is just one and the same (Female 27 years).

It becomes clear that the way in which they regard and experience religion changes. As they become increasingly imbedded in "mainstream" society in the new setting and are subject to its social and cultural influences, they begin to question issues regarding the interconnection between elements of the tradition in which they were raised. Some elements are emphasised, others are reinterpreted and some are rejected, even if this leads to conflict between generations and genders.

Although this particular group faces similar challenges to other second and third generations of women in Denmark (and diaspora in general), I would like to argue that this group's response to such challenges is shaped in a unique way by their status as Sri Lankan Tamil Hindu women in Denmark. The negotiation between being Hindu (religious identity), Tamil (cultural and social identity) and

Danish (social and cultural identity) is continuously present and shapes their particular understanding of belonging, not only to a place in history or in the world but also in the mind. They seem reluctant to relinquish these anchoring points and they appreciate this form of cultural hybridity. They understand them as important resources, which appears to be the primary motivation behind their wish to marry a Sri Lankan Tamil Hindu man; a man who shares the same relations to these elements of belonging.

Conclusion

It is not new to claim that young Sri Lankan Tamil Hindus in Denmark (who were either born in Denmark or came to Denmark as small children) have a different relationship to tradition and culture than their parents; however, what I have tried to demonstrate in this chapter is that their self-understanding as young Sri Lankan Tamil Hindus negotiates the process of encompassing and renewing elements from the tradition in such a way that the tradition is still understood as a collective memory they share with their parents.

Through my interviews with second-generation Sri Lankan Tamil Hindus in Denmark, it has become clear that the language, the texts, and the temple institution play an important role in the process of storing tradition as something they not only relate to in their self-identity as being either Tamil and/or Hindu, but also as something they wish to pass on to their children.

In relation to cultural hybridity, the second generation of Sri Lankan Tamil Hindus in Denmark appears to have no difficulty in connecting to at least four forms of identity-givers: as a Tamil (cultural, ethnic, and social identity), as a Tamil-Hindu (locally anchored cultural and religious identity that differentiates them from Tamil-Christian and Muslims), as a Hindu that links them to the global Hindu tradition, and as a Dane (social and cultural identity). Most second-generation Sri Lankan Tamil Hindus understand this as a privilege, provided they can themselves select how to connect to these different identities and pass this patchwork on to their children within a normative, yet deliberate framework – which, in this chapter has been referred to as collective memory – that in itself is not static, but fluctuates. Even if what the second generation of Sri Lankan Tamil Hindus put into this category differs from their parents, they still view it as a form of meeting point or mutual point of departure that they can use in the discussion of what it means to be a Sri Lankan Tamil Hindu in Denmark and what should be emphasised or downplayed within this shared reservoir of meaning. I appealed to the discussion between caste relation and education level as an example of how young intellectual Sri Lankan Hindu women use ideals from within the tradition to overrule others that fail to fit either their new society or their own life ideals. This emphasizes the way in which Appudurai's ethnoscape (which is associated with language, ethnicity, and locally based religiosity) is occasionally overruled by what Dwyer calls religioscape; Dwyer explores this concept in her research on British Asians, who she claims often define themselves primarily by religion and only to some extent by caste (Dwyer 2004: 197).

Let us now return to the question that formed the title of this paper: Why not become multi-cultural? The answer is that second-generation Sri Lankan Tamil Hindus don't mind and even appreciate becoming multicultural, but only on premises that communicate both with the culture they are linked to diachronically (through history or collective memory) and synchronically (in relation to their being in Denmark, being a Danish citizen, and their upbringing in Danish society). Their multiculturality is primarily formed by six identity givers: a) being a Hindu (global religious/cultural identity, b) being a Tamil (ethnic identity but also local cultural and social identity), c) the particular combination of being Tamil-Hindu (local religious, cultural but also social identity), d) being a Danish citizen (local social and cultural identity), e) being a young second generation immigrant in Denmark, f) being a young Dane. These identity givers or providers by which they become Danish "with a twist" are interwoven in such a way that young second generation Sri Lankan Tamil Hindus differ in some respects from other groups in Denmark, from their parents and also from other second generation Sri Lankan Tamil Hindus situated elsewhere in the world; however, at the same time, they also share many of the same problems, possibilities, ideals, and wishes for the future.

■ References

Assmann, J. *Religion and Cultural Memory*. Stanford: Stanford University Press, 2006.
Bauman, Z. *Liquid Modernity*. Cambridge: Polity Press, 2000.
Beckford, J.A. *Social Theory & Religion*. Cambridge: Cambridge University Press, 2003.
Beyer, P. "The Future of Non-Christian Religions in Canada: Patterns of Religious Identification among Recent Immigrants and their Second Generation, 1981-2001." *Studies in Religion* 34 (2005): 165-96.
Bhabha, H. *The Location of Culture*. London: Routledge, 1994.
Bhatia, S. and A. Ram. "Culture, Hybridity and the Dialogical Self: Cases from the South Asian Diaspora." In *Mind, Culture and Activity* 11, 3 (2004): 224-40.
Bramadat, P. "Beyond Christian Canada: Religion and Ethnicity in a Multicultural Society." In *Religion and Ethnicity in Canada*, ed. P. Bramadat and D. Seljak. Toronto: Pearson Education, 2005.
Breton, R. *Different Gods. Integrating Non-Christian Minorities into a Primarily Christian Society*. Montreal/Kingston: McGill-Queen's University Press, 2012.
Campbell, C. *The Easternization of the West. A Thematic Account of Cultural Change in the Modern Era*. Boulder/London: Paradigm Publishers, 2007.
Connerton, P. *How Societies Remember*. Cambridge: Cambridge University Press, 1989.

Dwyer, R. "The Swaminarayan Movement." In *South Asians in the Diaspora: Histories and Religious Traditions*, ed. K.A. Jacobsen and P.P. Kumar, 181-99. Leiden: Brill, 2004.

Fibiger, M.Q. "Young Tamil Hindus in Denmark and Their Relationship to Tradition and Collective Memory." *The Finnish Journal of Ethnicity and Migration (e-journal)*, 2010.

Fibiger, M.Q. "When the Hindu-goddess Moves to Denmark – The Establishment of a Sakta-tradition." *Bulletin for the Study of Religion* 41, 3 (2012): 29-36.

Halbwachs, M. *Les Cadres sociaux de la mémoire*. Paris: PUF, 1952.

Heelas, P. *Spiritualities of Life*. Blackwell, Oxford, 2008.

Heelas, P. and L. Woodhead. *The Spiritual Revolution. Why Religion is Giving Way to Spirituality*. Malden/Oxford/Victoria: Blackwell Publishing, 2005.

Hervieu-Léger, D. *Religion as a Chain of Memory*. Cambridge: Polity Press, 2000.

Hole, E. "Ethnicity and Symbolism among Hindu Women in a Small Diaspora Community." In *Hindu Diaspora: Global Perspectives*, ed. T. S. Rukmani, 443-69. New Delhi: Munshiram Manoharlai, 2001.

Jacobsen, K.A. and P.P. Kumar. "Introduction." In *South Asians in the Diaspora: Histories and Religious Traditions*, ed. K.A. Jacobsen and P.P. Kumar, ix-xxiv. Leiden: Brill, 2004.

Jacobsen, K. A. "Establishing Ritual Space in the Hindu Diaspora in Norway." In *South Asians in the Diaspora: Histories and Religious Traditions*, ed. K.A. Jacobsen and P.P. Kumar, 134-48. Leiden: Brill, 2004.

Jenkins, R. *Rethinking Ethnicity*. London: SAGE Publications, 2003.

Knott, K. "Hinduism in Britain." In *The South Asian Diaspora in Britain, Canada and The United States*, ed. H. Coward, J. Hinnels, and R. Williams, 89-108. New York: New York Press, 2000.

Knott, K. "Hindu Women, Destiny and Streedharma." *Religion* 26 (1996): 15-35.

Lorenco, I. "Religion and Gender: the Hindu Diaspora in Portugal." *South Asian Diaspora* 3, 1 (2011): 37-51.

Rayaprol, A. *Negotiating Identities: Women in the Indian Diaspora*. New Delhi: Oxford University Press, 1997.

Rayaprol, A. "Gender Ideologies and Practices among South Indian Immigrants in Pittsburgh." *Sagar: South Asian Graduate Research Journal* 2, 1 (1995): 268-70.

Sen, A. "Social Exclusion: Concept, Application, and Scrutiny." Social Development Papers No. 1, Office of Environment and Social Development, Asian Development Bank. Manila: Asian Development Bank, 2000.

Singleton, M. *Yoga Body. The Origins of Modern Posture Practice*. Oxford: Oxford University Press, 2010.

Vertovec, S. "Religion and Ethnic Ideology: The Hindu Youth Movement in Trinidad." *Ethnic and Racial Studies* 13, 2 (1990): 223-49.

14 The Entanglement between Religion and Politics in Denmark

Niels Kærgård

All members of society have attitudes, values and views on life and society. Some of these attitudes and views are normally classified as religious, while others are political or ideological. But it is far from certain that individuals actually make such distinctions between their attitudes (e.g. regarding immigration of refugees or the environment).

It is difficult to define both religion and policy. But it seems obvious that religion includes some elements which deal with attitudes towards behavior and society. In some religions, attitudes are very specific and concrete, while in others they are more implicit. In the Danish case, the evangelical Lutheran attitudes to morals and society are very implicit. A clear separation between the religious and the secular regime is normally seen as a key element in Luther's theology. Nevertheless, the Lutheran influence is so important also in secular matters that some researchers and authors talk about a "Lutheran work ethic", while others consider the Danish welfare state to be a result of a Christian attitude towards the weak and poor in society.

How can politics and political attitudes be defined? What is the difference between political ideology and religion? There is no obvious, simple answer to this question. However, perhaps the core of religion deals with individual responsibility and with nature, health and other uncontrollable elements of human life, while the core of policy and ideology is related to attitudes to society and elements of society which are controllable by human acting and decisions. But the border between religion and policy is not so obvious and clear, that it is irrelevant to analyze the entanglement between these two elements of human life.

Such an analysis seems more complicated in Denmark than in many other countries. The Danish church does not have any official spokesman or formulated program, and Denmark never had a Christian political party of any importance. This means that influence of Christianity in the Danish society, if existing, is very implicit.

The Danish model of religion

Until very recently, the religious life of the Danes has been organized in the public Evangelical Lutheran Church, which includes up to 99 per cent of the population. Since the 1970, an irreligious minority and the number of Muslims have been fast growing, but the public church still includes about 80 percent of the population, see table 1.

Table 1: Religious affiliations in Denmark, percentages of the population

Year	Total number of inhabitants	State Lutheran Church	Jews	Roman Catholics	Muslims	Others
1880	100%	99.1%	0.2%	0.2%	0.0%	0.5%
1901	100%	98.7%	0.2%	0.2%	-	1.2%
1921	100%	97.9%	0.2%	0.7%	0.0%	1.2%
1974	100%	94,3%	0.1%	0.5%	-	5.1%
1983	100%	91,6%	0.1%	0.5%	0.8%	7.0%
1990	100%	89,3%	0.1%	0.6%	1.5%	8.6%
2000	100%	85,1%	0.1%	0.6%	3.2%	11.0%

Source: Kærgård (2006a).

There is a close relation between the church and the state. The church is mentioned as supported by the state in the constitution and plays an important role on a number of official occasions – the opening of Parliament, the Danish holidays are mainly of Christian origin, etc. The registration of birth and death is taken care of by the church and cemeteries are often taken care of by the church even for non-members. Since 1849, the Danish constitution has included freedom of religious belief, but the different religious communities are not treated equally. The official church is closely related to the state and mainly managed by the political systems and the Minister of Ecclesiastical Affairs. A considerable number of other religious communities are publicly approved which means that the members get tax-reduction for their membership fee. Whereas it is clear that the public church and others religious communities are treated differently, it is far from clear which of the arrangements are the most advantageous to the religious community. The public church has a number of obligations in relation to the state, and has had to accept some – for a number of members of the church – controversial decisions from the political system (e.g. female ministers in 1948 and same sex marriages 2012). Calculations seem to indicate that the economic net transfers between the official church and state are beneficial to the state (see Kærgård and Pedersen 2012; 2012a), while the tax reduction is a clear advantage to the other religious communities. The Danish system is discussed in more details in Christoffersen (2010).

All this means that the Danish Evangelical Lutheran Church is one of the religious communities in the world, which includes the biggest part of the population. But it also means that the members have very different attitudes towards religious questions. In Denmark, there have been religious conflicts regarding virgin birth, female priests, same sex marriages, etc., but they have all taken place within the public church. As investigated by Andersen and Lücau (2004; 2011) and Zuckerman (2008), the Danes have one of the most relaxed attitudes in the world towards religious questions. In 2008, only 10 per cent of the members went to church regularly, 19 per cent believed in paradise, and only 9 per cent in hell, but 72 per cent considered themselves as "believers", see Andersen and Lüchau (2011: 80-81).

Such a church with a big majority of the population as members, but a loose relationship between the church and its members can of course be considered differently. From a national and economic point of view it is an advantage for the cohesion of society that almost everybody is a member of the same religious community, and that this community has a relaxed attitude towards the secular institutions. But others would find most Danes' relation to Christianity uncommitted and impassionate. The famous Danish philosopher Søren Kierkegaard is quoted for stating that "Christianity is phased out in line with its diffusion".

The Danish church has been described as a remote and retired church which is normally not seen, but never the less is always implicitly present in the background (Jensen 1995).

The Danish political system

Since 1915, Denmark has had a proportional election system where every party with more than 2 per cent of the voters becomes part of the Danish Parliament. Since 1953, the Danish Parliament has been a one chamber system. This means that the number of parties in Parliament has been considerable (table 2).

In relation to the topics of this article it is important to stress that Denmark never had a Christian party of any importance. Germany has the Christlich Demokratische Union with 40-45 per cent of the votes and has formed government from 1982-1998 and since 2002. In Norway, the prime minister was from the Kristeligt Folkeparti from 1997-2000 and 2001-2005, and in 1997 the party received 13.7 per cent of the votes. In Denmark, Kristeligt Folkeparti (now Kristendemokraterne) was represented in Parliament from 1973-2005, but never with more than very few per cent of the votes.

Table 2: Members of the Danish Parliament 1960-2008

	Right wing	Liberal party	Conservative party	Center parties	Christian parties	Social democrats	Left wing
1960	6	38	32	11	-	76	11
1964	5	38	36	10	-	76	10
1966	0	35	34	17	-	69	20
1968	0	34	37	27	-	62	15
1971	0	30	31	27	0	70	17
1973	28	22	16	39	7	46	17
1975	24	42	10	17	9	53	20
1977	26	21	15	23	6	65	19
1979	20	22	22	21	5	68	17
1981	16	20	26	24	4	59	26
1984	6	22	42	18	5	56	26
1987	9	19	38	20	4	54	31
1988	16	22	35	19	4	55	24
1990	12	29	30	16	4	69	15
1994	11	42	27	13	0	62	19
1998	17	42	16	15	4	63	18
2001	22	56	16	9	4	52	16
2005	24	52	18	17	0	47	17
2007	25	46	18	14	0	45	27
2011	22	56	8	17	0	44	28

Note: Danish names of parties: Right wing (De uafhængige, Fremskridtspartiet, Dansk Folkeparti), Liberal party (Venstre, Liberal Alliance), Conservative party (De Konservative), Centre parties (Det radikale venstre, Retsforbundet, Liberal Centrum, Centrum Demokraterne, Ny Alliance), Christian parties (Kristeligt Folkeparti), Social democrats (Socialdemokratiet), Left wing (Socialistisk Folkeparti, Danmarks Kommunistiske Parti, Venstresocialisterne, Fælles Kurs, Enhedslisten). The Danish Parliament has 179 members, but four are elected in Greenland and the Faroe Islands, and one for some periods from the German minority. Only the Danish parties are included.
Source: Folketinget (the Danish Parliament) (2008).

Kristeligt Folkeparti was founded in 1970 mainly as a protest against free abortion and the cancellation of the ban against pornographic pictures and the generally less restrictive sexual moral after 1968. Denmark canceled the ban against pornographic pictures in 1969 and a law about free choice of abortion passed Parliament in 1973. Kristeligt Folkeparti's programme as formulated in Folketinget (1998) includes three main points:

- The embryo has infinite value
- We shall take care of the weak
- We shall take care of the environment and resources

Since then, conflicts between more right wing people stressing a. and more left wing people stressing b. and c. have divided the party, and in the last decade it has not even been close to getting members elected to Parliament. This means that one has to look for religious influence in the "normal" secular political parties.

The Christians and the political parties

In Danish society where the church has no explicitly formulated statement, and a Christian point of view is hidden in the background rather than standing out as a high-profile statement in the debate, it is of course difficult to document the entanglement between policy and Christianity. What may be done, however, is to look at people with a university master degree in Theology who have been members of the Danish Parliament since 1960.[1] These people are found in the biographies of the members of parliament published by the Parliament just after each election. Among the members of the Parliament there have been 26 theologians (a Greenlandic member outside the Danish political parties is excluded); of these 26, 24 hold a university master degree in Theology and 2 have a supplementary theological education.[2] 23 were directly elected parliament members, 2 entered parliament as substitutes for a period, and 1 became minister without being elected beforehand. Of these 26, 4 have worked as politicians or with different forms of teaching or research during the entire period, while 21 have worked as ministers in the Danish public church.

The first question is of course whether these official "Christians" are related to specific political parties. This distribution is shown in table 3. The figures seem too small to make more precise and relative calculations. However, just to get an indication of the size of the parties, the total number of seats in parliament in connection with the party's best election between 1960 and 2011 is shown. Other

---

1. The focus in this paper is not the ordinary voter or church member, but the decision makers, politicians and the educated theologians. There can be a difference between these two groups. Lüchau (2011) investigates the attitude among voters and its relation to the recent focus on national and Christian values in the political debate about e.g. immigration. His conclusion is that "Religion has returned to the political arena in Denmark, but it has not returned to the general public".
2. Asger Baunsbeck-Jensen and Jesper Langballe have this "særuddannelse" (supplementary education) and are included. Jens Møller, who got an education as missionary, is not included. A number of other members of parliament have studied theology, but never finished the education. They are not included.

indicators could be shown but they are either as problematic or very complicated (ideally the total number of members from 1960-2011 should be counted, but this is rather time consuming) and the figures are too small to make more precise statistical calculations anyway.

Table 3: Christian theologians in the Danish Parliament 1960-2012 and their political party

Political party	Theologians among Parliament members	Total number of members of Parliament in best election
Socialist Party – SF	3	27
Social Democrats – Socialdemokratiet	6	76
Social Liberals – Radikale Venstre	1	27
Christian Democrats – Kristeligt Folkeparti	3	9
Liberals – Venstre	7	56
Conservatives – Det Konservative Folkeparti	3	42
Danish People's Party – Dansk Folkeparti	3	25

Nevertheless, it is possible to observe that all the major parties have ministers of the church among their Parliament members. There is perhaps a few more on the right wing side than on the left wing side but this is far from statistically significant. The conclusion must be that there are no correlations between active Christianity and political attitudes.

A survey among Danish priests before the election in 2011 made by the Danish newspaper *Kristeligt Dagblad* shows a trend towards the left wing side, see table 4, but still the number of priests is distributed very broadly among all political parties. It is perhaps most remarkable that the liberal party (Venstre), which according to table 4 has been the most popular party in the church milieu, is so modestly represented.

Table 4: Survey among priests of Danish National Evangelical Lutheran Church before the election to Parliament 2011

Party	Number of voters among priests, per cent	Number among all voters, per cent
Socialists	18.0	15.9
Social Democrats	14.5	24.8
Social Liberals	19.5	9.5
Kristeligt Folkeparti	5.0	0.8
Liberals	10.0	26.7
Conservative	9.5	4.9
Danish People's Party	5.0	12.3
Others and don't know	18.5	5.1

Note: Socialists include both SF and Endhedslisten. Liberal Alliance is included in "Others".
Source: Johansen (2011). The survey was sent to 2170 ministers of the church and 597 answered.

Another possible hypothesis is that the theological studies at the university and their treatment of political questions has changed over time; in the 1970s a number of professors were Marxists, and in other periods other attitudes have been dominating. To investigate this, table 5 contains an overview of the theologians classified both in relation to political party and year of their master's degree. Here as well, there is no significant structure. Perhaps the right wing has been dominating among the candidates before 1945, but this is still far from being significant.

Table 5: Christian theologians in the Danish Parliament 1960-2012 classified after political party and year of university degree

Year of university degree in theology	Right wing parties	Kristeligt Folkeparti	Left wing parties
1944 or before	7	0	3
1945 or after	6	3	7
Total	13	3	10

Note: Right wing: Liberal, Conservative and Danish People's Party. Left wing: Socialists, Social Democrats and Social Liberals.

A last possible question is whether the political activity among theologians or the parties' interest in engaging them has changed over time. As shown in table 6, it is not possible to find such a tendency. That the largest group is from 1930-1969 seems natural. Some of the candidates before 1929 had already retired in 1960, and some of the candidates after 1970 were still at the beginning of their careers.

The evident main conclusion of the investigation must be that the active Christians (the priests) are divided almost equally among all the political parties in Denmark.

Table 6: Christian theologians in the Danish Parliament 1960-2012 classified by year of university degree

Year of university master's degree	Number of parliament members
-1929	3
1930-1949	7
1950-1969	8
1970-1989	4
1990-2009	4

The Christians and the political debate

An alternative to the formal analysis of the relation between priests and political parties is to consider the Christian spokesmen's participation in the public debate about political matters. Explicit Christian points of view have been found mainly in relation to four political areas.

- Family and sexual moral (family law, divorces, pornography, abortion, same sex marriages, etc.)
- Social problems (the welfare state, attitudes to the poor and weak citizens, social laws)
- Environment policy (biodiversity and protection of nature)
- Immigration and integration

Besides these "secular" questions, the Christian spokesmen have of course participated in the debate regarding questions of more direct religious relevance like education and ecclesiastical topics.

In none of the four areas it is possible to see a united Christian point of view that has dominated the public debate and legislation. Some Christian groups were strongly opposed to abortion and pornographic images and literature, but the ban against pornographic images was cancelled in 1969 and free choice of abortion was passed by parliament in 1973, at a time where 95 per cent of the population were members of the public church, and the protest movement organized in Kristeligt Folkeparti got a maximum of about 5 per cent of the votes. The big majority of the members of the Danish public church and the secular part of the votes were united in the liberal attitude to these questions.

The social questions have also always divided the Danish church. Already in a debate in the 1870s, the two most prominent bishops participated. H.L. Martensen argued for a Christian socialism:

> One has to go into the material interests of the workers. They must be supported both by spiritual guidance and by material support for the improvement of their circumstances. When our Lord and Saviour fed the 5,000 men in the desert, he fed them not only spiritually by his words, but he satisfied them materially too. It is this double feeding which is needed by the poor (Translation of Martensen 1874: 53).

But his colleague D.G. Monrad was of a different opinion:

> The Christian kingdom is not of this world, and this means the Christian people, when they spoke not in their own name as humble mortal men, as simple citizens, ought not to talk too much about politics, not to judge about government systems and constitutions and not to strive for changing the civil society and to search Christian-ethical arrangement and politics (Translation of Monrad 1878: 144).

And both these opinions are still found in the church as indicated by the ministers' very different attitudes to the political parties.

There have been a number of theologians who have participated in the environment debate from a Christian point of view, arguing that we need to take care of the creation. Professor K.E. Løgstrup and his students Ole Jensen (Jensen 1976; 1980; 2011) and Jacob Wolf (Wolf 1997; 2012) are representative of this school. Member of the European Parliament, Margrethe Auken, and the former Danish Minister of Environmental Affairs, Ida Auken, are both theologians and members of the green sector of the Socialist People's Party. But it seems wrong to say that a Christian stewardship of nature has played a dominant role in the Danish political debate.

The most heated debate in Denmark during the last decade has been related to immigration and integration policy, however the church has been strongly divided on this issue. The most critical attitude towards open borders has been represented by the Danish People's Party with its two priests Søren Krarup and Jesper Langeballe as the main ideologists, arguing that a Christian humanistic attitude towards refugees is an unchristian mixture of the secular and the Christian regime as Luther in his time argued against the peasant rising and the social-radical part of the reform movement with Thomas Müntzer. But during Christmas of 2005, a considerable number of ministers of the church supported a more positive human treatment of refugees under the motto "there is still no room for them in the inn". Different aspects of the political debate about immigration, integration, and multiculturalism are discussed in Lüchau (2011) and Kærgård (2010).

It does not seem possible to find any political topics where the church or most of the church has a common attitude which has marked the development in Danish society. But this does not mean that Christian attitudes are without consequence on political matters. There have been specific religious groups with important influence. To investigate this a bit further, let us look at the history of the Danish welfare system.

The establishment of the Danish welfare state 1870-1924: Christian influence

As already discussed, there has never been Christian influence via specific political parties. This does not mean, however, that Christian attitudes were without influence in the creation of the Danish Welfare state. Some of the main pioneers in the debate about social matters were individual Christian spokesmen; most prominently Hans Lassen Martensen (1808-84), Harald Westergaard (1853-1936), and Fernando Linderberg (1854-1914), see (Kærgård 2005; 2006).

Hans Lassen Martensen was at the pinnacle of the official Danish church. He was professor of theology at the University of Copenhagen 1840-1854 and bishop of Zealand which includes Copenhagen 1854-1884. From 1845, he combined these positions with being Chaplain-in-Ordinary to the royal family.[3] In the 1870s, Martensen worked on Christian ethics. He published a more general volume in 1871 and, in 1878, two volumes on specific topics. One of these was his social ethics ("Den Sociale Etik"), a book of 475 pages. But already in 1874 he published a 78-page pamphlet about socialism and Christianity ("Socialisme og Christendom"). He himself did not consider the pamphlet as being of a more polemical nature, but rather a part of his "official" Christian ethics; almost all the pages in the pamphlet were included without any changes in the 1878 volume of his ethics.

Martensen was extremely critical towards the capitalist market economy and towards liberalism and rather positive towards socialism; and the pamphlet was published in 1874, at a point in time where the first Danish socialists were in prison

---

3. The ecclesiastical history of Denmark in the 19th century was strongly marked by reformers in the periphery of the official church, notably Søren Kierkegaard (1813-1855) and Nikolaj Frederik Severin Grundtvig (1783-1872), but Martensen is probably the most important representative of the official Danish church in this century.

for political activity, and where support for the international socialist movement was forbidden. Martensen's point of view was that individualism is the curse of modern society:

> Social egotism has in our time, behind the shield of Liberalism, grown strong through the progress of science and the associated control of nature, and through the ever-growing advance of industry and capital (Translation of Martensen 1878: 127-28).

From this position, Martensen considered mainstream economics and especially Adam Smith very critically. Martensen was not blind to the benefits of the market economy in the form of economic growth and international development, but he considered the costs of this system to be greater:

> It is not possible to deny, that the free competition has contributed to developing much power and given wealth to many people; neither is it possible to deny that capital is important to society, to the great companies and a universal economic coherence, a world economy in contrast to an national economy; but neither is it possible to deny that the free competition has made many more miserable and poor, that thousands upon thousands have fought a desperate battle for their daily bread in which they finally succumbed to the stronger (Translation of Martensen 1878: 172-173).

Martensen was rather positive towards socialism and mentioned both Marx and Engels' descriptions of the modern society which "have not been disproved" (Martensen 1878: 176). But Martensen was not simply a socialist. After having described the problem of modern capitalism, he provided a critical description of the socialist movement as well. He considered himself a kind of socialist, but not a revolutionary socialist of the Marxian type. For him there was a third way, "ethical socialism".

Martensen's contributions were widely debated both in 1874 in relation to the publication of *Socialisme og Christendom*, and in 1878 when *Den Christelige Ethik* was published. One of the most prominent of Martensen's critics was his episcopal colleague D.G. Monrad (1811-1887). Monrad was one of the most remarkable personalities in 19th century Denmark; member of the Danish Parliament 1849-65 and for many terms a cabinet minister. He was the main author of Denmark's first democratic constitution in 1848-49 and Prime Minister in 1863-1864. In 1878, Monrad published, as already mentioned, a long pamphlet (about 150 pages) called *Liberalismens Gjenmæle til Biskop Martensens Sociale ethic*. (The Reply of Liberalism to Bishop Martensen's Social Ethics). According to Monrad, one should not foolishly defy the great economic laws given by God to constitute human society. According to Monrad, Martensen's policy would not change society – at least not in any positive direction.

Neither Martensen nor Monrad participated further in the debate. They were, so to say, too prominent to participate in the public debate. But the debate continued among their pupils and supporters. This means that the social Christian point of view was represented by others in the decades after the 1870s, particularly the economist and statistician Harald Westergaard (see Kærgård 1997; Kærgård and Davidsen 1998). Westergaard was educated as a mathematician and an economist, and he, in fact, made a number of contributions to mathematical economics in the 1870s. He obtained a position as full Professor of Economics and Statistics at the University of Copenhagen in 1886, a position he held until 1924.

In 1875, as a student, Westergaard undertook work as a statistician for an important governmental poor law committee. There he met some of the most important people involved in the Danish social debate at that time, and his concern with social matters began as early as this. In 1878-1879, he studied in different European countries. This journey was of decisive importance for his entire future. He visited England, where he met the English Christian socialist John Malcolm Ludlow.[4] This meeting was to become of tremendous importance to Westergaard. From that time onward his religious and social engagement became strong and his scientific work was mainly in statistics and often concerned social matters. Harald Westergaard was from now on and until his death frequently used in numerous contexts by the Christian movement as speaker, administrator, etc. Perhaps his main efforts were made as the leading member of a small circle (of only 5 laymen and theologians) who founded Københavns Kirkefond (The Copenhagen Church Foundation). This originally private foundation has since played an important role in the Danish church both with regard to practical matters (church-building) and to theology. The problem facing the church in Copenhagen at that time was one of a fast-growing city with huge poor working-class districts without any churches. Their aim was to build small, humble churches with socially-engaged clergymen. The organization was a success; in Westergaard's lifetime, 38 churches were established without public support.

For Westergaard, however, the foundation was not just a theological movement. He and his friends were leading advocates of social reform and of protection of the workers by law (Sundays free from work, safety at work, protection of children, etc.). The movement was more humanitarian than socialist, but in 1899, when the first major conflict between the newly-formed trade unions and the employers took place, Westergaard and a number of clergymen supported the workers in the public debate and supplied food to the workers on strike, see Kærgård (1997).

The start of the work with Københavns Kirkefond derived from the correspon-

---

4. For a decription of Ludlow's life and work, see Christensen (1962) and Masterman (1963).

dence between the above-mentioned circles of 5 members in the period 1888-1891. In one of these letters from 1888, Westergaard formulated his point of view about social problems very precisely:

> The Christian who has acknowledged the injustice which the society commits against a single class ought to try to awaken the conscience of the society, and it must always be possible for the injured to feel confident about contacting Christians. The issues of the length of a working day, of the work of women and children, etc. will often be mentioned in the church, but these are questions for the whole civil society. But the Christians can do a great job by the creation of a social ethic. ... My opinion is consequently that one should not go and organize a socialist Christian political party, for politics and Christianity are opposites, but when a man stands up with a political program dictated by love for the humbler members of the society, he will primarily find support among the Christians (Kærgård 1997: 143).

There were a number of other socially-oriented influential people among the Danish Christians in the period 1870-1914, often pupils of either Martensen or Westergaard, and there was a comprehensive debate among both economists and theologians about the social problems, and a debate between the two groups was also common. A number of both economists and theologians can be mentioned, among others Fernando Linderberg, who with Harald Westergaard tried to establish an organization for the dissemination of information about social problems around 1890. In the years before the turn of the century, Linderberg established a Christian trade union for farm workers, which existed in 1888-1895, but he gave up and joined the Social Democratic Party. Linderberg contributed with a considerable number of articles and books characterized by strong positive engagement in both Christianity and social arrangements.

Even if the development in the period 1870-1924 did not form anything like a modern welfare state, a number of important social reforms which provided the foundation for the future development were established. In 1873, industrial work for children under the age of 10 was prohibited, and children between the ages of 10 and 14 were only allowed to work 6 hours per day. A pension system for poor, elderly people was established in 1891. A law about sick-benefit associations (*sygekasser*) was approved by the Danish Parliament in 1892, and members of these associations got half of the cost at hospitals paid by the state. In 1907, unemployment insurance associations were established and got public support. A number of land reforms were adopted; small pieces of land were given to the farm workers by law in 1899, 1904, 1907, and 1919.

The development of the welfare state since 1924: the Christian influence

In 1924, Denmark got a Social Democratic government for the first time, and the Social Democratic Party dominated the entire period from 1924-1973 when the Danish welfare state was built (about 75 per cent of the time during this period, the Prime Minister was from this party), and it is customary to see the Danish welfare state as a mainly Social Democratic construction. The Social Democratic Party supported a complete separation of state and church, like the French *laïcité*. Religion was seen as people's private matter (Jacobsen 2012). The church and Christianity are not seen as having any important role. It was the left side of the political spectrum which forged ahead with the construction and expansion of the welfare state and social security. A number of the best known Christian spokesmen, on the contrary, were very critical regarding publicly arranged social security (see e.g. Petersen and Petersen 2010). The mainstream history of the period after 1924 is that Christianity does not play any important role in the development of the welfare state.

It is questionable, however, whether this history is true. Even if Christianity was not seen as present in the public debate, and even if politicians made their arguments as Social Democrats without mentioning their religious attitudes, a number of leading Social Democrats and the architects of the Danish welfare model were strongly related to Christianity. In the following, this will be documented by a number of cases.

The main architect of the modern Danish welfare state is perhaps K.K. Steincke (1880-1963). He was a minister in the Social Democratic government in 1924-26 and 1929-1939, and Chairman of the 2nd chamber of the Danish Parliament in 1948-50 and 1951-52. He is mainly known for the perhaps most important reform of the Danish social system in 1933 when he was Minister of Social Affairs. If one man is to be mentioned as the father of the Danish welfare state, he is obviously a serious candidate. And his relation to Christian socialism is clear. He was strongly inspired by Fernando Linderberg (Christensen 1998: 38-42). One of his typical remarks was: "Had there never been any Christianity in the world, nor would there have been any socialism." He openly said: "I have always, whatever life has been for me, said my Lord's Prayer and I intend to continue to do so" (Bomholt 1963: 44).

Another leading Social Democratic spokesman Frederik Borgbjerg (1866-1936) – second only to Thorvald Stauning at the beginning of the 20th century, MP from 1898, editor of the main Social Democratic newspaper from 1911, and a member of the government 1924-26 and 1929-35 – had studied theology and was a priest for a short period of time, and moreover very inspired by Nikolaj Frederik

267

Severin Grundtvig, and considered himself the last true Grundtvigian, see Jacobsen (2012: 226).

Such cases are not only found in the early period of the history of the Social Democratic Party. A number of declared Christians are also found among leading Social Democrats after World War II. Orla Møller (1916-79) was member of the Parliament 1964-77, Minister of Ecclesiastical Affairs (1966-68), of Defence (1973), of Defense and Justice (1975-77), Chairman of the Social Democratic group in Parliament 1971-73, and he almost became Chairman of the party and Prime Minister in 1972, when Jens Otto Krag resigned (see Hansen 1995: 16). He was a priest of the public church and before his political carreer he held a considerable number of positions in ecclesiastical relations, Secretary General in a Christian youth organization (KFUM and KFUK) in 1951-56, in the board of the Home Mission (a big part of the Danish church with a more fundamentalist interpretation of Christianity) in 1952-56, in the Christian youth world organization 1950, etc.

A less known example is Knud Heinesen (b. 1932). He was the dominant economist in the Social Democratic governments in the 1970s and Minister of Education 1971-73 and of Economic Affairs 1975-1979 and 1981-82. He began his career as a co-editor of some Christian folk high school journals, where he argued that the welfare state is closely related to Christianity. This is described in details in his memoirs in a session with the headline "We have chosen Jesus but vote for H.C. Hansen" (H.C. Hansen was the Social Democratic Prime Minister of the time) (Heinesen 2006: 48-51).

A more complicated case is the leading Social Democrat in the post-war period, Jens Otto Krag (1914-78), who held various positions in the governments 1947-50, 1953-58, was Foreign Minister 1958-62, and Prime Minister 1962-68 and 1971-72. He had a similar starting point in the Christian folk high school movement (see Heinesen 2006: 48-49; Lidegaard 2001: 45-51; Krag 1969), but in contrast to Heinesen, Christianity seems only to have been important to the very young Krag. "Krag long ago changed his persuasion, while I continued to have my partout card to both the Social Democratic Party and the Danish Lutheran Church", writes Heinesen (Heinesen 2006: 49).

It seems right to say that the debate about the development of the Danish welfare state in the period 1870-1924 was characterized by a number of high-profiled Christian spokesmen, while the period 1924-1973 was dominated by the Social Democrats. But this does not necessarily mean that a Christian way of thinking was unimportant even after 1924. It was the, mainly veiled, foundation for a considerable number of the main Social Democratic profiles.

This section is concentrated on Social Democrats, partly because the analysis deals with the Danish welfare state, and in this context the Social Democrats were the main actors, and partly because this party is the most secular of the big traditional Danish political parties. It is obvious and less surprising that there have been a number of active Christians in the Liberal and Conservative parties. If only one shall be mentioned, Poul Hartling (1914-2000) can be chosen. He was Chairman of the Liberal Party 1965-1977, Foreign Minister 1968-1971, and Prime Minister 1973-1975, and after a university degree in theology in 1939, he was a priest 1941-1950. He was a leading figure in the Christian students' movement in the 1930s.

The investigation in this papers stops in the 1970s. At that time the Danish welfare state was fully developed, and what has happened since is mainly modifications and adjustment caused by necessary budget cuts. If one should investigate the Christian influence in the more recent decades one has to look at other topics e.g. immigration and multiculturalism. But this is a completely different story which should not be discussed here – this will need a separate investigation which is done partly in Kærgård (2010; 2010a).

Conclusion

Denmark has never seen any Christian political party of any importance. The Danish church has never had an official attitude to more policy-related questions. In almost all important political and religious debates, the active members of the Evangelical Lutheran Church in Denmark, the minister and the bishops have disagreed about what the true Christian points of view should be.

But this does not mean that Christian points of view have been without influence on the political development. The influence has, however, been related to specific groups within the church. An illustrative case is the welfare state. The Christians have since the debate between H.L. Martensen and D.G. Monrad in the 1870s disagreed about social questions, nonetheless there has been an important and influential tradition from H.L. Martensen to Harald Westergaard and Fernando Linderberg and from Linderberg to K.K. Steincke.

The entanglement between Christianity and politics is complicated, and it is often very difficult, perhaps impossible, to decide whether the attitudes behind a discussion are inspired by a Christian belief or a political attitude. Some secular interests can be legitimated by religion, and in other situations religious attitudes are hidden behind secular "rational" arguments. Sometimes people are unaware that their attitudes are founded on a religious tradition.

References

Andersen, P.B. and P. Lüchau. "Tro og religiøst tilhørsforhold i Europa." In *Danskernes Særpræg*, ed. P. Gundelach, 245-68. Copenhagen: Hans Reitzels Forlag, 2004.

Andersen, P.B. and P. Lüchau. "Individualiseringen og aftraditionaliseringen af danskernes religiøse værdier." In *Store og små forandringer – Danskernes værdier siden 1981*, ed. P. Gundelach, 76-96. Copenhagen: Hans Reitzels Forlag, 2011.

Bomholt, J. "Eksistentialisten." In *G.K.K. Steincke. Socialismens Aristokrat*, ed. Gert Munch, 36-46. Copenhagen: Stig Vendelkærs Forlag, 1963.

Christensen, J. *K. K. Steincke – Mennesket og politikeren: En biografi*. Copenhagen: Christian Ejlers Forlag, 1998.

Christensen, T. *Origin and History of Christian Socialism*. Aarhus: Aarhus Universitetsforlag, 1962.

Christoffersen, L. "State, Church, and Religion in Denmark." In *Law & Religion in the 21st Century – Nordic Perspectives*, ed. L. Christoffersen, K.Å. Modéer, and S. Andersen, 141-61. Copenhagen: Djøf Publishing, 2010.

Folketinget. *Folketinget efter valget*. Folketinget (various years).

Hansen, S. "Regeringen fortsætter – om statsministerskiftet i 1972," *Arbejderbevægelsens Bibliotek og Arkiv – Årsskrift 1995*: 11-18.

Heinesen, K. *Min krønike 1932-1979*. Copenhagen: Gyldendal, 2006.

Jacobsen, B.A. "De politiske partiers religionspolitik." In *Fremtidens danske religionsmodel*, ed. L. Christoffersen, H. Raun Iversen, N. Kærgård, and M. Warburg, 217-36. Copenhagen: Anis, 2012.

Jensen, J. I. *Den fjerne kirke*. Copenhagen: Samlerens Forlag, 1995.

Jensen, O. *I vækstens vold. Økologi og religion*. Copenhagen: Fremad, 1976.

Jensen, O. *Frem til naturen og andre essays*. Copenhagen: Fremad, 1980.

Jensen, O. *På kant med klodens klima – om behovet for et ændret natursyn*. Copenhagen: Forlaget Anis, 2011.

Johansen, T.S. "Præster vil have radikal statsminister." *Kristelig Dagblad*, 31. August 2011.

Krag, J.O. *Ung mand i trediverne – Erindringer*. Copenhagen: Gyldendal, 1969.

Kærgård, N. "Tre økonomiske professorers teologi". *Kirkehistoriske Samlinger* (1997): 129-97.

Kærgård, N. and T. Davidsen. "Harald Westergaard: From Young Pioneer to Established Authority." In *European Economists of the early 20th Century* vol. 1, ed. W.J. Samuels, 349-69. Cheltenham: Edward Elgar, 1998.

Kærgård, N. "Economists and Theologians about Social Justice: The Debate in Denmark after 1870." Paper presented at the conference European Society of History of Economic Thought, Stirling, 2005.

Kærgård, N. "The Founding Fathers of the Danish Welfare State: Mathematical Economists and Christian Believers." Paper presented at the conference European Society of History of Economic Thought, Porto, 2006.

Kærgård, N. "The Foundation for the Danish Welfare State: Ethnic, Religion and Linguistic harmony." Paper for International Economic History Congress, Helsinki, 2006a.

Kærgård, N. "Social Cohesion and the Transformation from Ethnic to Multicultural Society: The Case of Denmark." *Ethnicities* 10, 4 (2010): 470-87.

Kærgård, N. "Etik og dilemmer i indvandrerpolitikken." In *Grænser for solidaritet*, ed. T. Bak, M. Bock, and J.H. Schjørring, 31-70. Copenhagen: Anis, 2010a.

Kærgård, N. and J.H. Petersen. "Folkekirken, staten og økonomien." In *Fremtidens danske religionsmodel*, ed. L. Christoffersen, H. Raun Iversen, N. Kærgård, and M. Warburg, 259-73. Copenhagen: Anis, 2012.

Kærgård, N. and J.H. Petersen. "Den ideelle kirkeordning, Folkekirken og fremtiden – et økonomisk perspektiv". In *Fremtidens danske religionsmodel*, ed. L. Christoffersen, H. Raun Iversen, N. Kærgård, and M. Warburg, 357-70. Copenhagen: Anis, 2012a.

Lidegaard, B. *Jens Otto Krag I: 1914 – 1961*. Copenhagen: Gyldendal, 2001.

Lüchau, P. (2011) "Religiøse politikere og sekulære vælgere? Den religio-nationale dimension i dansk politik." *Politica – Tidsskrift for politisk videnskab* 43, 1 (2011): 91-109.

Masterman, N.C. *John Malcolm Ludlow*. Cambridge: Cambridge University Press, 1963.

Martensen, H.L. *Socialisme og Christendom*. Copenhagen: Gyldendal, 1874.

Martensen, H.L. *Den Sociale Ethik, Den Christelige Ethik, Den Specielle Deel*, Vol. 2. Copenhagen: Gyldendal, 1878.

Monrad, D.G. *Liberalismens Gjenmæle, Politiske Breve 14-18*. Copenhagen: C.A. Reitzel, 1878.

Petersen, J.H. and K. Petersen. "Kirkefolk og velfærdsstat i Danmark ca. 1945-1965 – med udblik til Storbritanien og Norge". In *I himlen således også på jorden? Danske kirkefolk om velfærdsstaten og det moderne samfund*, ed. N.G. Hansen, J.H. Petersen, and K. Petersen, 201-42. Odense: Syddansk Universitetsforlag, 2010.

Wolf, J. *Etikken og Universet*. Copenhagen: Anis, 1997.

Wolf, J. *Det ubevæbnede øje – Essays om fænomenologi, videnskab, økologi og teologi*. Copenhagen: Anis, 2012.

Zuckermann, P. *Society without God*. New York: New York University Press, 2008.

15 Cultural Diversity and the Resilience of Nations

John Hutchinson

Much of the scholarship views nationalists as cultural homogenisers whose goal is to make ethnographic and political boundaries congruent. Scholars differ on the consequences: Elie Kedourie (1960) maintains that the effects are wholly destructive, whereas for Ernest Gellner (1964) nationalism provides the cultural cement that makes it possible for industrial society and liberal pluralism to meet at the global level. However, both Gellner and Kedourie view national cultures as modern inventions with little relationship to earlier cultural forms. Accepting these two assumptions, that national cultures are homogenising and recent constructs, many scholars claim the contemporary proliferation of identity conflicts suggests we are shifting into a post-national phase (Nora 1996). Because of globalisation, state sovereignty has become fictional and we are losing confidence in the metanarratives of the nation-state. Our horizons are now often supranational (e.g. European) or local when we participate in the identity politics of sub national groups (see Guibernau 2001).

Such claims, I believe, are exaggerated. Cultural differences are intrinsic to nation-building and although they may indeed relate to the rise of global interdependence, globalisation has long preceded nationalism and the nation-state (Hopkins 2002). I operate with a broad definition of globalization as a set of structured processes that widen, intensify and accelerate the interconnectedness between the populations of the world (Held et al. 1999: 16-20). These processes, including imperial expansion, transnational religious missions, patterns of interregional trade and migration, have shaped nation-formation in several ways. First, when nationalists emerged with the goal of constructing the culturally distinctive, territorially unified and politically autonomous units we call nations, they had to struggle to disentangle their targeted populations from such networks. National identities and polities do not obliterate, but rather are overlaid on older and often resilient forms of attachment and networks, with which they may remain in tension. Secondly, conflicts arising from imperial conquest and between religions making rival global claims have often been ethnogenetic. For example, the confessional wars of 17th century Europe resulted in various states and communities identifying a national identity as distinctive guardians of 'true religion' against their heretical neighbours. Third, in many countries, as a national consciousness forms we see the existence of embedded differences that arise from global processes that result in wars, civil wars, colonisations and revolutions. Such differences may give rise to competing definitions of the nation and, once institutionalised, they take on a recurring character, erupting into cultural wars (see Hutchinson 2005).

In this chapter I wish to examine the origins and significance of cultural wars in the making and remaking of nation-states in several countries, and also to see their role in shaping populations when faced with contemporary global problems. I will suggest that although they often result in social polarisation, they also articulate alternative options for populations as they experience the contingencies of the modern world. In doing so, I will first outline a configuration of recurring conflicts in Russia, France, and Greece and then consider three questions:

- How do we explain the origins and persistence of such differences?
- Are these positive or negative in their effects: do they institutionalise cultural pluralism or a dangerous polarisation?
- Why do such repertoires of difference survive in spite of immense social changes in the modern world?

Three cases: France, Russia, and Greece

I have chosen just three out of a huge range of cases, where we see recurring and systemic conflicts that, though they sometimes have class or regional aspects, go beyond them to offer very different visions of the nation. (For more examples, see Hutchinson 2005). I should hasten to add these are not the only competing national visions, but are perhaps the most significant.

In France the major divisions for modern French nationalism crystallised during the French revolution. At the time the republican myth of France was born as a bearer of a universal mission to emancipate, in the name of a democratic people, first Europe and then humanity at large from an irrational *ancien régime* of monarchy and clerical obscurantism. It was countered early on by a counterrevolutionary myth of France having an ancient mission through its alliance of Crown, altar and nobility to defend the cause of Christian civilisation in Europe. A third and lesser tradition was of the Bonapartist Empire, invoking Napoleon Bonaparte as the national saviour who, transcending the divisions of republicanism and monarchism, established French leadership of the European nations, in the manner of a modern Charlemagne. These competing projects dominated the modern history of France, obtaining a variety of social constituencies and producing recurring political instabilities. They produced the First Republic (1792-4), Napoleon's Empire (1804-14), the Bourbon restoration (1815-30), constitutional monarchy (1830-48), the Second Republic (1848-51), the Second Empire (1852-70), the Third Republic (1871-1940), Occupation and Vichy (1941-45), the Fourth Republic (1945-58) and de Gaulle's Fifth Republic (1958-) (see Gildea 1994).

In Russia, we find in the late 18th and early 19th centuries a Russian nationalism emerging both within and outside the imperial regime that divided into two tendencies. First a Westerner conception that claimed that Russia must be raised from its Asiatic backwardness by developing according to the norms of Western Europe. This was opposed by a Russianist or Slavophile tendency that rejected Western statism in favour of restoring a rural social order based on Orthodox religious values and a harmonious co-operation between Tsar, Church, and peasantry. The imperial regime during the 19th century censored and sought to co-opt these two cultural projects, shifting between the two. Under Alexander II, after the defeat in the Crimean war, in the 1860s there was a swing to the Westerner perspective resulting in the emancipation of the serfs, the extension of education, and limited meritocratic reforms of the army. However, as the reforms stalled, there was a shift to repression at home and an aggressive Pan-Slavism in foreign policy. Initially the debate between these two tendencies was largely confined to the gentry (vividly depicted in Turgenev's *Fathers and Sons*) but with the growth of education this extended to a broader radicalised intelligentsia drawn from the lower classes (Neumann 1996: ch. 2). Such visions divided leftist opposition to the regime (Russian Populists vs. Western-oriented Marxists) and have continued into the present, when under Putin there has been a return to Orthodoxy and an authoritarian state after the Westerner bias of Yeltsin.

In Greece, nationalism took anti-Ottoman forms, but there were tensions between secular republicans who aspired to a state with its capital in Athens as the embodiment of a revived Hellas, whereas an Orthodox conception of Greece existed among the clergy and peasantry, who dreamed of a restored Byzantine empire with its capital in Constantinople (Herzfeld 1982: ch. 1). The first ideal was to be found in the diaspora in Western Europe and the small secular stratum that led the revolt against the Ottomans, but the millenarian dreams of the latter provided the driving force of the independence campaigns (Frazee 1969: chs. 2, 3). The independent state was weakened by conflict and by factions, which had allies in the great powers linked to Britain and France on the one hand, and Tsarist Russia on the other. The struggle was resolved by the Megali Idea (Great Idea), according to which the new state had a mission to re-unite all Greeks in a single state which would have a civilising mission directed to the East. However, conflicts remained over which language should be adopted by the state – the demotic version of the peasantry or an archaic version based on the classical antiquity. The expansionist projects resulted in a series of damaging wars with the Ottomans, and although Kemal Ataturk's defeat of Greek armies and subsequent forced exchange of populations in 1922-3 seemed to bring these to an end, the tensions between republicans and Orthodox have re-appeared in the contemporary period (Augustinos 1977: chs 1, 2).

Explaining the origins of these persisting differences

How does one account for the rise of such competing conceptions of the nation? I argue that such differences have their origins in foundational events that arise from larger transnational processes. These include geo-political pressures to modernise societies that result in state-church schisms; revolutions generated by the rise of universalist ideologies that in turn produce civil wars; imperial conquests that lead to colonisations and crisis of existing identities. Such experiences became institutionalised and the memories disseminated down the generations.

In the case of Russia, the divisions go back to the attempts of Tsar Peter the Great (1682-1725) to transform Imperial Russia into a great European power. Aware of Russian military and economic backwardness in a period of incessant European interstate warfare, he attempted to modernise his empire, engaging in an onslaught on Russian traditionalism which he believed had held it back. Adopting the pagan Roman title of Imperator/Caesar he sought to subordinate the Orthodox Church to the state, abandoned his capital, holy Moscow, to build a new European city, St. Petersburg, overlooking the Baltic, imported foreigners into a new civil bureaucracy and imposed on his downgraded nobility European norms of dress. The result was an alienation of a significant section of Russian society from the state and the transfer of the Russian messianic idea (of Russia as the Third Rome) from the state to the Russian people (Hosking 1997).

By the late 18th century the Russian tendency emerged within official circles (with support of the military and intellectuals), led by Admiral Shishkov, President of the Russian Academy. Rejecting French influences among the elite, this defined Russia not in terms of Tsar and bureaucracy, but of the cultural practices of people, notably the Russian language. The arguments that followed focused on the proper bases of the Russian language (Church Slavonic or the demotic) and on the place of Russia in European history, with protagonists viewing Russia as either the Christian saviour of an increasingly Godless Europe or as an embarrassing Asiatic outsider. This was the setting of the later conflicts that examined the degree to which Russia could pioneer a new path to progress based on its unique Orthodox heritage and communal institutions such as the *mir*, or whether it must engage in a large-scale adoption of ideas and institutions from the advanced Western European societies (Seton-Watson 1977: 82-5). The debate was institutionalised around the rival capitals and polarised in answer to the question "where was Russia to be found: in the character of the Tsar and bureaucracy or the people and their religio-cultural practices?" The Slavophiles were drawn from leading Muscovite landowning families for whom St. Petersburg's court and society represented the divorce of the Tsarist regime from a partnership with the Russian nation based on the land (Riasonovsky 1952: 29-30; Lieven 2000: 207). These contentions for long remained among the gentry, but by the late 19th century the intellectual class was growing from within the peasantry, among whom the messianic ideas of Russia as the Third Rome still lived.

The causes of the French revolution were complex. This period of cleavage was preceded by increasing conflicts between monarchy and the nobility, and other estates which date back to the 17th century. The triggers of revolt were the bankruptcy of the state from a series of ruinous wars and the outbreak of famine, but an important factor was the violent ideological assault of a new secular rationalist universalism (embodied in the enlightenment philosophies) on the dead weight of the Catholic Church which sustained the ancient regime. The profound experiences of the revolutionary period instituted the long lasting battle of cultures in France. On the one hand, there were the heroic liberation myths of the storming of the Bastille, the rallying of the people to defend in arms the republic against a perfidious monarchy and aristocracy allied to foreign monarchies, the establishment of a national citizenship, the triumphs of French arms and ideas in Europe. Royalist and Catholic supporters remembered the "blasphemous" execution of the King, the terror, the assault of the secular and religious rights of the clergy, and the violent crushing of the Vendee in 1794. Two antithetical myths were created – one of France as the inaugurator of a new age (Year 1) of reason with its centre in Paris against a timeless primordial defender of Christianity (the *France profonde* of the provinces, particularly in the west and south). The failures of the Revolution and its replacement by Napoleon produced a third myth based on his military glories, of a France as the heroic defender of the nations (see Hobsbawm 1962: ch. 3).

During the 19th century the bitter struggles between republicans and their opponents in France resulted in a symbolic as well as a cultural war (dubbed a 'statuomania') in urban spaces. In Paris a monumental split developed between liberal, secular republican East Paris (site of the Pantheon and the Bastille) and military, imperial West Paris (Place Vendôme, Étoile, Invalides) (Agulhon 1998: 535). In villages in 1860-1910 combined town hall-school buildings were built opposite churches, and in the cities government buildings and statues of Marianne and republican heroes confronted churches and representations of the virgin (Langlois 1996: 125). Even the fallen soldiers fought this iconographical war, as republican neo-classical heroic images vied with symbols of Christian suffering in the cemeteries.

The third case of Greece is one of conquest following a conflict between two Empires, the Byzantine and the Ottoman, representing rival global claims, Orthodox Christian and Islamic. The fall of the holy city of Constantinople in 1453 and the subsequent subjugation of the Orthodox population of the Byzantine territories to the Muslim yoke was an event commemorated in song and legend down the centuries. Among the clergy a millenarian tradition persisted that Constantinople would rise again (Campbell and Sherrard 1968: ch. 1).

But this also triggered a major division within the Greek population.

In some ways the Ottoman overthrow of the Byzantine Empire strengthend the sway of Orthodoxy over the Greek largely peasant-based population. The collapse of the Empire was blamed on the treachery of the Latin West that reinforced in a largely illiterate and peasant population hostility to the European Christendom that had betrayed the people of God. The millet system strengthened the power of the Constantinople patriarchy since it exercised secular as well as religious power over the Orthodox community; and it gave the Greek planariot class a privileged position in the Imperial administration.

However, there was an alternative conception of Greece looking back to Hellas developing in the substantial diaspora of merchant colonies that from the 15th century formed in all the major European cities and was active in the Balkans. These were exposed to a different conception of Greece as a result of the rise of European Renaissance humanism that idealised classical antiquity as an embodiment of human perfection. By the 18th century philhellenic intellectual currents adopted republican models as the basis for a reformation of Europe. Within this tradition invidious comparisons were regularly drawn between the virtuous Greeks of antiquity and their present decadence. Such ideas had a deep impact on the Greek diaspora, especially after the French Revolution, who now saw it as their duty to rescue their fallen compatriots from religious (Orthodox) obscurantism and to throw off the Ottoman yoke. Although many clerics sponsored the revival of Greek learning and the wave of publications that poured into mainland Greece from the diaspora, Hellenic nationalists saw Greece's revival as dependent on rejoining the West. Their Orthodox equivalents looked east to their co-religionists in the Balkans and Russia, hoping to reconquer the Byzantine Empire (Jusdanis 2001: ch. 4).

What this suggests is that cultural wars are shaped by powerful collective experiences such as state-religious schisms (Russia); revolutions and/or civil wars (France and England); wars and colonisations and religio-national conflicts (Greece) the memories of which are carried by various social strata and institutions (legal, religious, literary, and political). Around these mythical memories rival repertoires develop as mobilisers of collective action. These repertoires have internal and external dimensions. They offer different perspectives about the nature of politics, the status of social groups, relations between regions, the countryside and the city, economic and social policies and also foreign policy. It is notable that not all these projects were of similar weight. The "memories" of ancient Greece were not substantiated in a living culture as were their Orthodox equivalents.

The significance of these persisting differences: 1 cultural pluralism

What then were the consequences of the crystallisation of these opposing national conceptions? There were two obvious effects. One was to institutionalise cultural pluralism. No modern nation would long survive unless it contained a plurality of traditions. But what of those cases where the consciousness of having a differentiated past does not feed in a diffuse manner into national debates but configures antithetic competition, as say in France and Russia? Even in these cases, I will suggest we can find evidence of patterns of alternation between rival movements that mobilise different social energies by which to overcome crises, thereby strengthening the nation as it navigates the many challenges (political, economic, military, and ideological) of the modern world.

In France, Republicanism has been the dominant tradition but has had to compete with right wing religious nationalist and Bonapartist alternatives, each of which puts forward a vision of France as a society and defines a European mission. Republicanism defines France as a nation one and indivisible, as the guarantor of the democratic liberties of its citizens and because of its revolutionary heritage the bearer of a world mission to spread enlightenment modernity. It has produced a Parisian-dominated and centralist state, suspicious of regional and religious liberties as covers for political reaction (Gildea 1994: 169). Anti-republican opponents whose core institution has been the Catholic Church have articulated a strongly patriarchal, religious and rural vision of a France of provincial liberties, rooted in a golden medieval age that stands against the moral and social chaos of secular modernity. It gives weight to France as an ancient, virtually primordial, European community, descended from Clovis, and to its great legacy as defender of European Christendom in the Crusades. Catholic France has retained powerful support in the West and Midi regions (Johnson 1993: 53-4). The third Bonapartist tradition looks to a charismatic hero like Napoleon who, in alliance with the Church, restored social order. The tradition moreover looks to France's military glories and drawing on the legacy of Charlemagne, celebrates established France as the imperial ruler of Europe, though one that professed to respect the liberties of nations (Fontana 2002).

The persistence of these traditions indicates the co-existence of at least three Frances, each of which in crisis may seize hegemony. As the First Republic dissolved in chaos, Napoleon used its missionary enlightenment ideology to justify his imperial expansion, and at home he instituted a concordat with the Church and his civil code. But as a usurper he was undone by military defeat. The return of the Bourbon monarchy that followed, preserved the existence of France as a great power within a restored European balance of power system and engaged in military adventures. But the traditional *ancien régime* could not be restored, and after the revolutions of 1830 and 1848, a Second Republic was declared. Social breakdown justified the seizure of power of Napoleon III in 1851, just as it had his uncle, and the former promised to restore order and revitalise France's mission to Europe as the defender of the liberties of oppressed nations. However, he was similarly undone by military humiliation at the hands of Bismarck in 1870, leading to a (Third) Republic that restored a middle class democracy.

Determined to regenerate France, republicans sought to nationalise the people by mass patriotic secondary education, military conscription, and the economic unification of the territory (Weber 1976). The extension of secular state education led to prolonged conflict with the Church in the late 19th century, and the Republic was tested by scandals and economic depression. These produced challenges from class-based socialist and syndicalist movements and on the right from monarchists and the Action Française. The latter favoured a racial hierarchical Catholic nation and tapped traditional anti-semitic and anti-capitalist prejudices (Gildea 1994: chs. 6, 7).

There were similar alternations in the 20th century. Victory in the First World War vindicated the republic, which survived the Depression, but the humiliating collapse of France in 1940, resulted in Marshall Pétain's Vichy regime that promoted a national regeneration based on Catholic piety, respect for social hierarchy and the superior life of the land. The victory of the allies, however, brought to power a Fourth Republic, which in turn after a period of weak governments and the debacle in Algeria came to an end with the triumphant return to power of the charismatic de Gaulle. Marrying Bonapartist with republican traditions, he founded a Fifth Republic based on a presidential democracy that would restore France's great power status and its leadership of Europe.

There is a comparable pattern of alternation in Russia during the 19th and 20th centuries, as a despotic Imperial state sought to co-opt at different times Russianist or Slavophile and Westerner projects in defining Russian development and its external relations, above all with Europe. Iver Neumann (1996: ch.1) argues three main positions developed in the 19th century. The first viewed Imperial Russia as the protector of a European Christian *ancien régime* threatened by secular revolution and was suspicious of nationalism, but was forced to create an official nationalism by the late 19th century to broaden its dynastic appeal. Russianists argued that there was a distinctive Russian character drawn from Orthodox Christianity and its rural communal institutions that must provide the model first of Russian and then European development. This sought to strengthen a Russian society against the erosion of European secular ideas and looked early on to countries like Britain as successful conservative landed models (Pipes 1974: 268; Riasonovsky 1952: 104-5), and veered from a rejection of dynastic great power adventures to visions of leading a league of Slavic nations (Lieven 2000: 219, 247). Westerners claimed that for a backward and Asiatic society to progress it must tap the advanced technologies of Western Europe and adapt them to Russian conditions, if needs be by revolution.

The state's reaction, shaped by the revolutionary waves in Europe in the 1820s and 1830s, was to isolate Russia and try to re-arm against European ideas, embodied in the principles of autocracy, orthodoxy, and nationality propounded by Count Uvarov, Minister of Education. During the 1830s and 1840s a debate raged between the Slavophiles and the Westerners, both of which were suppressed by the state as a threat to its authority (Neumann 1996: ch. 3).

In response to the 1848 revolutions the regime at first moved to co-opt the Slavophiles' cult of Holy Russia, but its attachment ended with the Crimean War, which exposed Russia's military inferiority to European powers. Under Tsar Alexander II there was a switch to Westerner policies from 1861 to advance the modernisation of Russian society, but after his assassination there was a shift to repression and an aggressive Pan-Slavist foreign policy. Opposition movements, divided into liberal and socialist wings, and the socialists themselves espoused the rival visions: a Russian Populism formed that rejected industrialisation for a rural socialism based on the *Mir* opposed by Marxists who looked to Germany and the development of a proletariat as the basis of successful class revolutions (Neumann 1996: ch. 5; Pipes 1974: 269-78).

After the collapse of the state during the First World War brought the Bolsheviks to power, on Lenin's death, they divided between Stalin's advocacy of Socialism in One Country and Trotsky's failed advocacy of World Revolution. In practice, the Bolshevik regime married Russian messianism to communist utopianism, and although a Russian nationalism and Orthodox church were anathematised, a national Bolshevism survived, and at times of crises such as the Nazi invasion in 1941, Stalin invoked these latter themes to mobilise support for the regime. After the collapse of communism, debates have revived between Liberal Westerners who sought constitutional freedoms and a liberal capitalism (dominant under Yeltsin) and neo-Slavophile nationalists defending Orthodoxy (increasingly influential under Putin).

In summary, these examples indicate that rival traditions offered repertoire for states and for elements of a developing civil society by which to articulate options to face continually changing external and internal challenges. Failure in warfare resulted in a switching between options, as the formerly excluded took up the baton of saving the nation, and alienated social classes were recruited by different national factions and their energies mobilised for the national cause.

The significance of these persisting differences: 2 polarisation

However, such cultural debates produced an intense polarisation that could entail that options were dichotomised and a simplification of the national past in black or white terms so that the synthetic qualities of national cultures was downplayed, and with this the possibilities of productive accommodations of differences. This had the potential to lead to civil wars.

McDaniel (1996) has argued that the development of a pluralist Russian modernity was inhibited by a clash between two visions – of a Petrine bureaucratic modernisation from above versus an archaic idealisation of a land of small-scale rural communities. The result was a lurch from one fanaticism to another, from despotic government to utopian anarchism. In France the intensity of the schisms resulted in a winner-takes-all attitude to political power in which opponents were subject to extremes of violence. There was also an over-centralisation of French society as republicans (representing the dominant political tradition in modern France) feared pressure for devolution to the regions as covert plots to undermine the unity of the republic. The dogmatic secularism of French republicanism also produced a venomous anti-republican culture among right-wing Catholics that contributed to its defeat in 1940 and its smooth replacement by the Vichy regime in the south.

Against this, one could argue that the problem was not cultural difference as such, but rather the setting in which cultural difference was played out. The problem in Russia was the autocratic context which prevented a proper testing of rival nostrums, and in France the linkage of one side (the counterrevolutionaries) to foreign invasions which delegitimized them in the eyes of republicans as political actors. In Greece the divisions we saw were cloaked by a Hellenic-Byzantine irredentist crusade against the Ottoman Turks to unify Greeks in their new state.

What prevented these cultural divisions from producing a complete social breakdown in France and Russia? There were periodic internecine conflicts as we have noted. Nonetheless, there was reconsolidation as the cultural wars revealed to at least some of the major protagonists that they shared unwittingly many assumptions about the uniqueness of their land and its people. In these polemics, each side sought to validate its position by referring to an authentic past, which resulted in an increasing knowledge of the "national" history, its cultural achievements, social institutions, practices, and topography. In France after the instabilities of the first republic and the subsequent Bourbon restoration, during which France was subject to invasion, both republicans and their opponents sought to ground their projects in an older golden past of French greatness and unity in the 14th century. Both singled out as heroine, Joan of Arc. For republicans she was a woman of the people who embodied the democratic spirit of France and defeated foreign invaders only to be betrayed by Church and monarchy. For anti-republicans she was the pious daughter of the Catholic Church of which France was the eldest daughter in Europe. During the 19th century all emerging political groups sought to appropriate her legacy, including socialists, communists, supporters of Action Française, Fascists and most recently the Front National (Gildea 1994: 154-65). The battle to claim her implied the existence of a larger enfolding national spirit in which all factions participated and which they acknowledged as exercising a power over them.

Similar arguments can be made with respect to the Westerner-Slavophile debates in 19th century Russia. Whether they favoured Petrine or Russian traditionalist models, the polemics over their consequences for Russian social development and its status as a great power identified for better or for worse what was distinctive about Russian institutions *vis-à-vis* Western Europe – Orthodoxy, autocracy, the Mir, and that it lacked a commercial and participative middle class. These visions have alternated in power both at the level of state and of "educated society", with groups, at times switching positions, in part affected by the sense of place and security of the national territory. Over time the opposing sides internalised the assumptions of the other, resulting in a switching between positions. The Westerner Alexander Herzen, uneasy at the prospect of wholesale importation of European ideas, especially after the failure of the liberal European revolutions in 1848, declared that Westerners would be cut off from the people, as long as they ignored the questions posed by the Slavophiles (Neumann 1996: 170). By the 1860s in similar vein, Dostoevsky, advocate of Russia's Orthodox mission and its Eastern destiny, reveals the ambivalence of a new wing of conservative nationalists, "enthusiasts of the soil". He repudiated the dogmatism of earlier Slavophiles and agreed with the more "realistic" Westerners about the need for a greater liberalism (freedom of thought) in Russian society, and the need to reach out to the people among whom education and literacy must be promoted (Thaden 1964: 59-63).

At various times, too there are signs of a synthetic identity developing. In Greece the sense of an unfulfilled national mission and external enemy (the Ottoman Empire) brought the two together in the Megali idea – to unite all Greeks in a national state and possibly regain Constantinople. Similarly, among intellectual circles the concept of Russia as Eurasian power developed in the 1920s arguing that Russia was neither European nor Asiatic but both.

Persisting differences

Finally, what explains the persistence of these rival repertoires in spite of vast social and political changes over time? Is it not the case that events dictate the emphatic triumph of one side over another? Alternatively in more peaceful and stable democratic societies will the process of debate not result in the forming of common ground and a fading of intensities? In some cases, this indeed does happen: The Greek defeat in the war against the Turks of 1919-22 and the resulting mass transfer of populations between Turkey and Greece ended effectively the Byzantine dream. Yet even in such cases tensions between a Hellenic ideal oriented to Western Europe and a vision of Greece as distinctive by virtue of its Eastern Christian heritage persists, flaring up in 2001 when Archbishop Christodoulos rallied millions of Greeks against a secularising campaign of the Socialist PASOK government to detach the nation from its Orthodox heritage (by the removal of religious affiliation from citizens' identity cards).

A brief answer is that such repertoires have staying power because they reflect something of continuing importance in the life of their societies. The rival visions are often embedded in key national institutions: in constitutions, the selection and architecture of capital cities, the political system, religious institutions and canonical works of history or the arts. We should note that in these three cases, the divisions have a basis in secular-religious cleavages, and that in spite of what many secularisation theorists have assumed, the religiously-inspired visions of community retain deep roots within Europe, and even more so in the rest of the world.

These older repertoires also have resonance because nations are embedded in *enduring* geographical milieus and are exposed to neighbours whom they shape and by whom they are shaped. Although the interactions produced by the increasing global interdependence of peoples remain a challenge to states, the effects are always mediated by geography. The diverse heritages arise in part out of their territorial location that may expose them to unpredictable challenges from several directions. Nations are also situated in time with layered pasts, which offer different repertoires by which to cope with shifting challenges. There can be no final definition of a national identity.

In recognition of this nationalists have often declared a special position for their nation as mediator between different culture zones, one that implies a creative role as synthesiser and one that also "protects" them from being absorbed into dominant surrounding cultures. It expresses the hope that the nation will not continue to be a battleground between opposing states or blocs. As we have noted, some Russians have attempted to synthesise the Westerner-Slavophile debate by conceiving of their country as Eurasian, drawing on the best in both traditions to articulate their interests with respect to their "Western" and their "Asian" neighbours. In part this acknowledges that Russia has been formed by its military, political, economic and cultural interactions with Western and Central Europe and also with Asia, and that Westerner and Slavophile perspectives may be complementary rather than antithetical. Similarly, Kolettis in the 19th century presented the Greeks as the bridge between Europe and East. Its destiny would be to enlighten the East by its rise, just as it had done for Europe by its fall (Augustinos 1977: ch. 1). There are other examples. The 19th century Czech historian Palacky, declared Czechs to be the bridge between the powerful Germans and the Slavs (including Russia). Today Czech intellectuals such as Milan Kundera perceive themselves to be in the centre of Europe, wishing to "rejoin" the West after suffering the Eastern yoke, without succumbing to its technological superiority and materialism (Holy 1996: ch. 6). Such rival visions thus promise to offer a route by which countries with diverse heritages can productively participate in an interdependent world.

■ References

Agulhon, M. "Paris: A Traversal from East to West." In *Realms of Memory: Vol 3 Symbols*, ed. P. Nora. New York: Columbia University Press, 1998.

Augustinos, G. *Consciousness and History: Nationalist Critics of Greek Society 1897-1914*. New York: East European Quarterly, 1977.

Campbell, J. and P. Sherrard. *Modern Greece*, New York: Praeger, 1968.

Fontana, B. "The Napoleonic Empire and the Europe of Nations." In *The Idea of Europe: From Antiquity to the European Union*, ed. A. Pagden. Cambridge: Cambridge University Press, 2002.

Frazee, C.A. *The Orthodox Church and Independent Greece*. Cambridge: Cambridge University Press, 1969.

Gellner, E. *Thought and Change*. London: Weidenfeld and Nicholson, 1964.

Gildea, R. *The Past in French History*. Yale: Yale University Press, 1994.

Guibernau, M. "Globalisation and the Nation-state." In *Understanding Nationalism*, ed. M. Guibernau and J. Hutchinson. Oxford: Polity Press, 2001.

Held, D. et al. *Global Transformations*. Cambridge: Polity Press, 1999.

Herzfeld, M. *Ours Once More; Folklore, Ideology and the Making of Modern Greece*. Austin: Texas University Press, 1982.

Hobsbawm, E.J. *The Age of Revolution*. London: Weidenfeld and Nicholson, 1962.

Holy, L. *The Little Czech and the Great Czech Nation*. Cambridge: Cambridge University Press, 1996.

Hopkins, A.G. "The History of Globalization and the Globalization of History." In *Globalization in World History*, ed. A.G. Hopkins. London: Pimlico, 2002.

Hosking, G. "The Russian National Myth Repudiated." In *Myths and Nationhood*, ed. G. Hosking and G. Schopflin. London: Hurst, 1997.

Hutchinson, J. *Nations as Zones of Conflict*. London: SAGE Publications, 2005.

Johnson, D. "The Making of the French Nation." In *The National Question in Europe in Historical Context*, ed. M. Teich and R. Porter. Cambridge: Cambridge University Press, 1993.

Jusdanis, G. *The Necessary Nation*. Princeton, NJ: Princeton University Press, 2001.

Kedourie, E. *Nationalism*. London: Hutchinson, 1960.

Langlois, C. "Catholics and Seculars." In *Realms of Memory: Vol 1 Conflicts and Divisions*, ed. P. Nora, 109-44. New York: Columbia University Press, 1996.

Lieven, D. *Empire: the Russian Empire and Its Rivals*. London: John Murray, 2000.

McDaniel, T. *The Agony of the Russian Idea*. Princeton, NJ: Princeton University Press, 1996.

Neumann, I.B. *Russia and the Idea of Europe*. London: Routledge, 1996.

Nora, P. "General Introduction: Between Memory and History." In *Realms of Memory Vol 1*, ed. P. Nora, 1-10. New York: Columbia Press, 1996.

Pipes, R. *Russia under the Old Regime*. Harmondsworth: Penguin, 1977.

Riasonovsky, N.V. *Russia and the West in the Teaching of the Slavophiles*. Cambridge, MA: Harvard University Press, 1952.

Seton-Watson, H. *Nations and States*. London: Methuen, 1977.

Thaden, E. *Conservative Nationalism in Nineteenth Century Russia*. Seattle: University of Washington Press, 1964.

Weber, E. *Peasants into Frenchmen: the Modernization of Rural France (1870-1914)*. Stanford: Stanford University Press, 1976.